# RECOGNISING THE MARGINS

# Recognising the Margins: Developments in Biblical and Theological Studies

ESSAYS IN HONOUR OF SEÁN FREYNE

*Edited by*
Werner G. Jeanrond
and
Andrew D. H. Mayes

the columba press

First published in 2006 by
the columba press
55A Spruce Avenue, Stillorgan Industrial Park,
Blackrock, Co Dublin

Cover by Bill Bolger
Origination by The Columba Press
Printed in Ireland by ColourBooks Ltd, Dublin

ISBN 1 85607 549 4

# Table of Contents

Preface   7

## I BIBLICAL THEMES

1. Who is the Teacher in Isa 30:20 who will
   no longer remain hidden?
   *Joseph Blenkinsopp*   9
2. The Messianic Secret in Mark
   *Martin Hengel*   24
3. The Exodus as an Ideology of the Marginalised
   *Andrew D. H. Mayes*   48
4. Mark and Empire
   *Stephen D. Moore*   70
5. Crossing Border: Speaking about the
   beginning in Genesis 1 and John 1
   *Ellen J. van Wolde*   91

## II THEOLOGICAL THEMES

6. 'The Eye of the Soul': The Doctrine of the
   Higher Consciousness in the Neoplatonic and
   Sufic Traditions
   *John Dillon*   112
7. The Lapses in Christian Theology
   at the End of the Second Millennium
   *James P. Mackey*   123
8. Rootedness: Reflections on Land and Belonging
   *John D'Arcy May*   146
9. An Other Name for G*d
   *Elisabeth Schüssler Fiorenza*   160

## III CULTURAL THEMES

10. The Future of Christianity in Europe
    *Werner G. Jeanrond*   182

11. Interreligious Dialogue and Global Ethic in
an Age of Globalisation
*Karl-Josef Kuschel*                                    201
12. Theatre, Tragedy and Theology
*Enda McDonagh*                                        215
13. The Galileans of the South
The Untouchables at the Margins
*Felix Wilfred*                                        229

IV ETHICAL THEMES

14. Specifying the Meaning:
Jesus, the New Testament and Violence
*Nigel Biggar*                                         251
15. The Quest for Freedom in a Culture of Choice
*Stephen J. Duffy*                                     274
16. Virtues and the God who Makes Everything New
*Maureen Junker-Kenny*                                 298
17. The Role and Backgrounds of Religious, Ethical,
Legal and Social Issues in the Progress of Science
*Dietmar Mieth*                                        321
18. 'It is part of a process. It is part of a pilgrimage':
Text in Context and Conflict
*Elaine M. Wainwright*                                 335

List of Contributors                                   352

# Preface

To mark the occasion of Seán Freyne's 70th birthday in 2005 some of the finest biblical and theological scholars in the world were invited to contribute to this anthology. Its title, *Recognising the Margins*, reflects significant dimensions in Seán Freyne's academic work and personal concern: his radical openness to new experience and new ideas, his academic rigour as a biblical scholar, his theological interpretation of the biblical heritage, his hermeneutics of suspicion over against all claims to represent the centre, and his conviction that the encounter with truth always finds a place, although not always within the framework of conventional authorities.

Seán Freyne's changing pastoral and academic contexts and his international experience as scholar and teacher have made him increasingly sensitive to the influences of shifting contexts on the reception of biblical texts. His education at the interface of a propositionalist approach to the Bible within Roman Catholic theology and the emerging openness towards wider academic and cultural horizons during his years of study at Rome, coinciding with the Second Vatican Council, challenged him to investigate all emerging approaches to the biblical texts: textual, historical, form- and redaction-critical methods; literary, hermeneutical, philosphical, contextual, feminist, liberationist, theological and inter-religious approaches to the Bible. In his academic life, and in his wider experience, Seán Freyne has lived and worked in the tension between accepting the given and the restless pursuit of the yet to be discovered.

His work as a teacher and researcher in Europe, America, Australia and the Middle East, as well as his active participation in the editorial group responsible for *Concilium* exposed him to the demands of different academic interest groups, including those who approach the biblical texts with expectations of liberation, such as African-American communities in the United States and marginalised groups of people in and beyond Ireland. The question that remained constant in all these years of increased exposure and experience was: how can a responsible reading of the Bible contribute to critical and self-critical theological reflections on human life and vocation in our time, and *vice versa*. Moreover, Seán Freyne became aware of the urgency to promote a deeper conversation between Christian and Jewish thinkers, beyond traditional anti-Jewish biases and Christian ignorance of the rich and complex post-biblical Jewish intellectual culture. Thus, the Bible becomes the focus for disclosive and transformative meeting between cultures, religions and traditions, both ancient and post-modern.

The response to our invitation was overwhelming: eighteen scholars from Ireland and many parts of the world co-operated with us in producing a significant work. The chapters of this book develop the biblical, theological and ecclesiological concerns of Seán Freyne. We are certain that this collection will document the fact that this internationally celebrated Irish scholar has been an effective and successful promoter not only of a re-assessment of the place of theology in Ireland, but also of the significance of Irish theology in the contemporary world.

It is our hope that this collection of articles should not only manifest the contributors' appreciation of Seán Freyne as scholar and friend, but also invite and encourage many readers to engage in the kind of theology that has been so important to him as teacher, researcher and academic leader. Those of us who have had the privilege of working closely with Seán in establishing the School of Hebrew, Biblical and Theological Studies at Trinity College Dublin, in shaping *Concilium*, or in promoting the research programme of the Trinity College Centre for Mediterranean and Near Eastern Studies, of which he is founding director, can witness to his great talent for drawing people into an always deeper biblical and theological inquiry. Our anthology arose out of this spirit.

We wish to thank first of all our contributors for joining us in this collaborative work in honour of Seán Freyne. We are grateful to Peter Kenny for his help with the translation of Martin Hengel's contribution. We are very much obliged to our publisher Seán O Boyle of The Columba Press in Dublin who has supported this project with enthusiasm and generosity.

*Lund and Dublin, Pentecost 2006*
*Werner G. Jeanrond*
*Andrew D. H. Mayes*

CHAPTER ONE

# Who is the teacher in Isaiah 30:20
# who will no longer remain hidden?

## Joseph Blenkinsopp

I

There is a type of rabbinic exegesis which begins with a text ostensibly remote from the passage to be interpreted and works its way round by a kind of exegetical *tour de force* to the text under consideration. The title of the present essay may suggest something of the sort since it appears to be remote from what one would expect to find in a volume dedicated to a scholar of early Christianity. But my esteemed friend and colleague Professor Freyne is one such scholar who, most clearly in his recent study of Jesus the Galilean, has noted the unique importance of Isaiah for the identity and mission of early Christianity. I therefore dare to hope that this brief essay in Isaianic interpretation may be of interest to him.

My text is one of several cryptic passages in Isaiah which seem to presuppose an audience or readership limited to those who can be expected to grasp the point. Isa 30: 19-21 reads as follows (my translation):

> You people in Zion who dwell in Jerusalem,[1] you shall weep no more. He will surely show you favour when you cry for help, and he will answer when he hears you. The Sovereign Lord may give you the bread of adversity and the water of affliction, but your teacher will no longer remain hidden. Your eyes will see your teacher, and whenever you turn aside either to the right or the left your ears will hear a word spoken behind you: 'This is the way, keep to it.'[2]

It may seem paradoxical to say that the history of the interpretation of Isaiah begins in the book itself, yet there is a great deal of interpretative activity going on throughout the book including

---

1. Reading *yoshev* for MT *yeshev* with BHS.
2. On the translation, and the passage in the context of Isa 30:18-26 see my *Isaiah 1-39. A New Translation with Introduction and Commentary* (New York: Doubleday, 2000), 418-22.

several passages, almost all in prose, which serve as commentary on sayings immediately preceding, the latter generally in the
kind of high rhythmic diction or recitative characteristic of
prophetic discourse. The address to some inhabitants of
Jerusalem in Isa 30:19-21 is one example of such expansive commentary, and one which practically all critical commentators as-
sign to the Second Temple period, and later in that period rather
than earlier.[3] The saying immediately preceding (30:18) provides the assurance that, appearances to the contrary notwithstanding, Yahweh is waiting to show favour to those who wait
for God and with God:

Therefore Yahweh waits to show you favour,
therefore he bestirs himself to have compassion on you;
for Yahweh is a God of justice,
blessed are all those who wait for him!

The link between the two passages is apparent: repeating the
same verb (*hnn*, 'show favour' or 'show mercy'), 30:19-21 states
what form the divine favour anticipated in the previous passage
will assume. It is addressed to those who, though in distress,
continue to wait for God and with God, a prominent theme in
Isaiah.[4] It is therefore not addressed to all and sundry but to the
'remnant', those who, in the Isaianic context, form the core of the
new community which comes increasingly into view throughout the redactional history of the book, and is most clearly in evidence in the last two chapters.[5] They will have more to suffer,

---

3. For example, Bernhard Duhm, *Das Buch Jesaia* (Göttingen: Vandenhoeck & Ruprecht, 1922 4th ed.), 221-25; Georg Fohrer, *Das Buch Jesaia.
II Kap.* 24-39 (Zurich: Zürcher Bibelkommentare/Stuttgart: Zwingli),
102-3; Ronald E. Clements, *Isaiah 1-39* (London: Marshall, Morgan &
Scott, 1980), 250 (Persian period); Jacques Vermeylen, *Du Prophète Isaïe à
l'Apocalyptique* (Paris: Gabalda, 1978), I 419 (reflects the aspirations of
the post-exilic 'pious'). Otto Kaiser, *Isaiah 13-39. A Commentary*
(Philadelphia: Westminster, 1983 2nd ed.), 301-2, attributes the saying
to an eschatological teacher comparable to and contemporary with the
*maskilim* of Daniel who was forced into hiding during the persecution
under Antiochus IV.
4. Isa 8:17; 25:9; 26:8; 30:18; 33:2; 40:31; 49:23; 64:2-3.
5. The same 'people who dwell in Zion' are addressed in Isa 10:24, introducing a passage which is continuous with 10:20-23 (*laken*, 'therefore') which speaks about the 'remnant' more clearly and insistently
than in any other Isaianic text and concludes with language reminiscent
of the book of Daniel (Isa 10:23 cf Dan 11 :36). It is not surprising that its

and there will be more uncertainty and disorientation (turning to the right or the left), but they will have a teacher to guide them and keep them moving in the right direction. We are reminded of the twenty years of disorientation (groping like the blind) of the Damascus sect which came to an end when the Teacher of Righteousness appeared among them to guide them (CD I 8-11).[6]

Debate about the overall meaning of the passage understandably focuses on the identity of this teacher. MT *moreka* could be singular or plural, and in fact both LXX (*planontas se*) and 1 QIsa[a] (*mvr'yk*) have the plural. But in the context it is certainly singular since the verb, *yekanef*, is singular. What the text tells us is that this teacher is associated with those addressed, that he is at present hidden, assuming this to be the meaning of the hapax legomenon *knf* (Niphal),[7] but that he will come once again into view, at which time he will instruct those whom the writer is addressing. But the strangest bit of information is that he will speak and be heard from behind them (*me'ahareka*). Since Yahweh gives instruction (e.g. Isa 2:3; 48:17; 54:13), and is therefore a teacher (*mi kamohu moreh*, 'Who is like him as a teacher?', Job 36:22), it is understandable that many commentators, following the lead of the Targum and Rashi,[8] have identified the teacher in our passage with God.[9] God was certainly associated

implications for their own situation were seized on by the authors of the Qumran pesharim (4QpIsa[a] 2-6 II 1-9; 4QpIsa[c] II 1021). This suggests that the Assyrian and Egyptian oppressors mentioned in the passage could be a coded allusion to the Seleucids and Ptolemies respectively.

6. Another Isaianic image: 'We grope like the blind along a wall, we feel our way like the sightless; we stumble at midday as at twilight, like the walking dead among the healthy.' (59:10)

7. The older commentators, for example August Dillmann, *Der Prophet Jesaia* (Leipzig: S. Hirzel, 1890 5th ed.), 276, took it to be a denominative verb from *kanaf*, 'wing', and therefore to have the meaning of hiding in order to protect and, in the context, with a passive rather than reflexive sense.

8. The Targum paraphrases as follows: 'He (God) will no longer remove his Shekinah from the sanctuary, but your eyes will see the Shekinah in the sanctuary, and your ears will hear the word behind you.' Similarly Rashi.

9. Among earlier commentators Dillmann, *Der Prophet Jesaia*, 276; Karl Marti, *Das Buch Jesaia* (Tübingen: J. C. B. Mohr, 1900), 225; Duhm, *Das Buch Jesaia*, 223; Johann Fischer, *Das Buch Isaias* (Bonn: Peter Hanstein, 1939), 203-4; more recently Clements, *Isaiah 1-39*, 250; Brevard S. Childs,

with those addressed in a special way, and is often said to be hidden, or to hide his face from his devotees, either on account of sin or for reasons more inscrutable; but what would it mean for God to speak and his voice to be heard from behind them? Moreover, the Sovereign Lord (*'adonay*) is named in the same sentence, which suggests that access to the guidance of a *human* teacher is precisely the way in which God will answer their prayers and show them favour.

It must be said that attempts to explain this peculiar image with reference to God have not been very convincing. Bernhard Duhm and John Skinner, two of the great names in Isaianic interpretation, had the idea of God as a father guiding his children as they walk ahead of him, while Fohrer opted for God as maternal guide.[10] Others had in mind the less appealing figure of a farmer walking behind a herd of cattle or sheep and nudging them in the right direction. Edward Kissane, the most distinguished Irish commentator on Isaiah in the modern period, seems to have pictured God as a shepherd. But when he realised that shepherds, biblical shepherds at any rate, lead their sheep from the front, he emended *moreka* to *ma'arahka*, 'your pathfinder, guide', a form not otherwise attested in Classical Hebrew.[11] More recently, Wim Beuken took the first *moreka* to refer to human teachers and the second to God, resulting in the somewhat peculiar translation: 'Your teachers shall not be pushed aside any more, but your eyes shall be looking upon your Teacher'. I am not sure how Beuken arrived at 'push aside' for *yikkanef*, but in any case the riddle of the voice that will be heard behind those addressed remained unsolved.[12]

It is tempting to find the subtext for this figure in the wilderness narratives, at the point where the alternative modes of guidance, by the angel (*mal'ak ha'elohim*) and the column of smoke (*'ammud 'anan*), come together. Both these providential

---

*Isaiah. A Commentary* (Louisville: Westminster/John Knox, 2001), 227.

10. Duhm, *Das Buch Jesaia*, 223; Skinner, *The Book of the Prophet Isaiah: Chapters I-XXXIX* (Cambridge: Cambridge University Press, 1915 2nd ed.), 246; Fohrer, *Das Buch Jesaia* II, 103.

11. Edward Kissane, *The Book of Isaiah I* (Dublin: Browne & Nolan, 1960 2nd ed.), 338, 346.

12. W. A. M. Beuken, 'Isaiah 30: A Prophetic Oracle transmitted in two successive paradigms', in C. C. Broyles and C. A. Evans (eds), *Writing and Reading the Scroll of Isaiah* (Leiden: Brill, 1997) II, 371.

agents lead from the front (Ex 13:21-22), but as the critical encounter with the Egyptians nears they move behind the Israelites (Ex 14: 19). Both here and in Isa 30: 19-21 there is the theme of guidance, but the crucial point in the latter is guidance *by means of teaching* while the purpose of the manoevre in the wilderness is protection, with the cloud column acting as a smokescreen.

A more promising point of departure is the extraordinary experience of Ezekiel which was both visual and auditory. Ezekiel sees and describes in detail the great and sublime vision of the chariot throne (Ezek 1:3), but he hears the sound of the winged living creatures and the wheels, which accompany and guide him into the Babylonian diaspora, behind him (3:12). Likewise, John, exiled in Patmos, witnesses phantasmagoric scenarios and, like Ezekiel, actually sees the living creatures round the throne (Rev 5:6), but at the outset hears a voice like a trumpet behind him (1:10), a voice which gives him his mission. These are no more than chance clues, but they may indicate the existence of a trope according to which auditory revelations were thought to come from behind the recipient. There is the further point that the preposition *'ahar* (*'ahare, me'ahare*) can have a temporal as well as spatial connotation ('after' as well as 'behind'), or a temporal sense can be expressed in spatial terms, as when we say, for example, 'I now have that experience behind me.' This suggests the possibility that those addressed in Isa 30:19-21 are being assured that the guidance they will receive from their teacher will come to them from the past.

The proposal to which these considerations are leading, and the solution which seems to me least open to objection, is that those addressed, a minority group which thought of itself as the holy remnant (cf Isa 65:8-10, 13-16; 66:5), are being promised an expression of divine favour in the form of the teaching and example of a prophetic figure, a leader, now inaccessible in person, perhaps in hiding, perhaps imprisoned, more likely dead. The cryptic *me'ahareka* would therefore have a temporal rather than spatial sense. After a period of sorrow and deprivation they will see him not in person, as they no doubt had done in the past, but as an inspiring presence in their lives, and they would find strength and guidance in his remembered teachings. If this is an acceptable reading of the passage, it would be an early example of a pattern familiar from the Qumran sectarian texts and the

New Testament. But we should now go on to inquire whether it finds support elsewhere in the book, especially in those passages generally thought to belong to its later redactional stages

## II

The idea of a charismatic, prophetic figure whose personality and teaching attract a following which, to a greater or lesser extent, segregates itself from the society at large and deviates from generally accepted social norms, is a recurring theme in the history of the Second Temple period. The pattern was anticipated during the time of the kingdoms by those 'sons of the prophets' (*bene hannevi'im*) who lived a coenobitic-type existence in segregated settlements. The Rechabites, by some considered forerunners of the Essenes, fit the same pattern, as also the Nazirites, fanatical opponents of state-sponsored syncretism in ninth-century BC Israel.[13] All three groups owed allegiance and obedience to a charismatic leader. Elijah and Elisha are both addressed as 'father' (*'av*) by their prophetic adherents (2 Kgs 2:12; 13:14), and we find Elisha presiding over the assemblies of the *nevi'im* (2 Kgs 4:38; 6:1; 2 Kgs 9:1). The story of Samuel's birth presents him in the guise of a Nazirite, and he is explicitly so designated in the 4QSam[a] reading of 1 Sam 1 :22 though the story may have originally been about Saul. At any rate, we find the adult Samuel presiding over a seance of ecstatics in the manner of a sheik presiding over a Dervish *tawaf* (1 Sam 19:18-24). Jonadab, founder of the Rechabite order, is still being referred to as 'father' by his followers almost two and a half centuries after his *floruit* (Jer 35:6). We are in no position to write the history of these movements, but Jeremiah's acted-out parable of offering the Rechabites wine in the temple precincts, and the persistence of the Nazirate down to the dawn of the Middle Ages, demonstrates that such

---

13. On the 'sons of the prophets' see 1 Kgs 20:35-41 and 2 Kgs 1:8, 13; the Rechabites participated in the bloody purge carried out by Jehu (2 Kgs 10:15-17) and served for Jeremiah as examples of fidelity to tradition (Jer 35:1-10); Samson exemplified comprehensively how not to be faithful to the traditions and prescriptions of the Nazirate (Jdg 13-16). On the view of Matthew Black that Essene asceticism had its ultimate origin in the 'nomadic' lifestyle of the Rechabites and Kenites, see the critical remarks of Chris H. Knight, 'The Rechabites of Jeremiah 35: Forerunners of the Essenes?' in James H. Charlesworth (ed), *Qumran Questions* (Sheffield: Sheffield Academic Press, 1995), 86-91.

movements could continue to find inspiration in the teaching of the founder long after the founder's death.[14]

The book of Isaiah refers only once to disciples (*limmudim*) of Isaiah where, after the failure of his intervention in international politics under Ahaz, he is told to secure the message and seal the teaching[15] among his disciples, no doubt to authenticate it at the time of future fulfilment (Isa 8:16). Whether this injunction to secure and seal is to be taken literally of a written text, as with the tablet of Maher-Shalal-Hash-Baz written with a stylus and duly notarised (8:1-2), or metaphorically with reference to disciples committing it to memory, it was at a later point reinterpreted in the context of the reception or non-reception of written prophecy:

> The vision of all these things has become for you like the words of a sealed book. When they hand it to one who knows how to read saying, 'Read this', he replies, 'I can't, for it is sealed.' When they hand the book to one who can't read saying, 'Read this', he replies, 'I don't know how to read.' (Isa 29:11-12)

This cryptic text gives little away, but it is a reasonable surmise that it refers to the non comprehension of the book of Isaiah as it existed at the time of writing. We recall that the book carries the title 'the vision of Isaiah' (1:1) and was known in the Second Temple period by the same title (2 Chr 32:32). And since the Isaianic tradition moves in the direction of the apocalyptic world view, in which esoteric book knowledge and sealed prophetic books are prominent motifs,[16] the sealed book referred to here may be the book of Isaiah to be read as an apocalyptic prophecy of the end time, as in fact the Qumran *pesharim* and the gospel writers interpreted it.

The leader-disciple relationship appears again in Isa 50:4-9, the third of Bernhard Duhm's *Ebed-Jahwe-Lieder*.[17] Like Isa 8:16,

---

14. On these prophetic groups and their leaders see my *A History of Prophecy in Israel* (Louisville: Westminster-John Knox, 1996, 2nd ed.), 48-64.

15. As elsewhere in the book (1:10; 2:3; 5:24; 30:9), *tora* refers to prophetic teaching.

16. Dan 12:4,9; 1 En 81:1-2; Odes Sol 9:11; 4 Ezra 14:44-48; 4QMyst[b]; Rev 10:1-4; 22:10.

17. A curious title since, whatever else these passages are, they are not songs.

this statement is in the prophetic first person. The speaker, who is identified as Yahweh's Servant only in the comment attached to the statement (50:10-11), has been given the tongue of the instructed (*limmudim*) so that he himself may sustain the dispirited by word of mouth. He is therefore a teacher and a leader, and he discharges this mission in the face of opposition which has reached the point of physical abuse. He is, notwithstanding, confident that God will be his vindicator (*matsdiq*, v. 8a). The comment attached to this declaration (50:10-11) refers to the prophetic Servant in the third person and, in addressing the public, distinguishes between the God-fearers who heed the voice of the Servant and those who choose to ignore it. The speaker clearly belongs to the former category and is therefore, in all probability, a disciple of the abused Servant. The syntax leaves it unclear as to whether the walking in darkness (v. 10b) refers to the condition of the Servant or to the wilful incomprehension of those who choose to go their own way. If the former, it would parallel the hiddenness of the teacher in 30:20, but in any case both passages reflect the theme of prophetic teacher and disciples.

The same teacher-disciple relationship is implicit in the fourth of the Servant texts (Isa 52:13-53:12). It opens and concludes with first-person discourse of Yahweh (52:13-15; 53:11b-12) but the central part, the panegyric, is spoken by one who, after sharing the common interpretation of the Servant's sufferings as divine punishment (53:1, 3-4), arrived at an understanding of their unique significance, in all probability only after the death of the Servant. The intensity of the language and its arcane, recondite character mark it as the language of discipleship no less clearly than in the previous Servant passage. On the reasonable assumption of a degree of coherence in the book, these two texts would refer to one and the same prophetic figure. From casual abuse in the first we move to fatal injuries in the second. As the Servant of the earlier text anticipates that God will be his vindicator (*matsdiq*, 50:8a), so the Servant of the last of the *Ebed-Jahwe-Lieder* will vindicate the Many, but will do so posthumously (*yatsdiq tsaddiq 'avdi larabbim*, 'My righteous Servant will vindicate the Many', 53: 11). And both passages speak of the Servant as engaged in teaching (50:4; 53:11).

The allusion to the *rabbim* deserves further consideration. In this instance the Masoretes read this substantive in the determined state, with the article, but they were not the first to do so. In the course of the fourth and final vision in Daniel we are told that the *maskilim*, that is, the teachers and leaders of the group from which the book comes, will instruct the Many (*yavinu larabbim*, Dan 11:33), and towards its conclusion we hear that 'the *maskilim* will shine like the brightness of the firmament, and those who vindicate[18] the Many (*matsdiqe harabbim*) like the stars for ever' (12:3). The connection with Isa 53 is too close to be coincidental. Towards the end of Isa 53 there is considerable textual and prosodic confusion, but v. 11 should probably read as follows: *beda'to yastdiq [tsaddiq] 'avdi larabbim*, 'By his knowledge my [righteous] Servant will vindicate the Many'.[19]

There is therefore reason to believe that Isa 53:11 offers the first instance of *rabbim* as a technical term for a group of disciples, and that this usage was adopted in the group in which and for which the book of Daniel was composed. The same usage was then taken up in the Qumran sectarian rule books and the New Testament.[20]

Another interesting feature of this verse is the description of the Servant as righteous which, even if the adjective *tsaddiq* was inserted into the verse at a later time, calls for an explanation. One reason for the putative insertion may be to make an intertextual link with another of those cryptic, apparently disconnected texts which occur so frequently in Isaiah:

1. The Righteous One has perished, and no one takes it to heart;
the devout are swept away, and no one gives it a thought.
It was on account of evil that the Righteous One was swept away.
2. He enters into peace.

18. The verb could also convey the idea of leading to righteousness (*tsedeq, tsedaqa*) by example and by instruction. This is probably the meaning implied in the title *moreh hatstsedeq*.
19. Since *tsaddiq* overloads the verse and the adjective generally follows the noun, it was probably added; see my *Isaiah 40-55. A New Translation with Introduction and Commentary* (New York: Doubleday, 2002), 346, 348-49. For one explanation see below.
20. 1QS VI 1,8,11-12; VII 10,13; CD XIII 9; XIV 8-9; XV 5. In the New Testament the term is restricted to contexts dealing with the significance of the death of Jesus, and drawing on the fourth Servant passage, e.g. Mt 20:28; 26:28; Mk 10:45; 14:24; 1 Cor 11 :24.

They repose in their last resting places.
He is upright in his conduct. (57:1-2)

While *tsaddiq* can be a collective singular, its occurrence here
with the article, and at the beginning and end of v. 1, permits the
suggestion that reference is being made to an individual righteous person in association with a group of the devout (*'anshe-
hesed*, the equivalent of *hasidim*). Commentators have struggled
to make some consecutive sense of v. 2, often by recourse to
drastic surgical procedures. My proposal is to read the verse as a
collection of three glosses on the preceding verse arranged in the
same order, that is to say, the first and third referring to the individual *tsaddiq*, the second to the *'anshe-hesed*, the devout. The
pattern is therefore a-b-a in both verses. If we read it with the
Servant of Isa 53 in mind, the affinities are easily detected. The
Servant and the Righteous One are, respectively, 'taken away'
(53:8a) and 'gathered', euphemisms for death; their passing goes
unregarded and unconsidered (53:8a); and in both cases evildo-
ing plays a role though the Servant and Righteous One have
done no evil (53:8b, 9). Both passages refer to burial (53:9a),[21]
and while the Righteous One enters into peace, the Servant will
see light and be satisfied (53:11a). Finally and for our theme most
importantly, as the Righteous One is associated with a group of
the devout, so the Servant is promised descendants (*zera'*,
'seed'), namely, discipleship.

### III

Duhm was quite clear that his *Ebed-Jahwe-Lieder* were compositions distinct from the rest of Deutero-Isaiah, not least in applying the term *'eved* to an individual prophetic figure rather than
to Israel as a whole. These four *Lieder* were composed later than
Deutero-Isaiah, some time in the early fifth century BC, and
were inserted into the book wherever there was space on the
papyrus roll.[22] Nowadays, however, the tendency is to look for
indications of inner consistency and coherence in the so-called
Deutero-Isaiah, and therefore to seek ways of integrating the
four Servant passages into this segment of the book. One line of
enquiry, which bears on the present argument, starts out from

---

21. In addition to 'bed', 'couch', 'coition', the substantive *mishkav* can
also mean 'final resting place', 'grave', as Ezek 32:25.
22. Duhm, *Das Buch Jesaia*, 19, 311.

those occasions where we hear the voice of an individual prophet, sometimes in association with a prophetic following. The second and third of the *Ebed-Yahwe-Lieder* (49:1-6; 50:4-9) are in the prophetic first person, but there are other instances. The opening words, among the most familiar in the Bible ('Comfort, O comfort my people, says your God', 40:1), are addressed to a prophetic plurality (there are five imperatives in the plural), but the voice of an individual prophet is also heard asking for and receiving the message he is to proclaim in preparing the way for the coming of the glory of Yahweh, the parousia (Isa 40:1-8).[23] This first encounter with the text sets the tone for what is to follow.

Other instances are, or appear to be, more detached from their context. At the conclusion of a Yahweh discourse dealing with the mission of Cyrus we find what appears to be an incomplete statement of mission by a prophet: 'And now the Sovereign Lord Yahweh has sent me, and his spirit ...' (48:16b).[24] In somewhat similar fashion a response by Yahweh to a community complaint is followed by address to an individual prophet (59:21):

> As for me, this is my covenant with them, declares Yahweh: my spirit that rests upon you and my words that I have put in your mouth will not be absent from your mouth or from the mouths of your descendants (literally 'seed', *zera'*) or from those of the descendants of your descendants declares Yahweh, from this time forward and for ever more.

This assurance of the validity and permanence of spirit-endowment is here addressed to an individual prophet as an expression of God's covenant with those referred to in the verse immediately preceding, the penitents of Israel, those who turn from transgression (*shave pesha'*).[25] Here as elsewhere in the book, the spirit is the spirit of prophecy (cf 61:1). The placing of the re-

---

23. Those addressed are prophets, not members of Yahweh's heavenly court; see my *Isaiah 40-55*, 279-80.

24. See my *Isaiah 40-55*, 294-95.

25. This is one of the more common self-descriptions in the Qumran sectarian writings, distinguishing them from the unregenerate majority; see 1QS I 17; X 20; CD II 5 = 4Q266 2 II 5; XX 17; 1QH[a] VI 24; X 9; XIV 6. The same term, or the variant *shave yisra'el*, 'penitents of Israel', is applicable in a special way to the Zadokite priests who formed the core of the group (CD IV 2-3).

vealed word in the mouth brings to mind the Moses-like
prophet promised in Deut 18:15-18 (cf Jer 1:9), and therefore at-
taches the promise to one of the great figures of the tradition and
one of the great moments of the past. In the context of the book
as a whole this is not an isolated statement. A comment attached
to the second of the *Ebed-Jahwe-Lieder* describes the Servant as 'a
covenant to the people' (49:8), and the Servant whose suffering
and death are lamented in Isa 53 is also promised descendants:
'He will see posterity (literally 'seed', *zera'*), he will prolong his
days' (v. l0b). The reference in both cases is unmistakably to disciples, in the sense of a prophetic succession which perpetuates
the spirit and the teaching of the master. The individual
prophetic voice is then heard for the last time in 61:1-4, the passage from which Jesus read in the Nazareth synagogue and
which he appropriated for himself (Lk 4:18-19). Reading Isa
30:19-21 as addressed to prophetic disciples is therefore consistent with indications in the book that prophetic groups owing allegiance to a master prophet and teacher played a significant
role in the evolution of the Isaianic tradition in the direction of
the sectarian[26] and apocalyptic world view which comes to
classical expression in the book of Daniel. Those addressed in
30:19-21 who now weep and suffer adversity, referred to elsewhere in the book as 'those who mourn over Zion' (61:2-3; 66:10),
will be guided by the remembered instruction and example of
their teacher no longer present in person. The non-self-referential
character of prophetic discourse makes it difficult to be more
precise, but it would be reasonable to posit a connection of some
kind with the Servant of Yahweh whose voice is heard in 49:1-6
and 50:4-9 and whose death is lamented in 53:1-11, probably
also in 57:1-2. This prophetic individual taught, exhorted, encouraged (49:2; 50:4), and he had disciples whose voices can be
identified and who continued to revere his memory after his
death. As some commentators have supposed, the hiddenness
of the teacher of Isa 30:19-21 could imply actual concealment
during a time of persecution, a situation which would be
consistent with the physical abuse and violent death suffered by
the Servant, together with other indications of opposition and
persecution directed, for example, against those who tremble at

---

26. The terms 'sect' and 'sectarian' are standard in the sociological literature and do not imply a negative evaluation of the phenomenon in
question.

God's word (66:5). The forensic language used in describing the treatment of the Servant in the last two *Ebed-Jahwe-Lieder* have led others to think of imprisonment.[27] This is by no means improbable, but the Servant's death is also recorded, and we have seen that guidance coming to the disciples from the past is more consonant with the wording of 30:19-21.

IV

There can be no doubt that the author of the book of Daniel had in mind the Isaianic Servant of the Lord in relation to the Many in presenting the *maskilim* who teach and vindicate (or lead to righteousness) their followers, also known as the Many (Dan 11:33; 12:3). The *maskilim-rabbim* relationship is hinted at in the opening chapter which presents the Israelite youths at the Babylonian court as comprehensively learned while at the same time assigning a special status to Daniel as skilled in the interpretation of visions and dreams (Dan 1:4, 17). This earliest interpretation and appropriation of the Servant texts is only one aspect of a major interpretative trajectory originating in the book of Isaiah which reaches early Christianity after passing through the Danielic cycle, the Qumran sectarian texts, and other more or less related texts from the late Second Temple period. This is a large subject awaiting further investigation; at this point we can do no more than present one or two examples. In the first place, the language of eschatological judgement in Daniel draws extensively on Isaiah, and early Christian writers, in their turn, draw on the book of Daniel. In particular, the idea of a predetermined final annihilating judgment is expressed most clearly in late strands of Isaiah and in Daniel, and in practically identical language.[28] A further point, not unconnected with the preced-

---

27. On this point Isa 51:14 may be relevant:

The one who now cowers will soon be released;
he will not go down to death, to the pit;
he will not lack for food.

However, the verse is textually and linguistically obscure; the context permits but does not demand this reference; see my *Isaiah 40-55*, 329-30, 334.

28. Examples: Isa 10:23 *kala veneheratsa 'adonay YHVH tseva'ot 'oseh beqerev kol-ha'arets* ('The Sovereign Lord YHVH of the hosts will bring about the decreed destruction in the midst of all the earth') and the practically identical prophetic utterance in 28:22b; with which compare. Dan 9:26-27 *neheretset shomemot ... ve'ad-kala veneheratsa tittak 'al-shomem*

ing, is that the book of Isaiah hinges on the exile and the formation of a new or renewed community after the return. This
community of penitents (*shavim*, Isa 1:27; 59:20)[29] is the prototype of the new community with which the Danielic group and
the Damascus community (CD I 3-8) identify. The call to
*metanoia* proclaimed first by John the Baptist, then by Jesus,
could then be seen as a way of appropriating the idea of a peni-
tent community (*shave pesha'*, 'those who turn away from iniquity',
Isa 59:20) and taking it out into the wider society. This self-des-
ignation is used quite frequently in the Qumran sects.[30] Another
Isaianic image frequently exploited in the Qumran sectarian
writings and in other late Second Temple texts is that of the new
community as an organic growth planted by God:

> Your people, righteous one and all,
> will possess the land forever,
> the shoot that I myself planted,
> the work of my hands, that I might be glorified (60:21).[31]

An echo of this figure can be heard in the gospel parables of

---

('desolations are decreed ... until the decreed destruction is poured out
upon the desolator') and Dan 11:36 *vehitsliah 'ad-kala za'am ki neheratsa
ne'esatah* ('He [Antiochus IV] will flourish until the time of wrath [for
the persecuted] is finished, for what has been decreed will be done');
note that the use of the passive is a common form of indicating divine
activity, cf Isa 10:23 above. The Isaianic image of judgment as a flood
passing through the country also appears in Daniel (Isa 8:8; 28:15, 18; cf
Dan 9:26; 11:10, 40).
29. The designation exploits the polyvalence of the verb *shuv*, meaning
'return' in a physical sense but also metaphorically returning or turning
to God; hence the substantive *teshuva*, 'repentance', 'turning' (Buber);
there is also occasionally a play on the similar verb *shvh* ('take captive')
and the corresponding substantive *shevi* ('captivity'). Hence the *shavim*
are penitents but also 'returnees' from captivity.
30. CD II 5; XX 17; 1QS I 17; X 20; 1 QH[a] VI 24; X 9; XIV 6.
31. See CD I 5-8, 'A shoot of (God's) planting sprouted from Israel and
Aaron in the time of wrath to possess his land'. According to Martin
Hengel, *Judaism and Hellenism* (Philadelphia: Fortress, 1974), I 175, this
*shoresh matta'at* refers to the *asidaioi* of 1 Macc 2:42 and 7:14. 1 En 93:9-10
speaks of an 'eternal plant of righteousness' which appeared at the end
of the seventh week of years; Jub 1:12-18 says that those who survive
the exile will be transplanted as a righteous plant, etc. According to 1QS
VIII 5, the council of the *yahad* was established as 'an eternal planting'
(*matta'at 'olam*).

growth and in Paul's words to the Corinthian Christians: 'I planted, Apollo watered, but God made it grow' (1 Cor 3:6).

Isa 30:19-21 is one of the more cryptic texts in the book which seems to have puzzled interpreters from early times. In translating the passage, the LXX took a quite different line – perhaps dictated by a contemporary situation no longer apparent according to which those addressed are being threatened by false teachers who will try to blindside them by approaching them from behind. The Vulgate stays closer to the Masoretic text but in his commentary Jerome has no explanation of *me'ahareka*, 'behind you'.[32] In this article I have argued that the passage can be read together with other texts in the books, especially but not exclusively those in which the Servant of Yahweh speaks or is spoken of, as contributing to the image of the prophetic master whose disciples are sustained by his teachings after his death at the hands of his persecutors, even long after his death. This pattern is replicated throughout the late Second Temple period, beginning with the *maskilim-rabbim* of Daniel, then the *moreh hatstsedeq* of Qumran, the martyred John the Baptist and his following, Jesus and the first Christians. Among the many portrayals of Jesus currently on offer – marginal Jew, Galilean peasant sage, peripatetic Cynic philosopher, etc – this interpretative trajectory with its point of departure in the book of Isaiah may strengthen the case for the presentation of Jesus as martyred prophet whose disciples are sustained by his spiritual presence among them and his remembered teachings. It should, at any rate, provide one more reason for integrating our understanding of the early Christian movement more completely into the history of the Jewish people in the late Second Temple period.

---

32. Roger gryson, *Commentaire de Jérome sur le prophète Isaïe. Livres VIII-XI* (Freigurg: Herder, 1996) 1091-95.

CHAPTER TWO

# The Messianic Secret in Mark

## Martin Hengel

More than almost any other scholar, Seán Freyne has extensively researched the homeland of Jesus, Galilee in the time between the 4th century BC and the 2nd century AD. In this he has made significant contributions to the understanding of Jesus and early Christianity.[1] Among the topics treated by him is the theme 'Messiah and Galilee', a topic that contains within it a seeming paradox – one could even say a secret – to which the author already refers in his first sentence: he begins his study with the objection of the Jewish opponents of Jesus: 'Surely the Messiah does not come from Galilee. Does not the scripture say that he is of the seed of David, and the Messiah comes from Bethlehem, the village David is from?'[3] The 'Messiah from Galilee' was already at that time a point of contention. This is also so today, because many would wish to have a completely unmessianic Jesus, who would be only a Jewish teacher and prophet. Against this, in his most recent book on Jesus, our *honorand* has rightly emphasised that Jesus appeared as a 'Galilean eschatological prophet' and was influenced by the 'suffering servant' of the book of Isaiah.[4] Now that the Qumran texts have substantially extended the breadth of our knowledge about Jewish messianic expectations in the time of Jesus, these concepts appear thoroughly compatible with the idea of an 'anointed one,' a figure who at that time did not yet have dogmatically unified form.[5]

---

1. See the bibliography in his most recent work, *Jesus a Jewish Galilean* (London: T & T Clark, 2004), 193.
2. Freyne, *Galilee and the Gospels: Collected Essays*, WUNT 125 (Tübingen: Mohr Siebeck, 2000), 230-270.
3. Jn 7:41f.; Ibid., 230.
4. Freyne, *Jesus*, 166–177.
5. See Johannes Zimmermann, *Messianische Texte aus Qumran*, WUNT II/104 (Tübingen: Mohr Siebeck, 1998); William Horbury, *Messianism Among Jews and Christians* (London and New York: T & T Clark, 2003),

In the following, it is not our intention to treat the very complex and much disputed problem of the messianic claim of Jesus as a whole.[6] Rather, we wish to focus on one controversial theme within this area, the messianic secret in the oldest gospel. We argue that it cannot be simply traced back to the christological presentation of the evangelist, nor does it represent an artificial construction of the post-Easter 'community' behind which an originally 'unmessianic' Jesus is hidden. It has its origins in Jesus' activity itself, so that one may speak of the 'secret of the Messiah from Galilee', for it is founded ultimately in the question already posed by the isolated Jewish province regarding the craftsman, miracle worker and preacher from the unimportant village of Nazareth: 'Who then is this?'[7] It is not simply a matter of a later literary or theological theory, but also of a historical problem that begins with the public ministry of Jesus in Galilee.

### I THE QUESTION MARK RAISED BY WREDE

A decisive reference point in the disputed question about the historical Jesus is the study of William Wrede, *Das Messiasgeheimnis in den Evangelien*.[8] In terms of method, this book marked a greater break from the older psychologising Jesus research than the major work of Albert Schweitzer, that carried in its first edition the subtitle 'From Reimarus to Wrede.'[9] In the same year as Wrede's book, there appeared also Schweitzer's programmatic work *Das Messianitäts- und Leidensgeheimnis. Eine Skizze des Lebens Jesu*.[10] Wrede's study anticipated the methods of the later *Redaktionsgeschichte* and by itself determined the path

34–64, 125–156, 275–288; Horbury, *Jewish Messianism and the Cult of Christ* (London: SCM Press 1998); John Collins, *The Scepter and the Star: The Messiah of the Dead Sea Scrolls and Other Ancient Literature*, (New York and London: Doubleday, 1995).

6. See Martin Hengel, *Studies in Early Christology* (Edinburgh: T & T Clark, 1995), 1–117; Martin Hengel and Anna Maria Schwemer, *Der messianische Anspruch Jesu und die Anfänge der Christologie*, WUNT 138, (Tübingen: Mohr Siebeck, 2001), 1–131.

7. Mk 4:41; cf 8:27 and 6:14f.

8. Göttingen: Vandenhoeck and Ruprecht, 1901 (3rd ed. 1963). For the dispute with Wrede, see also Hengel and Schwemer, *Anspruch Jesu, passim*.

9. Schweitzer, *Geschichte der Leben-Jesu-Forschung*, 2nd ed. (Tübingen: J. C. B. Mohr, 1913) [1st ed. 1906].

10. Tübingen, J. C. B. Mohr, 1901.

of research in the 20th century. By contrast, Schweitzer's research was basically oriented to the past, and with its psychologising methods was still bound to the deficiencies of the old 'Life
of Jesus' research of the 19th century. This approach followed
too trustingly the threads of the Marcan narrative, as if it was a
case here of a continuous biography. Nevertheless, Schweizer
went beyond Wrede's restrictive skepticism on a decisive point,
namely, that he consistently asked about the messianic self-consciousness of Jesus and what this meant for the path of Jesus.[11]
Wrede himself was admittedly much more cautious in his conclusions than the 'radical criticism' stemming from Bultmann
and his school, which itself then fell into disagreement over the
theological significance of the Jesus question. With Wrede, it
was mainly a question only of 'the testing' of the 'evangelical
tradition about Jesus as the Messiah'; he pushed aside the question about his 'messianic consciousness'. Further study of this
topic could not be undertaken due to his premature death at age
47 on November 23, 1906. According to a recently published letter to Adolf von Harnack on January 2, 1905, he seemed, however,
to have changed his opinion, perhaps under the influence of his
friend Bousset.[12] Already at the end of his book on the messianic
secret he expressed himself only guardedly, for he knew that he
was contradicting the general consensus of the time. Thus, he asserted only: 'The question, whether Jesus took himself to be the
Messiah and proclaimed himself as such, has not been conclusively answered up to now.'[13] His own research led then to the

11. Here he arrives at the factually correct result, opposing Wrede, 'that
the influence of the faith of the early Christian communities upon the
synoptic accounts is not as deep as one was inclined to accept up to
now.' (Das Messias- und Leidensgeheimnis, IX). On this judgement, see
also Martin Dibelius in his review of Bultmann's Geschichte der synoptischen Tradition 2nd ed. 1931, DLZ Dritte Folge, 3. Jg. Heft 24, 1109: 'The
Gospels show in the clearest way how small the influence of the new
theological ideas upon the material in the Gospels [Evangelienstoff]
basically was; otherwise, the Kyrios faith and the sacramental theology
would have had a much stronger influence.'
12. 'I am more inclined than before to believe that Jesus had considered
himself to be the Messiah ...' See Hans Rollmann and Werner Zager,
'Unveröffentlichte Briefe WILLIAM WREDES zur Problematisierung
des messianischen Selbstverständnisses Jesu,' Zeitschrift für neuere
Theologiegeschichte 8 (2001), 274–322 (317) and Hengel and Schwemer,
Anspruch, IX f.
13. Wrede, Messiasgeheimnis, 207.

result: 'If Jesus really recognised and characterised himself as the Messiah, then the genuine tradition is so much interwoven with the later traditions that it is not easy to identify this.'[14]

Although he himself supported an 'adoption christology' brought about by the Easter appearances, he does not wish to claim that Jesus did not possess any messianic consciousness: 'It is not the intention here to reach a decision on whether Jesus really took himself to be the Messiah ... My intention in these remarks was *to raise a question mark over it*.'[15] In order to raise this question mark Wrede admittedly draws upon what he finds fault with so mercilessly in his opponents: a 'Jesus psychology':

> The difficulty is only relocated to another point, namely, the *psychological plane* ... How can we conceive such a certainty in Jesus ...? How can he know that, i.e. believe it in a firm and certain way? If all he had was hope, how could he have explicitly raised a messianic claim? And he must have done that in some sense, if he had really expressed his declaration before the High Priest and as the Messiah received the death sentence.[16]

With this, Wrede contradicts the ruling opinion of the exegetes of the time, which would not admit 'the standard of popular psychology ... for a religious personality such as Jesus'.[17] In his short study 'Zum Thema 'Menschensohn''[18] he again takes up the psychological argument that was usually rejected by him. If it is a matter of being forced to play one psychology of Jesus off against another, then it is probably better to prefer the strange-sounding solution, the one that is foreign to our everyday understanding. Our normality, in the form of a popular 'enlightened' apologetic, should not be transferred to Jesus.[19]

The work of Wrede was valued for its penetrating analyses, but the hypothesis of an unmessianic Jesus was nevertheless rejected by almost all well-known New Testament researchers of that time, even by such critical scholars as Heinrich J. Holtzmann, Adolf Jülicher, Julius Wellhausen, Johannes Weiss,

---

14. *Ibid.*, 208. One can easily agree with this conclusion.

15. *Ibid.*, 221f; my emphasis.

16. *Ibid.*, 221; my emphasis.

17. *Ibid.*

18. ZNW 5 (1904), 359f.

19. This problem was already raised by H. J. Cadbury, *The Peril of Modernizing Jesus* (New York: Macmillan, 1937/London: SPCK, 1962).

Paul Wernle and Hans von Soden among others. This was true
even for his friend, Wilhelm Bousset.[20] In his Foreword to the
2nd edition of Wrede's short work on Paul, he points out that
Wrede had ended his work on the messianic secret

'with a great question mark' and that Wrede, even though he
inclined toward a negative answer to the question whether Jesus
had held himself to be a Messiah, was 'rather too careful and
conscientious to pronounce this 'No'.' He had not yet 'considered all the possibilities, or researched the broad field of the
transmission of the dominical sayings ... He remained stuck at
the halfway point.'[21]

Bousset, the scholar of Jewish apocalyptic, remained critical
towards Wrede's thesis of the unmessianic Jesus.[22] He also
expressed himself very cautiously, but did not share his negative judgment,[23] but rather wanted to hold on to the messianic
claim of Jesus. Later it was Rudolf Bultmann who first picked up
Wrede's thesis, taking it up without any limitations,[24] indeed,
sharpening it even more. The result was that after the Second
World War, it had penetrated throughout Germany, and in part

---

20. See the evidence for this in Hengel and Schwemer, *Anspruch Jesu*,
17–27.
21. Printed in the Introduction from W. Wrede, *Vorträge und Studien*
(Tübingen: J. C. B. Mohr, 1907), VIII.
22. *Kyrios Christos*, 5th ed. (Göttingen: Vandenhoeck & Ruprecht, 1965),
2ff, 5, 9f, 18 n. 2, 35, 37f. [1st ed. 1913].
23 See also for this Bousset, *Jesus* (Halle/S: Gebauer-Schwetschke:
1904), 87f.
24. 'Die Frage nach dem messianischen Bewußtsein Jesu and das
Petrus-Bekenntnis,' *Zeitschrift für neutestamentliche Wissenschaft* 19
(1920): 165–174 [republished in Bultmann, *Exegetica. Aufsätze zur
Erforschung des Neuen Testaments* (Tübingen: J. C. B. Mohr, 1967), 1-10].
His presentation of the evidence is quite weak. In line with this, in his
*Geschichte der synoptischen Tradition* all passages where a 'messianic consciousness' might be seen are classified from the outset as inauthentic.
This pre-judgment determines the 'historical-critical' result. See also his
*Theologie des Neuen Testaments*, 9th ed. (Tübingen: Mohr Siebeck, 1984),
26-34, where he turns a conjecture of Wrede into a certain thesis: 'That
the life of Jesus was not messianic soon became no longer understandable ... and *thus the gospel account of his activity is set within the light of the
messianic faith*. The contradiction of this conception to the material in the
tradition comes to expression in the *theory of the messianic secret*' (33);
emphasis in original.

in even more radical form than that held by Wrede and Bultmann, for a large number of their school, Ernst Käsemann, Hans Conzelmann, Philip Vielhauer among others, have denied all the 'Son of Man' sayings to Jesus. Today, this viewpoint is represented especially in the flourishing speculation in America about Q and the Gospel of Thomas.

II THE COMMAND TO KEEP SILENT
AND THE DISCIPLES' LACK OF UNDERSTANDING

Wrede in his work concentrated on the gospel of Mark, because this oldest source was generally used at his time as the foundation for a biographical presentation of Jesus and his messianic secret, in order to construct a psychological development in the messianic consciousness of Jesus. It also was seen by Albert Schweitzer as furnishing the key for understanding Jesus.

Wrede brought under the heading 'messianic secret' a great variety of items that in our opinion can be held together as one topic only by force. He sought in Mark motifs that cannot be completely explained from one source.[25]

(i) The first such motif he calls the 'messianic recognition of the demons'.[26] Now it certainly seems reasonable that during the spectacular procedure of an exorcism the ill person, through the presence of the healer or through his touch, would become greatly agitated and would express this excitement by crying out. It is just as understandable that one would explain these exclamations as the cry of the demon in the possessed, who knows the power of his opponent and tries to defend himself. This does not have to be understood as 'messianic', i.e. texts such as Mk 9:20 and 1:34 do not of themselves fall into this category of the messianic secret, but rather first through the wider context of the gospel.

The recognition of the messianic status of Jesus by the demons appears *expressis verbis* only in three texts: Mk 1:23-25, where Jesus is given the puzzling title 'the Holy One of God', which does not exactly correspond to an established 'messianic

---

25. This inconsistency was clearly seen by Heikki Räisänen thirty years ago; see 'Die Parabeltheorien im Markusevangelium', *Suomen Eksegeettisen Seuran julkaisuja* [SESJ] 26, (1973); 'Das 'Messiasgeheimnis' im Markusevangelium', SESJ 28 (1976); both studies are collected in : Räisänen, *The Messianic Secret in Mark* (Edinburgh: T & T Clark 1990).
26. Mk 1:23-28; cf the summary accounts in 1:34; 3:11f.

dogmatics'.[27] It is rather a case of a traditional scene. The second attestation is the redactional summary Mk 3:11f, where the demons name Jesus with the title which characterises the christology of the gospel: 'You are the Son of God', whereupon he warns them[28] 'that they should not make this known'. Now here the evangelist sets down in a clear way his understanding of the 'messianic secret': Jesus' true status should not be made known to outsiders through demonic powers.[29]

Apart from this passage, one could also interpret the connection between recognition and the command to keep silent as that Jesus does not want to accept any 'confession' from the mouths of the demons. On account of their supernatural knowledge, the demons know and fear the 'stronger' one, the one who holds power over them.[30]

In 5:6f with the possessed of Gerasa we have the confession 'Son of the Most High God.'[31] The command to keep silent is missing; Jesus actually permits a discussion with the demon and requests that the healed man 'proclaim what the Lord has done for him' to the townspeople. Here perhaps it is a case of a gentle hint of the later mission to the gentiles through the evangelist.[32]

---

27. Lk 4:34 par; cf Jn 6:69. The designation 'the Holy One of God' can be applied to the High Priest: Ps 106 (LXX 105):16; cf Sir 45:6 and his golden plate Ex 28:36; 39:30 (LXX 36:37); further to the Nazirites Jdg 16:17 LXX cod B; and only secondarily to the Davidic ruler: Ps 89 (LXX 88): 36 according to the LXX in contrast to the MT. On 'Jesus als der messianische Hohepriester,' see Schwemer in Hengel and Schwemer, *Anspruch*, 226ff.
28. 3:12.
29. The title 'Son of God' describes for Mark more than 'Christos' and 'Son of Man' the real status of Jesus; see 1:11; 9:7; 13:32; 14:61; 15:39. Cf also the double address of the devil to Jesus, Lk 4:1–13 = Mt 4:1–11.
30. Cf 1:24: 'You have come to destroy us' and 5:7: 'I adjure you by God, do not torment me.'
31. On this address, cf. 1:24: Here Mark uses a LXX formula. 'God Most High' was the official designation of the Jewish God before or by non-Jews. On this, see Hengel, *Judentum und Hellenismus*, 3rd ed., WUNT 10 (Tübingen: Mohr Siebeck, 1988) 554ff and the index, s. v. 687.
32. The closest parallel, to which Wrede (30) correctly points, is Acts 16:16ff. On this, see Friedrich Avemarie, 'Warum treibt Paulus einen Dämonen aus, der die Wahrheit sagt? Geschichte und Bedeutung des Exorzismus zu Philippi, Act 16,16-18,' in: *Die Dämonen – Demons. Die Dämonologie der israelitisch-jüdischen und frühchristlichen Literatur im Kontext ihrer Umwelt*, ed. Armin Lange, Hermann Lichtenberger and K. F. Diethard Römheld (Tübingen: Mohr Siebeck, 2003), 550–576; cf also 19:15.

It is thus clear that Mark at two points (clearly in Mk 3:10-12 and greatly abbreviated in 1:34, where one can grasp the meaning only on the basis of 3:12), introduces into the exorcism narratives the motif of the 'messianic secret' in the sense of a keeping secret of his status. Yet these narratives themselves vary too much for one to place them exclusively under this one theme. That Jesus' 'messianic authority' is revealed in the exorcisms emerges completely independently of the Marcan theory from the Logia tradition in sayings such as Lk 11:20 or 10:18-20 and the interpretation of his person as the more powerful one.[33] In addition there is the saying about the messianic liberation of Isa 61:1f which stands at the heart of Jesus' first preaching in Nazareth where he presents himself as the 'prophetic anointed one'.[34]

(ii) The command to the demons to keep silent should be clearly distinguished from the command to those healed not to tell about their healing further, for in contrast to the former, *with the healings of Jesus, messianic status is not involved at all*. It is a case of only four (or better, three) texts in total. Mk 8:26 does not contain a command to keep silent, rather only the request to the healed man not to return to the village of Bethsaida, from which Jesus had led him out. It was the *secondary*, strongly varying textual tradition that first added to this a command to keep silent.[35] This account, narrated in a lively fashion, does not fit the picture of the usual miracle stories. The variety of these narratives in Mark is often overlooked.

This theme is encountered in the healing of the leper, 1:43-45, where Jesus after an emphatic command to silence, adds the atypical direction that the healed man should show himself to the priest and offer up the sacrifice associated with healing.[36] It is a case of a direction that actually contradicts the sense of the command to keep silent. For the obvious consequence is that this man would spread the news abroad about the wonderful

---

33. On Jesus as the 'stronger,' see Mk 3:27 = Mt 12:29; cf Lk 11:21f, but also Mk 1:7 = Lk 3:10 = Mt 3:11.

34. Lk 4:17ff, cf 7:22f = Mt 11:4-6, see also Mt 5:31. One should also refer to 4Q 521.

35. The latter is missing in the best textual witnesses: Sin, B, W, L f[1] pc sy[s] sa bo[pt].

36. Mk 1:44 = Lk 5:14 = Mt 8:4; cf also Lk 17:14. The priest thus becomes an 'official' witness to the miraculous healing; see Mt 8:4.

healing. It creates dramatic intensification and contrast: Jesus can no longer openly enter into Capernaum, but must rather retreat to an uninhabited place: 'even so they came to him from every quarter.' It happens in a similar way with the healing of the deaf-mute whose narrative is differently structured.[37] Jesus takes him away from the crowd and requests that the healed man and his companions tell no one about what happened. They, however, do it 'even more'.

In Mk 5:35-43, the raising of the daughter of Jairus, Jesus expressly orders the parents (and the three disciples), who are beside themselves in amazement, to keep the event secret. The pragmatic request that follows, to give the girl something to eat, underlines the reality of the miracle. In all three cases, the command to keep silent had nothing strictly speaking to do with Jesus' messianic mission, about which there is nothing said in this context, the more so since the people according to 6:14f and 8:28 already hold Jesus to be an especially important prophet. It is clear that the isolation of the deaf-mute in 7:36 and the eviction of the mourners in 5:40 is meaningful within the narrative: the miracle worker does not want to be disturbed while he is working. For Mark, the command to keep silent may emphasise in an effective way the contrast between Jesus' reserve and the contemporary impact whereby his fame was spreading, but the original meaning of the trait is to be developed from 1:45; the miracle worker seeks to defend himself from crowds that increase with every healing, but he has no success in this. The motif whereby Jesus withdraws to a lonely place[38] has nothing to do with the messiah question; it is understandable by itself. In our view, the command to keep silent given to those healed goes back to the memory of Jesus' deeds. That Mark uses it more for narrative effect than for the 'dogmatic' reasons that Wrede continually imputes, is shown by the fact that he can dispense with it without any problems in other healing stories.[39] In order to obtain a Jesus free from 'messianic dogma', Wrede read into the second gospel far too much a supposed Marcan 'messiah-dog-

---

37. 7:32-37; according to 7:31, for Mark the cure actually takes place outside of Galilee in pagan territory.

38. 1:45b; cf 1:12f, 45; 6:31f, 46f.

39. Cf 2:1-11; 31-5; 7:24-30; cf also 8:22-25; 9:14-27; 10:46-51. In the numerous summary accounts there is never a general command to keep silent given to those healed.

matics'. Others then followed him in this. Naturally Mark is always also writing with a theological intent, but he is at the same
time a very talented dramatic narrator. He narrates 'Jesus stories'
and does not compose a 'theological treatise' about timeless
truths, but reports about an event in space and time. Only one
who takes him seriously as a tradition-bound narrator, can also
understand him as a 'theologian'.

(iii) This holds in a similar way for the '*lack of understanding of
the disciples,*' which, despite the fact that the disciples know who
Jesus is, increases up until the bitter end, the betrayal of Judas,
the falling asleep in Gethsemane, the flight of the disciples, and
the denial of Peter. It has *absolutely nothing* to do with the 'messianic secret' in the sense of Wrede's theory where a bridge is
created between the completely unmessianic original Jesus tradition and a later image of Jesus where the messiah theme has
been painted in. The disciples indeed know Jesus' stature even
before the messianic confession of Peter, which only articulates
the conviction to which they have already come. Thus John, who
took exception to this contradiction in Mark, transfers the confession of Jesus' messiahship to the opening scenes.[40]

Since Mark assumes that at least the earliest disciples called
in Mk 1:16ff are present at Jesus' healings, he also presupposes
that they see in him from the beginning the eschatological redeemer and Son of God. He presupposes a 'development' in a
biographical-psychological sense neither by Jesus nor by the disciples. Ancient biography did not yet know about modern ideas
of development. In 2:10, 17, 19f, 25, 28 the Marcan Jesus (leaving
totally aside the 'confessions' of the demons) has already said
what was decisive for christology, and he did this in the presence of the disciples and before his adversaries who must reject
the claim made by Jesus. Above all, the 'bridegroom' in 2:19 can
be properly understood only as a messianic metaphor. It does
not fit a 'rabbi' or a 'prophet'. Mark probably assumes that 'son
of man' was a code term that Jesus could use as a self-designa-
tion, because it was not a universal and generally recognised

---

40. Jn 1:35-51; cf Lk 5:8ff (esp v. 8) and 4:18ff, where he allows Jesus with
the quote from Is 61:1f to refer to his 'spiritual anointing' and the fulfilment of this promise. Mary (and the family of Jesus?) know of this from
the beginning. On the other hand, John and Luke, even after the revelation of his messiahship can still describe him as a 'prophet': Jn 4:44;
6:14; 7:40; 9:17; Lk 7:16, 39; 13:33; 24:19.

term for the Messiah, though he nevertheless still presumes that the disciples knew what Jesus meant by it.[41]

On the other hand, one gets the impression that the lack of understanding of the disciples, despite the clear revelation of his messiahship, does not decrease as the gospel progresses toward the passion, but rather *intensifies*. In a similar way, from chapter 2 onwards the enmity of the religious leaders against Jesus *increases*.[42] In this way, the fate of Jesus takes on a unique significance. *It is at the same time the 'salvation' and the crisis for Israel* that affects everyone without exception, even the circle of his closest disciples. The climax lies in the events on Golgotha. There Jesus dies abandoned by God and men as the 'servant of God' 'for the many'.[43]

In all this there also arise tensions and contradictions that are probably consciously intended. Thus after the call of the twelve, 3:16-19, the disciples in the closest circle are his representatives and successors who surround him continually like a family, because they do God's will.[44] According to 4:11, they are still the chosen ones, to whom 'the secret of the Kingdom of God' has been given, while 'those outside,' the stubborn crowd, as in Isa 6:9, are given only parables as puzzling words. In 4:34 the group of the twelve in a straightforward way are identified as 'his own disciples'. To them alone does he interpret the true meaning of his puzzling parables. It is striking that while Mark indeed does speak once of the 'secret of the Kingdom of God', he never speaks about a 'secret' in connection with the messiahship of Jesus.

(iv) This questionable Marcan 'parable theory', which Wrede also wants to subsume under the 'messianic secret', is something that in its present form is a secondary Marcan theologumenon. As in Jn 12:40, Acts 28:26f and Rom 11:8, it is meant to explain the scandal of the unbelief of God's people in the face of the God-sent Messiah which, on the basis of Isa 6:9, is to be seen as hardness of heart brought about by God. The 'secret of the

---

41. On this problem, see Horbury, *Messianism Among Jews and Christians*, 125-155: 'The range of meaning of the phrase allowed it to be both self-referential and messianic; in its aspect of opacity which the hearer was invited to pierce, it resembled the parables' (151).
42. 2:10; 3:6, 21, 23.
43. Mk 10:45; 14:24.
44. 3:34f.

Kingdom of God' is proclaimed alone to the disciples, to whom Jesus unlocks the parables.[45] To the people, on the other hand, he speaks in riddles 'so that ... they hear and do not understand'.[46] For that reason they are not able to believe in his message. The unbelief of Israel is ultimately grounded in the mystery and predestination of God. This really secondary Marcan theory has very little directly to do with a supposedly unmessianic Jesus and the real Marcan 'messianic secret', which in reality is limited to very few passages. It tends rather to contradict it.

(v) A certain criticism of the disciples is first hinted at in a question of Jesus in 4:13: 'Do you not understand this parable? Then how will you understand all the parables?' This criticism increases in 4:40; 6:52; 8:17ff and reaches its first high point in the objection of Peter to the first prediction of the passion directly after the messianic confession, and the brusque rejection of the disciple as Satan by Jesus in 8:31-33. From then on, the lack of understanding is focused on the predictions of Jesus' suffering (and resurrection)[47] and secondarily on the disciples striving for positions of prominence, although both are linked.[48] The disciples thus become a warning for the community, which also confesses its faith in Jesus and yet in view of the expected last trials – the Roman community had just passed through the terrible persecution under Nero in 64 AD – still lies in danger of denying Jesus and of falling away.[49] The 'carrying of the cross' during this persecution had become a cruel reality.[50] Mark chose the traditions that fit into this schema and he in part also reshaped or expanded the material, such as the individual predictions of the passion, and also arranged it in a narrative framework. Behind this, nevertheless, there usually stand concrete traditions which go back to the band of disciples, especially to Peter, the most important guarantor of the tradition. To these traditions

---

45. 4:13, 34.

46. 4:12; cf Isa 6:10. Isa 6:9f was a fundamental text for the early community, only comparable with Isa 53, which also speaks of the failure of the followers of the Suffering Servant. See on this Mt 13:14f; Lk 8:10; Acts 28:26f; Rom 11:8.

47. 9:10, 32; 10:32; 14:18f, 27, 37, 40, 50, 68ff.

48. 9:5f, 14ff, 33; 10:35-45; 14:29.

49. 8:34-38; cf 9:42-48; 13:12f, 19; 14:38.

50 See Tacitus, *Annals* 15, 44, 4f; Martin Hengel, *Crucifixion* (Philadelphia: Fortress Press, 1977), 26: *aut crucibus adfixi et flammati.*

belong, among others, the scene in Gethsamene,[51] the denial of Peter and the request of James and John, sons of Zebedee.

Except for the messianic confession at Caesarea Philippi, the puzzling transfiguration account and the prophecies of the coming suffering of the 'Son of Man,' these narratives have no direct relation to the question disputed by Wrede and particularly his successors, whether with the pre-Easter Jesus there was already associated a 'messianic' claim. That the disciples in Mark's gospel are so often portrayed in an unfavourable light is certainly not a malicious invention of later Christian authors. Rather, it is linked with the deep impression made by the message of Jesus which, after his death and resurrection appearances, opens their eyes to their own fault, their failure, and their stupidity. They become without exception 'justified sinners', their spokesman Peter above all the others. In Luke this insight is transferred already to the confession of Peter at his calling.[52] With Mark these remembrances and impressions are paradigmatically and paraenetically shaped. The later apocryphal gospels and Acts of the Apostles sketch here predominantly a different picture.

(vi) There is also no doubt that the prophecies of the passion, broadly prefiguring the passion of Jesus, are *vaticinia ex eventu*. It is nevertheless too facile to declare all the prophecies of Jesus' suffering from the start as unhistorical. This presupposes that – after the execution of John the Baptist – he went up to Jerusalem without any apprehensions. One should not turn him into an unworldly dreamer.[53] Besides the actual prophecies of the passion, we have other texts which by their form and content show themselves to be authentic, such as the sharply delineated and disturbing doublet Lk 12:49f, 13:33, and the whole last supper section. Would the later community have placed in the mouth of Jesus (now elevated to the right hand of God) such an unusual word image as Lk 12:50 with the reference to his deep struggle? In addition, a basis for the words of the suffering Son of Man in Mark can be traced back to Jesus himself.[54] Finally, here Mk 12:1-9

---

51. On this, see Reinhard Feldmeier, *Die Krisis des Gottessohnes. Die Gethsemaneerzählung als Schlüssel der Markuspassion*, WUNT II/21 (Tübingen: Mohr Siebeck, 1987).

52. 5:8.

53. See on this point Seán Freyne, *Jesus*, 165 f.

54. See on this J. Jeremias, *Neutestamentliche Theologie I* (Gütersloh: Gerd Mohn, 1971), 264 ff.; Hans F. Bayer, *Jesus' Predictions of Vindication and Resurrection*, WUNT II/20 (Tübingen: Mohr Siebeck, 1986). Cf also Mk 10:38.

must also be mentioned,[55] which in our opinion goes back to a genuine parable of struggle from Jesus.

The theories of Wrede and Schweitzer are diametrically different, and yet their mistakes have the same root. Both believed that the disputed question about the messianic consciousness of Jesus could be solved through one comprehensive theory drawn from the gospel of Mark. The former believed that he grounded this theory well, the latter that he had refuted it. In reality, neither one nor the other is possible. The only possible way of approaching this lies in the interaction of numerous, quite different texts from Mark and from the Logia tradition with reference to four areas: (a) the witnesses to the Jewish messianic expectations, which have been considerably extended through the Qumran discoveries; (b) the relations of Jesus to his 'precursor', John the Baptist; (c) the passion of Jesus and its prehistory in Jerusalem after Jesus' entry and (d) the question of the emergence of the earliest christology and its rapid taking shape in the post-Easter circle of the disciples of Jesus, where the words and deeds of Jesus were still a living memory.[56] Wrede had neglected all four points and the same is even more true for his followers, Rudolf Bultmann and the majority of his students. One must give Wrede credit that, in contrast to his imitators, he only raised a large question mark but did not answer the question with a great 'no', as some did later with historically less justification. Rather, he worked and reflected on the theme further so that in the end, as the letter to Harnack shows, he began cautiously to reconsider his former opinion.[57] Against the popular thesis that 'the community' after the Easter appearances had made the crucified one into the Messiah, there stands the fact that we possess no Jewish parallels for this. The martyrs can be raised up to be close to God, but through this they do not become a messianic figure.[58]

---

55. See on this M. Hengel, 'Das Gleichnis von den Weingärtnern Mk 12:1-12 im Lichte der Zenonpapyri und der rabbinischen Gleichnisse,' *ZNW* 59 (1968) 1–39; Bayer, *Jesus' Predictions*, 90ff. K. Snodgrass, *The Parable of the Wicked Tenants*, WUNT 27 (Tübingen: Mohr Siebeck, 1983). See now also J. S. Kloppenborg, 'Self-Help or *Deus ex machina* in Mark 12:9', *NTS* 50 (2004): 495-518, which only wants to exclude 12:9 as 'part of its secondary allegorization' (495).

56. On this, Hengel and Schwemer, *Messianischer Anspruch, passim*.

57. See footnote 12 above.

58. For this, see Martin Hengel, "Setze dich zu meiner Rechten!'. Die

### III THE REAL MESSIANIC SECRET

There remain the two only real 'texts on the messianic secret' in the strict sense in Mark: the confession of Peter and the transfiguration account. Only in these does Jesus forbid people that they should speak about him as the Messiah and Son of Man.

(i) Both narratives are widely seen as resurrection stories that were incorporated into the gospels. This conjecture does not testify to the critical sense of its proposers. With regard to the transfiguration story on the mount of revelation, neither Moses nor Elijah nor the voice from heaven,[59] nor the preferred disciples, nor the foolish behaviour of Peter can be linked to a resurrection narrative. One needs a lot of imagination to see such a story here. Ultimately, the resurrection appearances lead to a confession of faith and to mission, not to misunderstanding and more failure. The best way to describe the transfiguration is as the further development of an account of a pre-Easter vision.[60] Visions did not emerge first only in the early community as a result of Easter, but rather already with Jesus himself and in the pre-Easter band of disciples. We can refer here to his baptism,[61] to the temptation narratives, to the account of Jesus walking on the water or to Logia such as Lk 10:18f, Mt 18:10 and the words about the future revelation of the Son of Man, Lk 17:24. The apocalyptic enthusiasm of early Christianity begins with Jesus himself and continues in the early community, and also with Paul. After Pentecost, the community of disciples believe themselves to have received the Spirit of him who was raised to the right hand of God, in whose fullness he himself had been working. There is little reason to admit the significance of visions for the disciples after Easter while at the same time denying them for the time of companionship with Jesus. Clearly Mark placed this text, with the voice of God to the disciples: 'This is my beloved Son, listen to him',[62] at the end of the Petrine confession as the decisive mid-point of the gospel, and directly linked it

---

Inthronisation Christi zur Rechten Gottes and Psalm 110:1', in *Le Trône de Dieu*, M. Philonenko (ed), WUNT 69 (Tübingen: Mohr Siebeck, 1993), 108–194 (188ff).

59. They play absolutely no role in the Easter tradition.

60. Seán Freyne, *Jesus*, 159ff refers to the parallels in the visions of 1 Enoch 12-14, which he places in a Galilean context.

61. Mk 1:10.

62. 9:7; cf 1:1, 11; 15:39.

with the voice of God at the baptism, working it out theologically with great care. The voice of heaven from the cloud, the place of God's presence already on Sinai,[63] in contrast to the Petrine confession in which only what was already known to the disciples was openly expressed for the first time, brings about a genuine 'advance in revelation'. Jesus, the Messiah of Israel, is at the same time the Son, who, inseparable from God, speaks in God's place. For this reason, the disciples – and the whole Jesus community – should listen to him, to him alone.[64] Just as with the Petrine confession, there follows here also a command to keep silent. By itself it is thoroughly plausible that Jesus should have forbidden the disciples to speak of visionary experiences. In the interpretation of Mark – what lay before him in the tradition, we cannot know in detail – the central command to keep silent about the messiahship in 9:9 signifies that the disciples only after Easter really understand this revelation, and that means above all the heavenly voice that asks them to listen only to the Son of God. It is first through the encounter with the risen one that they are confirmed in their faith in Jesus as the Son, one who is inseparably joined with the Father.[65] As long as they have not been witnesses to the resurrection of the Son of Man and Son of God, they do not understand at all what 'resurrection from the dead' really means,[66] even when every pious Jew of that time would have known texts such as Isa 26:19 or Dan 12:2f. Through Jesus' resurrection, 'resurrection from the dead' becomes a living experience for the disciples and is no longer only a shadowy apocalyptic knowledge. Behind Mk 9:10 and other texts of misunderstanding, there may lie the early Christian idea that the disciples received the Spirit only after the raising of Jesus and that it is first this action, as John in his paraclete sayings of the farewell discourse emphasises, that opens up the full mystery of the person of Jesus. Mark also can speak in several places about

---

63. Ex.19:6-20:1; 24:15ff; cf 40:34ff (35 = Mk 9:7).

64. This advance in revelation will be blurred in Mt 16:16 ff through the extensive confession of Peter and Jesus' response.

65. Rom 1:3f; cf Acts 2:34-36; on this, see Martin Hengel, *Sohn Gottes*, 2nd ed. (Tübingen: Mohr Siebeck, 1977). Cf also Lk 24:19-21 and for this Ulrike Mittmann-Richert, *Der Sühnetod des Gottesknechts. Die lukanische Interpretation von Jesaja 53* (Tübingen: Mohr Siebeck, 2006) forthcoming in the WUNT series.

66. 9:10.

the post-Easter gift of the Spirit.[67] Moreover, it becomes clear
that for Mark it is not so much '*Christos*' but rather 'Son of God'
that is the real, the only adequate christological title for Jesus.
This, in contrast to 'Son of Man' (and '*Christos*'),[68] never appears
in the mouth of Jesus, but is pronounced by God himself twice,
by the demons, by the High Priest, and finally by the pagan centurion. In Mk 12:6ff this occurs still indirectly in the parable and
in 12:36f we find in connection with Ps 110:1 the title '*Kyrios*' for
the Messiah. The messianism of Mark has more layers and is
more complex than Wrede realises. In addition, Mark, as a rule,
generally excludes the post-Easter events more than the later
evangelists,[69] just as he also does not narrate any resurrection
stories of his own.

(ii) In addition, the Petrine confession in the villages around
Caesarea Philippi[70] and Jesus' subsequent rejection of Peter cannot be simply traced back to Mark as the first author of a
Christian, kerygmatic Jesus novel, or simply to 'community formation'. Who would have later 'composed' this scene, which in
its detail does not fit with the surrounding material? Mark is
here working – as usual in a theologically reflective and dramatic
way – on significant older tradition. No more than the transfiguration narrative is it 'an Easter story projected back by Mark into
the life of Jesus'.[71] Against this weighs already the very unusual
localisation, 'in the villages of Caesarea Philippi', which

---

67. Mk 1:8; 13:11; cf 3:29.
68. Mk 9:41; 12:35.
69. Exceptions are relatively clearly visible, thus 2:20; 14:9; 13:9ff.
70. Mk 8:27-33. One notices the precise location, behind which stands
geographical knowledge.
71. Thus Rudolf Bultmann (*Theologie* 27f, 48; cf *Exegetica* 1-9; *Synoptische
Tradition* 275–278) supposes 'that Mt 16:17–19 in view of Mk 8:27-30'
'originally formed the conclusion of the confession scene' (277), and
wishes to characterize the 'narrative ... as an Easter story.' Bultmann
completely misunderstands *that there exists no connection at all in the
Jewish religion between resurrection and messianic status* and that the question of Jesus to the disciples (!) does not fit into an Easter story. In the
latter, there is always a spontaneous reaction to the seeing or recognition from the person involved. We can only characterise his – influential – hypothesis on this point as adventurous. Further conjectures are
found in Gerd Theissen and Philipp Vielhauer, (eds) *Die Geschichte der
synoptischen Tradition. Ergänzungsheft* 4th ed. (Göttingen: Vandenhoeck
& Ruprecht, 1991), 90f.

presupposes historical-geographical knowledge on the part of the author or his informant. It refers to the capital of the Kingdom of Philip, the former Hellenistic Polis Paneas, which Philip had renamed in order to honour Augustus. It lay at the foot of the snow-capped Mount Hermon, which already in the Enoch tradition is a mount of revelation.[72] The town designation 'Caesarea Philippi' still appears in Josephus,[73] then suddenly disappears soon after. Agrippa II founded the town anew after 53 AD and gave it the name Neronias. So, on the basis of the place name, which was in use for only a short time, it must be a case of an older tradition. The opinion of Bultmann, that 8:27 belongs to the previous narrative of the blind man of Bethsaida, contradicts the Marcan style.[74] Also the view of Conzelmann, that the motif of the 'withdrawal' to Caesarea Philippi is the 'messianic secret' misses the sense of the text. In Mark, there is no talk of a 'withdrawal'; the information about the destination is not theologically motivated and is not to be explained theologically. Only readers who know the local geography really well, such as modern exegetes, could suppose a 'withdrawal'. In Rome, where the gospel was written, no one could know about this. Rather, Mk 8:27 marks a narratively decisive turning point in the gospel. The views of the crowd about Jesus correspond fully to the Jewish-Palestinian milieu and fit perfectly with the context, but would hardly be understood by the Roman community. In 6:14f there is a similar tradition artificially inserted in order to create in the gospel a transition to the strange narrative of the execution of John the Baptist. The further claim of Conzelmann that 'The whole scene is christological reflection set within a narrative. Peter pronounces the faith of the community',[75] is also in this categorical form without support. First of all, it is misleading to consider christological reflection and the historicity of a narrative as fundamentally incompatible, since with

---

72. Freyne, *Jesus*, 56-58, 71-75, 134, 160. Its height is 2814 m.

73. Josephus, *JW* 3, 443; 7, 23; *JA* 20, 211; *Life* 74; cf in contrast the simple form 'Caesarea' in *JW* 2, 168 = *JA* 18, 28; *JW* 2, 510.

74. 'And he went on' with the place name is clearly a new beginning; cf 1:21; 2:1, 13; 3:1; 5:1; 6:1; 7:17; 9:33; 11:10, 12; 14:26.

75. Conzelmann, *Grundriß der Theologie des Neuen Testaments*, 4th ed. (Tübingen: Mohr Siebeck, 1987), 93; cf Hans Conzelmann and Andreas Lindemann, *Arbeitsbuch zum Neuen Testament* 11th ed. (Tübingen: Mohr Siebeck, 1995) 367 [1st ed. 1975].

Mark basically all the narratives of his 'gospel' are reported on the basis of christological reflection. With him, there are no 'christology-free zones'. Yet Mark remains a historical narrator bound by space and time. Moreover, the Petrine confession 'You are the Messiah' is no longer '*the* confession' of the community of the evangelist in Rome. For the title '*Christos*' has become in the Greek-speaking communities a proper name.[76] Already in Paul it is no longer used as a title.[77] In addition, for Mark it is not the *Christos-title* that is foundational, but rather 'Son of God' and along with this *Kyrios*.[78] That for 'the community' this confession was not sufficient is shown by its elaboration in Mt 16:16: 'You are the anointed one, the Son of the Living God.' Behind this is meant to stand God's *revelatio specialis* (16, 17). Luke also senses its incomplete character and expands it 'biblically' from the Old Testament: 'You are the Anointed One of God.'[79]

What the 'prototype' of Mark looked like is clearly not open to discovery. The command to keep silent, along with 9:9, is the only complete evidence for the messianic secret. One cannot simply identify it with the totally differently motivated command of silence to the demons,[80] for – in contrast to the latter – here Jesus himself asks this.[81] He provokes this confession, which then comes out of the mouth of his first disciple, for he wants this to be heard from the mouths of the disciples. In contrast, the demons as a rule do not speak at all, unless to acknowledge his divine status. The subsequent command of Jesus to his disciples to keep silent is indeed formulated by Mark in a way

---

76. Cf in Mk itself 1:1 and 9:41.
77. Cf Rom 1:3f; Heb 1:1ff; on this, 1 Clement 36:4. Martin Hengel and Anna M. Schwemer, *Paulus zwischen Damaskus und Antiochien*, WUNT 108 (Tübingen: Mohr Siebeck, 1998), 340-350; Hengel and Schwemer, *Anspruch*, 1–17; Martin Hengel, *Paulus und Jakobus, Kleine Schriften III*, WUNT 141 (Tübingen: Mohr Siebeck, 2002), 240–261.
78. Cf already 1:1. '*Christos*' has already long become for him, as 1:1; 9:41 show, a proper name, even when he naturally is aware of its significance as a title. On '*Kyrios*' see 1:3; 5:19; 11:3; 12:36.
79. 9:20. This holds especially true for Jn 6:69: 'You are the Holy One of God'. Jn 1:41 is still insufficient. In Jn 20:31 in contrast, the emphasis lies, as in Mt 16:16, on 'the Son of God'.
80. Thus Dieter Lührmann, *Das Markusevangelium*, Handbuch zum Neuen Testament 3 (Tübingen: Mohr Siebeck, 1987), 146.
81. What the disciples according to Mk 9:2-8 'saw' and should not 'spread further' also goes back to the initiative of Jesus.

similar to the command given to those healed. However, there it is of their healing that they should not speak, which is not a matter of the eschatological status of Jesus, while here it is said 'that they should speak to no one about him.' The 'about him' is found only here;[82] from the context it signifies 'about his messianic status'. They alone are supposed to recognise and understand him as the Messiah, as the 'Suffering Servant', who follows the path of suffering, but in reality they do not do this, as the reaction of Peter in 8:32 already shows.

Mark took up from the tradition the variously motivated commands to keep silent; these were certainly not all invented by himself, though he may have given them a similar (but not identical) formulation and set them in a certain interconnection. In the case of the command to keep silent given to the disciples, the closest connection is with the summary report composed by Mark about the expulsion of the demons, where Mark gives the rationale: 'so that they do not make him known',[83] which, however, does not appear like this anywhere else. We have to distinguish here between Marcan interpretation and the original tradition, where the individual motifs were still distinct.

What can also be rejected is the conjecture that in the pre-Marcan tradition the Petrine confession was followed originally by 8:33, the rejection of Peter as 'Satan', because Jesus had fundamentally rejected the title of Messiah. In that case, then the frequent use of the title and the name after Easter would appear as a betrayal of the reality of Jesus,[84] and moreover Mark would also contradict himself by his straightforward use of the title and name.[85] A narrative, in which Jesus provokes his disciples through an unmotivated question and then rejects the speaker of the disciples as Satan in the most brusque way, must appear meaningless. This was certainly not 'pre-Marcan tradition'. Behind all these attempts to exclude the Messiah question from the activity of Jesus there appears to be a modern, thoroughly dogmatic

---

82. 8:30.
83. 3:12.
84. See on this Martin Hengel in Hengel and Schwemer, *Anspruch*, 16f. Logically, in this case one would then have to make Caiaphas and Pilate 'founders' of christology, for in the execution of Jesus as 'King of the Jews', i.e. as a messianic pretender, they would have laid the groundwork for the emergence of christology.
85. 1:1; 9:41; 12:35; 13:21; 14:61; 15:32.

desire that the person of Jesus should have as little as possible to do with Jewish messianic expectations, which are understood in a very one-sided, political way[86] which does not correspond to the variety of the messianic conceptions before 70 AD.

When one evaluates Wrede's critical analysis of Mark, which led with Bultmann and his pupils to a complete denial of the messiahship of Jesus, one must finally not overlook the point that only Bultmann follows the positive explanation of Wrede that the early community or Mark wished with the messianic secret to overcome the scandal of a historically unmessianic Jesus. Today there is a consensus only on the negative aspect of this thesis; the explanations on the other hand are widely diverse.

Already in 1939 Hans-Jürgen Ebeling had criticised Wrede's explanation of the Marcan secrecy theory. Here, in the spirit of a purely kerygmatic interpretation that did not pay attention to history and was influenced by dialectical theology, he emphasised that this secrecy theory is not 'a reflection on historical situations and events in the life of Jesus'. That means, it does not aim at covering up the later historical situation when an unmessianic Jesus was considered a scandal, but explains the fact that the earthly and risen Lord are one and the same, and that he gave up his life in death for the salvation of all men and women. The messianic secret becomes the encompassing mystery of revelation that the evangelist develops in his work, which is oriented entirely toward the death of Jesus on the cross.[87]

Conzelmann also sees in the messianic secret a basic concept of Marcan christology, which expresses 'the paradoxical character of revelation'. In this the 'significance of Jesus' does not come from the miracles, but develops first from the faith 'that sees Jesus properly from the viewpoint of the cross and the resurrection'.[88] Yet, both for Mark and the entire early Christian community was not the resurrection a miracle and do not the 'miracles' of Jesus, especially in Mark, lie closely linked together with faith?[89] Is there not again with this theory a modern fear of miracles at work?

---

86. On this see Hengel in Hengel and Schwemer, *Anspruch* 25f.
87. Ebeling, *Das Messiasgeheimnis und die Botschaft des Marcus-Evangeliums*, BZNW 19 (Berlin: Töpelmann, 1939), 220f.
88. Conzelmann, *Theologie*, 150; *Arbeitsbuch*, 249.
89. Typical here is Mk 6:5: in Nazareth on account of their unbelief, Jesus 'can' do no miracle, cf 9:23f; 2:5 etc.

Admittedly, with these corrections the intention of the evangelist Mark is supported with a better argumentation than with Wrede. Yet just as with Wrede, the origin of the motif is still not sufficiently explained, since Mark, in contrast to John,[90] does not write any relatively free-standing 'christological poetry', but rather intensively reworks older traditions. This includes the command to keep silent in its various forms – this much Wrede saw clearly – which are not simply invented by Mark, but arise out of the tradition, whose Palestinian-Jewish origin is easy to see and which in our opinion goes back to Peter.[91] Rather, Mark expands in a fruitful way the various traditional historical motifs for his considered christology and has shaped them accordingly – as with all his material. He did not simply invent them for they are too diverse in their detail and thematically different. If the commands to keep silent really were a theologically and narratively new creation of Mark, then this would have been accomplished in a more unified way. In our opinion, these commands are founded in Jesus' messianic activity.

It lies in the nature of the situation that with the exorcism of the 'demon' in the sick man that it 'had to be brought to silence'. As long as the sick man continued to cry out, he was not healed, and the exorcism would be a failure. That here and there Jesus had forbidden those healed from proclaiming their cure to everyone, and that he sometimes withdrew into solitude, is also understandable. He did not yet want to stir up the crowds. Every successful doctor must at times close his practice, when it overflows, for there are only twenty-four hours in a day. This has nothing to do directly with the messianic question. In other words, from the texts about the 'messianic secret' gathered by Wrede, which for the most part do not fit in this schema, one can

---

90. He does this at various times in his work; see Martin Hengel, *Die Johanneische Frage. Ein Lösungsversuch* (Tübingen: Mohr Siebeck, 1993). [ET: *The Johannine Question.* (London: SCM Press; Philadelphia: Trinity Press International, 1989).]

91. On this see Martin Hengel, *The Four Gospels and the One Gospel of Jesus Christ,* (London: Trinity Press International, 2000), 65ff, 78ff. The numerous Latinisms and the church tradition of the second century suggest Rome as the place of composition. Syria, the place often proposed as the origin of the gospel, has no support in the sources. The origin of Matthew, on the other hand, is probably found in southern Syria or the border region with Jewish Palestine, cf Mt 4,24.

produce no argument against a 'messianic claim' of Jesus. H. J. Ebeling at the end of his study emphasised:

> Thus, based on our results, it is not permitted for us to have a positive or negative position in the conflict of opinions about whether or not Jesus had a messianic consciousness. Wrede's *arguments for an unmessianic consciousness* clearly are not valid. But the whole problem calls for a much broader investigation and interpretation of the gospel.[92]

In our opinion, up until today this has still not been accomplished in a satisfactory manner.[93] It would also go beyond the limits of our presentation. Conzelmann also rightly objects against Wrede (and *cum grano salis* against his own teacher Bultmann): 'The material worked over by Mark, especially the miracle narratives, do not in any way show an unmessianic picture of Jesus. More than this: an unmessianic Jesus tradition does not exist.'[94]

It becomes, then, completely incomprehensible how Conzelmann, even more clearly than Wrede and Bultmann, still arrives at an originally completely unmessianic Jesus. If an 'unmessianic Jesus tradition does not exist'[95] – a judgment with which we fully agree – how can he then distinguish neatly between the 'messianic' and the 'unmessianic' in order to arrive at a historically 'cleaned-up' picture of Jesus free of titles? How will he filter out from the completely messianically coloured tradition the supposedly historically true 'unmessianic' Jesus? The radical, more consistent conclusion would then be rather that he would deny all pre-Easter tradition about Jesus and declare the man Jesus to be an ungraspable phantom. But

---

92. Ebeling, *Messiasgeheimnis und die Botschaft*, 221. Emphasis found in Hengel and Schwemer.

93. See nevertheless Gaëtan Minette De Tillesse, *Le secret messianique dans l'Evangile de Marc*, (Paris: Éditions du Cerf 1968); Räisänen, *Parabeltheorien*; Räisänen, *Messiasgeheimnis*; the expanded English version: Räisänen, *Messianic Secret*. His thorough research of the problem leads nevertheless to false conclusions, since his attempts at historical solutions which ascribe to Mark the invention of the Messianic secret are too far fetched and no more convincing than the theses of Wrede.

94. Conzelmann, *Arbeitsbuch*, 249.

95. This 'unmessianic picture of Jesus' is found in his Jewish and pagan opponents, such as Celsus and his Jewish informants who describe Jesus as a magician and deceiver, who received his just punishment.

Conzelmann did not want to be that radical. His long article in the RGG[96] contains many worthwhile and factually correct observations even when, through his denial of the messianic claim of Jesus, he falls into insoluble contradictions.

The messianic secret in the gospel of Mark is neither a unified, secondary construction of the evangelist, nor the product of an unidentifiable post-Easter community. It goes back in its core to the personal mystery of Jesus himself and is inseparably linked with the 'messianic' activity of Jesus in Galilee. It forces us to take seriously historically 'the Messiah from Galilee', who was crucified during the Passover festival in Jerusalem 30 AD and appeared to his disciples in Galilee.

---

96. Conzelmann, s. v. 'Jesus Christus', RGG, 3rd ed., III, 619-653; for Jesus' self-consciousness, 629ff. For him, Jesus understands himself as 'the last herald'. His status is unique, for after him comes nothing more – than God himself. Yet was not John the Baptist 'the last herald', and Jesus the 'more powerful one' who was to come after him, cf Lk 7:19 = Mt 11:3? God neither comes after a last prophetic herald, nor does he wear sandals that one can untie and carry away: Mk 1:7; Lk 3:16; Mt 3:11.

CHAPTER THREE

# The Exodus as an Ideology of the Marginalised

## Andrew D. H. Mayes

It is common to understand the exodus tradition as paradigmatic
for the theme of liberation from political, social and economic
oppression, and, moreover, as having its roots in a clear and specific historical event: escape from Egypt interpreted as an act of
deliverance by Yahweh. This is certainly what the exodus tradition became; its origins, however, are more complex. An exploration of this complexity is also an exploration into one aspect of
the way by which that which is marginal may achieve centrality,
those who are on the borders achieve recognition: through the
appropriation and re-interpretation of tradition.

### A INTRODUCTION

Insofar as Israel does not trace her origins through the patriarchs
to Mesopotamia, she finds them in the exodus and Egypt. The
biblical presentation is clearly very schematic, and the skeletal
framework which gives it unity and coherence is genealogical:
Abraham migrated from Mesopotamia to Palestine; his grand-
son Jacob with his family went to Egypt; there, having become a
great people, they suffered oppression; from there they were led
out by Moses and returned to Palestine. When the skeletal
framework disintegrates, simply on the basis of the observation
that peoples do not originate as the Bible describes, then the
schematic account collapses into its component elements. This
separation of its parts is then reinforced by further study which
shows the tenuous nature of the literary links which hold the
whole together. For our present purposes it is sufficient to note
that the exodus tradition has only weak connections with the
patriarchal tradition, on the one hand, and with the Sinai tradition, on the other, so that it may be viewed as having had its own
history of development before it became part of the present continuous story.[1]

1. For the basic work, cf R. Rendtorff, *Das überlieferungsgeschichtliche*

These observations do not in themselves cast doubt on the essential historicity of the sojourn in Egypt and the exodus, however serious they may be for the historicity of any relationship between exodus and Sinai covenant; in fact, it becomes perfectly possible to see the exodus tradition as representing the experience of a core element of later Israel, the house of Joseph or a significant element of that group, which, because of the social and political significance of that group, came to be accepted as part of the tradition of origins of the whole. For a number of reasons, however, this picture has come under criticism. In the first place, there is now an increasing tendency to view the biblical record as a late construction, and, moreover, as one which is expressive of the ideological interests of a group whose relationship to any historical Israel is problematic. Secondly, it is argued that the only reliable basis for understanding Israel's origins and history is to be found in archaeology and non-biblical sources, and these not only make no reference to any exodus from Egypt but also suggest an origin for Israel that lies within the land of Canaan.[2]

This tendency in Old Testament scholarship has not gone unchallenged. My purpose here is to develop this challenge, with reference particularly to the contexts and processes by which the exodus tradition came to its present form.

---

*Problem des Pentateuch* (BZAW 147; Berlin: de Gruyter, 1977) = *The Problem of the Process of Transmission in the Pentateuch* (JSOTS 89; Sheffield: JSOT Press, 1990).

2. For a clear account cf S. Finkelstein, *The Archaeology of the Israelite Settlement* (Jerusalem: Israel Exploration Society, 1988); for a slightly modified version, setting the appearance of Israel within the larger context of long term cyclic processes of nomadisation and sedentarisation of indigenous groups, cf *id*., 'The Great Transformation: The 'Conquest' of the Highlands Frontiers and the Rise of the Territorial States', in T. E. Levy (ed), *The Archaeology of Society in the Holy Land* (London: Leicester University Press, 1995), 349-65. Note also, from the same volume (320-31), S. Bunimovitz, 'On the Edge of Empires – Late Bronze Age (1500-1200 BCE)', where the process of sedentarisation leading to the appearance of Israel is set within the framework of the increased security situation in Palestine effected by the Egyptian Pharaohs of the 19th and 20th dynasties, who took vigorous measures to establish stability.

B THE EXODUS AND HISTORY

(i) A recent, robust defence of the historicity of the exodus has come from Graham Davies who refers to four elements of the tradition that have commonly been thought to provide its historical core. The most important of these is the reference in Ex 1:11 to the people of Israel having been enslaved in the building of Pithom and Rameses as store cities for the Pharaoh. The second of these cities, with the prefix Per- or Pi-, is the name of the dynastic capital, constructed by Rameses II on the site of the Hyksos capital Avaris. Since this capital lost its significance in the mid-11th century BC, when it was replaced as the capital of Egypt by Tanis, it is more likely that the reference to Rameses in the biblical tradition is early rather than late. The location of Pithom is uncertain, but Tell er-Retabeh, a significant site for Rameses II, is plausible. In any case, 'If we consider the two names Rameses and Pithom together, it has to be said that they are more likely as a pair to belong to a tradition that originated in the Ramesside period than to a later time. Exodus 1:11 remains an important historical datum for the Exodus tradition.'[3]

The second element of the exodus tradition supporting its historicity is that which deals with Moses in Midian, a tradition that is unlikely to have arisen from an Israel that was rooted solely within the borders of Canaan. It points at least to the existence of influential 'proto-Israelites' in regions far to the south of Canaan. The third element is constituted by the frequent use in Exodus 1-2 of the term 'Hebrew' as an alternative name for the people of Israel. This must derive from a stage in the growth of the tradition which antedates the 'Israel' perspective which is now dominant. Finally, one must point to the Song of Moses in Ex 15:1-17 which, on the basis of its archaic language combined with its reference to Jerusalem, must come from the early monarchic period, thus providing evidence of belief in a deliverance from Egypt from that point. The Song of Miriam which follows it in Ex 15:21, is older still, and brings that belief back into the period of the judges.

Other, indirect, evidence is also important: the numerous references to 'apiru in Egypt in the New Kingdom, some of whom were brought as prisoners of war and set to work on state building projects; the record of the admission to Egypt of shasu as

3. Cf Davies, 'Was there an Exodus?', in J. Day (ed), *In Search of Pre-Exilic Israel*, (JSOTS 406; London: T. & T. Clark/Continuum, 2004), 30.

pasture seeking Bedouin; the report of runaway slaves escaping from Egypt into Asia. Yet, however important these may be in setting the context, the case for the historicity of the exodus rests on the other more direct evidence: 'The tradition is *a priori* unlikely to have been invented; the biblical evidence is widespread and can be followed back to a respectable antiquity, within at most two hundred years of the supposed event; some elements of it have a particular claim to authority; and in various ways what is said corresponds more closely to the realities of New Kingdom Egypt than one would expect from a later wholly fictitious account.'[4]

It must be noted that while Davies is indeed concerned to promote the evidence for the historicity of the exodus, his investigation takes its starting point from the perceived trend in Old Testament scholarship to see Israel's origins as lying wholly within Canaan, and indeed most of the evidence brought forward by Davies, both direct and indirect, relates in the first instance to this more general point rather than to showing the historicity of the exodus as a specific event which took place at a particular point in time. Thus, the tradition of Moses in Midian, the use of the term 'Hebrews' for Israelites, the widespread occurrence of the term '*apiru* in Egyptian texts, even in connection with slave labour in Egypt, serve in the first instance to support the view that one cannot understand Israelite origins solely within the boundaries of Canaan. As far as the exodus event is concerned, this evidence is thus in the main circumstantial. Even texts such as Ex 15:1-17, which are notoriously difficult to date, can witness reliably only to the tradition of a deliverance from Egypt regarded by Israel at some stage in its monarchic history as foundational.[5] About the origin of that tradition in any historical event it says little.

We are left then with Ex 1:11.[6] It is doubtful, however, that this verse can bear the weight that is laid on it. The identification

4. Davies, *op. cit.*, 36.
5. On the Song of Miriam in Ex 15:21 see below n. 47.
6. The identification of Moses with Beya, a highly placed Egyptian official of Syrian origin at the end of the 19th dynasty, proposed by E. A. Knauf, *Midian: Untersuchungen zur Geschichte Palästinas und Nordarabiens am Ende des 2.Jahrtausends v.Chr.* (Wiesbaden: Harrassowitz, 1988), 135-41, and J. C. de Moor, *The Rise of Yahwism: The Roots of Israelite Monotheism* (Leuven: Leuven University Press, 1990), 136-51, is too speculative to contribute anything of evidential value.

of these sites, which might allow Ex 1:11 to be linked to the time
of their flourishing, remains uncertain. Rameses is indeed probably the site Piramesse, founded by Rameses II, but while that
site declined after the Ramesside period, the name lived on, and
the site was replaced by Tanis, some thirty kilometres to the
south, to which Ramesside monuments were brought. The site
of Pithom, if Pithom is to be taken as a specific place rather than
a generic term (such as 'Pharaoh') which could be and was attached to a variety of specific locations, is most likely Tell el-
Maskhuta which was founded by Necho II of the 26th dynasty at
the end of the seventh century. Rameses II can be at best only a
*terminus post quem* for the references in Ex 1:11.[7]

(ii) The exodus tradition is one of national liberation by
Yahweh from bondage in Egypt. It is this that identifies the people Israel and sets them off from both Egypt and their neighbours. A consideration of the development of this tradition must
start with the recognition of its national dimension. The earliest
reliable references to the exodus in these terms are to be found in
the eighth-century prophets of the northern kingdom, Hosea
and Amos. In both cases, the references have polemical intention. For Hosea it is Yahweh and not Baal who brought Israel up
from Egypt and gave her the land (2:8, 15; 9:10; 11:1-4; 12:9, 13;
13:4). The focus of Amos is more on social than religious observation, but he too claims the exodus for Yahweh (2:10; 3:1), and
also that it is to Yahweh indeed that the Philistines and Syrians
owe parallel experiences (9:7). Both prophets also condemn the
existing state cult as practised at the sanctuaries of Bethel and
Samaria, and again it is Hosea who most clearly dissociates this
cult from Yahweh (8:4-6; 10:5f; 13:2; cf Amos 4:4f; 5:4f).

According to the deuteronomistic historian in 1 Kings 12, the
installation of this state cult, involving bull calves, was carried
out by Jeroboam at the two sanctuaries of Bethel and Dan, an innovation made in order to provide a counter attraction to
Jerusalem: 'You have gone up to Jerusalem long enough. Behold
your gods, O Israel, who brought you up out of the land of
Egypt' (1 Kgs 12:28). This is clearly a deuteronomistic polemical

---

7. Cf J. S. Holladay, Jr, 'Pithom', in D. B. Redford (ed.), *The Oxford
Encyclopedia of Ancient Egypt* (Oxford: Oxford University Press, 2001),
50-3; C. A. Redmount, 'Bitter Lives: Israel in and out of Egypt', in M. D.
Coogan (ed.), *The Oxford History of the Biblical World* (Oxford: Oxford
University Press, 1998), 88.

composition, part of the generalised condemnation of the northern kingdom.[8] Yet in a number of respects it undoubtedly reflects reality of the pre-prophetic period in the northern kingdom: the installation of a bull image in Bethel, and the veneration of such images elsewhere in the northern kingdom,[9] and indeed also the association of the exodus from Egypt and gift of the land with such worship. This association is presupposed in Hosea's polemic where he claims for Yahweh that with which Israelites have hitherto been crediting Baal.

Modern scholarly interpretation of 1 Kings 12 understands that the cult of Jeroboam was Yahwistic, that it was part of a political revolt against the house of David in Jerusalem, and that in choosing the bull symbol Jeroboam was opening the way to misunderstanding and syncretism in the popular mind. Jeroboam intended the bull not as a divine image but as a throne or pedestal of the invisible Yahweh, parallel to the role performed by the cherubim in the temple in Jerusalem. The bull, however, had associations with fertility and the cult of Baal,[10] and when Jeroboam proclaimed before it, 'Behold your God O Israel who brought you out of the land of Egypt', he opened the way to a syncretistic and idolatrous form of Yahweh worship.[11]

This understanding makes a number of assumptions that are uncertain. In particular, it presupposes that by this time the worship of Yahweh was the national religion of Israel and that Yahweh was identified as the God who brought Israel out of Egypt, so that Jeroboam's revolt involved an appeal to traditional religion. These assumptions, however, reflect essential elements of a historical understanding of Israel which no longer com-

---

8. For this, cf R. Albertz, *A History of Israelite Religion in the Old Testament Period,* vol. I, From the *Beginnings to the End of the Exile* (London: SCM Press, 1994), 139-40, with references.

9. Presupposed in Hos 10:5. If Judges 17-18 contains the ancient cult legend of the sanctuary of Dan, then its 'graven image' may also have been a bull image (cf Albertz, *op. cit.*, 305 n. 7); relevant also is the discovery of the bronze figure of a bull in an open cult place in the hill country of Samaria from Iron Age I (for which cf A. Mazar, ''Bull' Site', *The New Encyclopedia of Archaeological Excavations in the Holy Land* (Jerusalem: Israel Exploration Society & Carta, 1993), I, 266-67, which suggests that the bull image was a traditional element of cultic worship.

10. On the Baal background of the bull iconography, cf especially M. S. Smith, *The Early History of God* (San Francisco: Harper & Row, 1990), 51.

11. Cf especially Albertz, *op. cit.*, 143-6.

mands agreement. When it was possible to think in terms of a pre-monarchic federation of Israelite tribes, whether or not on the analogy of the classical amphictyony, within the framework of which the worship of Yahweh spread and a symbiosis was achieved between that worship and traditions of Israel's origins, particularly in this instance an exodus from Egypt, then also it was possible to think of a national Yahwistic religion of Israel, in which Yahweh was worshipped as the God of the exodus. This model, however, depends on a classical form of Pentateuchal criticism, which traces the Pentateuchal sources J and E back to a pre-monarchic *Grundlage*, a view which is no longer tenable. Even the least radical departure from that critical orthodoxy leaves the Pentateuchal sources later than is required by this view of Israel's history. One of the most detailed and compre-hensive recent attempts to establish the origin and development of the Pentateuch, which Albertz[12] takes as his own starting point, is that of E. Blum. For Blum, however, the Pentateuch goes back to late deuteronomistic (KD) and priestly (KP) compos-itions from the post-exilic period, behind which stand traditions of uncertain age and provenance which have in some cases been merely linked together but in other cases completely reshaped. Albertz believes that one of these earlier traditions is a narrative of the plagues and the exodus which, following Schmid,[13] he dates to the exilic period; another, earlier tradition is the remains of a Moses narrative in parts of Ex 1-2:4, some of which 'displays striking parallels to the revolt of Jeroboam and probably comes from the northern kingdom of this period'.[14] Albertz acknowl-edges that apart from this small amount of tradition, the 'main mass of the text is of exilic and early post-exilic origin, i.e. separ-ated from the events by between 700 and 800 years'. There is a fundamental problem in Albertz's fine study in that he then can write: 'So we will have to qualify quite considerably the concep-tion of the beginnings of Israel presented by the Pentateuch. In principle, however, this conception is not to be doubted ...'[15] It is clear that if Blum is right in his view of Pentateuchal origins, the basis is removed for maintaining the classical scholarly view

---

12. *Op. cit.*, 42-3.
13. H. H. Schmid, *Der sogenannte Jahwist. Beobachtungen und Fragen zur Pentateuchforschung* (Zürich: Theologischer Verlag, 1976), 44-56.
14. Albertz, *op. cit.*, 43.
15. *Ibid.*, 43-4.

of the early history and religion of Israel to which Albertz adheres.[16] In principle, the Pentateuchal conception of the beginnings of Israel is very much open to doubt. Rather, the polemic of the prophets, including the silence of the pre-classical prophets on any connection between Yahweh and the exodus, suggest that the national religion of the northern kingdom of Israel involved the worship of Baal, and that Baal was credited with bringing Israel out of Egypt and giving them the land.

(iii) The earliest stage to which the exodus tradition, as a tradition of national liberation, can be traced is the time of Jeroboam. Albertz[17] has noted the close parallels between the account of Jeroboam's revolt and the Moses story in the book of Exodus: both Jeroboam and Moses are depicted as royal figures who, on behalf of their fellow-countrymen, rebel against oppression (Ex 2:11-15; cf 1 Kgs 11:26-8); on both occasions the rebellions failed, and both rebels had to flee abroad to escape punishment (Ex 2:15; cf 1 Kgs 11:40); both return only after the death of the king (Ex 2:23; 4:19, 20; cf 1 Kgs 11:40; 12:2, 20); subsequent negotiations with the successor lead only to an increase in the burden (Ex 5:3-19; 1 Kgs 12:3-15). One should add that the appearance of Egypt, whether as place of oppression or as place of refuge, is a further link between the stories of Jeroboam and Moses. A further element of the Moses story, the account of the golden calf in Exodus 32, is clearly composed in the light of, and condemns as an idolatrous innovation, the cultic innovations of Jeroboam. That the Jeroboam episode is a clear background and context to the Moses story, even if it does not provide the whole explanation for that story, is a clear and persuasive justification for associating the exodus tradition with Jeroboam.

That it also justifies an association of Yahweh with the tradition at this time is much less clear. The story of 1 Kings 12 implies otherwise, and it certainly fits with the political dimension of the action of Jeroboam that it would have involved not only a rejection of the rule of the Davidic house, but a rejection also of that ideology, the worship of Yahweh in the Jerusalem temple, by which the Davidic house justified its authoritarian and op-

---

16. J. J. Collins, 'The Development of the Exodus Tradition', in J. W. van Henten & A. Houtepen (eds), *Religious Identity and the Invention of Tradition* (Assen: Van Gorcum, 2001), 146-7, has rightly noted this conflict in Albertz's position.
17. *Op. cit.*, 141-2.

pressive rule. The Jerusalem cult of Yahweh had no original
focus on Yahweh as God of the exodus; rather, through its promotion of the notion of Yahweh as king, by means of concepts
carried over to Yahweh from the pre-Davidic cult of El Elyon,
Yahweh was here worshipped as creator and universal sovereign, whose rule was realised through his earthly representative
the Davidic king. Jeroboam's rejection of Davidic rule necessarily
involved also the rejection of that ideology which was its foundation. That rejection involved not some subtle alternative understanding of the nature of Yahweh, but rather a claim that Baal is,
first, the god of Israel, and, secondly, the god who brought them
up from the land of Egypt and gave them the land.

(iv) The worship of both Baal and Yahweh were well established in Israel, and it was not until David and Solomon that an
attempt was made to create a state religion in the cult of
Yahweh, an attempt rejected by Jeroboam. Even for the time of
Saul it is evident that Yahweh was assigned no particular status
over against Baal. The theophoric elements in the names of his
family members (1 Sam 14:49-51; 2 Sam 2:8-10 [1 Chr 8:33]; 2
Sam 4:4; 21:8 [1 Chr 8:34]) indicate the diversity of their religious
practice: beside one name containing the element Yahweh
(Jonathan), two contain Baal (Meribaal, Eshbaal), one contains El
(Abiel), and four contain elements that may be family or ancestral deities (Abiel, Abner, Ahimaaz). There is no exodus tradition
or association of Yahweh with the exodus in the Saul tradition.

Jeroboam's promotion of Baal as the god of Israel in opposition to Judah is well rooted in Israelite tradition and experience.[18] Baal was not only a god familiar to Israelites, but a god
close to their everyday concerns. The closeness of Baal to ordinary Israelite experience, in agriculture and fertility, meant that
he provided an attractive alternative to the Yahweh cult of the
Jerusalem temple. The association of Baal with the exodus represents not a displacement of Yahweh (whose connection with the
exodus cannot for this stage be demonstrated), but rather what
may be the first articulation of a national tradition in the form of
what has been called a 'charter myth'.[19] Through this national

---

18. On the antiquity of the bull symbolism cf Albertz, *op. cit.*, 143-6.
Albertz believes, however, that this was traditional symbolism which
Jeroboam associated with Yahweh.
19. Cf K. van der Toorn, *Family Religion in Babylonia, Syria and Israel*
(Leiden: Brill, 1996), 287-315. Van der Toorn, however, thinks of this as

tradition the attempt is consciously made to forge a common identity for the diverse elements of Israel as a radical alternative to its southern neighbour. It should be noted that at this stage the connection of Baal to the Egyptian past was just as, if not more, possible than was the connection of Yahweh. The reference to Egypt and the exodus was merely an historical backdrop to possession of the land; it was on the land and Israel's life in the land that the emphasis lay. Moreover, it must be remembered that Baal worship was known in Egypt, especially from the 18th dynasty when there was a cult and priesthood of Baal at Memphis.[20] It had been brought to Egypt earlier, perhaps especially with the Hyksos when Baal was absorbed into Seth, many of whose characteristics he shared. The worship of Baal was practised there, undoubtedly chiefly by Asiatic immigrants, until the close of the Ramesside period. From this perspective, an association of Baal with the exodus is more understandable than one involving Yahweh.

The nature of the state cult and its object of worship was the

---

a form of the worship of Yahweh, *ibid.*, 279. Cf also *id.*, 'The Exodus as Charter Myth', in van Henten & Houtepen (eds), *Religious Identity and the Invention of Tradition*, 113-27. In his discussion with van der Toorn, Albertz ('Exodus: Liberation History against Charter Myth', in van Henten & Houtepen (eds), *Religious Identity and the Invention of Tradition*, 128-43) gives some reason for thinking that his view is not completely out of line with what is being suggested here. So, he writes (140): 'I cannot see any evidence that the Exodus tradition was used for defining a particular religious identity, promoting the Yahweh cult, and curbing local and family religion, before the time of Josia', and (*ibid.*, 142): 'In my opinion the Exodus tradition was a charter myth so far, as it motivated and justified the revolt against and the separation from the House of David. It legitimated the northern kingdom as the truer Israelite state over against Judah.' These statements sit very awkwardly with the view Albertz has expressed in his book; they conform with the position argued for here insofar as (i) it is suggested that the exodus tradition did not always involve Yahweh, and (ii) the exodus tradition functioned, without reference to Yahweh, as a charter myth of the northern kingdom. For a wide-ranging study of the function of myths, including charter myths, cf G. S. Kirk, *Myth. Its Meaning and Functions in Ancient and Other Cultures* (Cambridge: Cambridge University Press, 1970), index s.v. 'charters, myths as'.
20. Cf G. Hart, *A Dictionary of Egyptian Gods and Goddesses* (London: Routledge, 1986), 50; S. Morenz, *Egyptian Religion* (Ithaca: Cornell University Press, 1973), 238-9.

focus of social and political struggle through the history of the
northern kingdom. The extent to which it played a role in the
dynastic revolutions which marked this history from the beginning cannot always be determined, but it is reasonable to suppose that what has been identified as a conflict between different social systems, characterised as 'Canaanite' and 'Israelite',[21]
came to expression as a conflict between Baal and Yahweh. This
conflict, however, has no immediate focus on the exodus from
Egypt. Elijah and Elisha make no reference to Yahweh as the
God of the exodus; exodus concepts and terminology play no
role in their conflict with the rulers of the Omride period. Even
in the contest between Elijah and the prophets of Baal on Mount
Carmel (1 Kings 18), it is not the God of the exodus on whose behalf Elijah came forth. His altar was built with 'twelve stones, according to the number of the tribes of the sons of Jacob, to whom
the word of the Lord came, saying "Israel shall be your
name"'(v. 31), and his appeal was not to the God who delivered
his people from oppression in Egypt but rather: 'O Lord, God of
Abraham, Isaac and Israel, let it be known this day that thou art
God in Israel, and that I am thy servant, and that I have done all
these things at thy word.' This lack of reference to the exodus in
a prophetic tradition very much to do with deliverance from oppression, is startling if the God of the exodus as the national
charter myth of Israel was Yahweh. It is rather clear that at this
time Yahweh's association was with a people understanding itself in tribal, patriarchal terms, rather than with a nation identifying itself as having originated in an exodus from Egypt.

We may conclude, therefore, that Yahweh's association with
the exodus came about as part of that process by which he came
to be accepted as the national God of Israel, a process of much
conflict in the religious and social history of the northern kingdom. Claims and counter-claims are at work here, the primary
issue being 'who is Israel's God?' The identification of the god of
the exodus follows on from that issue, for that is the charter
myth of the northern kingdom. In its earliest stages as a national
tradition, it is probable that the god of the exodus was Baal. This
was an identification made credible by the familiarity of the cult
of Baal both in Egypt and in Israel, and in any case by the primary
focus of the exodus tradition, which was on Israel and her life in

21. Cf my *The Old Testament in Sociological Perspective* (London: Marshall
Pickering, 1989), 13-14.

the land. Israel got its identity from an ideological expression of its ongoing concerns, life in the land, and not solely from its origins.

### C THE EXODUS TRADITION: ORIGINS AND DEVELOPMENT

The matter cannot, however, be left at that point. If the exodus tradition, as a national charter myth of Israel, is to be traced to the establishment of the northern kingdom under Jeroboam I, the question of the foundation and later development of that tradition still remains. Van der Toorn, to whom we owe the characterisation of the exodus tradition as a 'charter myth', even if one associated with Baal rather than, as with Van der Toorn, with Yahweh, has written: 'We must be careful to distinguish, however, between use and origin. It is one thing to say that the exodus tradition was promoted, along with Yahweh as the national god, as a national charter myth; it is something else to imply that the tradition grew out of the political need for it. The available evidence warrants the conclusion that the exodus motif was appropriated by the state religion as the national myth; there is also sufficient evidence to say that the motif was originally Ephraimite. It is harder to determine, however, in which particular segment of the early Israelite society the tradition originated and developed. Both the Egyptian background of the name of Moses, and the data concerning the presence of Western Asiatic people in 13th century Egypt, argue in favour of the historicity of an exodus of some kind. The most satisfactory solution is to assume that the sojourn in and the flight from Egypt were historical realities for a limited group of immigrants to Israel. Their particular history was gradually transformed into a national past of sheerly mythical proportions.'[22]

This says at the same time too much and too little. It is too much in terms of the suggestion that 'the sojourn in and flight from Egypt' were a historical one time experience of a group of people. It is too little in that it is possible to say more about those elements of later Israel for whom an Egyptian experience was part of their historical background and cultural memory, and for whom an appeal to this cultural memory would serve as a unifying force.

(i) At this stage and in this context it is not necessary to enter into all the problems surrounding the emergence of Israel in Palestine. Yet, insofar at any rate as Davies' discussion of the

---

22. Van der Toorn, *Family Religion*, 301.

historicity of the exodus takes its starting point with the observation that for some the origins of Israel are to be accounted for
wholly within the framework of Canaan without any need for
an exodus from Egypt, it must at least be ascertained if the most
reasonable and credible account of Israel's origins does in fact
make any connection with Egypt both unnecessary and unlikely.
One author who is quoted by Davies to this effect is William
Dever, though the latter's most recent study of the subject does
perhaps leave a little more latitude than is apparent in his earlier
writings.[23] Dever sets out to give an account of Israel's origins
from an archaeological perspective, combined with a critical
rather than a dismissive attitude to the biblical text. Building especially on the work of L. E. Stager,[24] Dever notes the astonish-
ing increase in settlement sites in the Iron I period (1200-1000BC),
especially on the highlands of Palestine, including Upper and
Lower Galilee, the central highlands and the Judean hills.[25]
There is an increase from a LBA total of 58 sites to an Iron I total
of some 350, an increase which amounts to a population explos-
ion not to be accounted for simply by natural growth, but presupposes an influx of people into the highlands in the 12th and
11th centuries. The nature of the settlements is uniform: they are
agricultural villages or hamlets with animal husbandry. The
material culture of these settlements is rural, agricultural, family
based and egalitarian. The best clue to the origin of these settlers
lies in the pottery, and this reveals strong continuity with LBA
Canaanite society.

The most probable explanation for the origin of the Iron I
culture is a process of withdrawal from a disintegrating city-
state culture, in which former members of the city state
Canaanite society, already experienced in farming, agriculture

---

23. W. G. Dever, *Who were the early Israelites and where did they come from?*
(Grand Rapids: Eeerdmans 2003); for his earlier views, cf e.g. 'Is there
any archaeological evidence for the exodus?', in E. S. Frerichs and L. H.
Lesko (eds), *Exodus: The Egyptian Evidence* (Winona Lake: Eisenbrauns,
1997), 67-86; 'Archaeology and the Emergence of Early Israel', in J. R.
Bartlett (ed), *Archaeology and Biblical Interpretation* (London: Routledge,
1997), 20-50.
24. Cf L. Stager, 'Forging an Identity: the emergence of ancient Israel', in
M. D. Coogan (ed), *The Oxford History of the Biblical World* (Oxford:
Oxford University Press, 1998), 123-76.
25. Dever, *Who were the early Israelites...?*, 97.

and the storage of grain surpluses, moved to new settlements in the highlands in pursuit of a new mode of agricultural life.[26] That this culture may be further identified as 'proto-Israelite' is indicated[27] by the continuities between Iron I and Iron II, the period of the Israelite monarchy, in which there is no mass abandonment of Iron I sites but a gradual movement from ruralism to urbanism, and in which at least a dozen Iron I sites (such as Hazor, Megiddo, Shechem, Bethshemesh and others) have become fortified cities in Iron II, in which there is a steady growth of population and development of technology, and in which the characteristic pillar courtyard house of Iron I continues into Iron II in both rural and urban sites, and in which, finally, there is religious continuity in the worship of El, Baal and Asherah.

Dever has undoubtedly constructed a powerful case for the indigenous Canaanite origins of Israel as the dominant paradigm for our understanding Israel's emergence. Yet, one can maintain this overall paradigm while giving more room than Dever allows to aspects of and contributors to the movement which provide a necessary external dimension.[28] I refer here to those elements of the population of Palestine which contributed to the constitution of Israel and which also show close connection with Egypt and Egyptians both in Egypt and in Palestine. These include the *'apiru* and the *shasu*, but also indeed other elements of the population at the higher end of the social scale.

It is probably true that the role of the *'apiru* in the origins of Israel has been considerably exaggerated in some treatments of the subject,[29] and it is also true that the linguistic connection between *'apiru* and Hebrew is by no means established.[30]

26. Dever (*ibid.*, 182-9) elaborates on this by taking up the work of Marvin Chaney who, applying the results of studies of modern peasants in class structured societies, understands the process involved as a peasant revolt.

27. Cf Dever, *Who were the early Israelites...?*, 194-200.

28. Towards the end of his book (229-32), in order to account for the Old Testament Joseph story, Dever does allow for the possibility that elements of the house of Joseph had formerly been in Egypt. This, however, is left wholly undeveloped, no doubt in the interests of emphasising that 'there is no longer a place or a need for the Exodus as a historical explanation for the origins of Israel' (232).

29. Cf D. B. Redford, *Egypt, Canaan and Israel in Ancient Times* (Princeton: Princeton University Press, 1992), 263-9.

30. A. Kuhrt, *The Ancient Near East* (London: Routledge, 1995), vol. II, 436; Dever, *Who were the early Israelites...?*, 74.

Nevertheless, the *'apiru* remain highly relevant to the issue of Israelite origins, and the use of the term 'Hebrews' of Israelites in Genesis, Exodus and 1 Samuel, relates to circumstances in which such Israelites could easily be understood as *'apiru*. They appear throughout the Ancient Near East in the second millennium, with particular concentration in the Amarna period in central Palestine. Many references to the *'apiru* present them as social bandits and outlaw groups, so that a generally accepted definition now is that they were groups of refugees, without particular ethnic affiliation, who lived out of reach of the urban settled areas, but nevertheless preyed on such areas. In the New Kingdom period, the land between the Orontes and the Mediterranean was under nominal Egyptian control but was not administered on their behalf by any local vassal. The area, known as Amurru, became the haunt of *'apiru* from the reign of Amenophis III, and under the leadership of Abdi-ashirta and his son and successor Aziru it posed a real threat to neighbouring states and was the subject of repeated complaints to the Egyptian overlord.[31] But such dangers were posed not only to the states immediately bordering on Amurru, for the activities of the *'apiru* penetrated also into the central and southern highlands of Palestine. So, Milkilu king of Gezer wrote to the Pharaoh:

> Say to the king, my lord, my god, my Sun: Message of Milkilu, your servant, the dirt at your feet, I fall at the feet of the king, my lord, 7 times and 7 times. May the king, my lord, know that the war against me and against Suwardata is severe. So may the king, my lord, save his land from the power of the *'Apiru*. Otherwise, may the king, my lord, send chariots to fetch us lest our servants kill us. Moreover, may the king, my lord, ask Yanhamu, his servant, about what is being done in his land.[32]

31. The activities of Abdi-ashirta and Aziru can be followed especially through the letters to Pharaoh from Rib-Addi, the king of Byblos who constantly sought Egyptian help against them. On the *'apiru*, cf J. K. Hoffmeier, *Israel in Egypt* (Oxford: Oxford University Press, 1996), 112-6; R. B. Coote, 'Habiru, Apiru', in D. N. Freedman (ed), *Eerdmans Dictionary of the Bible* (Grand Rapids: Eerdmans, 2000), 549-51; M. L. Chaney, 'Ancient Palestinian Peasant Movements and the Formation of Premonarchic Israel', in D. N. Freedman and D. F. Graf (eds), *Palestine in Transition: The Emergence of Ancient Israel* (Sheffield: Almond Press, 1983), 72-83; Redford, *Egypt, Canaan and Israel in Ancient Times*, 170-2.
32. EA 271; W. L. Moran, *The Amarna Letters* (Baltimore: Johns Hopkins University Press, 1992), 317.

As part of their approach to control of Syria-Palestine in the New Kingdom, the Egyptians practised population deportation. Numerous sites which had been inhabited in the MBA in Palestine were destroyed under the 18th dynasty rulers and the population deported to Egypt.[33] Figures for these deportations are given in the annals of the New Kingdom pharaohs on the walls of the Karnak temple: so, from the Palestinian campaign of Amenophis II in his 9th year 89,600 prisoners of war were brought to Egypt. Among those taken prisoner by Amenophis II were 3,600 *'apiru*. From the reign of Rameses II there is a notice in Papyrus Leiden 348 of 'the *'apiru* who are dragging stone to the great pylon of ... Ra'messe-miamun, Beloved of Ma'et'.[34] Another record, Papyrus Leiden 349, mentions *'apiru* as labourers: 'I have taken note of my lord's message to me saying: Give rations to the soldiers and to the *'apiru* labourers who are drawing water from the well of Pre of Rameses II l.p.h. south of Memphis. Farewell.'[35] Prisoners of war, deported to Egypt in large numbers in the New Kingdom period were in the main assigned to temple estates and put to state building projects, including, as the illustration from the tomb of Rekhmire, the vizier of Thutmoses III, makes clear, the making of bricks. Such historical experience on the part of the *'apiru* cannot be irrelevant to the later formulation of Israel's exodus tradition.

Like the *'apiru*, so the *shasu* are an unsettled people, living not far from the sedentary population, having contact with the towns but living outside the fabric of society.[36] Yet they are not to be identified with the *'apiru*. They are referred to separately in Egyptian texts: Amenophis II's list of prisoners of war taken from Palestine refers not only to 3,600 *'apiru*, but immediately following to 15,200 *shasu*. Moreover, while the *'apiru* appear in both Egyptian and other documents as spread throughout the Ancient Near East in the second millennium, the *shasu* are men-

---

33. Cf Redford, *Egypt and Canaan in the New Kingdom* (Beer-sheva: Ben Gurion University of the Negev Press, 1990), 37-9.
34. Papyrus Leiden 348; cf R. A. Caminos, *Late-Egyptian Miscellanies* (Oxford: Oxford University Press, 1954), 491; M. Greenberg, *The Hab/piru* (New Haven: American Oriental Society, 1955), 56.
35. E. Wente, *Letters from Ancient Egypt* (Atlanta: Scholars Press, 1990), 124.
36. On the *shasu* cf R. Giveon, *Les Bedouins shosou des documents Egyptiens* (Brill: Leiden, 1971); Redford, *Egypt, Canaan and Israel in Ancient Times*, 269-80.

tioned only in Egyptian documents, and indeed are presupposed as belonging to the New Kingdom period from Thutmoses II to Rameses III, and their more limited movement within Syria-Palestine can be traced.

The documents of the 18th dynasty show the development of the *shasu* from being a hostile group to become a people referred to beside the most powerful enemies of Egypt. More than half of the references to them relate to the time of Rameses II, recording his actions against the *shasu*, their massacre, the pillaging of their country and the imposition of tribute. According to the most ancient surviving documents they lived in south west Palestine, in southern Transjordan, connected with Edom and Seir. All other references that put the *shasu* in other parts of Asia or Egypt should be understood in the light of this: the presence of the *shasu* outside this south western area of Palestine is the result of emigration or their being carried away as prisoners. The *shasu* are later found participating in the battle of Kadesh, when they are auxiliaries with the sedentary population in the war against Egypt under Rameses II. They are also found, again in the time of Rameses II, in Palestine proper, where they are brigands infesting the central mountain region: 'The narrow pass is dangerous, having *shasu*-bedouin concealed beneath the bushes, some of whom are of four cubits or five cubits (from) their nose to foot and have fierce faces. They are unfriendly and do not take to cajolery while you are alone having no aid with you nor soldiery backing you up'.[37] The *shasu* are an urgent problem for the Egyptians. They are described as rebels, implicated in rebellions in Palestine, and getting ready to approach the frontier of Egypt.

In addition, the *shasu* are remarkably important because two Egyptian texts of 14th and 13th centuries refer to them in connection with *yhw'*. One of these texts refers twice to 'the land of the *shasu* of *yhw''*; the other, from the time of Rameses II, refers to 'the land of *shasu* of *yhw''*. The word *yhw'* is probably a place name; in both instances reference is being made to an area in the mountainous district of Seir east of the Arabah where the *shasu* are located. There are parallels, however, for a god and a place sharing the same name,[38] which makes it very probable that in

37. Papyrus Anastasi I, cf Wente, *Letters from Ancient Egypt*, 108.
38. R. de Vaux, *The Early History of Israel* (London: Darton, Longman & Todd, 1978), 334; S. Herrmann 'Der Name JHW in den Inschriften von

this instance we have the first extra-biblical references to 'Yahweh' the God of Israel. This must be connected to those biblical references which locate Yahweh in the same region: 'Lord, when thou didst go forth from Seir, when thou didst march from the region of Edom ...'(Jdg 5:4); 'The Lord came from Sinai, and dawned from Seir upon us ...'(Deut 33:2). This, as Redford has noted,[39] is 'a most precious indication of the whereabouts during the late fifteenth century BC of an enclave revering this god'. Seir, the mountainous region east of the gulf of Aqabah, inhabited originally by the Horites and later by the Edomites, is the home of Yahweh-worshipping *shasu* who later spread north and west, creating a major threat for the Egyptians who reckoned them among their chief enemies, mounted expeditions against them, and carried off thousands as prisoners of war to labour in Egypt. By the beginning of the 19th dynasty they expanded across the Arabah and into the Negev and northern Sinai, threatening Egypt's coastal route. During the 13th and 12th centuries they are reported along the eastern delta frontier whence they migrated with their cattle to gain access to water in the Wadi Tumeilat.

It goes beyond the evidence simply to identify the *shasu* as 'proto-Israelites'.[40] Nevertheless, like the *'apiru*, they represent a significant element in that mixed population of Palestine in the Late Bronze Age out of which Israel emerged. They cannot be identified with Israel; Israel is already an entity in the time of Merneptah independent of reference to the *shasu*. But in their wandering homelessness and their threatening status to Egypt, they represent a hostile force such as the Israel defeated by Merneptah; and in their veneration of Yahweh they came to form a core element of the later Yahweh-worshipping people that bore that name.

Relationships between Egypt and Palestine also took a different form, involving a very different layer of the population of Palestine. The measures used by Egypt to maintain control of Syria-Palestine included not only punitive expeditions and mili-

Soleb: Prinzipielle Erwägungen', *Fourth World Congress of Jewish Studies* (Jerusalem: World Union of Jewish Studies, 1967), 216.

39. Redford, *Egypt, Canaan and Israel in Ancient Times*, 273.

40. Redford, *Egypt, Canaan and Israel in Ancient Times*, 269-80, probably makes too close a link. In what is the main study of the relevant texts, Giveon, *Les Bedouins shosou des documents Egyptiens*, 267-71, also emphasises the parallels between the *shasu* and the biblical story.

tary outposts, but also the forcible transfer to Egypt of members of the royal families in Palestinian cities. So, the Amarna texts[41] record the sending to Egypt of whatever sons or relatives of the vassal king that the Pharaoh might have demanded. Undoubtedly, these individuals were often if not usually hostages for the good conduct of the vassal, but there was also an additional purpose: the inculcation of Egyptian ways was intended to influence future relations to Egypt's benefit, for these 'hostages' included those who would in time succeed to the throne in their Palestinian city-state homes. The tomb of Rekhmire, vizier of Egypt in the reigns of Thutmoses III and Amenhotep II, includes a scene[42] where Canaanite children are shown with Egyptian officials, with the apparent gloss: 'the children of the chiefs who are to be put in their fathers' places'.[43] Such relationships add to that range of on-going contacts which brought Egypt and Palestine into ever closer association through the New Kingdom period. Jeroboam I's flight to Egypt to escape the attentions of Solomon, and his subsequent return to become the first king of the northern kingdom, thus stand in a long tradition of relationships which embraced the top level of society as well as that of the 'apiru and the shasu.

(ii) Israel's population thus comprised different elements, many of which had, as part of their cultural memory, experience of captivity in Egypt and hostile relationships with Egypt while living in Palestine. A story of common origin in Egypt would therefore have been an effective tool for national unification.[44] That it was an ideology originally associated with Yahweh has already been seen to be doubtful. Not only was this ideology conceived as a resource for self-identification over against Judah where Yahweh was worshipped in the Jerusalem temple, but 1 Kings 12 itself explicitly relates the ideology to bull images more immediately associated with Baal than with Yahweh.

---

41. EA 156.10; 180.4-5; 187.22f; 194.30f; 254.30f; 270.15ff.; cf Moran, *The Amarna Letters*, 242, 263, 269, 272, 307, 316-7.

42. Plate 61 in N. G. Davies, *The Tomb of Rekh-mi-re at Thebes* (New Hampshire: Ayer Company, 2002).

43. Cf Redford, *Egypt and Canaan in the New Kingdom*, 27-36.

44. The degree to which the theme of 'liberation from oppression' featured in the original charter myth is impossible to say; it may be that the charter myth spoke simply of origins (cf Amos 9:7), while it was in its later appropriation by the Yahweh-alone party that the theme of liberation from oppression achieved prominence.

Moreover, the cult of Baal was officially established in the northern kingdom, and attempts to oppose this in favour of the worship of Yahweh alone did not, as the Elijah-Elisha stories indicate, appeal to Yahweh as the God of the exodus.

The social location and content of the worship of Yahweh in
the early monarchic period in Israel can be described here only
in very schematic terms. Yet enough may be ascertained to
indicate a probable framework within which the relationship
between Yahweh and the exodus from Egypt may be understood to have become established. Yahweh was already widely
venerated in monarchic Israel, along with Baal, El and Asherah.
As has already been clearly recognised, however, there also existed those for whom the worship of Yahweh *alone* was legitimate.[45] This was a demand that reflected social and political as
well as religious concerns, for it was clearly aimed against the
ruling house, especially that of Omri, and expressed support for
those in the rural population marginalised and oppressed by the
ruling urban elite. Although the lines of relationship cannot now
be traced, it is not improbable that these rural Yahweh-worship-
pers were descendants of the old *shasu* element in the population, through whom the worship of Yahweh had been introduced to Israel.[46] It is this group which came to constitute the
'Yahweh-alone' party, that alienated and marginalised group
represented by Elijah and Elisha in their opposition to the ruling
house. For this group Yahweh was the God of the oppressed, in
opposition to Baal, the god of the ruling party. The veneration of
Yahweh lay in the rural tribal elements of Israel for whom an
origin in Egypt was true only insofar as these *shasu* people had a
cultural memory of opposition to Egyptian oppression experienced not only in Egypt but perhaps mainly in Palestine. Their
self-identification, however, was much more strongly a matter
of being the people of Yahweh. Among this group an exodus

---

45. The evidence has been presented especially by M. Smith, *Palestinian
Parties and Politics that Shaped the Old Testament* (2nd edition, London:
SCM Press, 1987), 11-42; cf also B. Lang, *Monotheism and the Prophetic
Minority* (Sheffield: Almond Press, 1983).

46. The Yahweh-alone movement was, as Smith (*op. cit.*, 31) has clearly
shown, socially diverse in its composition in the later stages of its history,
so that membership of the group was indeed 'a matter of conversion,
not mere adherence' (*ibid.* 22). In the 9th century, however, this would
have been much less the case, and the worship of Yahweh alone would
have been characteristic of a more clearly defined social group.

from Egypt under the leadership of Baal, as proclaimed by Jeroboam, served only as a secondary framework of national belonging rather than as a primary expression of self-understanding.[47]

The association of the exodus with Yahweh is a prophetic achievement, which was a necessary corollary of the claim that it is Yahweh, not Baal, who is God of Israel. If Yahweh is God of Israel then it is Yahweh and not Baal who delivered Israel from Egypt. The exodus was an ideology appropriated by the marginalised. Its origins lie in the need to create a national unifying ideology; with the fragmentation of the nation and the alienation of Yahweh-worshipping elements, this ideology lost its binding and unifying character. Prophecy, as the protest of the marginalised, came to appropriate for Yahweh this significant element of national tradition, but only in the context of the claim that it is Yahweh who is God of Israel. The socially marginalised, in making their rightful claim to their place in Israel, do so at least in part through appropriating and also re-interpreting for themselves what had been the charter myth of the nation.

D CONCLUSION

Jeroboam's foundation of the northern kingdom with a 'charter myth' that expressed the unity of the people in terms of a common background in Egypt thus appealed to and built upon a historical experience which was undoubtedly a more or less significant element in the cultural memory of large sections of the population. There is no clear indication that there was any earlier formulation of such a 'charter myth' or that at any earlier stage a group had expressed its common adherence to a god who had

---

47. As far as the content of this Yahwistic faith is concerned we are very much in the dark, so overlaid is the tradition by what was later ascribed to Yahweh. Nevertheless, given the social location and background of this Yahweh-alone movement, it is not improbable that already here Yahweh was worshipped as one who upholds, supports and delivers from distress. It is even possible that the Song of Miriam in Ex 15:21 is an old hymn of this movement. What is notable about this hymn is the lack of any explicit reference to the exodus. Its association with the exodus is elaborately established by the preceding and much later Song of Moses in Ex 15:1-18, but this deliberate effort to provide an interpretative introduction to the Song of Miriam strongly suggests that the latter did not in fact have the exodus as its original point of reference.

brought them up from the land of Egypt. Such a belief is the expression of a group already in possession of its own land, contrasting its present with its past experience; it is not simply the expression of deliverance. It represents a breakthrough to a recognition of that which unites, in the face of that which worked against such unity (the rule of Solomon). That it was made in the name of Baal rather than Yahweh[48] is a reflection of a claim for the dominant role of Baal in the community, a claim which was itself to become the subject of bitter dispute. When that conflict was eventually resolved in favour of Yahweh as God of Israel, a resolution which emerged in the context of the opposition of early prophetic groups to the house of Omri, then also Yahweh appropriated those characteristics which had hitherto been attached to Baal. In particular, it was now Yahweh who gave Israel the land; it was Yahweh who had brought Israel up out of the land of Egypt.

---

48. The name Jeroboam is not Yahwistic, possibly derived from Jerubbaal; cf L. Koehler & W. Baumgartner, *The Hebrew and Aramaic Lexicon of the Old Testament* (Leiden: Brill, 1995), vol II, 434.

# CHAPTER FOUR

## Mark and Empire

### Stephen D. Moore

I. NATION

We begin on a lake as well known to Seán Freyne as any in his native Mayo:

> They went across the lake to the region of the Gerasenes. When Jesus got out of the boat, a man with an evil spirit came from the tombs to meet him. This man lived in the tombs, and no one could bind him any more, not even with a chain. … Night and day among the tombs and in the hills he would cry out and cut himself with stones. When he saw Jesus from a distance, he ran and fell on his knees in front of him. He shouted at the top of his voice, 'What do you want with me, Jesus, Son of the Most High God? Swear to God that you won't torture me!' For Jesus had said to him, 'Come out of this man, you evil spirit!' Then Jesus asked him, 'What is your name?' 'My name is Legion,' he replied, 'for we are many.' (Mk 5:1-9, RSV)

What's in a name, not least a name that gestures simultaneously to demonic possession and colonial occupation – if, indeed, it does? 'Since the text explicitly associates Legion with numerousness,' one leading Markan scholar has recently protested, 'we have no reason to think of a covert reference to the occupation of Palestine by Roman legions.'[1] No reason whatsoever, perhaps,

---

1. Robert H. Gundry, *Mark: A Commentary on His Apology for the Cross* (Grand Rapids, MI: Eerdmans, 1993), 260. R. S. Sugirtharajah notes that the Gerasene demoniac pericope 'has been exegeted in at least three ways that take no account of the colonial context'. First, the episode has been used to legitimate the missionary enterprise, Jesus' 'outreach' to this territory east of the Sea of Galilee, predominantly inhabited by Gentiles, being understood as both foreshadowing and authorising later missions to Africa, Asia, and Latin America. 'Another interpretation has the behaviour of the Demoniac explained in terms of social scientific categories and Western psychological theories,' while '[i]n a

unless our desire be for a Mark for whom the occupation of Palestine by Roman legions *is* a concern – or for *which* that occupation is a concern, 'Mark' now naming the text rather than the author; for even what cannot plausibly be ascribed to an author's intentions can always be ascribed to the text that invariably exceeds them. That, apparently, is the dual lesson of 'precritical' biblical exegesis and poststructuralist literary theory. Yet we need not break free of the current of mainstream biblical criticism in order to encounter readings of Mark's Gerasene episode attuned to colonial issues. Even the improbably prolonged moment in Markan scholarship of which Gundry's monumental commentary is a consummate product – the 'historical-critical' moment, with its single-minded preoccupation with the gospel's 'original' context, coupled with the evangelist's putative intentionality, and the corollary exclusion (necessarily incomplete) of contemporary contexts from the task of exegesis – yielded a small but significant trickle of assertions that Roman military occupation, no less than demonic possession, was indeed in view in this pericope. And in recent years, with the multiplication of 'political' readings of Mark, and of early Christian texts and traditions more generally, that assertion has become almost commonplace.[2] With the emergence of a newly sharp-

third interpretation, African biblical interpreters have recently tried to vernacularize the incident by reading it in light of African belief-systems regarding demon possession, witchcraft, and the spirit world' (*Postcolonial Criticism and Biblical Interpretation* [Oxford: Oxford University Press, 2002], 92). Even if none of these three interpretive trajectories engage explicitly with the ancient colonial context of the Markan pericope itself, however, it is probably safe to assert that the first and third, in particular, are implicitly engaged with modern colonial and postcolonial contexts, given the dense intersections between European missionary and colonial ventures, on the one hand, and between 'vernacular' hermeneutics and anti- or post-colonial consciousness, on the other. I would suggest, in addition, that there is a fourth way in which the pericope has been exegeted that takes no account of its colonial context, and that is the way epitomised by Robert Gundry in the quotation above, who himself speaks for a legion of European and North American New Testament scholars who have managed to write on Mk 5:1-20 for a century or more without explicit reference to any colonial framework, whether ancient or modern (although there have been exceptions to the rule; see n. 2 below).

2. See, for example, Ched Myers, *Binding the Strong Man: A Political Reading of Mark's Story of Jesus* (New York: Orbis Books, 1988), 190-94;

ened focus on 'empire' within New Testament studies, moreover[3] – a focus enabled, on occasion at least, by the conceptual
tools and critical vocabulary of extra-biblical postcolonial studies – we do have, *pace* Gundry, compelling reasons for hearing in
Mk 5:9 a dual reference to demonic possession and colonial occupation.

The fraught tale of the Gerasene demoniac, then, seems like a
logical enough place from which to launch a 'postcolonial' reading of the gospel of Mark, centred on the perennial and intractable issues of land, invasion, occupation, and liberation. If
the demons are, by their own admission, to be identified analogically with the Roman 'army of occupation,'[4] then the demoniac
may be identified in turn as the land and people under occupation – which, it may be argued, is why the demons earnestly en-
treat the exorcist 'not to send them out of the land [*exô tês chôras*]'
(5:10).[5] And if the act of exorcism is to be accorded anti-colonial
significance in this pericope, why should it not be accorded sim-

---

Herman C. Waetjen, *A Reordering of Power: A Socio-Political Reading of
Mark's Gospel* (Minneapolis: Fortress Press, 1989), 115-18; John Dominic
Crossan, *The Historical Jesus: The Life of a Mediterranean Jewish Peasant*
(San Francisco: Harper San Francisco, 1991), 314-18; Richard A.
Horsley, *Hearing the Whole Story: The Politics of Plot in Mark's Gospel*
(Louisville, KY: Westminster John Knox Press, 2001), 140-41; *idem, Jesus
and Empire: The Kingdom of God and the New World Disorder* (Minneapolis:
Fortress Press, 2003), 100ff; R. S. Sugirtharajah, *Postcolonial Criticism and
Biblical Interpretation*, 91-94.

3. A focus evident even in the titles of an increasing number of books in
the field; see, for example, Richard A. Horsley (ed), *Paul and Empire:
Religion and Power in Roman Imperial Society* (Harrisburg, PA: Trinity
Press International, 1997); *idem, Jesus and Empire*; Warren Carter,
*Matthew and Empire: Initial Explorations* (Harrisburg, PA: Trinity Press
International, 2001); Wes Howard-Brook and Anthony Gwyther,
*Unveiling Empire: Reading Revelation Then and Now* (Maryknoll, NY:
Orbis Books, 1999); R. S. Sugirtharajah, *The Bible and Empire: Postcolonial
Explorations* (Cambridge: Cambridge University Press, 2005).

4. A token force, to be sure, stationed primarily at Caesarea – but able to
call upon the Syrian legate and his legions whenever the paucity of its
numbers instills hope of effective armed resistance in the native populace.

5. 'The translation ['out of the land'] attempts to capture two nuances of
*chôra*: a region, especially the rural region surrounding a city ..., and dry
land as opposed to the sea ...' Joel Marcus, *Mark 1-8: A New Translation
with Introduction and Commentary* (New York: Doubleday, 1998), 345.

ilar significance in every other exorcistic episode in Mark, that most exorcistic of gospels (see 1:23-27, 32-34; 6:7, 13; 7:24-30; 9:14-29; cf 3:11-12, 14-15, 22-30; 9:38)? Jesus' earlier boast that his plundering of the property of the 'strong man' portends the end of Satan's empire (3:23-27) could then be read as equally portending the end of Rome's empire, the latter being implicitly construed as but an instrumental extension of the former. To begin to read Mark in this way is tantamount to using 5:9 ('My name is Legion ...') as a 'hermeneutical key' with which to unlock the gospel as a whole. Such keys generally break off in the lock, as the history of biblical scholarship never tires of telling us, and so I do not intend to overuse this one.[6] But it may at least open up a reading that will lead to an as yet unforeseeable destination.

To set foot, however tentatively, on this interpretive path is to begin to read the narrative of the Gerasene 'demoniac', and much else in the larger narrative in which it is embedded, as allegory, to read as the Markan Jesus himself has taught us to read (4:13-20) – a strategy that accrues added interest from recent (heated) debates concerning the extent to which so-called 'national allegories,' in which literary representations of individual colonial subjects stand in allegorically for the histories and destinies of entire colonised peoples, may be seen as a defining characteristic of contemporary postcolonial literatures.[7] Allegory, in any case, once unleashed, cannot easily be contained – not unlike the Gerasene demoniac himself whom no shackle or chain can restrain (5:4), and who thereby becomes an allegory of alle-

---

6. A determination reinforced by reading Laura E. Donaldson's 'Gospel Hauntings: The Postcolonial Demons of New Testament Criticism' (in Stephen D. Moore and Fernando F. Segovia (eds), *Postcolonial Biblical Criticism: Interdisciplinary Intersections* [New York: T. & T. Clark International, 2005], 97-113), which incisively underscores the hazards of imposing a unitary meaning on the gospel exorcisms. Not least among these hazards is a certain gender blindness. While the Gerasene wails at the top of his lungs, notes Donaldson, the demon-possessed daughter of Mk 7:24-30 is mute; while he engages in frenzied activity, she lays immobile on her mattress; and while he vividly inhabits the main narrative, she is absent from it. Such stereotyping subverts 'any attempt to yoke men and women indiscriminately together under the master term of 'the colonized'' (*ibid.*, 103).

7. See, for example, Stephen Slemon, 'Monuments of Empire: Allegory / Counter-Discourse / Post-Colonial Writing,' *Kunapipi* 9 (1987): 1-16.

gory itself. It would not be unduly difficult to track allegory's in-
exorable verse-by-verse rampage through this entire pericope,
should strategy demand it. In the event, a few sample steps will
suffice to relay a sense of the dance.

*They came to ... the country of the Gerasenes* (5:1). The Hebrew
root *grsh* means 'banish,' 'drive out,' 'cast out,' as more than one
commentator has observed, and so, by extension, commonly signifies exorcism.[8] The exorcist has landed, but on what shore?
Hardly 'the land of the exorcists'; 'the land in need of exorcism'
better suits the context. The very name of the country in which
he has just set foot 'hails' Jesus, then, and 'interpellates' him, as
the Marxist Louis Althusser might have said – and by which he
might have meant that the name, simultaneously a summons,
reaches out subtly yet imperiously to mould and manipulate the
one thus called.[9] Jesus has arrived among a people whose very
appellation constitutes a pre-existing appeal to (and hence a
covert construction of) his (now) manifest destiny to drive out
the powers that possess them.

*[A] man out of the tombs in an unclean spirit [en pneumati
akathartô] met him* (5:2). The peculiar *en* should be allowed its
full, engulfing force here.[10] It signifies that the possessed subject's identity has been utterly submerged in that which possesses
him – as is indeed evident from that fact that, in the dialogue
that ensues, it speaks in him, through him, and for him. One
would be hard pressed to find a more apt image – or allegory –

---

8. J. D. M. Derrett, 'Spirit-Possession and the Geresene Demoniac,' *Man*
n.s. 14 (1979): 287; Marcus, *Mark 1-8*, 342; cf Gundry, *Mark*, 256. While
'appropriate symbolically,' the name Geresa is 'difficult geographically,' notes Marcus (*ibid.*), since the place was not on the shore of the lake,
as the narrative would lead us to assume, but thirty-seven miles south-
east of it. The possessed swine would thus have had an exhausting run
indeed before plunging (not without relief?) into the lake. But it is the
very difficulty of the reading 'Gerasenes,' together with its superior attestation in the manuscript tradition (cf Metzger, *A Textual Commentary
on the Greek New Testament* [London and New York: United Bible
Societies, 1971], 23-24, 840), that makes it preferable to 'Gadarenes' or
'Gergasenes,' in accordance with the text-critical principle, 'prefer the
*lectio difficilior.*'
9. Louis Althusser, 'Ideology and Ideological State Apparatuses (Notes
towards an Investigation),' in *idem, Lenin and Philosophy and Other
Essays* (trs Ben Brewster; London: New Left Books, 1971), 121-73.
10. Cf Marcus, *Mark 1-8*, 187, 342, 348.

of the colonial subject's self-alienation when compelled to internalise the discourse of the coloniser.

*[N]o one could restrain him any more, even with a chain; for he had often been restrained with shackles and chains, but the chains he wrenched apart, and the shackles he broke in pieces; and no one had the strength to subdue him. Night and day ... he was always howling and bruising himself with stones* (5:3-5). Possession is *maddening*, eliciting spectacular acts of masochistic resistance. Here the national allegory projects onto the parallel screen the disastrous and increasingly desperate armed rebellion that culminated with the Roman decimation of Jerusalem and its temple. When the occupying power is too overwhelming, armed resistance can only effect self-annihilation – which, however, is also self-immolation; and from the ashes of martyrs rebellion is reborn.

*And the unclean spirits came out and entered the swine; and the herd ... rushed down the steep bank into the sea ...* (5:13). The reason for the pigs' lemming-like rush into the sea is unstated. The simplest explanation would seem to be that the exorcist has compelled them to do so, thereby cleansing the land of their polluting presence. Not to put too delicate a point on it, the Romans are here shown up for the filthy swine that they are, and triumphantly driven back into the sea from whence they came – the dream of every Jewish peasant resister, as one of our own sages has observed.[11] Cleansing the (com)promised land of unclean occupants so that God's people can possess it more completely is a theme thoroughly rooted in the Israelite myth of origins.[12] But whereas in the Israelite conquest narratives the invaders are charged with sweeping the land clean, now it is the invaders themselves who must be swept into the sea. Genocide and nationalism share a certain fastidious tidiness, it would seem – which, no doubt, is why the former has at times sprung fully formed from the head of the latter.

And it is not just the invaders who must be swept away, but the comprador class who have made the invaders' continuing control of the land and its people possible. The first step in ridding the land of the polluting Roman presence, it emerges (once

---

11. Crossan, *The Historical Jesus*, 314.
12. The companion theme of prior liberation from bondage is also discernible in the pericope, the phantasmic destruction of the Romans in the sea serving to evoke the mythic destruction of the Egyptians in the sea.

we begin to survey larger stretches of the narrative, employing
Gerasa as our vantage point), is to rid it of the collaborating local
elite. In due course, Mark's Messiah will embark on his single-
minded march to Jerusalem (cf 10:32-34). But to what end?
Primarily, so that he may enact the symbolic destruction of the
Jerusalem temple, essential seat of power of the indigenous elite:
'Then they came to Jerusalem. And he entered the temple and
began to drive out [ekballein] those who were selling and those
who were buying in the temple ...' (11:15). Again, we are faced
with an exorcism of sorts: the spectacle is one of expulsion,
cleansing, dispossession, and repossession. Thematically, at
least, this pericope is intimately imbricated with that of the
Gerasene demoniac. The 'cleansing' of God's house ('My house
[ho oikos mou] shall be called a house of prayer ...'– 11:17) performed with such passion by Mark's Messiah, and seen as so
threatening by the Jerusalem elite ('And when the chief priests
and the scribes heard it, they kept looking for a way to kill him
...'– 11:18), is a symbolic prelude to the 'cleansing' of the entire
land that properly belongs to the owner of the house (cf 12:1ff), a
cleansing that the exorcism at Gerasa anticipated.

The Messiah's symbolic destruction of the temple precipit-
ates his own destruction, however, his public annihilation upon
the colonial cross. But in engineering Jesus' own obliteration in
retribution for the symbolic destruction of their temple (11:18; cf
14:58; 15:29-30), the local elite unwittingly and catastrophically
engineers the actual destruction of the temple, according to
Mark, and as such their own inevitable eradication. Consider the
positioning of the 'temple-cleansing' incident. It interrupts the
two-part anecdote of Jesus cursing and thereby blasting an unproductive fig tree (11:12-14, 20-22). The 'temple-cleansing' material thus forms the filling in a narrative sandwich. It is, indeed,
one of the more notable examples of Mark's celebrated 'sandwich technique' (the menu also includes 3:20-21 [22-30] 31-35;
5:21-24 [25-34] 35-43; 6:7-13 [14-29] 30-32; 14:53-65 [66-72] 15:1-5),
and is generally regarded as one of the less enigmatic examples
of the device, the material in the two outer layers of the sandwich imposing a relatively transparent meaning upon the material in the middle layer: the destruction of the unproductive fig
tree portends the destruction of the 'unproductive' temple.[13]

13. The standard study detailing and advancing this interpretation is
William R. Telford, *The Barren Temple and the Withered Tree* (JSNTSup 1;
Sheffield: JSOT Press, 1980).

Mark thereby obliquely signals his conviction that the Roman annihilation of the temple and city that brought the Jewish rebellion of 66 AD to a catastrophic close was an act of divine retribution. The sandwich is followed almost immediately by the Parable of the Vineyard and the Tenants (12:1-12), which deftly reinforces the message: 'What then will the owner of the vineyard do? He will come and destroy the tenants ... [T]hey ['the chief priests, the scribes, and the elders'] realised that he had told this parable against them ...' (12:9, 12).

Of course, the Jerusalem temple's destruction is itself but the eschatological prelude to Jesus' parousia, as the ensuing apocalyptic discourse (13:1-37) makes plain. And what the parousia will signify, among other things, is the unceremonious cessation of the Roman empire, as of every other human *basileia*. Jesus will bump Caesar off the throne. Is this the *telos*, then, toward which everything in the Markan narrative is tending? Yes and no, it seems to me. Yes, because a reading of Mark along these lines is not only possible; in certain contexts – straitened contexts, especially, occasioned by overt state-sponsored oppression, akin to that experienced, or anticipated, by the Markan community itself – a reading of Mark as anti-imperial resistance literature, pure and simple, may be absolutely necessary. And no, because such a reading, in order to run smoothly, must aqua-glide over the intense ambivalence that, on an alternative reading, can be shown (and will be shown below) to characterise and complicate Mark's representations of empire. Practices of reading acutely attuned to such complexities are a signal feature of contemporary postcolonial theory, and not the least of its benefits for the biblical critic. Outside of biblical studies, postcolonial studies has tended to be infused and enabled by a generic poststructuralism, itself intimately attuned to the inherent instabilities of discourse and representation. Postcolonial biblical criticism has, to date, been less shaped by poststructuralism, tending instead, in some of its more notable manifestations, to operate under the aegis of a hermeneutic of suspicion and in the mode of ideology critique.[14] Like its extra-biblical counterpart, however, it brings complexly unstable texts into view. A defining feature of 'post-

---

14. Exemplified by such works as Musa W. Dube, *Postcolonial Feminist Reading of the Bible* (St Louis, MO: Chalice Press, 2000), and Tat-siong Benny Liew, *Politics of Parousia: Reading Mark Inter(con)textually* (Leiden: Brill, 1999).

colonial' biblical exegesis, indeed, as distinct from (although by
no means in opposition to) 'liberationist' biblical exegesis is a
willingness to press a biblical text at precisely those points at
which its ideology falls prey to ambivalence, incoherence, and
self-subversion – not least where its message of emancipation
subtly mutates into oppression.[15] We have seen, in miniature at
least, how an unreserved reading of Mark as anti-imperial resistance literature might proceed.[16] It remains to inquire how else a
reading of Mark attuned to issues of empire might unfold.

II EMPIRE

Let us begin again, then, this time by noting that Mark altogether
lacks the snarling, fang-baring hostility toward the Roman state
that possesses Mark's near-contemporary, and yet more apocalyptic, cousin, the Book of Revelation,[17] a text that shares with
Mark an intense preoccupation with the prospect of persecution,
and likewise proffers an apocalyptic solution to that problem:
'the one who endures to the end will be saved,' is Mark's sum-
mation of the solution (13:13), but it could just as easily be
John's. The face of Rome comes into explicit focus in Mark only
in 15:1-39, Jesus' trial before the Roman prefect of Judea and his
public execution at the hands of the Roman military. But the expression on that face is curiously difficult to decipher. How is
the figure of Pontius Pilate in Mark to be construed? As a basically benign but morally feeble official, who would release the
accused if he could, but is unable to out-manoeuvre, or is merely
unwilling to override, the Sadduceean elite and the vociferous
mob whose strings they control? Or rather as himself a consummate manipulator, who unblinkingly dispatches the peasant

---

15. Cf. R. S. Sugirtharajah, *The Bible and the Third World: Precolonial,
Colonial and Postcolonial Encounters* (Cambridge: Cambridge University
Press, 2001), 250-65 *passim*; *idem*, *Postcolonial Criticism and Biblical
Interpretation*, 103-23 *passim*.

16. One way, at least. Other strategies have been developed, and
fleshed out much more fully, in such important works as the following,
all of which read Mark as unambivalently anti-imperial: Fernando Belo,
*A Materialist Reading of the Gospel of Mark* (trs Matthew J. O'Connell;
Maryknoll, NY: Orbis Books, 1981); Myers, *Binding the Strong Man*;
Waetjen, *A Reordering of Power*; Horsley, *Hearing the Whole Story*.

17. And not only Revelation, of course. Two Jewish apocalypses roughly
contemporary with Revelation also predict the destruction of Rome: see
2 Baruch 36:1-46:7; 4 Ezra 11:1-12:39.

troublemaker, while skillfully contriving to make it seem as though he is simply acceding to the impassioned demands of the peasant's own countrymen?[18] The only other Roman official who makes an explicit appearance in Mark, albeit a cameo one, is, if anything, still more ambiguously delineated. What does the Roman centurion's celebrated pronouncement in 15:39 actually amount to? In declaring the bloody corpse dangling before him to have 'truly [been] a Son of God' (*Alêthôs houtos ho anthrôpos huios theou ên*) is he, in good crypto-Christian fashion, succeeding spectacularly where Jesus' own disciples have so singularly failed, effortlessly coupling the concepts of divine sonship and dishonorable death where they could not, and thereby giving climactic and definitive expression to Mark's *theologia crucis*? Or is he merely engaging in grim gallows humour ('Some Son of God!'), unwittingly giving expression thereby to a 'truth' that is not his but belongs to the evangelist/ventriloquist instead? Unaware that he is a dummy, is the centurion simply parroting the derision of everybody else in the vicinity of the cross (15:29-32), not least the local elite with whom his commander is in cahoots: 'Those who passed by derided him ... In the same way, the chief priest, along with the scribes, were also mocking him among themselves and saying, "... Let the Messiah, the King of Israel, come down from the cross now ..." Those who were crucified with him also taunted him' (15:29-32)? Jesus' sole explicit pronouncement on Rome in Mark – 'Give to Caesar the things that are Caesar's, and to God the things that are God's' (12:17) – is itself no less enveloped in ambiguity, as its history of reception amply attests. It can be, and has been, read to mean that since, in accordance with Israelite tradition and theology, everything belongs to God, nothing is due to Caesar;[19] far more frequently, however, it been read unabashedly as an affirmation of the imperial status quo.[20] In consequence of these assorted un-

---

18. It is Matthew's Pilate who, of late, has been the more notable recipient of the latter line of interpretation (see Carter, *Matthew and Empire*, 145-68), although much of Carter's analysis applies *mutatis mutandis* to Mark's Pilate.

19. See especially Richard A. Horsley, *Jesus and the Spiral of Violence* (San Francisco: Harper & Row, 1987; rp Minneapolis: Fortress Press, 1993), 306-17; *idem, Reading the Whole Story*, 36, 43, 112-13.

20. See, for example, the survey of late nineteenth and twentieth century British biblical commentaries recently undertaken by Ralph Broadbent, which finds the 'render unto Caesar' logion, among others, almost in-

certainties, it seems to me, Mark's stance *vis-à-vis* Rome cannot plausibly be construed as one of unambiguous opposition. Turning now to less explicit or immediate representations of Rome in Mark, my working assumption instead is that Mark's attitude toward Rome is imbued with that simultaneous attraction and repulsion – in a word, ambivalence – to which the postcolonial theorist Homi Bhabha, in particular, has taught us to be attuned when analysing colonial or anti-colonial discourses.[21]

The clamour of Roman legionaries breaching the walls of Jerusalem and putting its inhabitants to the sword can dimly be heard in Mk 13:14-20, according to the dominant critical reading. Earlier in the apocalyptic discourse, Jesus' disciples are forewarned that they must stand before Roman governors or client kings, just as Jesus himself did, and possibly be executed for their testimony, just as he himself was (13:9-13). When the Son of Man returns 'in the clouds with great power and glory' (13:26), however, as he is soon destined to do, his behaviour and demeanor will be markedly different from his Messianic counterpart in Revelation, who, on his own return through an 'opened heaven,' will be riding at the head of the 'armies of heaven,' 'to judge and make war,' armed with the 'sharp sword' of his mouth 'with which to strike down the nations,' which will result in a nightmarish mountain of rotting human flesh upon which 'all the birds that fly in midheaven' will be invited to gorge (Rev 19:11-21). What of the parousia of the Markan Messiah? What pre-ordained plan of action will he execute when he makes his own appearance on the clouds? We are told only that 'he will send out the angels, and gather his elect from the four winds, from the ends of earth to the ends of heaven' (13:27). The Markan parousia is, in essence, a search-and-rescue mission, not a punitive strike, as in Revelation. Nowhere in Mark are Roman officials who have persecuted Christians, nor even Judean collaborators with Rome who have conspired to murder their

---

variably accommodated to imperial ideologies ('Ideology, Culture, and British New Testament Studies: The Challenge of Cultural Studies,' *Semeia* 82 [1998]: 47-55).

21. See Homi K. Bhabha, *The Location of Culture* (London and New York: Routledge, 1994), 85-92, 129-38. Further on Bhabha and the Bible, see my 'Questions of Biblical Ambivalence and Authority under a Tree outside Delhi; or, the Postcolonial and the Postmodern,' in Moore and Segovia, *Postcolonial Biblical Criticism*, 79-96.

Messiah, threatened explicitly with a post-parousia reckoning.[22] Whereas in Revelation, Rome's imminent destruction, and its eschatological consignment, in the guise of the Beast, to 'the lake of fire and sulphur' (20:10) is an immense and intense preoccupation, in Mark the only characters threatened with the Son of Man's displeasure upon his return and with the everlasting torments of hell are Jesus' own disciples (8:38; 9:42-49). In marked contrast to the Apocalypse of John, Mark's 'Little Apocalypse' (ch 13) predicts not the destruction of Rome, but rather an act of destruction by Rome (the demolition of city and temple, that is, and the concomitant decimation of the Judean populace) – a particularly arresting symptom of the profound ambivalence that attends Mark's representation of the empire.

Mark's anti-imperial invective really only extends to the local elite.[23] Indeed, far from predicting divine punishment of Rome for the destruction of Jerusalem and its temple and the attendant massacre of its people, Mark appears to interpret this destruction and slaughter as divine punishment of the Judean elite for their exploitation of the common people (7:9-13; 11:12-21; 12:38-44), as we have already seen, coupled with their rejection of the Galilean Messiah (12:7-12). So whereas Rome in Revelation embodies and epitomises intractable opposition to and alienation from the God of Israel and his salvific interventions in human history, Rome in Mark is merely God's instrument, his scourge, which he employs to punish the indigenous Judean elite. (Rome therefore occupies roughly the same role in Mark's deuteronomistic theodicy as in that of his contemporary Josephus, as the latter's *Jewish War* 5.395 in particular suggests: 'Indeed, what can it be that hath stirred up an army of the Romans against our nation? Is it not the impiety of the inhabitants?') Mark thereby falls prey spectacularly to the divide-and-rule strategy entailed in the Roman policy of ceding administrative authority to indigenous elite in the provinces. As has been remarked with regard to the advantages to modern European empires of indirect rule in colonial Africa, 'popular resentments and hatreds could

---

22. Although the latter are threatened implicitly with a pre-Parousia reckoning, as we have seen: the destruction of their city and temple.

23. Cf Mary Ann Tolbert, 'When Resistance Becomes Repression: Mark 13:9-27 and the Poetics of Location,' in Fernando F. Segovia and Mary Ann Tolbert (eds), *Reading from This Place; Volume 2: Social Location and Biblical Interpretation in Global Perspective* (Minneapolis: Fortress Press, 1995), 336.

be deflected on to the local officials while the ultimate authority could remain remote, unseen and 'above the battle'[24] – at least until, as in the case of the Jewish revolt and its suppression many centuries earlier, the ultimate authority finds it necessary temporarily to relinquish its godlike remoteness and relative invisibility in order to intervene decisively and irresistibly in the corrupt affairs of its creatures, in an attempt to contain the chaos that its own administrative policies have created.

And yet, even if Mark lacks the explicitly hostile attitude toward Roman rule evident in Revelation, he also lacks the explicitly 'quietist' attitude toward Roman rule evident in at least two other first-century Christian texts, namely, the letter to the Romans (cf 13:1-7: 'Let every person be subject to the governing authorities; for there is no authority except from God, and those authorities that exist have been instituted by God. Therefore whoever resists authority resists what God has appointed, and those who resist will incur judgement ...') and 1 Peter (cf 2:13-17: 'For the Lord's sake accept the authority of every human institution, whether of the emperor as supreme, or of governors, as sent by him to punish those who do wrong and praise those who do right ...').[25] Generally speaking (and putting it rather too mildly), Mark does not enjoin its audience to respect human authorities.[26] Every human authority in Mark, indeed, whether 're-ligious' or 'political' (a distinction largely meaningless, however, in the context) is a persecutor, or potential persecutor, of John, Jesus, or the disciples of Jesus, aside from three incidental, but rule-proving, exceptions: the synagogue leader, Jairus (5:22ff);

---

24. Peter Worsley, *The Third World* (2nd ed.; Chicago: University of Chicago Press, 1970), 38. Cf Richard A. Horsley, 'The Imperial Situation of Palestinian Jewish Society,' in Norman K. Gottwald and Richard A. Horsley (eds), *The Bible and Liberation: Political and Social Hermeneutics* (2d ed.; Maryknoll, NY: Orbis Books, 1993), 397-400, which also has recourse to Worsley.

25. William R. Telford, *The Theology of the Gospel of Mark* (Cambridge: Cambridge University Press, 1999), 206, groups Mark's 'Render to Caesar ...' pericope (12:13-17) with these two texts, and not without reason, given the uses to which the Markan passage has primarily been put down through the ages. As we have seen, however, the passage does admit of alternative readings, and far more readily than the Romans or 1 Peter passages.

26. Cf Tolbert, 'When Resistance Becomes Repression,' 335; Lieu, *Politics of Parousia*, 86-93 *passim*.

the scribe commended by Jesus for not being 'far from the empire of God' (12:28-34); and the Sanhedrin member, Joseph of Arimathea (15:42-46). In addition, Jesus is repeatedly represented in Mark as urging his followers not to aspire to authority, glory, power or wealth (9:33-37; 10:17-31, 35-44; cf 12:41-44), but to adopt for emulation instead such liminal role models as the child (*paidion*) and the servant (*diakonos*) or slave (*doulos*) (9:35-37; 10:13-16, 42-45; cf 13:34). Mark's relentless narrative undermining of Jesus' own elite corps of disciples (4:13, 40; 6:52; 7:18; 8:21, 32-33; 9:5-6, 33-34, 38-39; 10:35-45; 14:10-11, 32-46, 50, 66-72), themselves the repositories of significant authority by the time the gospel was written, may be regarded as a further component of this elaborate anti-authoritarian theme.

There *is*, however, one major human authority figure in Mark whose authority is not the object of repeated narrative erosion but rather of constant reassertion and reification, that figure being, of course, Jesus himself. The question then arises: in attributing absolute, unassailable authority to Jesus, is Mark merely mirroring Roman imperial ideology, deftly switching Jesus for Caesar (to replay the ending of the reading performed earlier), but thereby undercutting the gospel's anti-authoritarian thematics, and inaugurating an empire of God that inevitably evinces many of the oppressive traits of the Roman empire it displaces?[27] This question is best addressed within the framework afforded by another, more encompassing question: what does the empire of God in Mark actually amount to?

Arguably, Mark's deployment of the term *basileia* ('empire')[28] may be deemed an instance of what the postcolonial theorist Gayatri Spivak has dubbed *catachresis*, originally a Greek rhetorical figure denoting 'misuse' or 'misapplication.' As employed

---

27. As Tat-siong Benny Liew has, in effect, argued (*Politics of Parousia*, 93-108). Pivotal to his argument is a reading of the Markan parousia (13:24-27), in tandem with the Markan passage on Gehenna (9:43-48), as a show of ultimate force and authority that 'will right all wrongs with the annihilation of the 'wicked'' (*ibid.*, 107). As my earlier remarks indicate, however, I myself find Mark's parousia to be a much milder and more muted affair.

28. In common with a still small but growing number of New Testament scholars, I believe that *basileia* in Mark, as in other early Christian texts, is best rendered in English by the term 'empire' rather than by the more innocuous 'kingdom,' a term whose political edge has been all but rubbed smooth by centuries of theological usage.

by Spivak, the term designates the process by which the colonised strategically appropriate and redeploy specific elements of colonial or imperial culture or ideology; as such, it is a practice of resistance through an act of usurpation.[29] In any Roman province, the primary referent of *basileia* would have been the *imperium Romanum*.[30] Mark's practice of catachresis, as it pertains to *basileia*, can therefore be said to border on the parodic. 'The time is fulfilled, and the empire of God has come near,' Mark's ragtag peasant protagonist proclaims (1:15), marching through the remote rural reaches of southern Galilee, and drawing assorted other peasant nonentities in his wake, fellow builders-to-be of this latest and greatest of empires. The intrinsic, indeed surreal, unlikelihood of this Empire of empires begs elucidation, and as such is virtually the sole topic of Jesus' first extended public address in Mark (only one of two), namely, his parables discourse (4:1-33). (His other extended 'sermon,' the apocalyptic discourse [ch 13], also has the advent of God's empire as its topic, although it is delivered from the other side of the eschatological curtain.) The parables of the Seed Growing in Secret (4:26-29) and of the Mustard Seed (4:30-32) contrast the present concealment (cf 4:11-12) and seeming inconsequentiality of the empire of God with its impending and impressive public manifestation, as does the parable of the Sower (4:1-9, 14-20), albeit to a lesser degree. Mark's next explicit mention of the empire of God glosses its imminent public disclosure as the moment when the seemingly vanquished Son of Man will reappear in unequivocal majesty (8:38-9:1). But the next several occurrences of the term play again on the paradoxically inglorious character of the present as opposed to future empire of God. Physical deformity will pose no obstacle to membership in the imperial ranks ('better for you to enter the empire of God with

---

29. See, for example, Gayatri Chakravorty Spivak, 'Identity and Alterity: An Interview – Gayatri Chakravorty Spivak with Nikos Papastergiardis,' *Arena: A Marxist Journal of Criticism and Discussion* 97 (summer 1994): 70.

30. Even in the Jewish homeland and diaspora, presumably. Contrary to what the synoptic gospels and other early Christian writings might lead us to expect, the term *hê basileia tou theou* is highly infrequent in the extant extra-Christian Jewish literature. According to Burton Mack (*A Myth of Innocence: Mark and Christian Origins* [Philadelphia: Fortress Press, 1988), 73 n. 16), it is found only in Philo, *On the Special Laws* 4.164; *The Sentences of Sextus* 311; and *Wisdom* 10:10.

one eye ...' [9:45]), nor will childlikeness (which, on the contrary, will be a necessary qualification: 'whoever does not receive the empire of God as a little child ...' [10:15]). Social status, however, epitomised by wealth, *will* pose a near-insurmountable stumbling block to membership ('How hard it will be for those who have wealth to enter the empire of God!' [10:23]), which is to say that those who have benefitted most egregiously from participation in Caesar's empire will be least eligible for admittance to God's empire. The latter pronouncement occurs in the immediate context of others which, as we have already noted, proffer servanthood and slavery as the supreme models for Christian existence, in marked contrast to the practice of the 'Gentiles' (read: Romans) – a cluster of countercultural sayings and anecdotes (9:30-10:45 *passim*) that, in the absence of anything else approximating a Markan 'Sermon on the Mount,' gives much-needed (if still insufficient) substance to its singularly unimperial concept of divine empire, as it translates into Christian practice.

The present empire of God, then, dimly conjured up in Mark, seethes with countercultural valence. But is it effectively domesticated and defused by the coming empire of God? Is the Markan Jesus' self-proclaimed ethic of self-giving and self-emptying ('the Son of Man came not to be served but to serve ...'), culminating in his voluntary submission to torture and execution ('... and to give his life as a ransom for many' [10:45]), in the end but the means to an end, that end being (not to put too subtle a point on it) incomparable personal power and authority ('Then they will see the Son of Man coming in clouds with great power and glory' [13:26])? And what of Jesus' disciples? Neither Matthew nor Luke hesitate to extend the eschatological 'no pain, no gain' formula to disciples: 'You are those who have stood by me in my trials, and I confer on you, just as my Father has conferred on me, an empire, ... and you will sit on thrones judging the twelve tribes of Israel' (Lk 22:28-30; cf Mt 19:28).[31] Mark, however, in intriguing contrast, seems reticent about unequivo-

---

31. Compare, too, Mk 14:25 and Mt 26:29. If, with the majority, we assume Markan priority, then we see that Matthew has changed the Markan Jesus' declaration, 'Truly I tell you, I will never again drink of the fruit of the vine until that day when I drink it new in the kingdom of God,' to 'I tell you, I will never again drink this fruit of the vine until that day when I drink it new with you [*meth' hymôn*] in my Father's kingdom.'

cally promising eschatological power and glory to disciples who
successfully imitate Jesus' practice of embracing a self-abnegat-
ing way of life fraught with the risk of violent death: Jesus readily
promises the suffering ('The cup that I drink you will drink ...'),
but is noticeably evasive on the matter of the reward ('... but to
sit at my right hand or at my left is not mine to grant' [10:39-40]).
Mark's curious caution in this regard, whatever its motivation
might have been, arguably lends its ethics a 'contemporary feel'
that Matthew's and Luke's lack. To deal in broad generalisations
for a moment, from within the enabling assumptions and convictions that have characterised many modern experiments in
community (not least, socialist experiments), a teleology of
otherwordly reward has tended to be seen as serving only to devalue a community ethic built on egalitarianism and mutual service. The tendency instead has been to regard the community
thereby constructed as sufficient 'reward,' in and of itself, for the
sacrifices that subtend it. Mark comes closer than most early
Christian writings to approximating this perspective. Mark
10:29-30 is particularly notable in this regard: 'Truly I tell you,
there is no one who has left house or brothers or sisters or mother
or father or children or fields, for my sake and for the sake of the
good news, who will not receive a hundredfold now in this age –
houses, brothers and sisters, mothers and children, and fields,
with persecutions ...' (cf 3:31-35). The concluding clause – 'and in
the age to come, eternal life'– is interestingly akin to an after-
thought: in contrast to the painstakingly itemised rewards of the
present age, it is devoid of detail or substantive content. All of
this, too, contrasts starkly, yet again, with Revelation, whose
only real ethic is an ethic of endurance, and which so scrupu-
lously itemises the spectacular benefits due to those who, through
their endurance, have earned admittance to the heavenly city
(21:1-22:5).

## III APOCALYPSE

To the extent that Mark can be said to locate the primary rewards for the radical community experiment that it advocates in
the liminal communities themselves that will come into being in
consequence, must its christology be said to stand in tension
with its ethics? By insisting on returning 'with great power and
glory' (13:26), does Mark's Jesus betray Mark's own latent desire
for a top-heavy, authoritarian, universal Christian empire, an

über-Roman empire, so to speak – the kind that will arrive all too soon, anyway, unbeknown to Mark, long before Jesus himself does? By insisting on returning in imperial splendour (however muted, relative to Revelation and even the other synoptics), does Mark's Jesus relativise and undercut the radical social values that he has died to exemplify and implement? Can radical apocalypticism, in other words, only ever stand in tension or outright contradiction with radical ethics? Or to put it yet another way, can radical apocalypticism only mirror imperial or colonial ideologies (and reflect them in a convex mirror, what is more, so that what was oppressively oversized to begin with now towers above the heavens: 'And then they will see the Son of Man coming in clouds ...'), or can it instead be consonant with a counter-imperial or counter-colonial ethic?

Yes and no, it would seem to me (yet again); it all depends on how apocalypticism is to be construed. A radical ethic that shatters every previously imaginable social structure (not that Mark's ethic goes quite that far) is, in its own way, also radically apocalyptic, portending the end of the world as we know it. Mark's apocalyptic discourse (13:1-37) does not, however, portend the end of the Roman imperial order but rather its apotheosis.[32] To discover a counter-imperial apocalypse in Mark we must look elsewhere. Conveniently, however, we will find what we need on the very threshold of Mark 13. The Markan anecdote traditionally labelled 'The Widow's Mite' (12:41-44) may be read as encapsulating, or at least adumbrating, a counter-imperial apocalyptic ethic.

Traditionally, the widow's donation 'out of her poverty' (*ek tês hysterêseôs autês*) of 'everything she had, all she had to live on' (12:44), has been construed as an exemplary action enthusiastically lauded by Jesus, the woman's absolute self-giving dramatically prefiguring his own self-emptying in death. In recent years, however, a sharp reaction to this hallowed typological interpretation has set in, not least because the interpretation, at its least palatable, has traditionally been presented to the poor as an enticement to donate beyond their means to the church. In the revisionary recasting of the anecdote, the woman is read as epitomising instead the oppressed peasantry mercilessly bled dry

---

32. To this extent I am fully in agreement with Liew; see *Politics of Parousia*, 93-107.

by the indigenous, Rome-allied elite.[33] The latter reading, unlike
the former, enables interpreters to posit a high degree of narrative continuity between the anecdote about the widow and the
apocalyptic discourse that succeeds it: it is because of what has
been done to the weakest of the weak in its name that the
Jerusalem temple has been marked by God for demolition, as
Jesus immediately goes on to imply: 'Do you see these great
buildings? Not one stone will be left here upon another; all will
be thrown down' (13:2). The congeniality of this line of interpretation to an emancipatory reading of Mark is, however, severely
undercut, it seems to me, by Mark's neo-deuteronomistic theodicy, which, when pressed, promptly implodes in horrific absur-
dity: impoverished denizens of Jerusalem, such as this widow,
would have been among the first to fall victim, if not by slaughter then by starvation,[34] to the Rome-administered divine retribution against the city and temple – a retribution that the
Roman-Judean administration, through its exploitation of the
common people, had (in accordance with the theodicy imputed
to Mark) provoked in the first place. The divine response to the
unjust suffering of the poor, on this reading, is to escalate that
suffering beyond measure: 'For in those days there will be such
tribulation [*thlipsis*] as has not been from the beginning of the
creation which God created until now, and never will be' (Mk
13:19).

A third reading of the widow anecdote is, however, possible.
This one piggy-backs on the traditional ecclesiastical reading,
the first one summarised above, and similarly styles the woman
as an exemplary figure – not because she anticipates and dimly
adumbrates Jesus' self-emptying, however, but rather because
she exceeds it. The woman's voluntary self-divestment of
'everything she had, all she had to live on' – at once an absolute
and a thankless gesture – may be read as an act of epiphanic ex-
travagance whose immeasurable immoderation thrusts it outside every conventional circle of economic exchange. As Jacques

33. See, for example, Addison G. Wright, 'The Widow's Mites: Praise or
Lament? – A Matter of Context,' *The Catholic Biblical Quarterly* 44 (1982):
256-65; Donald H. Juel, *A Master of Surprise: Mark Interpreted*
(Minneapolis: Fortress Press, 1994), 81-82; Liew, *Politics of Parousia*, 73;
Horsley, *Hearing the Whole Story*, 216-17; cf Elizabeth Struthers Malbon,
*In the Company of Jesus: Characters in Mark's Gospel* (Louisville, KY:
Westminster John Knox Press, 2000), 166-88 *passim*.
34. Cf Josephus, *Jewish War* 6.199ff.

Derrida has remarked, apropos of his own liminal concept of a gift beyond reciprocity,

> the gift is precisely, and this is what it has in common with justice, something that cannot be reappropriated. A gift is something which never appears as such and is never equal to gratitude, to commerce, to compensation, to reward. When a gift is given, first of all, no gratitude can be proportionate to it. A gift is something you cannot be thankful for. As soon as I say 'thank you' for a gift, I start cancelling the gift, I start destroying the gift, by proposing an equivalence, that is, a circle which encircles the gift in a movement of reappropriation.[35]

Read from this angle, the widow's self-divestment, as expenditure without reserve and absolute gift, would represent (with only a minimum of hyperbolic torquing) the breaking through, or breaking out, of 'something inconceivable, hardly possible, *the* impossible' even.[36] In common with other radically counter-cultural currents in Mark that we have pondered – only more so – this gift beyond reciprocity would hint at liminal experiments in community that apocalyptically deconstruct the world as we know it. The anecdote of 'The Widow's Mite,' then (mighty mite, indeed!) would be the real site of apocalypse in Mark, not the so-called 'apocalyptic discourse' that follows, rather lamely, on its heels, and for which it ostensibly prepares. Having already surpassed that for which it prepares, the anecdote renders the apocalyptic metanarrative superfluous and hence expendable. And the non-imperial apocalypse pre-emptively unveiled in the anecdote, far from undercutting the radical ethic that informs much of the preceding narrative, instead epitomises it. What the widow's action prefigures, if anything, is not so much Jesus' self-divesting investment – the Markan cross, in the end, is merely a bold entrepreneurial wager that yields an eschatological empire – but rather the expenditure without reserve exemplified by yet another anonymous woman in the narrative, the one who 'wastes' on Jesus (*eis ti hê apôleia hautê ...;*) the 'alabaster

---

35. Jacques Derrida, 'The Villanova Roundtable,' in John D. Caputo (ed), *Deconstruction in a Nutshell: A Conversation with Jacques Derrida* (New York: Fordham University Press, 1997), 18.

36. John D. Caputo, *The Prayers and Tears of Jacques Derrida: Religion without Religion* (Bloomington: Indiana University Press, 1997), 177, his emphasis. Here I have been expanding and embroidering some passing, but illuminating, comments of Caputo on the widow's gift.

flask of ointment of pure nard, very costly' (14:3-4), and whose tale is told almost immediately after the (official) apocalyptic discourse. Sandwiched between two women of whom he is apparently in awe, Mark's Jesus nonetheless fails to learn the lesson wrapped up in the absolute gift that he lauds, not once but twice, and cancel his planned parousia accordingly. In the end, then, Mark's gospel refuses to relinquish its dreams of empire, even while deftly deconstructing the models of economic exchange that enable empires, even eschatological ones, to function.

CHAPTER FIVE

# Crossing Border
## Speaking about the beginning in Genesis 1 and John 1

### Ellen J. van Wolde

*Crossing border* is the name of an international festival in The Hague where literature, music, film and contemporary art meet each other. Because these arts originate in different cultures they may influence, irritate or mesmerise each other when they finally meet. Is not also 'crossing border' one of the main characteristic's of Seán Freyne's work? Since decennia he has been working in different cultures, in the New Testament world, in present day's theology at Trinity College Dublin and in the broadly varied international board of the journal *Concilium*, and he has been living in different environments, in the city of Dublin, in Ireland's wildest hidden corner or (mentally) in the landscape of ancient Galilee, and in these as well as in similar circumstances he expresses a 'crossing border' attitude. Because in the discipline of biblical studies borders are often seen as frontiers not to be crossed, it is liberating when someone like Seán Freyne gently but convincingly shows the margins for what they are and thus challenges people to rethink their positions in their clear cut areas. To write in his Festschrift is, therefore, an honour for me.

My intention is to study some aspects of two renowned biblical texts about the ultimate margin, i.e. the very beginning of it all: Gen 1:1-2:3 (abbreviated as Genesis 1) and Jn 1: 1-18 (abbreviated as John 1). These chapters tell about the beginning not only to convey information, but also to construct and convey significance. In a cognitive intertextual study, as will be presented here, attention will be paid to these texts' 'mode of cognition', that is, to their way of thinking or of constructing usable meaning in relation to their cognitive and theological backgrounds.

## SIMILARITIES AND DISSIMILARITIES BETWEEN GENESIS 1 AND JOHN 1

By way of introduction, some of the generally accepted analogies and differences between Genesis 1 and John 1 can be sketched. Both chapters are the opening texts of biblical books and they start with the same word 'in beginning', $b^e$*reshit* and *en arche* without the definite article. This opening immediately triggers in John's audience's minds the text of Genesis 1. Also these texts' relevant ending points show some similarity, because they end with a description of the results or consequences of the relation between the creative process and the created universe. In between, the creatures are being created through God's performative speech acts, which demonstrates the cause-effect relationship between God's words and their consequences. The same is true for John's prologue to the extent that the Logos expresses in one word a kind of résumé of the dynamic process of creation that originates in the divine speech acts. In addition to these general analogies, two of the main topics of God's creative activities in Genesis 1, viz. the creation of the light and the distinction between darkness and light, are explicitly referred to in John's prologue. And finally, although not conclusively, Genesis 1's totality of the created universe expressed in the collocation 'the heaven and the earth' is in John 1 indicated by *ho kosmos*, 'the world'. In sum, John's reference to Genesis 1 is obvious.

Apart from these similarities two differences may immediately be noticed. Genesis 1 narrates about the coming into being of the heaven and the earth, whereas John 1 is not concerned with the origin of the universe, but with the Logos' arrival into the already existing world. Another difference is that in Genesis 1 only the last day of creation (vv. 26-28) relates to the human beings, whereas in John's prologue all verses implicitly relate to the link between the Logos and the human beings. John's text is human centred, but Genesis 1 is not. In order to understand their different modes of cognition, first Genesis 1 will be studied and consequently John's prologue.

## A LINEAR OR A NON LINEAR APPROACH TO GENESIS 1

The text in Genesis 1 is usually read from a chronological and causal perspective. In a chronological view, the opening verse represents the beginning and, from then on, the counting of the days shows what happens subsequently. The first verse of the story, 'In the beginning, God created the heaven and the earth', shows that, at this very moment in the text, both heaven and earth are being created. Accordingly, v. 2 is read as a description of the situation that exists immediately after this creation: the earth was there but it was still without form and content, darkness laid over the deep mass of waters, and God's spirit hovered over the waters. Hence, about the situation before God's creation no information is provided: nothing, chaos or something else may have preceded this creation; all we know is that, according to vv. 1-3, with God's creation this previous state of (non-) being disappeared. After this first event, six days of God's creative activities follow an obvious chronological pattern.

The traditional view of the story of creation is not only characterised by a chronological view, but also by a causal view. Thus, one explains the first element told as the cause of the second element and the second element as the effect of the first, which is also the foundation of what is understood as the creation's main feature: God is the very first initiator who created all and everything through performative speech acts. A consequence of this causal understanding is that the last element told is regarded as the most valuable one. In the Jewish tradition this had led to the conclusion that the seventh and last day is the climax of the story.[1] In the Christian tradition most people infer that the human being is the pinnacle of creation, and the sixth day of the creation is considered to be the story's climax. On this day, God created the human being as the final creature and in this creature creation reaches its culmination, possibly even its goal. According to this causal conception, Genesis 1 is understood as an explanation of the unique position of the human being in the created universe: the heaven is made for the benefit of the earth, the earth for the benefit of the human beings, and all creatures, plants, and animals are made as the necessary conditions for the human being to live on earth. However, when this causal approach is also applied to Genesis 2-3, that is the story of paradise in which the woman is the last creature to be made, one has to infer that creation reaches its climax and ultimate end in the female creature! Illogically, the opposite conclusion is usually drawn.

---

1. N. M. Sarna, *Genesis* (Philadelphia: Jewish Publication Society 1989), 14, resumes this as follows: 'The ascending order of Creation, and the 'six-plus-one' literary pattern that determines the presentation of the narrative, dictates that the seventh day be the momentous climax. Man is indeed the pinnacle of Creation, but central to the cosmogenic drama is the work of God, the solo performer. The account of Creation opened with a statement about God; it will now close with a statement about God. The seventh day is the Lord's day, through which all the creativity of the preceding days achieves fulfilment.'

These two approaches, the chronological and causal conceptions of coherence-building, are of a linear nature. They reflect the still predominant Western convention of thinking. The question is whether this linear kind of inferring actually fits the story of creation in Genesis 1. Some shortcomings can easily be detected. If linearity were the fundamental device, how can it be explained that no mention is made of what existed prior to creation? From numerous discussions in Western history about the question of whether there was nothing or chaos before God started to create, one may conclude that such an explanation would have been indispensable. Another problem concerns the creation of light. Through the ages, people have wondered how God could possibly have made the light in v. 4, and the sun and the moon much later on (in v. 14). People in the Ancient Near East knew, of course, that the light originates from the sun. How is it possible that the text expresses the idea that the light came into being before the sun was created? Another question arises with regard to v. 1, 'In the beginning, God created the heaven and the earth.' Does the text, in the opening verse, tell about God's creation of the heaven and the earth, as claimed in the linear approach described before? In other words, do the earth and the heaven exist now, according to the story at this stage? If they do, it is inexplicable that God in vv. 6-8 makes a vault in the middle of the waters and calls it 'heaven', and that in vv. 9-12 God separates the waters from the dry land and he calls the waters 'seas' and the dry land 'earth'. Does God create them twice?

The most striking difficulty of this linear approach is how to understand Genesis 2-3 immediately after Genesis 1. It seems that Gen 2:4b starts from the beginning again. 'On the day YHWH God made earth and heaven, the earth was without plants and human beings, and he made the human from dust of the earth.' But this had already happened before, in 1:26-28! People who read linearly are completely baffled. In historical critical exegesis the repetition is explained from a text-external point of view and it is concluded that Genesis 2-3 were written by another redactor or group of redactors than Genesis 1. It presupposes that, from a linear perspective, this could not be explained text-internally. What if this linear conception is too limited a view?

In a non-linear perspective, some of the problems referred to can be solved. Coherence is not viewed to be built up chronologically or causally, but in such a way that a text starts with the most general characteristics, which may be presented as a title, a framework or setting, a summary, or a motto, and then the text goes on to highlight one or another aspect against this general background. Coherence in this view always reflects a continuous interaction between the general and the specified or between the setting and what is profiled. Thus, the first verse is considered to give a kind of caption of the entire story that expresses at the outset its main thought.[2] The camera shows us in v. 1 an overall shot of creation and, after a short description of the situation in v. 2, the lens zooms in on the creation of the light (vv. 3-5), on the creation of the heaven as a vault in between the waters (vv. 6-8), and on the creation of the earth bringing forth plants (vv. 9-12). Subsequently, the lens zooms in on the creation of the heavenly bodies in relationship to the earth (vv. 14-19), on the creation of the inhabitants of the seas and the sky (vv. 20-23), and on the inhabitants of the earth (vv. 24-28). Meanwhile, the setting remains stand-by, that is, the waters of the deep do not disappear, but remain present in the background. Actually, the heaven in vv. 6-7 and the earth in vv. 9-10 are profiled against these waters' setting. In the same way it is clear that the darkness does not disappear, but that the creation of the light profiles the light against the darkness' background, so that a distinction can be made between day and night, and between the bearers of the day-lights and the night-lights. This also explains why the days are viewed to start with the night: the days are profiled against the framework of darkness that is introduced first. In the same way can alertness to this non-linear form of coherence building solve the problem of how God could possibly have made the light in v. 4, and the sun and the moon much later on, in v. 14. First, in v. 4, an image of the whole is presented: God creates the light, whereas later on, in v. 14, the lens zooms in on the bearers of the light: the sun, the moon, and the stars.

In sum, in Genesis 1 traces of linear and non-linear forms of coherence building can be found. Traditionally, its texture is reduced exclusively to its linear features, which is to be regretted because this text shows clearly traits of a non-linear coherence

2. For a survey of modern biblical scholars who consider v. 1 to present a name, caption or motto, see: Bauks, M., *Die Welt am Anfang. Zum Verhältnis von Vorwelt und Weltentstehung in Gen 1 und in der altorientalischen Literatur* (WMANT, 74; Neukirchen-Vluyn: Neukirchener Verlag, 1997), esp 69-92.

building. It elucidates, too, that linear and non-linear forms of organisation and presentation are to be considered complementary: they do not necessarily exclude each other.

THE FRAMEWORK OF GENESIS 1 (VV. 1-3)

The grammatical construction of vv. 1-3 has caused great discussions in history[3] till the present time.[4] It all starts with the indefinite noun 'in (the) beginning' in v. 1 and continues with the preterit verb 'he created', that does not describe the action as taking place (in such a case an imperfect consecutive would have been used) but gives an overall-view.[5] At the same time the words 'heaven and earth' do have the definite article, implying that the terms refer to something definite, something previously known, that is, the heaven and the earth as the writer and reader

---

3. For a survey of the long and ongoing discussion about *bereshit* lacking the definite article in the Jewish tradition, see: *Bereishis, Genesis. A New Translation with a Commentary Anthologized from Talmudic, Midrashic and Rabbinic Sources* (ArtScroll Tanach Series; New York: Mesorah Publications, 1977), 28-30. The noun *bereshit* without the definite article is interpreted by Rashi and Ibn Ezra, and by modern Jewish exegetes, such as N. M. Sarna, (*Genesis*, Philadelphia-New York-Jerusalem: The Jewish Publication Society 5749/1989, 5) and R. Alter (*Genesis, Translation and Commentary* [New York-London: Norton, 1996], 3) as a noun in the construct state: 'In the beginning of God's creating.' This rendering of the Hebrew looks to verse 3 for the completion of the sentence. It takes verse 2 to be parenthetical, describing the state of things at the time when God first spoke: 'When God began to create heaven and earth – the earth was ... darkness was ... God's spirit was ... – God said: 'Let there be light.' The peculiar syntax of this Hebrew sentence, viz. a noun in the construct state with a finite verb, makes it, however, a less plausible solution. That is the reason why Ramban disagrees with the construct form interpretation of Rashi and Ibn Ezra. He holds that if *bereshit* were a construct form, a noun would be needed to which to be connected: 'In the beginning of 'all things', God created.' Also Rabbeinu Bachya concludes that *bereshit* should be rendered as an independent, rather than a construct word. The best proof for this is, in his opinion, the accented punctuation of the word which is a *tipcha* (similar to the English comma), indicating that it is not joined with the following phrase.
4. For an extensive discussion on the syntactic structure with all due literature, see: Bauks, M., *op. cit.*, 69-92.
5. Cf B. Isaksson, *Studies in the Language of Qohelet. With Special Emphasis on the Verbal System* (Stockholm: Almqvist &Wiksell International, 1987), 61.

know them. Because these two words constitute a 'merism' or an entirety created by two opposites (such as 'from a to z'), its meaning is not limited to the two geographic locations 'the heaven' or 'the earth', but includes everything to be found in it.[6] This entirety as the audience knows it is linked to its origin and God's creative action is presented here in one total shot.

Syntactically, the three nominal clauses in v. 2 describe a threefold situation. The first clause with the copula 'was', connects the condition or formless state in the past to the earth. The next two clauses relate to the same time frame. The second clause has a locative predicate (no verb form) and relates it to 'the darkness', thus expressing a static situation, whereas the third clause holds a participle ('hovering') and thus contributes a dynamic element into this static situation; it constitutes a hinge to the dynamic activity described in v. 3 ('God said'). Together they give an idea of the background for the actions that will take place from v. 3 onwards.[7] These actions in vv. 3, 4, 5, 6 etc. will be marked by imperfect consecutive verb forms, of which the first in v. 3, 'God said', performs the task of introducing a change: something new happens.[8] Consequently, after the caption in v. 1 and before the detailed picture of the actions that are executed in vv. 3-12, v. 2 gives a short description of the situation prior to these divine creative activities.

Semantically, v. 2a can be considered to describe the primeval state of the earth as *tohu wabohu*: *tohu* by itself means emptiness or futility, and in some contexts is associated with the trackless vacancy of the desert; *bohu* by itself means wilderness, a place devoid of living creatures.[9] Thus, the earth is described as lacking the elements with which it will be filled in v. 11 (the

---

6. Cf M. H. Narrowe, 'Another Look at the Tree of Good and Evil', *Jewish Bible Quarterly* 26, 3 (1998), 184-188, here 185.

7. Cf P. Weimar, 'Chaos und Kosmos. Gen 1, 2 als Schlüssel einer älteren Fassung der priesterschriftlichen Schöpfungserzählung', in A. Lange, H. Lichtenberger, D. Römheld (hrsg), *Mythos im Alten Testament und seiner Umwelt. Festschrift für Hans-Peter Müller zum 65. Geburtstag*, (BZAW, 278; Berlin, New York: Walter de Gruyter, 1999), 196-211, here 197.

8. Cf B. Isaksson, *op. cit.*, 61.

9. See T. A. Perry, 'A Poetics of Absence: The Structure and Meaning of Genesis 1.2', *Journal for the Study of the Old Testament* 58 (1993), 2-11; D. Tsumura, *The Earth and the Waters in Genesis 1 and 2. A Linguistic Investigation* (JSOTS 83; Sheffield: Sheffield Academic Press, 1989).

plants) and vv. 24-26 (the animals and the human beings), as an earth without vegetation and devoid of living creatures. Verse 2b characterises this situation prior to creation additionally as *tehom*; there exists a primeval deep ocean wrapped in darkness. Later on, in vv. 6-8, God will create a dam or vault between the vertical masses of waters, to separate the waters from the waters below, and he will call this dam or vault *sha-mayim*, (literally 'that which relates to the waters') or 'heaven'. Hence, the *tehom* or deep vertical ocean is described in v. 2b as lacking the separating element that it will contain later on. The characteristic of 'darkness' will be removed in God's first creative act. Finally, v. 2c depicts the primeval situation as God's spirit or 'breath'[10] hovering over the waters', which confirms the existence of waters prior to creation, so that we may conclude that vv. 2a, 2b, and 2c describe the situation prior to the creation as 'not yet': God is there, but not yet speaking and creating; the waters are there, but not yet separated; and the earth is there, but not yet filled with its future inhabitants.

How then does Genesis 1 describe the situation before God created the cosmos? Not as nothing, not as chaos, but as earth wrapped in water, water wrapped in darkness and God's breath hovering over what is present: the waters. Thus, in contrast to the linear chronological view, in which v. 2 was perceived as a description of the initial situation after creation, in this non-linear view, it is perceived as a description of the situation prior to creation, as a not-yet situation, viewed from the perspective of the following verses.

### GOD'S ACTIONS

Usually much attention is paid to God's speech acts in their capacity as constitutive acts of creation. The idea is that God speaks and that the next verse immediately shows its results, be it the creation of the heaven, of the light, or the creation of the plants and of the animals. This might be true for God's first speech act in v. 3, but it is not true for his second (vv. 6-8), fifth (vv. 14-19), sixth (vv. 20-23), seventh (vv. 24-25), and eighth speech act (vv. 26-28), that is, in 50% of the cases. In these, God's speaking activities are not sufficient in themselves, but they are followed by their actual implementation through the verbs 'making' (*asah*) in

---

10. Alter, *Genesis*, 3.

vv. 7, 16, 25 or 'creating' (*bara*) in vv. 21-27. Consequently, God's speech acts are not always performative speech acts.

Another remarkable aspect is that this story does not merely reflect on 'the making of', but that it also reflects, and very often so, on the act of separation. This is obvious from the beginning. In his first speech act (vv. 3-4), God creates and consequently he makes a separation between the light he just made and the pre-existing darkness. In vv. 6-8, the separation between the waters is indicated as the vault's main function, and its fulfilment is explicitly described. Similarly, in his fifth speech act in vv. 14-17, God addresses the lights on the vault of heaven 'so that they will be a separation between the day and the night', which is executed accordingly. Three elements are, therefore, clearly distinct in these divine actions, namely speaking, making and separating. And the conclusion is justified that God's creative speaking in relation to the heavenly realm does not merely consist of 'cause to be', but also of 'cause to be distinct' or 'to separate'. Creation and separation go apparently hand in hand.

How about the divine speeches that relate to the earthly realm? When God in vv. 9-10 addresses the earth for the first time, no creative activity is mentioned, because the earth is already there. Only the waters have to gather on one place so that the earth can appear. It presupposes, therefore, a separation of the waters from the 'dry material'. Subsequently, God addresses in his other speeches the earth's inhabitants, using the term *mîn* ten times; this word originates from 'part or partition'[11] and is usually translated with 'kind' or 'species'. He applies it to plants, trees, see-animals, birds, and land-animals: they are all made and are asked to reproduce 'after their own kind'. Thus, differentiation appears to be a necessary condition for life on earth.

Only when the human being's creation is described, the term *mîn* is not used. In fact, the human being is the only creature that God does not make 'after its own kind', but 'in our image' and 'after our likeness', with possessive pronouns that refer to God. This is an indication that the human being, unlike the other creatures, does not find a point of reference in him- or herself, but in God.[12] In the last two speech acts, God addresses the human be-

---

11. J. Barr, *The Semantics of Biblical Language* (Oxford:Clarendon Press, 1962), 104.
12. Cf D. Clines, 'The Image of God in Man', *Tyndale Bulletin* 19 (1967), 53-103; J. Barr, 'The Image of God in the Book of Genesis – A Study of

ings once more, and he relates them to each other, to the earth, the other animals and to the plants on earth.

## GENESIS 1'S MODE OF COGNITION

The hypothesis is defended here that Genesis 1 in content and in form testifies of the same mode of cognition: the interaction between the continuous background and the foreground with its profiled elements coheres with the text's option for creation and differentiation. In its non-linear way of coherence building, the overall view is presented first and subsequently aspect after aspect is highlighted, and at the same time the elements of the setting or overall view keep their value although not placed in a fronted position. Hence, the profiled elements are not only made or created as entities or units in themselves, but also differentiated from one another. For example, darkness is pre-existent and stays on the background, whereas light is created and projected on this ground, so that the lights of the heavenly bodies keep daylight and darkness apart and day and night can alternate; darkness does not disappear, but is still there, though distinct from the light.

In his impressive study, Paul Beauchamp explains some elements of Genesis' cognitive background and thus clarifies the concept of separation in the Hebrew thinking.[13] He resumes his view in the diagram opposite.[14]

This diagram shows the specific role of the fourth day: it repeats the creation of the light and the firmament (vault of heaven), but at the same time surpasses the days of the week structure, because it announces set times and seasonal festivals. Thus, this fourth day is related to the first and the seventh day. Still more importantly, this diagram elucidates three thematic lines or continuities in Genesis 1, namely, first, the line of calling and blessing, secondly, the line of separation, species (of every kind, after their kinds) and declaring holy, and, thirdly, the line of day and night, set times and the Sabbath.

---

Terminology', *Bulletin of the John Rylands Library of Manchester* 51 (1968), 11-26.

13. P. Beauchamp, *Création et séparation. Etude exégétique du chapitre premier de la Genèse* (Bibliothèque des Sciences religieuses ; Paris, Bruges: Ed. du Cerf, Desclée de Brouwer, 1969).

14. P. Beauchamp, *op. cit.*, 69 (diagram 3; translated by the present author).

| day 1 | day 2 | day 3 | day 4 | day 5 | day 6 | day 7 |
|---|---|---|---|---|---|---|
| call (2x) | call | call (2x) | | bless | bless | bless<br>and |
| SEPARATE | SEPARATE (2x) | distinct species (3x) | SEPARATE | distinct species (2x) | distinct species (5x) | DECLARE HOLY |
| light and darkness | | | light and darkness | | | |
| DAY and NIGHT | | | DAY, NIGHT and SET TIMES | ................................... | | SEVENTH DAY (SABBATH) |

These lines are closely related. In an extensive study of the occurrences of the word *hibdîl,* 'separate' in the Hebrew Bible, Beauchamp shows that this term is used exclusively in a religious or sacral context, where it denotes a distinction of the pure from the impure, a separation of the sacred from the profane, a distinction of the more holy from the less holy, a division of Israel from the other people, or an attribution of a sacred function to some people and not to others.[15] A second important characteristic is that the word *hibdîl* is often used (in the books of Leviticus, Deuteronomy, Ezekiel and Chronicles) in combination with 'consecration' or 'declaring holy'. What is classified as sacred or pure needs previously be separated from the less sacred and the impure. This also explains why in such a context (e.g. Leviticus 11, 20, Deuteronomy 14) the terms *hibdîl* and *mîn* regularly occur side by side: in the lists of pure and impure animals the verb 'separate' denotes the distinction between the animals, whereas the noun 'kind' is used in the legislation which founds the classes and categories. It clarifies why Leviticus is

15. P. Beauchamp, *op. cit.*, 235.

anxious to maintain the distinction between the animals' species as they existed from their origins.[16] Genesis 1's attitude towards differentiation and separation shows, therefore, great similarities to the other books in the Hebrew Bible, such as Leviticus, Deuteronomy, Ezekiel and Chronicles. Also the distinction into six creation days and a seventh day of rest originates in the same mode of cognition.

> ... we discover in this story a classification of values with a nice message: everything that is created is good. But everything is not equally good. And also, everything that is good is not blessed, only living beings, and the Sabbath. Above all, everything that is blessed is not holy, only the Sabbath is blessed and holy. The Sabbath is the object of a blessing in order to make the transition possible in this scale of values.[17]

In sum, Beauchamp's study of Genesis 1 and of its relationships to other priestly writings in the Hebrew Bible, makes it understandable why Genesis 1 lays as much stress on differentiation and separation as on creation, because it grounds the distinction between the seventh day and the six days of creation.

The other chapters of the book of Genesis pay a comparable attention to differentiation and separation. In the primeval history (Genesis 1-11) the different appreciations of the sacrifices of Adam and Eve's sons and of their various offspring according to their professions (Genesis 4), the distinction of pure and impure animals in the flood story and the acceptance of the sacrifices of pure animals only (Genesis 6-9), the classification of Noah's sons' descendants into differently valued ethnic groups and classes (Genesis 10), and the story of the tower of Babel that shows God's preference for differentiation in languages and peoples (Genesis 11), all these chapters of the primeval history testify of the necessity of differentiation.[18] This differentiation makes particularity possible and forms, therefore, a necessary condition for YHWH's election of one people in Genesis 12.

The conclusion is that in Genesis 1's mode of cognition, distinction and separation are as crucial divine activities as creation.

---

16. P. Beauchamp, *op. cit.*, 245.

17. P. Beauchamp, *op. cit.*, 239 (translated by the present author).

18. See E. J. van Wolde, *Words Become Worlds. Semantic Studies of Genesis 1-11* (Biblical Interpretation Series, 6; Leiden: Brill, 1994); and *id, Stories of the Beginning. Genesis 1-11 and Other Creation Stories* (London: SCM Press, 1996).

This explains why this text favours in the created world bio-diversity above monoculture and why it considers the existence of and the differentiation between the various phenomena as valuable and of major importance. The variety of phenomena forms the background for the selection of certain components that are profiled and thus serve as reference points for the char-acterisation of the foreground. This prominence building is pre-sent in every line in Genesis 1.

### THE FIRST PART OF JOHN'S PROLOGUE (VV. 1-5)

Although John 1 opens with the same word as Genesis 1, it shows a completely different orientation. In order to be able to understand John's mode of cognition and its differences with Genesis 1, a rather detailed syntactic analysis of some verses in John 1 is asked for. Its composition in three parts, viz. vv. 1-5, 6-13 and 14-18,[19] allows us to discuss it part by part.

Verse 1a introduces the subject, the Logos, with a definite article. It is usually translated as 'the Word'. Because the term 'Logos' functions in a complex conceptual network which the English 'Word' does not share, I prefer not to translate it. From its usage with the definite article here, one may conclude that the Logos is John's starting point and that John's audience has heard of it before and has a certain idea about it. This Logos is related to the predicate (the imperfect 'he/it was') that expresses continuity and stability, and it relates the Logos to the category of 'being'. A comparison between Jn 1:1a and Gen 1:1a shows that, first, both stories open with a description of the temporal conditions, secondly, in Genesis 1, 'the heaven and the earth' is the story's point of departure, whereas in John 1 the Logos is, and, thirdly, in Genesis 1 the active transitive preterit 'created' indicates that the beginning is viewed and presented from the perspective of a dynamic process of creation, whereas in John 1 the imperfect 'was' indicates that the beginning is viewed and presented from the perspective of a steady and sure situation.

In v. 1b the predicate pictures the Logos in its spatial condi-tion: it was 'with God'. The implication is, of course, that God

---

19. This distinction of John 1 into three parts is generally accepted and based on the clearly marked syntactic and semantic caesuras between vv. 5 and 6 and between vv. 13 and 14, and on the differences in subject: in vv. 1-5 the Logos is the main subject, whereas in vv. 6-13 the Logos does not occur; it reappears in v. 14.

was previously present as well. The syntactical structure of v. 1c is slightly different, because it starts with the nominal predicate, *theos*, 'God'. If *theos* were the grammatical subject of this clause, it would have had a definite article; this feature, together with its first position in the clause and the fact that it precedes the copula, explains its function as a nominal predicate that describes the subject's quality.[20] Thus, the Logos is attributed to the category of God, which qualifies its essence of being. Verses 1a, 1b and 1c can, therefore, be understood as a description of the close connection in time, place and quality between the Logos and God. Verse 2 recaptures these three features: 'this' Logos, just qualified as belonging to the same nature of God, shares with God the same time-frame and the same place.[21]

The perspective of vv. 1-2 is the relation between the Logos and God, which in the consequent vv. 3-5 shifts to the relation between the Logos and the (not-divine) reality. The Logos remains the main point of reference and the logical subject, as the triple use of 'him' in vv. 3-4 shows, although the syntactic subjects are 'all things'. In v. 3 the temporal stance moves to past historical tenses that establish the Logos' role in creation in the past, and then moves in v. 4a to an imperfect tense, which underscores that the event that happened in the past has continual relevance.[22] 'Both its beginning and continuing existence are attributed to the Logos.'[23] The spatial demarcation narrows 'all things' in v. 3 to humankind in v. 4 and the imperfect verb forms in v. 4a and 4b mark the action or situation as continuous and not yet concluded. Nevertheless, v. 4a is syntactically ambiguous: the subject, a nominalised perfect verb tense 'what has come into being' (*ho gegonen*), can and cannot be related to 'in him', which creates two possibilities: 'what has come into being in him, had life' or 'what has come into being, in him was life'.[24]

20. See Ph. B. Harner, 'Qualitative Anarthrous Predicate Nouns: Mark 15:39 and Joh 1:1', *Journal of Biblical Literature* 92 (1973), 75-87.
21. See M. Theobald, *Die Fleischwordung des Logos. Studien zum Verhältnis des Johannesprologs zum Corpus Evangeliums und zu 1 Joh* (Münster: Aschendorff, 1988), 222-224.
22. J. L. Resseguie, *The Strange Gospel. Narrative Design and Point of View in John* (Biblical Interpretation Series, 56; Leiden and Boston: Brill, 2001), 111.
23. R. Bultmann, *Das Evangelium nach Johannes* (KEK; Göttingen, 1968), 39.
24. Cf M. Theobald, *op. cit.*, 189.

Surprising is the shift to a present tense in v. 5a, 'shines' or 'lights', with 'the light' as subject. The emphasised final position of the verb in v. 5a confirms that the verb is the clause's main focus.[25] This shift from past tenses (perfect or imperfect tenses in vv. 1-4) to a present tense demonstrates that this v. 5a is its climax: the light shines in the darkness till the present day. The light, equated with life in v. 4b, which in its turn was equated with the Logos in v. 4a, has now taken over the subject position of the Logos. Life and light are apparently facets or faces of the Logos. Verse 5b describes the relationship between this light and the darkness: 'The light shines in the darkness, and the darkness has not *katelaben.*' The Greek *katelaben* is ambiguous. Like 'to master' in English, it can mean either overcome or understand.[26] To say that the darkness did not accept the light is a contrastive negative way to conclude the first part of the prologue. To say that the darkness did not master the light is, on the other hand, a positive way to conclude it. Some features make the second solution the most likely. The light or enlightenment is mentioned in vv. 4, 5 (*bis*), 7, 8 (*bis*), and 9 (*bis*), establishing an effulgent primacy. By contrast, darkness, which is mentioned only twice in v. 5, recedes into the distant background, unable to overcome the light even at the level of words and phrases. Further, in v. 5 the light surrounds the darkness (light : darkness :: darkness : light).[27] Another strong argument in favour of this positive reading is the present tense used with the subject 'light', in contrast to the past tense with the subject 'darkness'.

This syntactic analysis demonstrates that two oppositions constitute v. 5's foundation: the opposition between present and past and the opposition between light and darkness. Light belongs to the present and darkness belongs to the past. They exclude one another in time and place: it is either light or darkness, and it is the light (or the Logos) one has to choose, because light is life, and accordingly (but implicitly) darkness is death. Some similarities can be noticed between John 1 and Genesis 1. In both texts, darkness appears to exist prior to creation, which elucidates why in Genesis 1 God's first creation act is the creation of light and why in John 1 the Logos is first and foremost equated

25. M. Theobald, *op. cit.*, 189.
26. T. L. Brodie, *The Gospel According to John. A Literary and Theological Commentary* (Oxford, New York: Oxford University Press, 1993), 138.
27. Resseguie, *op. cit.*, 112.

with light. However, John's mode of cognition is different from
Genesis 1's in that it presupposes an exclusive way of thinking,
whereas Genesis 1's mode of cognition is inclusive. In Genesis 1,
the presupposition is that day and night are meant to alternate
and God does not favour the day or the light, because for the distinction in days, weeks, weekdays and Sabbath-days, festivals
and seasons both day and night are needed. John 1, on the other
hand, shows an exclusive preference for the light. He speaks in
terms of present and past, of prevailing or mastering. He sets
light, life and Logos on one line in opposition to the line of darkness, death and not acceptance of the Logos. His view is 'either
... or', and not 'and ... and'.

### THE SECOND PART OF JOHN'S PROLOGUE (VV. 6-13)

The second part of John's prologue opens with a new subject,
John the Baptist (below referred to as 'the Baptist'), and an
equally new topic, that shows that the text moves from the cosmic (in vv. 1-5) to the historical affairs of humans (in vv. 6-13).
The Baptist's singular role is underscored by a threefold repetition of his function ('witness', 'to testify' to the light, v.7), followed by a negative assertion of what he is not: 'He himself was
not the light' (v. 8).[28] The aim of his testimony is 'so that all
might believe through him' (v. 7c). The universal role of the
Baptist, who proclaimed a message directed at all human beings, is, therefore, obvious. The universality of the message is
echoed in v. 9b where the light is said, 'to enlighten everyone'.

From v. 9 onwards the Baptist disappears in favour of the
Logos represented by its function as 'the light', which is the subject of vv. 9-12. Verse 9 is an extremely controversial verse.[29] The
imperfect 'was' in v. 9a defines the light as 'the true light'. The
subsequent present tense verb form 'enlightens' in v. 9b relates
the thus defined light to the present situation, and may be compared with the present tense verb 'shines' in v. 5a.[30] Both verbal
tenses express continuity till the present time. In this way, vv. 9a

---

28. Resseguie, *op. cit.*, 112.
29. B. Bonsack, 'Syntaktische Überlegungen zu Joh 1:9-10', in J. K. Elliott
(ed), *Studies in New Testament Language and Text* (FS G. D. Kilpatrick)
(Novum Testamentum Series, 44; Leiden: Brill,1976), 52-79, presents
eleven possible solutions provided in history to solve the problems in
this verse.
30. See Theobald, *op. cit.*, 191-195.

and 9b identify the essential aim and quality of the true light as universally directed to all human beings. What defines the light as the true light is, therefore, its quality to enlighten the human beings made possible by the light's present and continuous shining in the world.

In addition to this temporal unity, the next three clauses describe the intensifying spatial relationship between the true light and the world, that starts with 'the coming of the light into the world' (v. 9c), continues with its 'being in the world' (v. 10a) and results in the event that 'the world came into being through him'(v. 10b). Thus, the spatial unity between the light and the world gradually expands into a world defining, qualitative unity, in which the world is said to have come into being through the light; a stronger identification is hardly possible. This tie is so strong that in the following clauses vv. 11a-11b, the world is called 'his own', and the human beings are referred to as 'his own people'. The tragic negative reaction comes, therefore, as a blow. The light came to his own people, but they did not accept him.

Finally, in v. 12 a positive ending prevails as it focuses on those who put their faith in the Logos. The perfect verb form *elabon* in v. 12a characterises this subject as 'those who accepted him' and these remain the subject of the other three clauses of v. 12. The perfect tense of the verbs continues in v. 12b and c ('he gave them power to become children of God'), but remarkably in v. 12d a transition is made to the present tense. If the author were commenting on v. 12a, the perfect verb form of v. 12a would have been continued in a perfect verb form in v. 12d. Therefore, the transition to another tense must be of significance.[31] This present participle, 'those who have faith', is set at the very end of all these events. It places the final vantage point in the present time, that is, in the time of John's audience: by accepting the name of the Logos, they have become God's children.

No similarities can be noticed between Jn 1: 6-13 and Genesis 1, only differences. John's prologue's temporal continuity between past and present times and the spatial unity of the Logos who creates through his arrival into the world a close relationship to his own people testify of a striving for unity which is unknown to Genesis 1, where all the time distinctions are made

31. Theobald, *op. cit.*, 194.

and defended. Also John's audience's movement towards this Logos, its acceptance and endeavour to be united, is totally unknown to Genesis 1.

### THE THIRD PART OF JOHN'S PROLOGUE (VV. 14-18)

After the Logos' reintroduction in v. 14a, a new subject enters the stage, namely 'we' (v. 14b, 14c, 16a). The perspective shared is, therefore, the people who believe in the Logos. The difference between the previous parts, vv. 1-5 and 6-13, on the one hand, and this part, vv. 14-18 on the other, is that the former are phrased in a proclamation style with identifying clauses and third person forms (verbs, personal pronouns and possessive pronouns) and testify of a universal perspective. Conversely, the latter is phrased in a confessionary style with first person forms and testifies of the perspective that shares the view of those who have experienced and confessed in the Logos. The transition between the two first parts and the last one is prepared by v. 12d through the present particle 'those putting their faith in his name'.[32]

In v.14a, two words that occurred previously in vv. 1-3 are repeated, viz. the Logos and *egeneto*. In addition to this, some other connections are visible. The Logos' 'being' in the beginning (v. 1a) defined as belonging to the category of God (v. 1b) is converted in v. 14a into the Logos' 'becoming' and his belonging to the category of the flesh. And the Logos' being 'with God' (v. 1b) is transformed in v. 14b into his living 'with us'. Thus, the prologue describes the Logos' move from an abstract, divine and universal existence with God into a limited, individual and human existence in the world. This transfer was pointed at in vv. 10 and 11 in general terms, but is articulated now in the 'flesh', which is concrete and imaginative at the same time. It defines an incredible link between the divine and one mortal human body, and allows us to share the perspective of those who believe and recognise in it 'the glory in the flesh'.[33] In these confessionary verses (vv. 14, 16-18), the Baptist's testimony is included as a direct speech (v. 15).

Though the text does not specify explicitly which event(s)

---

32. Theobald, *op. cit.*, 205-208.
33. Resseguie, *op. cit.*, 114: 'While some see only flesh and judge by appearances, others see the glory palpable in the flesh. The unfamiliar (the glory) must be seen in the familiar (flesh), yet some see only the familiar.'

manifested glory, it does emphasise a more basic, general point, that the glory in question is not human self-glorification but rather the glory which an only son receives from the Father.[34] The text goes on to add, as a culminating factor in its account of the incarnation that it was 'full of grace and truth'. The two-fold expression 'grace and truth' seems, almost certainly, to reflect *hesed* and *'emet*, two Old Testament words which together mean 'merciful love', 'loving-kindness.'[35] Together with the law or Torah, represented by Moses here, the reference to the Old Testament and its fulfilment in Jesus Christ are unmistakable.

Verse 18 concludes the prologue and the two expressions 'nobody' and 'ever' emphasise Jesus' uniqueness: he alone has seen God and no one else can make this claim. Further, Jesus makes God known because he is close to the Father's heart, which elevates his point of view above all other views.[36] This closing verse's reference to the prologue's opening verse is of utmost importance. In v. 18b, the view that the only son is God points at v. 1a, where the Logos was qualified as 'God' ('the Logos was God'). Verse 18c, the closeness to the Father's heart expresses metaphorically the Logos' closeness to God in v. 1b ('the Logos was with God'). And v. 18d, the very last word of the prologue, *exegesato*, 'who has made known' or 'who has explained in words' represent the noun *ho logos* ('the word') as 'a divine herald'.[37] Thus, v. 18 expresses in words what v. 1 evoked in an image and constitutes the overwhelming conclusion of a prologue that testifies of the Logos' incarnation as an 'Exegesis of God'.[38]

## JOHN'S MODE OF COGNITION

John shows in his prologue a close relation between three different time zones: the ultimate past with the Logos' pre-existent being; the past with the Logos coming into the world and the world's coming into being through the Logos; and the present time in which the Logos shines and enlightens all human beings and in which a selected group of believers testify of him. The

---

34. Brodie, *op. cit.*, 143.

35. Brodie, *op. cit.*, 143.

36. Resseguie, *op. cit.*, 115.

37. H. Lausberg, 'Miniscula philologica (VII): Das Epiphonem des Johannes-Prologs (J 1,18)', *NAWG, PH* (1982), 269-289, here 278.

38. Theobald, *op. cit.*, 208.

narrator's camera zooms in progressively. Its opening shot is taken from an outside position, at a point placed outside the time frame and spatial world known to human beings, with a universal and divine perspective. Subsequently it zooms in on a history related but still universal position of a past shared by all human beings. And finally the lens zooms in on a selected audience of Jesus-believers and shows the past from their present days' perspective. In other words, John shifts from a universal and history-transcending view to a historical perspective related to all human beings, and finally to a present time and people related perspective or immanent view.[39] This growing closeness between the past and the present and its relation to the self-definition of the community of believers in the present characterises John's prologue.

One can resume, therefore, the transformation that John's prologue presents as a transition in three stages: 'he was', 'he (be)came' and 'he made known'. The first stage describes how the Logos was in the beginning, was with God, and was God. The second stage shows the Logos' arrival in the world and the world's coming into being through him. And the third stage presents the Logos incarnated into Jesus Christ, who makes God known. The logical sequence is, however, the other way around, that is: first, because the word was made known, and because one knew through the Baptist's testimony, the community of believers realised that Jesus Christ was the Logos, the only born son of the Father; secondly, this made them aware of the fact that the world had come into being through the Logos; and, thirdly, this was possible because the Logos is God, is/was with God and was in the beginning. Thus, it can be demonstrated that a major characteristic of John's mode of thinking is its aim to bring about unity and conjunction. The temporal association between the beginning and the ultimate past, the past and the present has been sketched. The spatial association is clearly visible, too: the light came into this world and the world became through the light. The qualitative association is most clearly marked by the Logos' incarnation: though belonging to the divine world, the Logos became part of the human world. The foundation of the Logos' unity with the world is laid in the qualitative unity of the Logos and God. This explains the close relationship of Jesus Christ, the Son and God, the Father. Ultimately,

---

39. Theobald, *op. cit.*, 204-205.

the text's intention is to demonstrate that these three associations should finally lead to human beings' conjunction with Jesus Christ, with the Logos and with God.

Thus, it becomes apparent that John's mode of cognition contrasts fundamentally with Genesis 1's mode of cognition. Genesis is characterised by creation and differentiation: the non-unity of the created world, the distinction with God, the distinction and separation of the heaven and the earth and the earth's living beings, are qualified in Genesis 1 as wished, effectuated and approved by God. The differences between these chapters' final verses illustrate this. Although both texts describe the final relation between the human beings and the created world, Genesis 1 ends with a declaration of the holiness of the seventh day and thus incites to honour the Sabbath, to respect the distinction between the weekdays and the seventh day, to acknowledge the differences in the created universe and to respect the order based on distinctions and separations, while John 1 ends with the Logos' incarnation, the unity of God and the world. Genesis 1 marks and defends the borders between the distinctly created phenomena, and these borders are to be respected in order to do justice to God's creative and separating activities. Genesis 1's aim is, therefore, dissociation: to honour God is to respect the dignity of difference. Conversely, John 1 is fundamentally about border crossing. The Logos crossed the borders that are generally considered to be impossible to transgress, the borders between the human beings and God, between the human world and the divine world, and between the body and the word. John 1 points at the unique position of the community of Jesus-believers to be united in Jesus Christ with God. John's aim is, therefore, association: to honour God is to respect the unity between Jesus Christ, the Logos and God, and to participate in the community of Jesus believers. The conclusion to be drawn, therefore, is that these two biblical texts about the beginning do testify of completely different modes of cognition and of two opposite theologies indeed.

# CHAPTER SIX

## 'The Eye of the Soul':
### The Doctrine of the Higher Consciousness in the Neoplatonic and Sufic Traditions

### John Dillon

One of Plato's more striking images is that of the 'eye of the soul', that faculty with which the human being can contemplate true reality. In Book VII of the *Republic*, we find a number of references to this faculty, and to the necessity for cultivating its vision. At 518CD,[1] as we know, Socrates declares that education should not be seen as a matter of introducing sight into blind eyes, but rather of

> turning the mind's eye away from the world of becoming, until it becomes capable of bearing the sight of real being and reality at its most bright ... Educators should devise the simplest and the most effective methods of turning minds around. It shouldn't be the art of implanting sight in the organ, but should proceed on the understanding that the organ already has the capacity, but is improperly aligned and isn't facing the right way. (trs Robin Waterfield)

Plato himself, however, is not very specific as to how far this vision of the 'real world', the intelligible realm of Forms, and ultimately of the Good, leads to the unveiling of a new level of consciousness for the human being – though something such would seem to be implied in the process of turning one's focus of attention away from the sensible to the intelligible realm. But in fact Plato does not concern himself to dwell much on the possibility of attaining higher states of consciousness while still in the body (though the perfected Guardians do surely achieve some such state, with their vision of the Good, at the culmination of the dialectic process); he is more concerned with the nature of the soul in itself, and its life outside the body. Although Socrates, and Plato after him, had adopted the Delphic precept, 'Know Thyself', as a basic rule of procedure,

---

1. I use here the standard method of identifying Platonic texts, by the pages and subdivisions of the Stephanus edition.

they did not employ it in the search for a centre of consciousness within the living soul-body complex, but rather to isolate the soul from the body.

It is only, really, when we come to the later Platonist Plotinus (204-269 AD) that we find a concern for the identification of the seat of consciousness as such. Indeed, Plotinus – as, once again, we know – does not even have a ready-made term for this: he is compelled to make use of the ordinary Greek word for 'we', *hêmeis*. In the treatise that Porphyry, his pupil and editor, places first in his collection of his essays, the *Enneads* (though it is in fact a late treatise – no 53 out of a total of 54), Plotinus gives much attention to the precise delimitation of this concept of the 'we'. He locates the ordinary, 'vulgar' centre of consciousness around the mid-point of a spectrum, between what he identifies as the 'undescended intellect' (a concept to which we will return in a moment) at the higher end, and the purely vegetative soul at the lower end, comprising processes such as growth and digestion, of which we are not normally conscious. The range of our 'normal' consciousness has been compared famously by E. R. Dodds to a beam of light moving up and down around the middle of the range of the psyche. Dodds' remarks[2] are worth quoting at length, I think:

> Plotinus distinguishes sensation from perception more clearly than any previous thinker, and he has noticed that there are sensations which do not reach consciousness (IV 4, 8 and V 1, 12), thus anticipating the 'petites perceptions' of Leibniz. He also recognises in one place (IV 8, 8) the existence of unconscious desire (and here he begins to approach Freud). And again, in the discussion on memory he has a curious passage (IV 4, 4, 11) implying that those memories of which we are not aware are sometimes more powerful in their influence on our conduct than the memories of which we are conscious: 'not knowing what we have within us, we are liable to be what we have.' That is a profound observation for a pre-Freudian thinker.

Finally, is not Plotinus the first to have clearly distin-

---

2. Made in the course of commenting on a most useful paper by another great authority on Plotinus, H. R. Schwyzer, "Bewusst' und 'Unbewusst' bei Plotin', in the course of a colloquium at the Fondation Hardt, *Les Sources de Plotin* (Entretiens sur l'Antiquité Classique, V; Vandoeuvres-Genève, 1960), 385-6.

guished the concepts of soul (*psykhê*) and ego (*hêmeis*)? For him the two terms are not coextensive. Soul is a continuum extending from the summit of the individual *psykhê*, whose perception is perpetual intellection, through the normal empirical self, right down to the *eidôlon*, the faint psychic trace in the organism; but the ego is *a fluctuating spotlight of consciousness*.[3] This picture is surely a great advance on Aristotle's: for one thing, it does not break the continuity of *nous, psykhê*, and *physis* in the way that Aristotle's *nous thyrathen* appears to do. These are some of my reasons for regarding Plotinus as primarily a great psychologist.

These remarks of Dodds are of great importance. Plotinus is certainly, among other things, a great psychologist. So many issues bother him that do not appear to have bothered his predecessors, including Plato. One main one is the overall issue of the mode of interaction between soul and body, a totally immaterial entity with an essentially inert material one. For Plato, this does not seem to have been an issue. The soul simply does rule the body; that is its job. The body provides a source of distraction and corruption for the soul; that is its role. How each of these things happens is not problematic. The concept of the soul seems, certainly, to undergo significant development from the *Phaedo*, through the *Republic, Phaedrus* and *Timaeus*, to Book X of the *Laws*, but not in respect of the mode of its interaction with the body.

Later schools of thought, Aristotelians, Stoics and Epicureans, do not have the same problem as the Platonists, since they regard the soul either as a mere mode of the functioning of the living being (Aristotle), or as a material entity of some sort – albeit composed of a special sort of fire (Stoics), or of a special sort of small, round atom (Epicureans). Only the Platonists are left with the problem of the interaction of the immaterial with the material.

Plotinus, it must be said, does not actually solve this problem, but he does worry about it. I am not concerned on this occasion, in fact, with his views of this question. I mention them merely as background to what I am concerned with, which is his postulation, and exploration of the nature of, a higher state of consciousness above our 'normal' one, which is this 'we' that

---

3. Italics mine.

Dodds characterises as a 'fluctuating spotlight', moving up and down the mid-range of our psychic processes. Let us start with a passage from *Ennead* I 1 (on 'What is the Living Being, and what is Man?'), which is a good presentation of his general view (I 1, 10, 1ff):

> But if 'we' are the soul, and we are affected in this way,[4] then it would be the soul that is affected in this way, and again it would be the soul which does what *we* do.
>
> Yes, but we said that the 'commonality' (*to koinon*)[5] is part of 'us', especially when we have not yet been separated from body: for we say that 'we' are affected by what affects our body. So 'we' is used in two senses, either including 'the beast' (*thêrion*), or referring to that which even in our present life transcends it. The 'beast' is the body which has been given life.[6] But the true man is different, clear of these affections; he has the virtues which belong to the sphere of intellect and have their seat actually in the separable soul, separable and separate (*khôristê*) even while it is still here below.
> (trs Armstrong, slightly altered)

We see Plotinus here making a distinction between a higher and a lower 'we', the higher being identified with the 'true man' (*alêthês anthrôpos*), which is our separable soul – or rather, 'we' *qua* separable soul. But we have not yet probed the full complexity of Plotinus' concept of a higher consciousness. For that we may turn back, initially, from this very late treatise to one of his earliest, *Enn* IV 8 [2], 'On the Immortality of the Soul'. In ch 10 of that treatise, Plotinus is engaged in claiming that the soul is an immaterial entity, and is most truly what we are. By way of reinforcing this point, he urges us to consider soul in its purest form (10, 30ff):

> Consider it by a process of stripping away (*aphelôn*), or rather let the one doing the stripping look at himself and be per-

---

4. That is, by having some activities which are proper to the soul alone, and others which are the results of influences from without, such as sense-perceptions.

5. This is one of Plotinus' terms for the joint entity formed by soul and living body, his others being *to syntheton*, 'the composite', and *to synamphoteron*, 'the both-together'.

6. This is probably a creative application of the image used by Plato in Book IX of the *Republic*, characterising the irrational, passionate part of the soul as a 'many-headed beast' (588C).

suaded that he is immortal, when he looks at himself as he
has come to be in the mode of intelligible purity. For he will
see an intellect (*nous*) which sees nothing perceived by the
senses, none of these mortal things, but which apprehends
the eternal by its eternality (*to aidion*), and all the things in the
intelligible world, *having become itself an intelligible universe*
(*kosmos noêtos*) full of light, illuminated by the truth from the
Good, which radiates truth over all the intelligibles; so he
will often think this very well said,

> 'Greetings! I am for you an immortal god.' [7]

having ascended to the divine, and concentrating totally on
likeness to it.

We are now coming nearer to what Plotinus has in mind (and
plainly had in mind already by the commencement of his writing career, at least).[8] The statement that the person who looks at
him- or herself with true insight realises that they are 'eternal',
and 'an intelligible universe', brings us nearer to Plotinus' deepest thought.

What he has in mind is essentially this. Our common or garden consciousness is something that, ultimately, we have to
transcend if we are to attain true enlightenment. The first step,
certainly, is to realise that 'we' are a soul, not a body, nor even a
combination of (lower) soul and body. But that is only the first
step. What we then have to realise is that we are not just a soul;
we are an intellect (*nous*). For Plotinus this means the realisation
that there is a part or aspect of us that has never 'descended'
from the intelligible world, but remains rooted in *Nous*. It is true
that most people, for nearly all of the time, are not in touch with
this highest part of themselves, but Plotinus wishes to maintain
that it is there nonetheless, and it is something that he has plainly
achieved union with himself on numerous occasions.

Now what we have to realise about the intelligible realm, the
realm of *Nous*, is that it is a plane of existence which transcends
both time and space. It is eternal in the sense of being *timeless*
(rather than being *sempiternal*, a state with which it must not be
confused), and thus its inhabitants (which are pure intellects, or
Forms) enjoy a form of consciousness which cognises all its ob-

---

7. A quotation of a famous utterance of Empedocles (B112 Diels-Kranz).
8. He was, after all, already in his forties when he began to write down
his philosophy.

jects of thought simultaneously, not one after another, or 'discursively'. Secondly, it transcends spatial distinction, so that all its inhabitants *exist together* – are mutually implicated, one might say. That is, each in fact shares in the consciousness of all, while still retaining an individuality of some sort – an individual *point of view*. This is obviously a state of consciousness, and of existence, not easily comprehended by entities such as ourselves, bound as we are by distinctions of time and space; indeed, it is not normally comprehensible at all. Nevertheless, this is the state which Plotinus wishes to postulate as the proper home of the highest part of ourselves, and as something to which we should aspire. If we were to achieve this, even momentarily, then we would realise that we are in fact, each of us, an 'intelligible universe', and our limited 'vulgar' consciousness of self would simply wither away.

Let us look at a few Plotinian texts illustrative of this. First of all, *Enn* VI 4 [22], 14 (part of his large treatise 'On the Omnipresence of True Being'), where he is making a distinction between what he sees as the original core of our personalities and later accretions:

> But we – who are *we*? Are we that which accretes itself (sc. to the original) and comes to be in time? No, even before this coming to be came to be we were There,[9] men of a different nature, and some even gods, pure souls and intellect united with the whole of reality; we were parts of the intelligible, not marked off nor cut off, but belonging to the whole; and we are not cut off even now.
>
> But now another man, wishing to exist, has approached that man; and when he found us – for we were not outside the All – he wound himself round us and attached himself to that man who was then each one of us … and we have come to be the pair of them, not the one which we were before – and sometimes just the other one which we added on afterwards, when that prior one is inactive and in another way not present.

Here we have the remarkable image of an original 'core' man – the original 'we' – to which a bogus, secondary man has attached himself, becoming our 'vulgar' consciousness, and, in the great majority of cases, quite obscuring our original nature.

---

9. 'There' (*ekei*) is a basic Plotinian term for the intelligible world.

This concept is developed further in a later passage of the same treatise (VI 5, 7):

> For we and what is ours go back to real being (*to on*), and ascend to that and to the first which comes from it,[10] and we cognise the objects of that realm (*ekeina*), not as having images or imprints of them – and if we do not, we *are* those things.[11] If then we have a part in true knowledge, we *are* those, not apprehending them as distinct within ourselves, but we ourselves being within them. For since the others, and not only ourselves, are those, we are all those.
>
> So then, being together with all things, we are those; and so, *we are both all and one*. So therefore, when we look outside that on which we depend, we do not realise that we are one, *like faces which are many on the outside but have one head on the inside*. But if someone is able to turn around, either by himself, or having the good luck to have his hair pulled by Athena herself,[12] he will see God[13] and himself and the All. At first he will not see (himself) as the All, but then, when he has nowhere to set himself and limit himself and determine how far he himself goes, he will stop marking himself off from all being and come to the totality of the All without going out anywhere, but remaining there where the All is set firm.

This is certainly a difficult passage, but Plotinus here is presenting us with a concept of great importance and beauty. We are the universe, and indeed, in his terms, we are God. But it is important to realise that we have not dissolved into this great Unity as into some Nirvana; we are still ourselves, and our-

---

10. It is not quite clear to me what this refers to, but perhaps the hypostasis of Soul.

11. That is to say, at the level of *Nous*, the subject and object of intellection become identical. One is no longer simply receiving an impression of the object, as would be the case with a sense-object.

12. This is a reference to the famous passage of Homer's *Iliad* (Book I, ll. 197-8), where Athena swoops down from Olympus and tugs Achilles by the hair, to stop him from attacking Agamemnon – forcing Achilles to turn and look behind him, or rather, if Athena be thought of as a voice of conscience, to look within himself. Plotinus may well be drawing on a previous allegorisation of this passage, but on the face of it, it is a striking literary allusion.

13. 'God' here, as often elsewhere in Plotinus, is to be equated with the hypostasis of Intellect.

selves, not just as a small portion of this All, but rather as a 'point of view', identical with the totality of it, but viewing it from a certain unique angle.

There are various other passages which one could adduce to illustrate further Plotinus' remarkable doctrine of the higher consciousness, or 'true man', but this will, I hope, suffice to give us the picture. What I would like to do for the latter part of this discourse is to turn, instead, to the tradition of Islamic Sufism, to consider certain parallels which I discern in that tradition to Plotinus' theory.

One should remark at the outset that Sufism begins, in the eighth century of the Christian era, as a purely religious movement within Islam, involving an extremely world-negating style of asceticism, with no discernible philosophical content to it. The earliest generation of Sufis, men such as Al-Hasan al-Basri (d. 728 CE), Abu Hashîm 'Uthman bin Sharîk of Kufa (d. 776), who was the first to receive what is actually the nickname of 'sûfi', from his wearing of woollen garments (sûf, 'wool'), instead of cotton, and Ibrahim bin Adhâm (d. 777) were simply men who rejected the level of worldliness and luxury that had become common, especially among the elite, in the triumphant century or so after the death of the Prophet in 632. They sought to achieve union with Allah through comprehensive rejection of the joys of this world and the practice of every sort of self-denial. They were impelled by a love of God, and a desire to know him, and to be united with him. There was as yet no discernible theoretical aspect to the movement, though we find bin Adhâm talking of learning ma'rifa (gnôsis, mystical knowledge) from a Christian monk.[14] The content of the 'knowledge', however, turns out to be no more than how to live on as little as possible. Bin Adhâm also, when asked by a disciple for a definition of service, replied, 'The beginning of sevice is meditation and silence, except for the recollection (dhikr) of God.' This concept of dhikr, however, which may be approximately equated to the Platonist concept of anamnêsis, as understood by Plotinus, takes on considerable philosophical content in later centuries.

It is really only in the next century, in the person of al-Junaid of Baghdad (d. 910), that a degree of analytical thought seems to emerge within the movement. One important concept, however,

---

14. Quoted in A. J. Arberry, *Sufism: An Account of the Mystics of Islam* (London, 1950), 37.

that of *fanâ* (lit. 'passing away', 'extinction'), or losing oneself in union with God, seems actually to have been developed somewhat earlier, by the so-called 'intoxicated' Sufi Abu Yazid of Bistam (d. 875), though it acquires philosophic content only later.[15] *Fanâ* is understood by al-Junaid to involve a 'dying to oneself', which does not betoken a complete abandonment of consciousness on the part of the mystic, but rather a transmuting of his individuality into union (*tawhîd*) with God. *Tawhîd*, as al-Junaid defines it,[16] consists in 'the separation of the Eternal from that which was originated in Time', resulting in the return of man to 'the state in which he was before he was,' which is equated with 'continuance' (*baqâ'*) in God. This is all beginning to sound very much like what Plotinus was striving for some six centuries earlier!

The formalisation of Sufi doctrine, however, has to await such authorities as al-Qâsim al-Qushairî (d. 1072) and in particular Abû Hâmid Muhammad al-Ghazâlî (1059-1111), whose massive work *Ihyâ' 'ulûm al-dîn* ('The Revival of the Religious Sciences'), provides a comprehensive account of Sufi doctrines, with considerable philosophical underpinning. The summit of Sufi mystical thought, however, was achieved by the thinkers and poets Ibn al-Fârid of Cairo (1181-1235), and Muhyî al-Din ibn 'Arabî. This latter was born in Murcia, in Arabic Spain, in 1165, and after many travels through the Islamic world, died in Damascus in 1240. He is credited with at least 400 books, of which over 200 survive today. It is with an examination of one of his allegorical exegeses of the Koran that I would like to end, as it brings together most of the themes that I have been dwelling on.

Ibn Arabi developed the concept (which he must, I think, have picked up either from translations of Greek Neoplatonic works, or from works, such as those of his older contemporary Ibn Hasday, which are themselves dependent on such sources) of 'the Perfect Man' (*al'Insan ul-kâmil*). This is an entity, itself an aspect of the Logos, or First Intellect, of God (which he identifies also as the Form, or reality, of Muhammad [*al'Haqîqat al-*

---

15. The concept of *fanâ* was developed, it seems, from exegesis of the verse of the Koran, 'Everything on earth passeth away, save His face' (55: 26), which the Sufis understood as describing the passing away of human attributes through union with God.

16. Cf Arberry, *Sufism*, 57.

*Muhammadîya*]), which is the sum-total, or perfection, of human-ity, when all 'otherness', or individual characteristics, have been cut away, or shaken off. Since Ibn Arabi thinks very much in al-legorical terms (another trait that he must have picked up from Neoplatonic sources), it is natural for him to see indications of such a doctrine in passages of the Koran, such as *Surah* 20: 9-13:

9. Hath there come unto thee the story of Moses?

10. When he saw a fire and said unto his folk: 'Wait! Lo, I see a fire afar off. Perchance I may bring you a brand therefrom or may find guidance at the fire.'

11. And when he reached it, he was called by name: 'O Moses!

12. Lo, I, even I, am thy Lord. So take off thy sandals, for lo, thou art in the holy valley of Tuwa.

13. And I have chosen thee, so hearken unto that which is in-spired.'

Here, the injunction from God to Moses to remove his sandals is to be understood as the exhortation to the Sufi to divest himself of all traits and features that comprise his individuality, and thus rid himself of anything that constitutes 'otherness' from God.

God is presented as infinite Unity (*al-Ahadiyya*), and to indic-ate oneness with this unity, there is a Sufi saying as follows, with which I will end:

I am Ahmad without the letter *mîm*. I am an Arab without the letter *'ain*. Who hath seen me, the same hath seen the Truth.

The meaning of this is as follows. The letter *mîm* is the letter of death, that is, of ending, and the letter *'ain* is the letter of the source of creation, that is, of beginning. If both of these are re-moved from the Sufi, what is left is *ahad*, 'One', and *rabbi*, 'My Lord', and that symbolises the real Self, which is none other than God.

What we seem to have here, then, I would suggest, is a re-markable deepening of Sufi thought in the course of the eleventh century, in the direction of developing a coherent con-cept of a 'higher consciousness' very similar to that which had been developed in the Neoplatonic tradition after Plotinus, togther with an extensive employment of allegorisation of the text of the Koran which does not appear to stem from indigen-ous Islamic sources. I would like to suggest that there is some degree of Hellenic Neoplatonist influence lurking here in the background, though I am all too conscious that the precise channels of such influence are still very imperfectly known. One trace of a possible source, certainly, is to be found in a philosophical excursion in Ibn Hasday's work *The Prince and the Ascetic* (chs 32-5),[17] but more detailed analysis of this and other passages is still required – and some day soon, *insha'allah*, I shall do it. Meanwhile, I offer these shreds and tatters as a tribute to a noble Christian theologian.

---

17. See on this the most useful article of S. M. Stern, 'Ibn Hasday's Neoplatonist – a Neoplatonic Treatise and its Influence on Isaac Israeli and the Longer Version of the *Theology of Aristotle*', *Oriens* 13-14 (1961). I have had occasion to look at this vexed question of Neoplatonic influence on mediaeval Arabic and Jewish philosophers in an earlier article, 'Solomon Ibn Gabirol's Doctrine of Intelligible Matter', in Lenn E. Goodman (ed), *Neoplatonism and Jewish Thought*, (Albany: SUNY Press,1992), 43-59 (repr in *The Great Tradition: Further Studies in the Development of Platonism and Early Christianity* (Ashgate: Aldershot, 1997, Study XXIV), but without coming to any very satisfactory conclusions.

# CHAPTER SEVEN

# The Lapses in Christian Theology at the End of the Second Millennium

## James Mackey

Any balanced, critical retrospective account of the main moves in Christian theology during the 20th century could hardly fail to notice the gradual emergence of an interesting pattern: each move set out in turn in the same direction as the one before it, and by so doing seemed to record some gains for Christian theology. Some greater cogency and clarity seemed to accrue, if only because of an increase in *aggiornamento,* as good Pope John put it in the course of calling for the Second Vatican Council; some increasing openness and relevance to the cultures and conditions of the present and the impending future. But then each move in turn seemed to falter before its fullest promise could be redeemed, and some moves even seemed to take one step backward for each step forward. The list of main moves in 20th century theology with the analysis of these which follows, is designed to illustrate the common direction that seems to be have been taken, the gains recorded and then largely lost in the course of successive lapses. This list has been compiled of course by one who has lived and worked through the Christian theology of the second half of the 20th century, and who is well aware of the fact that the list of what are deemed to be main moves may seem somewhat arbitrary to others. Closeness can lend distortion to the view. Nevertheless, this list can serve to illustrate adequately enough the alleged lapsing, while leaving others free to add or subtract from both alleged lapses and alleged degrees of detriment sustained in the theological enterprise of the 20th century as a whole.

### HISTORY AND FAITH

At the dawn of the 20th century the quest of the historical Jesus was already over a hundred years old. During these years a number of problems had been posed to the portrait of Jesus painted by the faith of his followers, with the result that Jesus began to appear somewhat different from the all-knowing divine being whose claims to bring us the fullness of grace and truth were proved true by the miracle of his resurrection. Proffered solutions to these problems then seemed to have settled on Kahler's formulaic distinction between the Jesus of history and the Christ of faith. By mid-century this solution seemed to have solidified around Bultmann's peremptory pronouncement to the effect that Christian faith cannot be made to depend upon the historian's labours. Indeed such a solution seemed to be confirmed by the experience of readers and hearers of the Christian message; if only because the more history seemed to discover how human Jesus was, the less they seemed able to think of him as divine. For what else can history discover except our common humanity in its intercourse with the natural world? So that claims concerning the divinity of alleged agents in the natural world, history can only record, but cannot in the least degree verify. Is that not obvious?

In any case, at this point solutions to problems raised during the long quest for the historical Jesus seemed to require – or was it to re-instate? – something of an unbridgeable chasm between human reason (historical investigation being one of reason's major learning modes), and a Christian faith correspondingly thought to be entirely dependent upon special, supernatural divine revelation. Yet the quest of the historical Jesus, the second quest, as it came to be called, was continued, not least by Bultmann's own best pupils, for all that the master could say or do. But then, like other movements in the Christian theology of the 20th century, as we must see, this one also simply seemed to peter out. No final audit of the gains of this second quest was produced or published; no assessment attempted of the kind or quantity of the contribution these gains could make to the next phase of academic production in this sector of the business, the theology of divine revelation.

## REVELATION AND HISTORY

In the first decade of the second half of the 20th century René Latourelle realised that, although Christians had claimed from the beginning that they had their distinctive truth through special divine revelation; and although in the centuries between, all preaching, deployment, explanation and interpretation of this truth was accompanied by the insistence that it was especially revealed by God; and although theological expositions of every main element of that truth had been on offer since the third Christian century; no properly thought-out theology of divine revelation itself had ever appeared. Latourelle's own effort to fill this long-standing lacuna proved to be the beginning of a move that drew many of the best minds in Christian theology to this topic over the next two decades. Briefly the move began with a rather concerted and adverse critique of the propositional model of divine revelation or, more bluntly put, the verbal dictation model of the revelation of Christian truth, despite the support for such a model apparently offered by that synonym for divine revelation, the word of God. And the move ended, or rather it petered out, with a model of divine revelation as history.

In short, on this alternative model, God was revealed, and revealed what God wished to reveal, in and through events of history. In the case of Christianity it was the historical person of Jesus of Nazareth, his life, death and destiny, that offered to all those who would follow him the full and final revelation of God and of God's ways with the world. The words of Jesus, his parables and other preachings and propositions of his, were of course part of this revelation. There was talk of them as 'word event,' but that very phrase in itself suggested that the words were subsidiary, pointing up the true significance of the events which were primarily charged with the divine revelation. It was therefore not essential that the actual words of Jesus, the *ipsissima verba*, be recorded and retained verbatim. Suitable suits of words could always be found to clothe, present and interpret, especially to people who used a different language and a different idiom, the true meaning and significance of the human origin and the human journey of the one in whom, as Christians claimed, the Word of God was incarnate.

There was a problem about this conclusion to the recent move on the nature and incidence of divine revelation, the move, namely, to the view that divine revelation consists essentially of historical events, and that problem remains unsolved. That is part of what is meant by saying that this second move also petered out. The problem is this: when theologians talk of historical events as the prime medium of divine revelation, do they have in mind a special series of special events, and not just a series of events of the kind that are commonly and currently reduplicated, and that make up the stuff of ordinary history?

There had been much talk about 'salvation history' in the years before, and that phrase continued in common use during this move on the theology of revelation as history. Was this salvation history made up of a special sub-set of exclusively miraculous events then, that is to say, events which allegedly bore the signature of a special divine intervention? Not altogether, for certainly some of the central stories in the Christian Bible's history of the Israelites are in the main concerned with events that are quite common in the all too ordinary history of our race. A subjugate people escaping servitude and by a military campaign finally winning for themselves the freedom of life in their own lands; the execution, even the wrongful execution of a man judged guilty of threatening the security of the state. Yet the latter event, and often these two events together, with the former in the role of prophetic sign of the latter, are seen as God saving the human race from sin. But surely, since they are instances of common or garden variety historical events, one has to ask how a divine revelation, a revelation of the divine, can be seen in just these Jewish examples, and in none of the myriad of other examples of such events in history? Did God communicate to the mind of some prophet, or to the prophet Jesus, the message that what was really going on in that singular execution in Jerusalem long ago, was in fact God's saving of the whole human race from sin?

Some of the writers who seemed to have reached a view of divine revelation as history, still made room for such prophetic necessity. Which meant that they could not face up to the full implications of ordinary history as revelation of the divine. For did the actual divine revelation not now consist in some special divine communication-event conveyed to others through the prophetic office, rather than in the historical event as such? And how far had these theologians really come after all from the older and much criticised propositional view of divine revelation? Once more a move in modern theology had petered out without finally tackling the final problem it itself had raised. Once more, as in the case of the quest for the historical Jesus, a theological move towards the search for God in natural history re-introduced an older chasm between a natural and a supernatural realm, between the events that took place in the one and those that took place in the other, while still limping forward, for a while, towards some acceptance and assessment of the new sense of the religious relevance of the natural and the ordinarily historical.

THE BIBLE AS REVELATION, HISTORY, LITERATURE

That move on the theology of revelation was paralleled by yet another move in 20th century theology, a move this time on the theological theories concerning the Christian scriptures. Despite what mainline Christian churches, from Calvinist to Catholic, would have considered assaults upon these scriptures from historical Jesus questers, from modernists and from other assorted attackers boasting a heightened critical sense of either history or literature, or both, these churches at the outset of the 20th century still stood by the following view of their divinely inspired scriptures: a divine inspiration reserved from the human authors of these scriptures had the effect that the words they used, all the words they used, without exception, conveyed the revealed truth, the whole of that truth, and nothing but that truth. It was sometimes stressed, as it was by Calvin himself, that this did not amount to divine dictation of the text, so that the 'sacred' authors were no more than recording secretaries. This was not a theology of verbal, propositional revelation, for the inspired scriptures are not themselves, Qur'an-like, the actual revelation, the divinely revealed word of God. Rather did the doctrine of the divine inspiration of the scriptures amount to this: that those scriptures formed an absolutely and entirely inerrant witness to a divine revelation which took final form in the incarnation of the Word of God in Jesus of Nazareth.

Despite such assertions, however, it is hard to see how this theology of scriptural inspiration differed in the least degree in its overall outcome from a theology of direct divine propositional revelation. And it is correspondingly easy to understand just how the most faithful followers of those churches to this day think and talk about these scriptures as if these subtle theological distinctions between divine inspiration and divine revelation did not exist. And yet, as far back as Galileo and as recently as the most recent findings of scientific cosmology, to take but one class of example, the assumptions and assertions of the Bible concerning the form and coming-to-be of the cosmos came so far into question by science as to qualify, to say the least, those other assumptions and assertions of the absolute and entire inerrancy of the Bible. Gradually, as the 20th century rolled on, qualifications of this kind were officially sanctioned. For example, in the Roman Catholic Church it became acceptable to say that only what was directly asserted in the sacred text of the scriptures was made inerrant by divine inspiration. *Obiter dicta*, assertions incidental to those primarily intended, did not enjoy such protection; so that the former, but not the latter, would lead us unerringly to the truth divinely revealed. So, for instance, at the very outset of the Bible it is directly intended to assert that God created the world out of nothing; but the quaint ancient cosmology, a flat earth floating on an ocean with a sky-canopy stretched over it, is incidental to the main assertion, because that ancient cosmology, as it happened, was the best description of the created world that was available at the time to those who proclaimed, truly, that God created the world.

The distinction between direct assertions and *obiter dicta*, however, proved increasingly difficult to keep in line with any distinction between, on the one hand, religious assertions (God created the world) that constituted the directly intended assertions of a sacred text like the Bible and, on the other hand, those secular-type assertions concerning cosmology, history and so on, that are included in the Bible only incidentally, and by those less informed on such matters than we now are. When Yahweh, the Lord of Hosts, that is to say, the commander-in-chief of the Israelite armies, also commands them through prophets to engage in what can only be described as total ethnic cleansing, the untruth entailed in such texts is on the religious side of the religious/secular divide. It belongs firmly in that 'deposit of faith and morals' that Roman Catholics see as the yield of special divine revelation. Some of the most religiously conservative of Israeli Zionists provide an illustration of the contemporary currency of this kind of understanding of biblical revelation of the will of God. Little wonder then that Karl Barth, the greatest theologian of the 20th century, insisted that errors in the Bible cannot be confined to secular matters, but that errors in the domain of religion must be allowed there also. Yet Barth too insisted that the Bible, despite its proneness to ignorance and error, inevitable in view of its human authors, can still bear adequate and authoritative witness to the final revelation of God's Word in the man, Jesus, provided that the Spirit who inspired these authors to achieve such written witness enlighten our hearts also as we are drawn to seek the living God.

Once more, just as in the case of a theology of divine revelation, what seemed to be a move towards a theory to the effect that this revelation came in the public events of natural and human history, then seemed to be reversed in favour of an older theory of private divine communication. For now a set of scriptures, the very proneness of which to error and ignorance of various kinds seemed to show them up as thoroughly human in authorship, had their previous image as straightforward communication of divine revelation severely qualified by the added necessity of an inner divine communication to their readers to enable the latter to see only the truth, and the whole truth that they contained.

Yet scholars have continued to study the Bible by increasing, if anything, the usage of all those tools and methods commonly in evidence in any and all attempts to uncover all the truth about the natural world and the human race that natural and human history has to offer. In pursuit of the recovery of the overall import of the Bible these scholars apply to it, as to any other book, the standard methods of literary criticism. In pursuit of the social, political and geographical background against which the history of the Israelites and especially of Jesus was played out and can be better understood, they apply the critical methods of the social, historical sciences, including human geography. In pursuit of the particularly religious affordances of the Bible they apply the critical methods of comparative philosophy and religion. And all of this has unquestionably contributed, and continues to contribute to a clearer account of the faith that his followers believe comes to them from Jesus of Nazareth. It contributes also to a finer assessment of the ensuing Christian religion in which that faith came to be embodied; including in that a finer assessment of the fidelities and betrayals incurred in the very course of that continually changing embodiment; in particular from the point at which the faith of Jesus the Jew became fully and finally embodied in a new religion called Christianity.[1]

All of which confirms the character of the position in which we find ourselves at the beginning of a new millennium of the Christian era. The quest of the historical Jesus, and of the wider history of the times and places and peoples from which he emerged and of which he was such an integral part, or in which

---

1. It is to this area of Christian scholarship, perhaps the only area that has shown persistence despite the temporary stops and even the embargoes that have sought to block its way, that Seán Freyne has made one of the most distinguished of internationally recognised contributions.

he and his movement engaged in mutuality of influence, continues at least in the normal course of biblical studies. And it continues, at least in that particular specialisation of Christian theological studies, to let shine the light that this historical Jesus and
the faith he fashioned from his own Jewish tradition of faith,
throws upon the being of God and of God's ways with the
world. Yet the theology, and especially the theology of divine
revelation, that would underpin and correspond to this ever
clearer vision of the truth that came with the historical Jesus, and
that continues to result in its purification from subsequent religious, moral and political adulteration, still awaits adequate
formulation. It seemed as if it might emerge from the quest of
the historical Jesus, but it was blocked by the introduction of the
dichotomy between the Jesus of history and the Christ of faith.
Then the second quest of the historical Jesus, under that specific
title, simply petered out; and although the second quest could
be said to be continued anonymously as it were, in the general
area of biblical studies, nothing specific is yet being done to remove the theological blockage of the dichotomy between the
Jesus of history and the Christ of faith; just the kind of dichotomy
between history and faith that continued to keep its place in the
forms of the dichotomy between, on the one hand, reason and
history and, on the other, divine communication and other special interventions, in the theologies of revelation and of divine
inspiration.

## SIN AND SALVATION IN NATURE AND HISTORY

There were other moves that dominated for a while the theological landscape of the 20th century, and that were also allowed to
peter out before their best results could be established and
recorded, and brought into contact with other theological moves
of that century, such as those instanced already, for the
advancement of the whole of a unified and consistent Christian
theology for our times. There was, for example, the move on the
traditional Western theology of original sin. This move came
about almost accidentally, as follows. The developing sciences
of evolution had been causing problems for some time for the
traditional Christian understanding of its biblical account of
creation, when suddenly one angle of one of these sciences
caught in the dominant traditional Christian account of original
sin, and threatened to cause a large tear in it. The study of the

origin of the species suggested that the species, *homo sapiens*, as such species tend to do, evolved from a population and not from a single member or a single couple. And if this was so, it made little sense to say that anything passed from one original member or couple to all the rest of that species without exception through the very process of procreation itself. Now, whatever differences may have arisen between the main Christian churches of the West concerning the precise mechanisms of the transmission of original sin, or concerning the extent of the damage thereby done to human kind, and whatever explanations some of these may have come up with, in the matter of the sheer queer justice of God regarding a human neonate sinful as a result of simply being conceived, there remained a unanimity in the official teachings of these mainline churches, on the idea that something called original sin was transmitted from one man, Adam, at each conception of his progeny, and hence to all human beings without exception. But it was precisely this account of original sin that saw a serious challenge arise from the science of evolution that regarded polygenism as the favoured formula from all the evidence of origins of species, with monogenism a scarcely conceivable alternative.

The responses of Christian theology to this challenge, as with the responses to evolution theory in general, varied in kind as much as in their power of conviction: from the utterly reactionary insistence that biblical propositions must ever be held higher than scientific hypotheses, to new and creative theological efforts at saying just what this original sin consisted in, and how it was transmitted from generation to generation. For example, one type of theological suggestion would have it that original sin consists in effect in a form of idolatry; more specifically, a deifying of human self-interest, at the expense not merely of the rest of creation, but of other peoples or groups. The kind of thing one finds, for instance, in that worship of Mammon in which all of us at all times and to one degree or another engage, and which brings untold evils to the human race as well as to the natural world; a kind of endemic immorality that is transmitted culturally down all the sad centuries of human tenancy of this lean earth, but at all events certainly not transmitted at or through the fertilisation of women's ova.

This theological excursus also petered out before any generally agreed re-formulation of the traditional Western theology of original sin, widely thought to have originated in Augustine's writings on the subject, could be developed. With the result that this Augustinian formula remained in the more official teachings of the churches, and thence in the minds of the great majority of church members. Now one does not need to delve any deeper at this point into the details of this fourth main theological move of the 20th century – the challenge, the response, and the curtailed theological outcome – before one realises that it shares a certain characteristic with the other three. Just as theology seemed to be moving towards a position in which the substance of the Christian faith, or at the very least some central elements of that faith, appear to be accessible from the natural history of the natural world, the move peters out, fails to deliver the full potential outcome either for itself, or by linking up with the other moves in such a manner as to urge them forward also, in a direction in which they already seemed to be going, that is to say, towards what would most likely result in a combined position on the Christian faith, nature and history.

For whatever else might be said about this allegedly inherited sinfulness, in relation to a just God and so on, one thing is certain: since this original sin is not, and not even a result of, a sin committed after Adam, it is now and in itself entirely undetectable on the stage of nature and history. Some theologians persist in saying that it is detectable through its symptom, concupiscence, disordered sensual desire. But concupiscence stands in no more need of an essentially undetected causal explanation for its occurrence than do the disorders of any other human faculty or habit; a plentiful supply of detectable causal explanations are available for all of them. And there is an interesting corollary to this utter undetectability of original sin: the cure is equally undetectable. For its cure is said to consist in divine grace, and in particular the grace that is poured into the infant's soul, as normal theological idiom would have it, on the occasion of the infant's baptism. So divine grace and its operation is also undetectable on the empirical stage of nature and history? Apparently so; indeed even more undetectable than original sin, for the common theological view amongst traditionalists in this matter is that concupiscence continues even after original sinfulness is washed away in the waters of baptism.

The upshot of all of this must be that all of this activity, the transmission of sin, the ensuing state of sinfulness in every human neonate, and the forgiveness or washing away of this original sin, all take place in some supernatural, supra-historical realm, in some kind of alternative world and history that is, during our natural lifetime at least, invisible, inaudible, intangible to all earthlings. So that we certainly seem to have yet another example of a piece of modern theology that tried to talk of an element of the Christian faith that could be detected in natural history, but then let the matter drop, and allowed both original sin and God's grace in respect of it to recede once more into some realm of agents and activity above and beyond nature and history, to be known only through some special divine communication to a select few to be communicated to others. Before attempting a response to that point and to plot a way forward, ask one more question concerning the matter in hand. If the grace that washes away original sin is undetectable in this natural world and by our own normal means of perception, does the same apply to all of God's grace of whatever sort and purpose – saving, auxiliary, sanctifying? The answer, again from an analysis of the teachings of the mainline Christian churches, would appear to be in the affirmative. Although this does not imply that it was this outcome in the case of the grace of baptism for the wiping away of original sin that caused the undetectable condition to be extended to all of God's grace.

## NATURE AND GRACE

The text books of Roman Catholic theology that continued to be published well into the second half of the 20th century provide in ample profusion the evidence for the view that divine grace does not belong to the natural world and is not therefore detectable through our natural modes of perception. Textbook evidence is particularly important, for textbooks provided the common sources for the training of the clergy of the Christian churches, and their preaching in turn formed the minds of the generality of Christian believers on this and all other relevant matters. In these textbooks what was found was what the few theologians who dared to criticise it called the superstructure model of divine grace. Divine grace in all its forms – sanctifying, saving, and enabling both generally and during particular bouts of moral activity – was modelled on the structures of human nature. That nature was then understood to consist of the human essence or substance itself, together with its faculties or powers, and its characteristic activities. So the term, divine grace, referred to a created complex consisting of a new being or entity corresponding to the human essence or substance, new faculties or principles of operation, and the activations of these that then made up the active life of the human being endowed with the grace of God. A doppelganger nature, in short, added to the natural nature, essence or substance of the human being and to its natural faculties and activities. That is to say, a supernatural entity in its entirety, living a supernatural life; supernatural in the literal sense of something over and above (*super*) the human nature we directly experience in ourselves and in others. As such 'the supernatural life of grace' became a common phrase for a kind of superstructure raised above the structures that made natural life possible. As the matter was further explained: since the ultimate goal of human existence was in itself something supernatural, namely, the final union with God known as the beatific vision of God, the life of grace by which this goal beyond the grave could be reached, must of necessity be something equally supernatural and simply not accessible to natural powers of observation. And even though the imagery of this strictly supernatural model of divine grace sometimes included talk of 'elevating' our human nature with its characteristic powers and activities to the point of enabling these to be accommodated to the beatific union with God, no real prospect of a natural detectability of divine grace ensued. The overall doppelganger-supernatural structure of divine grace militated against such a possibility; and the beatific vision was, with the exception of occasional and very temporary divine favours for unique individuals, reserved for another life and another world. The history of this natural world, including the history of humanity, moved on a different and separate plane therefore from that of divine grace and its strictly super-natural ends.

As in the case of other elements of the Christian faith already analysed above, there was a move in the case of the Christian theology of divine grace also, to bring it closer, if not into the natural world and its history, where its presence and power would be more accessible to all. For example, Karl Rahner, conscious perhaps that Henri de Lubac's *Surnaturel* had been placed on Rome's index of prohibited books for arguing for continuity between nature and grace, argued instead that nature was a 'remainder concept'. By this he meant that God had from the beginning of creation destined humanity for a supernatural destiny, a return to a union with God called the beatific vision, and for no other goal. This divine decision then sets up a 'supernatural existential', as the inmost thing in concrete human existence in all of its concrete history; an existential structure consisting mainly in God's own immanent activity in humanity and its history and resulting first and foremost in all that we call divine grace – the life-structures, principles of operation and activities already mentioned. This inmost existential condition is then detectable to us in our concrete life and history in this world. In fact, it is so much a part of what we are and perceive in all of the actual and concrete conditions of our life in this natural creation, that it is only by revelation (a special revelation, presumably) that we can distinguish this supernatural existential from whatever in us and our history would remain as purely natural. In this sense then nature and natural are remainder concepts; the connotation of these concepts is complete in what is left over from our account of all that our nature and its history in this world tells us, once the supernatural existential, which we know from the same inspection of nature and history, but are told by special revelation is actually supernatural, has been subtracted.

This whole manoeuvre of Rahner's is little more than a fine example of sleight-of-hand, typical of Rahner when he wanted to introduce an idea he knew would be unacceptable to his ecclesiastical masters. In this case the idea that was unacceptable was that God's presence, power, light and grace was all of it detectable as an innermost existential in our history as part of the natural world. But Rahner still appeared to support the opposite, the authorities' professed idea, namely, that the supernatural existential was truly supernatural in that, although it could be detected in the course of our ordinary experience of our nature and history, we had special revelation to tell us that it was not part of the merely natural after all. Of course, some would deem this characterisation of Rahner's move to be unfair. But it does at least point up a problem with the other theological efforts of that era to get away from that dichotomous distinction between nature and supernatural grace that was endemic to the superstructure model of divine grace. The problem is this: why, as these new theologians investigated the incidence and extent of supernatural divine grace in the world and its history, did they stop short of including in this the very creation and thereby

God's free gift (*gratia*) of natural existence and natural life and all the abundance of sources for life and life ever more abundant for all?

Or, to put the problem in precisely parallel terms to the terminology of divine grace, to put it in the terminology of revelation: why, when it was admitted by all, including Calvin, that the one, true God was revealed in ordinary created nature and its ordinary, natural history, did theologians persist in driving a dichotomy between, on the one hand, special supernatural divine revelation accompanying the special creation and gift of the alleged grace-superstructure and, on the other hand, the natural knowledge of God's power and presence in the creation and gift of the natural structures of existence and life? When the problem is phrased in the terminology of divine revelation, the Calvinist answer is clear: the knowledge of God that is available from nature and history has always been sufficient in itself to light and empower our way to our eternal destiny in union with God; but then original sin entered upon that blissful natural world and so blinded us to the revelation of the life-giving God in the natural creation that a special supernatural revelation became necessary and was in fact vouchsafed. This special revelation, witnessed in divinely inspired scriptures, had essentially the same content as the original revelation in nature and history, except for the addition of a word concerning God's special arrangements for the forgiving of sin. The Roman Catholic answer, whether the problem is posed in the terminology of grace or of revelation, is less clear. But it does seem that a fear of reviving what was believed to be the heresy of Pelagius was the operative factor here.

This fear could then be outlined as follows: if the divine grace was thought to consist of God's free creative activity in giving existence and life and all the supports and affordances of life from time into eternity, and if the creation could then be seen correspondingly as sufficient revelation of this God and of God's power and presence, then surely the conclusion would somehow emerge that human beings can come to know God and to progress towards their destiny in eternal communion with God by, as it is sometimes put, pulling themselves along to this blissful goal of their whole existence by their own boot-straps. Nature itself and alone, and human nature in particular, enables the eternal God to be seen and reached; and that is thought to be the crowning error with which the good name of Pelagius has been besmirched to this day.

But that, as the necessary revisionism of modern historical theology has long proven, is not something that Pelagius's own thought either endorsed or entailed. For, particularly when divine creation is seen as it truly is, not a one-off act that long ago put the world in existence, but rather a continuous divine activity that gives origin to forms of finiteness and creatively empowers these to create others in what eventually becomes a living and hence a continually evolving universe, then the free initiative always remains with God in gifting all the life that stretches from time to eternity, and in concomitantly revealing God's self ever more fully to all those who possess powers of comprehension sufficiently developed to receive such revelation. Our activity, our living is therefore always a response to God's continuously creative initiative; our knowledge of God and of our destiny with God a response to the self-revelation of God that is conveyed through that same continuous creativity that is pictured in the scriptures in the imagery of the Word of God by which the world is created. But this is to anticipate the argument of the book that is to follow. For the moment it is necessary only to observe that, in the case of the theology of grace there is yet another example of a 20th century move towards seeing an element of the Christian faith revealed in nature and its varied history; yet another move of this kind and this general direction that was then once again aborted, or for one reason or another petered out before it could be finally tested, at the very least by being driven, in the company of other moves in the same direction, to its logical conclusions.

CREATION

So far it seems that the theology that the 20th century bequeathed to the new millennium was comprised in effect of a series of start-stop movements, each of which began by reaching out to the natural world, and particularly perhaps to humanity, and the history of that world and the history of humanity within it, in the expectation and hope of finding there true traces of the presence and power of such a being as one might deem divine; hoping to find the traces of that being's boundless grace for life and life forever more abundant, and of such blessed mutual knowledge and love of the gracious being as its infinite creative benevolence always initiates and correspondingly promises to fulfil. Yet each and every one of these theological movements, although each and all could boast some better insights into the content of the Christian faith, and some potential improvements in its social structures and communal practices, either ground to a halt or virtually reversed its direction. In either case, the kind of theology that was left in possession was a theology that located the substance, power and activity of God's grace, together with the source of our knowledge of this, in some supernatural realm, a realm which, even in its breaking into the realm of the natural world, remained quite distinct from it. No one seemed to think of following the clues provided by the very fact that all of these movements began in the same direction and recorded some striking insights into the Christian faith while moving in that direction. No one seemed to sense the promises that might be redeemed by bringing all of these movements together and then continuing in the same direction of the quest for God and for the highest of human prospects with God, in the natural history of the world.

There was one other movement in the course of 20th century theology that might have accomplished such a task. It was in fact a movement that concerned itself specifically with the theology of creation. But that movement seemed satisfied in the end with a re-positioning of the theology of creation within the overall prospectus of Christian theology. It did not attempt to pursue the whole of Christian theology as a theology of creation, that is to say, as a theology, a critical, investigative and analytic study of God and God's ways with the world, the results of which would be taken from and based upon the evidences afforded by the natural creation itself, its origin, continuous development, recurring destructions, savings from these, and ultimate prospects. Rather, the new theology of creation seemed to be happy to promote itself to priority over the theology of sin; just as certain moves in the moral theology of the 20th century sought to promote the priority of charity, or the priority of the scriptures, over the priority of law and obedience. In the course of this push for priority, the priority of sin in Christian theology was not taken to suggest that the sin of the creature took place before the creation of this material universe, even if certain early Christian theologians flirted with that idea. Rather was the priority of sin taken to mean that, in general, and particularly in certain crucial parts of Christian theology, if the idea of God having to respond to sin were to be the foundational consideration, then in these central parts of Christian theology, what might be called a sin-driven theology would promote the image of God having to respond to sin, and would situate this image so as to make it logically prior to the image of an eternal God ever understood as benign creator.

For example christology, which gives its distinctive character to the whole of any Christian theology, could be said to have been sin-driven in all the main churches of the West. The pivotal event in the earthly life of Jesus, his crucifixion, was read simply and solely as the redemption of the human race from sin. Correspondingly, in the dominant Anselmian theology of salvation, the incarnation itself, in which the Word of God became man, was said to be necessitated by that same requirement of paying the price for the sin of the race. Indeed the very theology of original sin that was derived from the Augustinian model in the West was itself seen to be a necessary presupposition of the theological model which saw Christ's crucifixion as the saving of all of mankind without exception from sin. Without a doctrine of original sin transmitted to all in the very process of procreation, how could we be sure that Jesus was the saviour of all human beings without exception? This question was often asked without any apparent awareness of the kind of totally sin-driven theology that same question presupposed.

These sin-driven theologies derived from epochal interpretations of the Christian sources, such as those provided by Augustine and Luther, theologians who were themselves obsessed with sin, at the very least in the sense that their assessment of themselves as persistent sinners persuaded them to describe all other members of the race – the *massa damnata*, as Augustine called it – in much the same terms and so wholeheartedly as to quite smother at birth any balancing assessment of themselves and all other human beings as equally persistent creators of good, and as naturally capable of that as they are of evil-doing. In just such ways sin takes priority over creation in most Christian theologies of the West. Sin drove and fashioned the whole of these Christian theologies through the dominant influence of soteriology in christology, and thereby relegated the theology of creation to the simple task of accounting for the existence of the stage and the actors on which and by whom this great cosmic drama of sin and redemption is played out.

Now any attempt to displace this priority of sin in Christian theology was welcome, and always is welcome, if only because these sin-driven theologies did spawn, and must always tend to spawn, extreme forms of exclusivism in the polity of the Christian religion. For the more exclusively Jesus is seen as the saviour of the whole race, the more must all other religions be excluded. Baptism in the name of Jesus, or at the very least faith in Jesus, is both necessary and sufficient for human salvation. Not surprisingly then, those who in the course of the move just mentioned, tried to re-position the Christian theology of creation in the pecking order of subject matters dealt with, were criticised on many counts: on the count of prioritising 'natural theology' at the expense of 'revealed theology', for instance, but principally on account of demoting the 'supernatural' revelation of God sending his only Son to save the world, with all that was thought to entail in terms of universal sinfulness. In the end, with such criticism to contend with, this final 20th century theology of creation petered out also. And it left us, as did the similarly aborted movements already mentioned, with the dichotomies of history and revelation, and nature and grace; and with the kind of superstructure model of Christianity in which both the divine givings and other actions designed to achieve our blessed destiny, together with the processes by which these are made known to us, take place in a kind of doppelganger universe, above and beyond the natural world of which we are such integral parts and knowers. Both the dichotomies and the superstructure models are designed, in reality if not consciously, to alert us to, and more crucially to lead us to a world quite other than this one.

### THE FRANCHISE THEOLOGY THAT THE LAPSES LEFT IN PLACE: AND SOME OF ITS TRAGIC CONSEQUENCES

Another way to sum up the Christian theology of the 20th century is to say this: that, together, these aborted or petered-out theological moves, each of which began by holding out such prospects for an ever-necessary reforming of Christian theology that would keep it faithful alike to the faith of its founder and to a human race that had discovered first history and then evolution, ended by inviting back what can only be called a centuries-old franchise theology, with all of its limitations and potentially damaging outcomes.

The term 'franchise theology' is hereby coined in order to characterise the kind of theology, and in particular the theology of church, the ecclesiology, that corresponds to the superstructure model of grace above and beyond nature, and of revelation above and beyond history. If the divine acts and their effects that constitute grace belong to a supernatural realm, then divine grace is not accessible in the natural world and by natural means. Neither in consequence is the knowledge of grace or of the God giving that grace, accessible by means of our natural powers of perception. Both the grace and the truth about it must then be conveyed either to each human being individually, or to some chosen individual or group in the first instance, who can then distribute both grace and truth to others across time and space. The fullness of grace and truth, according to the Bible, came with Jesus the Christ, and the Christian churches that have followed Jesus generally claim that they, and perhaps principally some leadership groups within them, have had entrusted to them the privilege and responsibility to make this grace and truth known and available to all nations and all ages, down to the last limit of place and time. It is with such a scenario in mind that the Christian theologies that promote or assume the superstructure model of nature and grace, history and revelation, are called franchise theologies.

Now of course these theologies, and the Christian churches that define themselves on their terms are not, all of them, quite as crudely exclusivist as the term, sole franchise, might of itself suggest. For the sole franchise refers to the fullness of grace and truth that came into the world with Jesus of Nazareth. So a particular church could say that God had granted some grace and truth to other peoples and religions, to Judaism in particular; or it might say that certain other Christian churches that had either broken away from it or strayed from fidelity to the fullness of Christ's grace and truth, had nevertheless retained some of that grace and truth. But in both cases such generous acknowledgments, as they are intended to be, could quickly be seen to imply that the partial possessions or remnants of divine grace and truth still detectable in other religions or churches, should have as their proper goal and essential *raison d'être* the divinely authorised impulse to drive their possessors towards the Christian fold, or back into the one, true church to which alone the fullness of grace and truth is solely franchised.

On such an understanding of the franchise theology, the sole franchise of the fullness of grace and truth that came with the Lord Jesus, whether one is talking about other Christian churches or other religions, and whether in the latter case one Christian church believes that the fullness of grace and truth already subsists in itself (as the Roman Catholic Church clearly and consistently asserted in Vatican II's *Decree on Ecumenism*), or that it will subsist once more in the one, true church that will come about only when the many-sided negotiations of the ecumenical movement reach final agreement, the upshot for non-Christian religions and for (all but one of) the Christian churches is the same: all are in effect instances of the *praeparatio evangelica*, the divine providential preparation of human kind for the fullness of grace and truth, divinely intended from eternity to be embodied in one, true, catholic or universal church, one *ecclesia*, one calling-out or gathering-in of human kind; so that all of these other religions and churches should disappear by merging into this one, true community of all people of the one, true God.

That is but one general illustration of the manner in which the failures of 20th century Christian theology to follow up on the recurrent directions and promises of so many of its start-up movements left Christians without the ability or willingness to appreciate the permanent value and future prospects of other religions or other Christian churches; and provided these Christians instead, even through the modified versions of exclusivism just outlined, with opportunities to denounce members of other religions and churches for their deficiencies of truth and goodness, shortcomings that are then described as forms of falsehood and sin. Take the case where such religious or ecclesiastical divisions correspond to other ethnic or social divisions, as in Christian-Muslim divisions, or the Catholic-Protestant divisions of Northern Ireland; between which animosities, even violent animosities, are already engendered both by natural concupiscence, the lust for self-aggrandisement, for the wealth by which that is achieved, and the power over others that wealth confers, and by the opposing natural desire for the freedom and justice of which the conquered and despoiled are inevitably deprived. In cases such as these, religiously derived judgmental attitudes to an allegedly ingrained falsehood and sinfulness of whatever kind or degree inevitably supply a range of supports to the most violent animosities that threaten to destroy both sides caught up in the ensuing madness. These can range from, at the lowest level, a simple unwillingness to break down divisions of purely religious or ecclesiastical origin, such as those that Christian churches maintain when they refuse to let their respective members sit together round the eucharistic table of the Lord, as they call it; or where different churches or different religions refuse to allow their children to be educated together. The range continues through higher supports for hate-filled and violent altercations that supply further justification for treating those on the opposite sides of ethnic or social divides with ever more extreme animosity and violence. Not all of this, of course, can be attributed directly in all cases to the modified exclusivism that is characteristic of Christian franchise theology. And yet, once one begins to talk in terms of endemic deficiencies of truth and goodness in other human groups, one is on a slippery slope well greased at times of emergent divisions and hostilities, to degrees that make ever more difficult any restraint upon slipping to ever more extreme positions.

In any case, there are further examples of the manner in which the franchise theology which the 20th century seemed about to replace, but instead left in the end in possession, contributed to further damage to both religion and humanity. These must then be counted as further failures of the theological community to pursue to the end the direction and promise that began to appear in so many individual theological moves: a direction away from the superstructure models of revelation and grace, and a promise of a replacement of the franchise theology with a theology of equal access of all and at all times to the fullness of God's grace and truth. Two further examples must suffice, for although there were many more, enough will then have been supplied to secure the general contention that a theology different from the franchise theology, so often seemingly heralded by so many of the moves of the 20th century, still awaits its formulation, and with this the end of theological lapsing for this time, and the end also of these lapses of Christian praxis consequent upon franchise theology and its implementation.

First, failures in the moral teachings of some Christian churches. Franchise theology assumes that, just as all the truth concerning God and God's ways with the world comes by special divine revelation, so does all the true moral guidance by which we must live in the world in order to reach our immortal destiny with God. For one Christian church this moral truth, in the forms of principle and precept and the example of Jesus and so on, is contained in its entirety in the infallible Bible. For another church it is contained in the Bible, but also in the natural creation, and it is infallibly interpreted in the former and read from the latter by the Pope as teacher of the whole church. In both of these accounts one can detect the sole franchise model of a morality delivered by God for the observance of the whole of human kind. One can also see how the moral deliverances from these beneficiaries of the sole franchise would be seen by them, and delivered to all, as unchangeable, absolute principles and precepts. A precept that God has delivered, man can neither reject nor alter. So, to narrow this further example down to one case: when Pope Paul VI read from nature that a 'safe period' is provided as an interval during which intercourse may not result in pregnancy, and he then interpreted the role of God the creator to mean that we may not interfere with God's creation of new human beings in any manner other than the one provided for us in human nature itself as created, he then decreed that any 'artificial' methods used for the avoidance of pregnancy are intrinsically sinful. And, as the Pope was teaching on a matter of faith or morals as head of the whole church, that is an infallible and immutable moral teaching.

The damage done by this regrettable decree to the lives of untold numbers of good Roman Catholics, to their consciences and their faith, and in many, many cases to their family lives, was increased exponentially when, in pursuit of the same porous logic by which the decree was arrived at, the Pope further decided that the use of condoms – intrinsically evil as it always is – could not be recommended as a deterrent to the spread of AIDS. This was an appalling affront to the very value of human life, particularly in places like Africa where AIDS is pandemic; apart from being a further abysmal denial to women of the most basic right to have their very lives protected from men who in any event and for their own macho pleasures could scarcely be persuaded to use condoms under any circumstances. A more graphic example would be difficult to find, of a failure of Christianity in the world which clearly derives from a franchise model of the Christian religion, and thence implicates a failure of Christian theology as it for so long proposed, defended, and finally allowed that model to survive every new move in 20th century theology that promised to modify, if not replace it.

THE CONSEQUENT CASE FOR A FULL-BLOWN
CHRISTIAN THEOLOGY OF CREATION

Such a critical survey of the main movements in Christian theology as it reached the end of the last millennium – if it be at all fair and reasonably accurate – surely suggests, and indeed it could positively promise, that some sustained attempt to follow to their full and combined conclusions the very similar direction detected in all of these movements, to find God's grace and truth in the natural history of the only world we know to exist, might very well result in a sketch of the whole of Christian theology that would at the very least avoid the lapses of 20th century theology, together with the tragic consequences of these as already in part exemplified. What is then at issue and in prospect is a Christian theology construed entirely and in all of its traditional constituent parts – Creation, Fall, Salvation in Christ, Trinity, Eschatology, Revelation, Faith, Grace – as a theology of creation. It would of course be necessary to derive, and to be seen to derive such a theology from the Christian scriptures, for these are the only fully authoritative sources for Christian belief accepted by all Christian groups. And as a consequence it would be necessary to show that such a natural Christian theology was fully in accord with the faith of the historical Jesus, for which these scriptures provide evidence without equal. For otherwise Christians would quite reasonably assume that all of this was just another case of over-educated theologians corrupting the Christian faith by the intrusion of secular philosophies. And in any event, if the case can be made from the Christian scriptures, the implications must go far beyond the ridding our new millennium of the worst excesses of the franchise theology. The relationships between the Christian churches, and indeed the relationship between Christianity itself and other religions must also expect the most searching revision.[2]

---

2. This piece is a version of part of a prologue to my *Christianity and Creation: The Essence of the Christian Faith and its Future among Religions* (New York and London: Continuum International, 2006).

CHAPTER EIGHT

# Rootedness: Reflections on Land and Belonging

## John D'Arcy May

*For an Aboriginal, surveying the landscape is like reading the Bible.*[1]

While trying to come to terms with the unique religious sensibil-
ity of Japan, I came across a study of a mountain landscape
steeped in the sacredness of Shinto *kami* which had become the
'enmountained text' of the *Lotus Sûtra*, now able to be 'read' as a
kind of geographic transliteration of the text itself with all its
transcendent Buddhas and Bodhisattvas.[2] Such powerful symbolic realities are deeply ambivalent: while rooting people, and
peoples, in place, they can become the objects of exclusive attachment, bringing about a rejection of the different and a refusal of the universal, as the transformation of Shintô into a
nationalistic ideology in Japanese history despite the universal-
ising influence of Buddhism shows.[3] Rootedness need not con-
note narrowness, however: land can become a metaphor for
wider experiences and values. Patrick White's *The Tree of Man*
(1956) begins with the arrival of a man driving a cart into the virgin bush: 'So the cart stopped, grazing the hairy side of a tree,
and the horse, shaggy and stolid as the tree, sighed and took

---

1. Eugene Stockton, 'The Mindful Land', in John Cameron (ed),
*Changing Places: Re-imagining Australia* (Double Bay: Longueville
Books, 2003), 234-242. I owe Eugene Stockton many insights into an
Australian 'spirituality of the land', such as the following: 'When I am
alert in prayer I am 'minding' the universe, just as a Zen practitioner is
said to be 'sitting' for the universe', *ibid*. I would also like to thank my
former schoolmate Robyn Reynolds for commenting on a draft of this
essay out of her lifelong experience as a missionary sister in northern
Australia.
2. I refer to Allan G. Grapard's essay 'The Textualized Mountain –
Enmountained Text: The Lotus Sutra in Kunisaki', in George J. Tanabe
Jr. and Willa Jane Tanabe (eds), *The Lotus Sutra in Japanese Culture*
(Honolulu: University of Hawaii Press, 1989), 159-189.
3. For a fuller discussion see J. D. May, *Transcendence and Violence: The
Encounter of Buddhist, Christian and Primal Traditions* (New York and
London: Continuum, 2003), 73-78.

root', thus establishing the place of the human drama of settlement to follow, while *Voss* (1957) pits a slightly deranged
German explorer against the unrelenting vastness of the central
desert, which he can penetrate but never appropriate. Place, as
what we set out from, though it defines us, can enable us to respond – with a sense of justice – to the promise of a wider world,
as Abraham did. Even if we have the privilege of mastering a
variety of idioms and imageries, we never finally leave but continually reappropriate our 'place' in inverse proportion to our
distance from it in space and time. Land, then, can be both liberating and enslaving, schooling us in both rootedness and openness.

Like Seán Freyne, I grew up in the country, in a place – the
Western District of Victoria in Australia – which, like County
Mayo (and Galilee!), most people would regard as out of the
way and unimportant. Yet over the long years I have been half a
world away from it, I realise how it formed me and how important it is to me to go back there occasionally and be reminded of
its sights and sounds, the tang of eucalyptus and the crunch of
dry bark underfoot. Though we were 'townies' who did not
work the land, and though I knew nothing about its previous indigenous inhabitants, that part of south-eastern Australia is 'my
place' and helped to make me what I am.[4] As many contemporary Australians from a variety of cultural backgrounds are dis-
covering, this sense of belonging can become morally ambivalent as the descendants of settlers and newly-arrived immigrants
struggle to feel 'at home' in landscapes very different from
Europe's, and awareness grows of the quite incomparable relationship to land experienced by Australia's indigenous inhabitants 'from the beginning' (*ab origine*).[5] In addition, the experience of living in Germany, the Pacific Islands and Ireland has

---

4. Sally Morgan's book *My Place*, though it is now regarded as a 'white-
wash' by some fellow-Aboriginal critics such as Jackie Huggins,
'Always Was Always Will Be', in Michelle Grossman (ed), *Blacklines:
Contemporary Critical Writing by Indigenous Australians* (Melbourne:
Melbourne University Press, 2003), 60-65, poignantly evoked for me as
a 'whitefella' the impact on identity of losing and finding one's true
'place'. For a development of this theme from both biblical and
Aboriginal points of view, see Geoffrey Lilburne, *A Sense of Place: A
Christian Theology of the Land* (Nashville: Abingdon Press, 1989).
5. Nothing I have read in recent years has got into the emotional guts of
the problem as movingly as Peter Read's *Belonging: Australians, Place*

brought home to me just how politically disruptive attachment
to land can be (*Lebensraum*, the *Drang nach Osten* and *Blut und
Boden* in Nazi ideology; land disputes and compensation sagas
in neocolonial Papua New Guinea; the loss of land as a source of
Irish grievances), and I have discovered that in the Hebrew as in
the Christian Bible the use and ownership of land is not only a
powerful metaphor but a fundamental religious and ethical
theme.[6] Seán Freyne's recent innovative use of the ecology and
geography of Galilee to modify our perception of Jesus in his
formative context[7] emboldens me to offer a meditation on belonging to land and the earth which may hint at solutions to
some of the most intractable problems of the era of globalisation.

As we explore this theme, still rather unfamiliar to theologians,
some terminological agreements are necessary. By 'land' I mean
not just 'landscape' – a concept born of the Renaissance aesthetic
and the Romantic movement of early modernity and associated
with paintings and postcards – nor 'property', the category of
ownership in Western jurisprudence, for both involve an objectification and alienation of land behind which I wish to go to
reach something more elemental. I wish to conceive of land as
'place' in the sense of the birthplace of identity, the primordial
point of departure and of return on life's journey, not just the object of possession and cultivation but the subject of genesis, giving birth, together with family and society, to the 'self' as a
formed individual. This can happen culturally in very different
ways, many of which characterise land as 'mother', the matrix of
identity.[8] Land as 'place' in this seminal sense is undoubtedly a
cultural artefact, but a primary one, providing the generative

---

*and Aboriginal Ownership* (Cambridge: Cambridge University Press,
2000). As we shall see, his interviews and analyses bring out every register of ambiguity and perplexity in making land that does not, in the
end, 'speak to us', is not 'ours', nevertheless 'home', in a sense that can
be shared with Aboriginal people as 'our place'.

6. Walter Brueggemann, *The Land: Place as Gift, Promise, and Challenge in
Biblical Faith* (Philadelphia: Fortress Press, 1977), has no hesitation in
saying that land 'is a central, if not *the central theme* of biblical faith', 3.

7. Seán Freyne, *Jesus, a Jewish Galilean: A New Reading of the Jesus Story*
(London and New York: T. & T. Clark-Continuum, 2004).

8. I tried to explore some of these in J. D. May, 'Education as Initiation?
Some South Pacific Perspectives', *Journal of Religious Education* 50/2
(2002), 45-52.

mythic context for the secondary ones of ritual, kinship and the constitution of persons.

Aboriginal people recapitulate most of this when they refer to land as their 'country', not just the site of the ritual enactment of their stories of origin and moral orientation but a participant in them, the geographically embodied presence of the Ancestor Beings who shaped the world and the Abiding Events by which they continue to do so.[9] Marcia Langton evokes this unique sense of place in a memorable paragraph:

> In this life lived under the stars, places are marked not through physical inscriptions, but through kin and dreaming ties that inscribe the self in place and place in the self. That is, places are inscribed through metaphysical relationships. Places are not simply 'out there', but experienced through relationships with the emplaced dreaming beings who gave rise to the original ancestors. Both sense of place and rights to place are marked by ancestral connections passed down through indigenous law, not simply through humanly created physical signposts. In turn, the places of memory and experience are sensual proof of the truth of Aboriginal law. Through the authority of the elders as keepers of law and customary land tenure, cultural memories become inscribed in the places of tradition, and such places become 'site-markers of the remembering process and of identity itself'.[10]

Country, for Aboriginal people, is the 'speaking land' which preserves, verifies and transmits the law, giving shape to every aspect of their lives.[11]

If Land connotes 'place' as a context of origin from which one can detach oneself while maintaining an abiding relationship to

---

9. The elusive Aboriginal worldview somewhat misleadingly known as 'The Dreaming' has been interpreted as a 'locative ontology' along these lines by Tony Swain, *A Place for Strangers: Towards a History of Australian Aboriginal Being* (Cambridge: Cambridge University Press, 1993).

10. Marcia Langton, 'Sacred Geography', in Max Charlesworth, Françoise Dussart and Howard Morphy (eds), *Aboriginal Religions in Australia: An Anthology of Recent Writings* (Aldershot: Ashgate, 2005), 131-139, 135, quoting A. Taylor.

11. The moral richness of this heritage is documented by Ronald M. Berndt and Catherine H. Berndt (eds), *The Speaking Land: Myth and Story in Aboriginal Australia* (Ringwood: Penguin Books, 1989).

it, Earth suggests, in a sense so fundamental that it is only just
beginning to dawn on us, 'home' as the fabric of our very existence, the bodiliness and materiality we humans share with what
Christians call 'creation', others 'nature' and still others the 'mutual dependency' of all that exists. To speak of Earth as the object
of domination and exploitation becomes not only sacrilegious
but morally repugnant. Indeed, in the perspective of those responsible for the *Earth Bible* project of learning to read the
Hebrew and Christian scriptures ecologically, Earth becomes
the voiced subject both of experienced suffering and hope and of
expected justice and liberation.[12]

These perspectives, I venture to suggest, are not only unfamiliar but disconcerting to many Christians. Are we faced
with a re-paganising of the Bible and a relapse into natural theology of the crassest kind? Let us reserve judgment on that, noting at the same time that a comparable degree of discomfort at
the irreversible dis-placement of indigenous peoples and up-
rooted individuals in a world of capital mobility and resource
exploitation is not always evident, not to mention outrage at the
irreversible damage done to Earth itself by the destruction of in-
tact ecologies and the pollution of the biosphere. Let us rather
move on to examine the resources provided by Christian tradition for developing a sense of belonging to land and rootedness
in the Earth.

Most Christians, I suspect, are at least vaguely aware of belonging to a universal faith – this is, after all, the meaning of
'catholic' – which transcends both ethnicity and locality, though
this is not to say that Christianity does not get dragged into endless disputes about both in places such as Northern Ireland and
the former Yugoslavia. The conflict in Israel-Palestine, indeed,
could be interpreted as a tussle over claims to land which is sacred
to Jews, Christians and Muslims. The very abstractness and absoluteness of the transcendence enshrined in the great monotheistic faiths, when brought to bear on the inescapable particularity
of claims to land, become terrifying in their intransigence.
However we might judge the relationship to land in Diaspora
Judaism and the State of Israel, in the Islamic *ummah* and the

---

12. See Norman C. Habel (ed), *Readings from the Perspective of Earth: The
Earth Bible Volume One* (Sheffield: Sheffield Academic Press, 2000), especially Habel's introduction, 25-37, and the description of the project's
guiding principles, 38-53.

Arabian heartland, Christianity must be said to lack a 'spirituality of the land' almost entirely. Even to raise the matter creates puzzlement: what could something as banal as land have to do with theology, especially for urbanised post-moderns with access to travel and communications? A moment's reflection suffices to show that the individualism and rationalism to which Europe's (formerly?) 'Christian' civilisation has given rise are not unconnected with the objectification and exploitation of the earth, its creatures and the cultures that nurture them. In a quite spectacular way, once one learns to see it, the animals other than the human and what we somewhat abstractly call 'nature' have gone right out of focus in Christian ethics and doctrine.

In the Book of Genesis, by contrast, land as 'earth' (*adamah*) is at the centre from the very beginning. Norman Habel goes to far as to call the first creation story a 'geophany', a narrative in which Earth is the primary character, emerging from the darkness of the primordial waters at the prompting of the *ruach* or breath of *Elohim*.[13] Towards the end of this first creation story, however, humans are introduced as a kind of narrative counterpoint, for they are to subdue the earth and rule over all the creatures it has brought forth: 'fill the earth and subdue it; and have dominion over ... every living thing' (Gen 1:28), a text which has been used to lay responsibility for ecological destruction at the door of biblical religion and whose hierarchical dualism cannot easily be explained away.[14] In other words, the story of humans, for whom the ready-made earth becomes the 'place' in which the human drama of coming to responsibility and awareness unfolds, is in tension with the story of the earth, which is already established as 'good', intrinsically valuable, and seen to be so by God ('And God saw that it was good', Gen 1:10b, 12b, 18b, 21b, 25b; 'And God saw everything that he had made, and behold, it was very good', 1:31). In the second creation narrative, by contrast, the human (*adam*) is crafted out of the earth itself (*adamah*, Gen 2:7) in order to live in the garden prepared by God for that

13. See Norman C. Habel, 'Geophany: The Earth Story in Genesis 1', in Norman C. Habel and Shirley Wurst (eds), *The Earth Story in Genesis: The Earth Bible Volume Two* (Sheffield: Sheffield Academic Press, 2000), 34-48.
14. See Norman Habel's response to the well-known accusations of Lynn White Jr. in his introduction to *Readings*, 29-31, and the fuller treatment in Habel and Wurst, *The Earth Story in Genesis*.

purpose and which becomes the setting for the ensuing drama of good and evil. 'The wordplay between *adam* and *adamah* is manifest, but beyond the wordplay lies the potentially subversive claim that the human is derived from soil.'[15]

And so the drama of human existence in and against the earth 'takes place': Cain, the tiller of the soil, having killed his brother Abel, the herdsman, out of envy, is 'cursed from the ground', which 'shall no longer yield to you its strength' (Gen 4:11-12). After preserving all living species from the flood sent to punish humans, 'the Lord said in his heart, "I will never again curse the ground because of man, for the imagination of man's heart is evil from his youth"' (Gen 8:21). In the light of the story of human solidarity in disobedience in Gen 2-3, the focus begins to shift towards humans as the point at which the earth and God, 'nature' and 'creation' become alienated. The covenant which God now concludes with Noah is a covenant 'between me and you and every living creature that is with you … a covenant between me and the earth' (Gen 9:12-13, although permission is given to kill in order to eat, Gen 9:2-3). The covenant with Abraham, by contrast, is not cosmic (earth) but local (land): it concerns land, the land, this land of Canaan (Gen 12:1, 7). It demands of Abraham an archetypal uprooting from his own ancestral land and a journey into a land where he is a stranger and from which – unlike Odysseus – he will never return. Moreover, he must constantly negotiate and reach arrangements with the people whose land he has to share. Each time the covenant is renewed, it becomes clearer that it is not simply a private agreement with Abraham, but already envisages all his descendants, for 'by your descendants shall all the nations of the earth bless themselves' (Gen 22:18). Yet this does not preclude such mundane measures as purchasing a plot of land as a burial place (Gen 23:17-20). So also with Isaac, and finally Jacob: 'The land which I gave to Abraham and Isaac I will give to you, and I will give the land to your descendants after you' (Gen 35:12). The earth, the primordial 'home' of the human species from which it was mythically 'cast out' by its own lust for power, is henceforth the land, an object of contention which each people must fashion into its own 'place'.

---

15. See Mark G. Brett, 'Earthing the Human in Genesis 1-3', in Habel and Wurst (eds), *Earth Story*, 73-86, 80.

The subsequent drama of emigration and exodus remains centred on the loss and repossession of the land, but when we come to the Book of Joshua the story has an entirely different, ideological tenor.[16] Here the land is not entered cautiously and its possession and use negotiated with its inhabitants, but it is systematically conquered and its inhabitants massacred – by divine command, a stance that is reflected in the Deuteronomic code. 'As owner of the land, Yahweh can drive out all those other people who had inhabited it, but who have no rights there', whereas in the covenant with Abraham 'there is no suggestion that these [peoples living in the land] have either to be conquered or driven out'.[17] In the words of Norman Habel: 'The 'giving of the land' and the 'conquest' are two discrete concepts; Israel need not have settled the land by conquest'.[18] Freyne continues: 'Abraham's is an essentially itinerant lifestyle, as he continues to journey through the land as a *ger*, or resident alien (Gen 20:1, 21:3, 23:4)',[19] whereas the Moses narrative provides Joshua with a title deed in advance. The Canaanites are not guilty of anything, nor do they deserve punishment, but as inhabitants of the land ceded to Israel they are enemies by definition and are to be eliminated: 'dispossession means genocide'.[20] The story becomes the prototype of Christian conquest and colonisation down the ages, and it is still invoked today by ultra-orthodox Jews to justify their settlements in the West Bank and Gaza.

These starkly contrasting accounts of a people's relationship to land prefigure the profound moral ambivalence of 'possessing' land. After Israel's landless wanderings in the wilderness the gift of the land of Canaan with its fruitful and well-watered valleys is of enormous significance, but it also represents a temptation to forget the giving and concentrate on the taking, identifying with the earth-based fertility cults of the Canaanites rather than the covenant with Yahweh.[21] Israel's history oscil-

16. See Seán Freyne, *Jesus*, ch 3, 'Stories of Conquest and Settlement'; Normal Habel, 'Conquest and Dispossession: Justice, Joshua and Land Rights', *Pacifica* 4 (1991), 76-92.
17. Freyne, *Jesus*, 67-68.
18. Habel, 'Conquest', 77, n. 2.
19. Freyne, *Jesus*, 69, with the implication that this provides the pattern for Jesus' itinerant existence.
20. Habel, 'Conquest', 83; see 81-83, 90. 'The Canaanites apparently do not deserve to die; they have to die, however, to make way for Israel', 85.
21. This is the theme developed by Brueggemann, *The Land*, 53-59,

lates between possession and exile, precisely in order to prevent
her from becoming identified with the land, thus forgetting the
covenant. Land is intimately bound up with Torah, and in the
various legal codes precisely the responsible use of the land is
legislated in detail. It is for this reason that the setting up of the
monarchy is so fraught with ambiguity and ends in exile, the apparently definitive loss of the land. The pain of loss and the joy
of restoration become the twin themes of the prophets of the
exile, and the next time around, as reflected in the Books of Ezra,
Nehemiah and Maccabees, Israel is reduced to a jealous separat-
ism in its determination to cling to the land and purify it of all
foreign influences, whether indigenous or Hellenistic. Israel's
challenge is to strike a balance between 'grasping' and 'waiting',
between Masada – armed but doomed rebellion – and the
Wailing Wall, enduring in hope sustained by memory.[22] There
remains a sense of alienation: the 'cosmic covenant' with Noah
between God and all the earth recedes into forgetfulness, while
the people's claim to a particular piece of land is purified of anything 'earthy' and reinforced by an ideology of resistance.

The theme of creation – the story of earth – is nevertheless
maintained, somewhat like the subversive stories about women,
in the praise of nature as the revelation of God's majesty in the
Psalms and the wisdom literature, particularly in the awe-in-
spiring vision of the grandeur of the universe at the climax of
Job's debate with God (Job 38-39). It may even be discovered as a
kind of counter-text in the New Testament. In central passages
the cosmic and eschatological dualisms of the heavens and the
earth, the present and the time to come are both posited and de-
constructed, thus giving earth *as such* a voice and a role in redemption. In the Lord's Prayer (Mt 6:9-13) the dualism of 'on the
earth' and 'in the heavens' is resolved into the immediacy of our

though his interpretation of the conquest is more benign than Habel's,
and like most theologians he neglects the reality that the Canaanites,
too, had a relationship to 'their' land which their rituals continually renewed; see the more recent work of Regina M. Schwartz, *The Curse of
Cain: The Violent Legacy of Monotheism* (Chicago: University of Chicago
Press, 1997), prompted by a student's question: 'What about the
Canaanites?' The remainder of this paragraph summarises Brueggemann's nuanced treatment of land as danger and opportunity.
22. Brueggemann, *The Land*, 169. He carries this right through to the
'central insight and mystery of the gospel – that letting go is to have and
keeping is the way to lose', 183.

'bread for the day' and our being 'put to the test' in our life context here and now. In Rom 8:18-25 the 'groaning of creation' clearly means the material universe ('and not only the creation, but we ourselves'), which is an actor in the eschatological drama whose outcome will be 'the redemption of our bodies' (Rom 8:23). The 'new heaven and new earth' of Rev 21:1-22:5 suggest a transformation of the earth into a 'new creation' ('Behold, I make all things new', Rev 21:5), repeating the original creation in definitive form as 'the holy city, new Jerusalem' (21:2), where there is no longer need of a temple or 'light of lamp or sun' (22:5), because this very earth will now be what it was originally intended to be, the 'dwelling of God ... with men' (21:3).[23]

Though it is seldom related to its biblical antecedents, in Australia a comparable conflict rages within the hearts of many. Negotiated sharing or assertion of possession? Separate nations or multicultural federation? From the descendants of the early settlers who have strong roots in particular pieces of land to the newest citizens of multicultural Australia, many are reluctant to cede actual land or social privileges to Aborigines simply because they were 'there first' and then dis-placed. A common complaint is that Aborigines simply make up stories about ritual relationships to land and change them opportunistically to suit their purposes – a strange notion in the light of Aboriginal convictions about the unchanging nature of law as embodied in land.[24] Very often, however, this resistance rests on hearsay about history and Aboriginal behaviour, not on accurate information about historical atrocities and first-hand knowledge of Aboriginal people where they live.[25] Though relationships are never easy across such a wide cultural gulf, as a rule the racism that is never far below the surface of Australian life is fuelled by fear and ignorance. In the country towns of the outback, not to mention city slums like Redfern in Sydney, contact can be trau-

23. See the corresponding chapters by Vicky Balabanski, Brendan Byrne and Duncan Reid in Habel (ed.), *Readings*.
24. See Francesca Merlan, 'Do Places Appear?', in Charlesworth, Dussart and Morphy (eds), *Aboriginal Religions*, 116-129, and for the broader Pacific context J. D. May, 'Human Rights as Land Rights in the Pacific', *Pacifica* 6 (1993), 61-80.
25. Read, *Belonging*, has vividly illustrated this from contemporary poetry and historiography and interviews with young people who love the country where they grew up and ecological idealists who struggle to find an authentic relationship with the land.

matic because anger and aggression are always ready to erupt, and even among academics resentments can run deep.[26]

Land as 'place', then, is not primarily a physical but a mental possession: it is a cultural artefact.[27] Territoriality is an inherited trait, but the fashioning of 'land' into 'place' is a cultural achievement, albeit one that can be disturbed and destroyed by invasion and displacement.[28] Land law and land use are thus cultural variables, heavily reliant on memory but by the same token vulnerable to abuse and fragile in the face of envy and the desire to dispossess. Land is precious not only because it provides the basis for physical life, but because it sustains imaginative life.[29] Transformed by memory, it remains a presence in memory, exerting a primary influence on people's self-understanding. 'Ethnic' strife, therefore, is often conflict over land as life itself, not just as 'property', something Westerners in general and Christians in particular have found it difficult to grasp. In Aboriginal Australia, both 'the work of the world' and 'ritual business' establish relationships between people and 'country' and are expressions of responsibility for land and earth as one seamless sacred space.[30] Whereas in the Dreaming of Aboriginal

26. Aileen Moreton-Robinson, 'Tiddas talkin' up to the white woman: when Huggins et al. took on Bell', in Grossman (ed), *Blacklines*, 66-77, documents the acrimonious controversy between the outstanding scholar of women in Aboriginal Australia, Diane Bell, and her Aboriginal opponent Jackie Huggins, who in effect tells Bell to 'mind her own (whitefella) business' after Bell had raised the question of violence by black men against black women.

27. See the deep reflection by Br Andrew SSF, based on long experience as a psychologist in Papua New Guinea, 'Territoriality and Land Disputes', *Catalyst* 34/1 (2004), 57-83, 59, in which he places 'territoriality', 'the strong affinity of animals, including man, to a particular place', 60, in the context of genetic evolution.

28. Br Andrew, 'Territoriality', 70-71.

29. This important but often neglected point is stressed by Paul Collins, *God's Earth: Religion as if Matter Really Mattered* (Dublin: Gill and Macmillan, 1995); see my comments in J. D. May, 'Ecology: Our Newest Religion?', *Doctrine and Life* 46 (1996), 578-585, 580.

30. See Deborah Bird Rose, 'Sacred Site, Ancestral Clearing, and Environmental Ethics', in Graham Harvey (ed), *Readings in Indigenous Religions* (London and New York: Continuum, 2002), 319-342, making use of Jane Goodale, *To Sing with Pigs is Human: The Concept of Person in Papua New Guinea* (Seattle: University of Washington Press, 1995); on contemporary transformations of the Dreaming, see Lynne Hume, 'The

tradition the unity of human, animal and topographical reality is so close as to constitute an 'ontology of place' (Tony Swain), in Melanesia there is often an opposition or complementarity between forest and clearing, gathering and gardening, hunting and cultivating, though each involves elements of ritual and is controlled by spirits (*masalai*).

Transposing the 'subjectivity' of earth – what James Lovelock proposed to an astonished world by characterising the earth as an organism and calling her Gaia, or what prompts Charles Birch to posit the subjectivity of sub-atomic particles[31] – into the sacredness of land as 'place' is not easy to do without falling prey to mythologisation, romanticism or even eco-fascism. As a theologian, one is likely to be accused of neo-paganism or worse. Yet all the 'universalist' religions of transcendence pay for their gain in clarity and scope by losing something of that rootedness in earth and land which complements their absoluteness (*ab-solutum*, 'loosed' from bonds) by 'earthing' them again in the 'biocosmic' dimension of religion, what I like to call 'completing' religion by overcoming the dualism of transcendence and immanence.[32] When we think, for example, of the fundamental Buddhist conception of 'dependent co-origination' (*paticcasamuppâda*), the reciprocal determinacy of all constituents of existence without an external origin or cause, which radicalises the notion of an endless cycle of rebirth (*samsâra* – what a contemporary Buddhist has called 'cosmic recycling'), we seem to have a religious equivalent of some of the most sophisticated

---

Dreaming in Contemporary Aboriginal Australia', in Graham Harvey (ed), *Indigenous Religions: A Companion* (London and New York: Cassell, 2000), 125-138, and her innovative book *Ancestral Power: The Dreaming, Consciousness and Aboriginal Australians* (Melbourne: Melbourne University Press, 2002).

31. Deborah Bird Rose has tried to appropriate the 'Gaia hypothesis' to broaden and deepen our understanding of Aboriginal land claims, see her *Dingo Makes Us Human: Life and Land in an Aboriginal Australian Culture* (Cambridge: Cambridge University Press, 1992); see also Charles Birch and John B. Cobb, *The Liberation of Life: From the Cell to the Community* (Cambridge: Cambridge University Press, 1981), ch 1.

32. See the Conclusion to May, *Transcendence and Violence*, 148-158, and J. D. May, 'Cosmic Religion and Metacosmic Soteriology: The 'Completion' of Interreligious Dialogue by Primal Traditions', in Robert Crusz, Marshal Fernando and Asanga Tilakaratne (eds), *Encounters with the Word: Essays to Honour Aloysius Pieris SJ* (Colombo: Ecumenical Institute for Study and Dialogue, 2004), 351-364.

theories of contemporary science, not least those developed by ecology. It takes a greater mental effort at this stage of theological development for Christians to see something comparable in *perichoresis*, the mutual relatedness of persons which for us is at the very heart of both the 'immanent' and the 'economic' Trinity. The implication is surely that the earth in all its materiality and life in all its physicality are suffused with divine life. There are sufficient theological safeguards to prevent us from falling into pantheism or naturalism, so why not take up the challenge as, say, Jürgen Moltmann has done in his work on Spirit in creation? Just as the theme of earth and its relationship to land can be discovered as a countertext throughout the Hebrew and Christian Bibles, so too in theology, if we had the imagination to give it its due.[33] Far from jumping on an ecological bandwagon, this would represent a reappropriating of traditions that are already there and a reconceiving of theology in the light of them, with as yet unforeseen results for political economy and ethics, as John Cobb has presciently proposed.[34]

We have come a long way from Hamilton and County Mayo, Galilee and Palestine, but just as one never loses the link to the land one identifies with, however far away from it life's journey leads one, so the journey of faith and our reflection on it in theology need not tarry indefinitely in the rarefied atmosphere of abstraction but can lead us back to places which have formed us and to earth as our home, both now and in the new creation that awaits us. In a rapidly globalising world more and more of us are dis-placed and coping with exile; indeed, it has been said that 'all Australians can be described as exiles', but this is a dilemma white Australians share with Aboriginal people by now: pondering the implications of graffiti saying 'Abos go home', Digby Hannah continues: 'The journey out of exile is not simply a 'return journey'. It is a journey home. But where is

---

33. I tried to do this in a 'thought experiment' along these lines towards the end of an essay entitled 'Buddhists, Christians and Ecology', in Perry Schmidt-Leukel (ed), *Buddhism, Christianity and the Question of Creation: Karmic or Divine?* (Aldershot: Ashgate, 2006) 93-107.

34. See Herman E. Daly and John B. Cobb, *For the Common Good: Redirecting the Economy toward Community, the Environment and a Sustainable Future* (Boston: Beacon Press, 1989), and John B. Cobb, *Sustainability: Economy, Ecology and Justice* (Maryknoll: Orbis Books, 1992).

'home'?'[35] Brian Friel's play *The Home Place* captures this poignantly when the well-meaning master of a decaying Big House in Donegal, already threatened by the encroaching Land War of the 1870s, wistfully refers to 'the home place' – in distant Kent, whence his ancestors came in a doomed attempt to make Ireland their own. There are other ways of coping than pining for our 'home place' as a lost paradise or allowing fierce attachment to the fusion of locality and ethnicity to blind us to other solidarities – with refugees and strangers, with the earth in the larger sense of our common home.

The journey is not without risk, but neither is our present precarious situation of blind global destruction in the name of economic rationalism. Belonging somewhere, spiritually and physically, is not a bad place to start, because it gives us a stable point of reference from which to enlarge our sensibilities in order to embrace wider belongings in all their physical, moral and spiritual complexity.

---

35. Digby Hannah, 'Experience of Place in Australian Identity and Theology', *Pacifica* 17 (2004), 297-310, 305.

CHAPTER NINE

## An Other Name for G*d[1]

### Elisabeth Schüssler Fiorenza

This Festschrift for Seán Freyne is appropriately entitled 'Recognising the Margins'. I am encouraged by this title to offer an experimental essay in feminist[2] biblical the*logy that transgresses the boundaries of biblical scholarship to which Seán has so richly contributed. As his former colleague on the editorial board of the journal *Concilium*, I came to know his theological contributions to biblical studies which otherwise I may have missed since Seán is rightly known for his historical-exegetical work. Hence, I hope, that Seán will accept this somewhat unusual biblical-theological essay as a token of my appreciation for his work.

#### KANNON – AN OTHER NAME FOR G*D

Two experiences stand out in my mind when I reflect on my visit and conversations in Japan in April of 2004: these are the image of Divine Wisdom and that of Divine Kannon.[3] The ques-

---

1. Elisabeth Schüssler Fiorenza, *The Open House of Wisdom: Critical Feminist Theological Explorations* (translated into Japanese by Satoko Yamaguchi *et al*; Tokyo: Shinkyo Shuppansha, 2005).
2. For further elaboration of a critical feminist hermeneutics of liberation see my books *But She Said: Feminist Practices of Biblical Interpretation* (Boston: Beacon Press, 1992); *Sharing Her Word: Feminist Biblical Interpretation in Context* (Boston: Beacon Press, 1998); *Wisdom Ways. Introducing Feminist Biblical Interpretation* ( Maryknoll: Orbis Books, 2001).
3. It always had been my desire to visit Japan but I did not want to do so as a Western tourist. Hence, I was more than delighted when I received an invitation for a lecture tour from the centre of Feminist Theology and Ministry in Tokyo. Dr Satoko Yamaguchi, the co-director of the centre and a close friend and translator of my books *In Memory of Her* and *Bread not Stone* into Japanese was the driving 'work' force behind this invitation. I am deeply grateful to her for this opportunity to get to know a part of her great country and to meet so many Christian feminists in Japan. I never will be able to sufficiently express my grateful-

tions that I was asked most often after lectures pertained to my understanding of Divine Wisdom-Sophia, whereas the encounter with the cult of the Bodhisattva or Boatsu Kannon in her/his manifold Japanese manifestations mostly took place during sightseeing. Both experiences raise the question of feminist G*d[4]–language and imagery. They concern the central theological problem as to how to speak about G*d and how to image the Divine. Both the shape-shifting figure of Kannon – Kuan Yin, which means 'S/he who hears/ sees all,' and the oscillating biblical rhetoric of Wisdom-Sophia, I suggest, provide religious resources for the refashioning of Christian theology which calls for intercultural and interreligious collaboration.

I was delighted to discover in Japan again the manifold images and worship of the Buddhist Bodhisattva or 'Goddess of Mercy' or of 'Compassion and Wisdom', whom I had already previously encountered as Kuan Yin[5] during my visits to Hong Kong and Korea and who had become for me the manifestation of Divine Wisdom-Sophia in other world religions. Since Kannon is ubiquitous in Japan, celebrated in many different images, and has numerous places of worship, this divine-like figure, it is safe to assume, must have great impact also on the subconscious of Japanese Christians, although they might not be consciously aware of it. The lively interest of diverse audiences in the figure of Divine Wisdom-Sophia, I reasoned, therefore might be due to the cultural-religious context of Japan that knows of and celebrates a divine female figure.[6] However, this experience is prob-

---

ness to Satoko without whose initiative, labour, and care this rich and rewarding experience would not have been possible.
4. To the consternation of copy-editors I have changed my writing of G-d which I advocated in *But She Said: Feminist Practices of Biblical Interpretation* (Boston: Beacon Press, 1992) and *Discipleship of Equals: A Critical Feminist Ekklesialogy of Liberation* (New York: Crossroad, 1993) since such a spelling recalls for many Jewish feminists a fundamentalist orthodox mindset. My new way of spelling G*d seeks to indicate that G*d is 'in a religious sense unnamable', and belongs to the 'realm of the ineffable'. God is not G*d's 'proper name'; cf Rebecca S. Chopp, *The Power to Speak: Feminism, Language, God* (New York: Crossroad, 1989), 32.
5. Other forms of her name are Guan Yin, Kwan-yin, Kun lam Kwun Yam or Avalokiteshvara. Kwok Pu-lan, *Introducing Asian Feminist Theology* (Sheffield: Academic Press, 2000), 72f writes Guanyin.
6. Like that of Kannon so also the gender of the archaic Divinity Amaterasu whose name is gender neutral is debated. However

ably repressed and never made explicit in Christian circles. Hence, it was not surprising that no questions were asked publicly about the relation of Divine Wisdom and Divine Kannon.

The hesitancy of Japanese feminists to critically engage the figure of Kannon might be due to their minority status as tiny minority within a minority (not quite 1% ), or to the fear of being accused of syncretism and heresy[7] or be because Kannon is not much known among Christian feminists,[8] although her figure and cult resemble in many ways the figure and veneration of the Virgin Mary in Christianity. Consequently it is important to make explicit and explore here – even though shortly – the affinities between Divine Wisdom and the 'G*ddess' Kannon and their significance for Christian theology in general and feminist theology in particular. However, I am well aware of the danger that an uncritical appropriation of the feminine Bodhisattva figure could result in a strengthening of the internalised structures of domination. For, as Haruko Okano has argued,[9] the Bodhisattva figure as seen in the amalgamation of Japanese Buddhism with Shinto is seen as the embodiment of the feminine principle of motherhood, because one of the most important attributes of the Bodhisvatta figure is wisdom and compassion which is envisioned as motherly embrace.

---

Amaterasu is mostly understood as Goddess. For literature and discussion see Thomas Immoos, 'Das Land der mächtigen Frauen. Archaisches im Gegenwärtigen – Frauen in schamanistisch-kultischen Funktionen,' in Elisabeth Gössmann (ed), *Japan – ein Land der Frauen?* (München: Iudicium Verlag, 1991), 13-33. For Japanese as a much less gendered language than English and the significance of this observation for feminist Christian G*d-language see Satoko Yamaguchi, 'Father Image for G*d and Inclusive Language. A Reflection in Japan', in Fernando F. Segovia (ed), *Toward a New Heaven and a New Earth. Essays in Honor of Elisabeth Schüssler Fiorenza* ( Maryknoll: Orbis Books, 2003), 199-224

7. In the article cited above Satoko Yamaguchi on the one hand points to the fear of syncretism instilled by white elite Western male theology and on the other hand to the oppressive history of political intentional syncretism in Japan. See also her article 'The Invention of Traditions: the Case of Shintoism,' *In God's Image* 18 (1998), 40-46.

8. I want to thank Rev Claudia Genung-Yamamoto who went out of her way to find more information for me about her.

9. Haruko K. Okano, *Christliche Theologie im japanischen Kontext* (Frankfurt: IKO Verlag, 2002), 168.

Since the word 'theology' literally means 'speaking about G*d', it is important to critically look at how the feminist awareness of cultural-religious particularity and global responsibility provides a rich opportunity to strengthen the Christian language about the Divine. Further, the question of how to speak about the Divine is a problem that is common to all Christian feminists around the world. We all have to face on the one hand the problem of deeply ingrained and internalised patriarchal and kyriarchal[10] language about G*d, and on the other hand a symbolically and socially entrenched dualistic gender system in which the feminine always is supportive of and supplementary to the masculine. Although issues such as neocolonialism, militarism and sex-tourism[11] are important feminist challenges, according to Satoko Yamaguchi the issue of G*d-language and imagination,

> in our religious traditions is a crucial and urgent issue to which we cannot but give priority in this unjust world. It is because the kyriarchal religious imagination inscribes and naturalizes kyriarchal values into the deep subconscious levels of our minds.[12]

Hence, the problem of how to speak about G*d in female language and imagery without re-inscribing the cultural feminine as divine – a problem that is common to all religious feminists around the globe[13] – must be addressed differently in different

---

10. I have introduced the analytical terms kyriarchy / kyriocentrism which are derived from the Greek *kyrios = Emperor, Lord, Master, Father, Husband* in order to specify that in western societies the system of domination and exploitation is not just patriarchal but kyriarchal, that is it is not just defined by gender, but also by race, class, ethnicity, imperialism, and age. For an analysis of the Japanese form of kyriarchy see the important work of Hisako Kinukawa, *Wo/men and Jesus in Mark. A Japanese Feminist Perspective* (Maryknoll: Orbis Books, 1994), 15-22.
11. In response to Kwok Pu -lan, *Introducing Asian Feminist Theology* (Sheffield: Academic Press, 2000), 69, who argues that concern for inclusive language is a preoccupation of Western but not of Asian women.
12. Satoko Yamaguchi, 'Father Image of G*d and Inclusive Language', 224.
13. For Asia see Abraham Dulcie *et al* (eds), *Asian Wo/men Doing Theology: Report from Singapore Conference, November 20-29, 1987* (Hong Kong: Asian Women's Resource Center for Culture and Theology, 1989); *Faith Renewed: A Report on the First Asian Wo/men's Consultation on Interfaith Dialogue* (Hong Kong: Asian Women's Resource Center for Culture and Theology, 1989).

cultural-religious contexts. Both the ubiquitous figure of Divine
Kannon, or more formally Kanzeon,[14] in Asia, as well as the vac-
illating biblical figure of Divine Wisdom, at one and the same
time display the possibilities as well as the problematics of using
cultural-religious resources for Christian G*d-talk. On the one
hand both seem to be figures that transcend and destabilise the
dualistic kyriarchal, naturalised sex-gender system. On the
other hand they seem also to embody typically feminine features and the virtues of the Lady such as mercy, beauty, self-
sacrifice, and motherliness. Like Mary they therefore can be easily (miss)used to re-inscribe the oppressive cultural gender
image of the Lady that inculcates decorum, docility, self-sacri-
fice, humility, subordination, or wifely devotion as the Divine
Feminine.

Kuan Yin or Kannon, however, seems to subvert these gender inscriptions. S/he is first mentioned in chapter 25 of the
*Lotus Sutra*, a Sanskrit writing dated around the 1st century CE
in India. S/he is pictured as the Bodhisattva Avalokitesvara, a
male figure, who postponed his/her final release into Nirvana
in order to hear the cries of the suffering world and to pour out
his/her compassion over all those in need of salvation. However,
according to the text this Bodhisattva can take any form be it
male or female, monk or nun, animal or human responding to
the needs of the suffering person, the time and the place. To ask
for her/his gender is like asking for the gender of wind or water.

Kannon is envisioned in this chapter of the *Lotus Sutra* as:
Wisdom's sun, destroying darkness,
Subduer of woes, of storm, of fire,
Illuminator of the world!
Law of pity, thunder quivering,
Compassion wondrous as a great cloud,
Pouring spiritual rain like nectar
Quenching all the flames of distress.[15]

Beginning with the 5th century AD in China and with the
7th/8th century in Japan one can find statues of Avalokitesvara,

---

14. Cf Martin Palmer and Jay Ramsay with Man-Ho Kwok, *Kun Yin.
Myth and Prophecies of the Chinese Goddess of Compassion* (San Francisco:
Thorsons, 1995). See also Ulrich Pauly, *Kannon. Wandel einer Mittler-
gestalt* (München: iudicium, 2003).
15. Martin Palmer and Jay Ramsay with Man-Ho Kwok, *Kun Yin. Myth
and Prophecies of the Chinese Goddess of Compassion*, 5

whose name was translated into Chinese as Kuan Shih Yin and
into Japanese as Kannon. In his/her earliest forms the Bodhisattva
of Mercy is depicted as male. Yet, by the end of the 8th century
Kuan Yin was portrayed as female and by the late 9th century
her cult was established. The cult of Kuan Yin grew, however,
not in the heartland of historic China but on the northwest borders from where it spread across China and to Japan. It is theo-
rised that her cult grew out of the ensuing rivalry between
Taoism and Buddhism:

> Buddhism is a male-dominated faith. At this time it lacked a
> divine feminine aspect. In the wider world of Chinese belief
> devotion to the Queen Mother of the West and other power-
> ful creator or local female deities had been taken over by the
> resurgent forms of shamanism, namely popular Taoism and
> especially the Mao Shan sect of Taoism, whose central scrip-
> tures were, interestingly enough, revealed to them by the
> spirit of a woman shaman, who it was believed had become
> an immortal.[16]

Around the same time Christianity in its Nestorian form arrived
on the scene in China (635 AD) and brought with it the figure of
the Madonna with child whose image in turn was patterned
after that of the Egyptian Goddess Isis and her divine child
Horus. Hence, it is safe to assume that the figure of Kuan Yin
and her cult probably was engendered by the confluence of the
traditions of Mary/Isis, the Great Mother of the West and other
female deities of old China with the predominantly male defined Avalokitesvara who was able to manifest her/himself in
different forms.

Bodhisattva Avalokitesvara-Kannon Boatsu arrived with
Buddhism in Japan first as a male figure. However, in the 9th
and 10th centuries Japanese travellers probably brought from
China female Kuan Yin statues. In Japan Kannon, like in China
Kuan Yin, crosses religious boundaries since she is found in
both Buddhist and Shinto temples. Most characteristic of
Kannon in Japan is the tradition that she has had thirty-three
major manifestations of whom the majority are female while
some are in the form of creatures such as a snake, a winged bird,
a horse or a dragon. Whereas in China these manifestations are

---

16. Martin Palmer and Jay Ramsay with Man-Ho Kwok, *Kun Yin. Myth
and Prophecies of the Chinese Goddess of Compassion*, 17.

seen as more symbolic, in Japan they are more understood as incarnational.

Kuan Yin has many manifestations and names. The most widespread image is that of the *White Clad Kuan Yin/Kannon*, the image of serene beauty, purity and compassion. A variation of it is Kuan Yin as a Child-bearer which resembles the figure of the Madonna. *The Willow Branch Kuan Yin/Kannon* is characterised by the willow, known for its ability to bend without breaking and its magical powers to cast out demons and to make contact with the spirit world. Kuan Yin/Kannon is also pictured as the protector of all creatures and of all life and her devotees are often practising vegetarians. The Kuan Yin/Kannon of the Southern Ocean has absorbed all the ancient sea goddesses and is the protector of fisher folk. *The Warrior or Armed Kuan Yin* is the protector in the struggle against evil demons and the forces of ignorance.

Finally, the *Thousand-Armed, Thousand-Eyed Kuan Yin/Kannon* embodies the all-embracing compassion and ability of Kannon to see the suffering of all. Whereas in China there is a three-headed Kuan Yin, in Japan Kannon is often eleven-headed, symbolising her ability to look stern and gentle over all parts and regions of the world simultaneously. Because of the G*ddess Kannon's ability to reveal herself in different manifestations and to be symbolised as both male and female and at one and the same time as neither male nor female, her tradition provides language and imagery that can be used by Christian feminist theology to express that G*d transcends gender, race, and class, that s/he is neither male nor female as well as both male and female and much more. The figure of Kannon with her many different, often grotesque manifestations and alternating gender incarnation thus fashions a discourse that does not define identity in essentialist feminine or masculine terms but at the same time sees the female body and feminine values as divine. A similar dynamics can be detected in the biblical Divine Wisdom rhetoric.

## WISDOM-SOPHIA AN OTHER NAME FOR G*D

The lively interest of many Christian feminists in Divine Wisdom-Sophia is probably due to the fact that Divine Sophia-Wisdom is not much known and worshipped in malestream Christianity but that she has nevertheless a foothold in the

Christian scriptures. While the biblical wisdom writings are part of the Catholic canon of holy scripture, they are for the most part absent from the Protestant canon. Although Catholics may have heard about Divine Wisdom, both Protestant and Catholic audiences are generally unfamiliar with this biblical divine image. It has been feminist theology that in the past thirty years or so has rediscovered the significance of Divine Wisdom-Sophia. Although biblical scholarship has pointed to the importance of the wisdom traditions for quite some time, it has been feminist theology and liturgy that have made Divine Wisdom present and recognisable again among the people of G*d.

In the past two decades feminists have rediscovered and recreated the submerged traditions of Divine Wisdom in all their splendour and possibilities. Feminist theologians have discovered anew the creativity of Wisdom and have searched for her presence in the spaces 'in-between,' the blank spaces between the words of the Bible. They have sought 'to hear Wisdom into speech,' to use the expression coined by Nelle Morton, one of the first feminist theologians and teachers of Wisdom, who recognised that 'Wisdom is feminist and suggests an existence earlier than Word.'[17]

In the Hebrew Bible, 'Spirit (*Ruach*)'-'Presence (*Shekhinah*)'-'Wisdom (*Chokmah*)' are all three grammatically feminine terms. They refer to very similar female figurations in the Hebrew Bible[18] who express G*d's saving presence in the world. They signify that aspect of the Divine which is involved in the affairs of humanity and creation:

> For within Her is a spirit intelligent, holy, unique, manifold, subtle,
> Active, incisive, unsullied, lucid, invulnerable, benevolent, sharp,
> Irresistible, beneficent, loving humans, steadfast, dependable, unperturbed,
> Almighty, all-surveying, penetrating all intelligent, pure and most subtle spirit.
> For Wisdom is quicker to move than any motion;

---

17. Nelle Morton, *The Journey is Home* (Boston: Beacon Press, 1985), 175.
18. I use Hebrew Bible instead of Old Testament and Christian Testament instead of New Testament because Old and New Testament are Christian expressions that announce the superiority of Christianity over Judaism.

She is so pure, she pervades and permeates all things.
She is a breath of the power of G*d, pure emanation of divine
glory.
Hence nothing impure can find a way into her ...
Although alone, she can do all; herself unchanging, she makes
all things new.
In each generation she passes into holy souls,
She makes them friends of G*d and prophets;
For G*d loves only the one who lives with Wisdom.
She is indeed more splendid than the sun, she outshines all
the constellations;
Compared with light, she takes first place, for light must
yield to night,
But over Wisdom evil can never triumph.
(Wis 7:22-25, 27-30)[19]

Whereas traditional malestream theology has focused on the
Spirit, who is in Latin grammatically masculine (he) and in
Greek grammatically neuter (it), Christian feminist theology
centres around Divine Wisdom-Sophia, while Jewish feminists
in turn have rediscovered a spirituality of *Shekhinah* because she
plays a significant part in some Jewish traditions. Christian, especially Catholic feminists, have elaborated the female figure of
divine Wisdom (which in Greek is called *Sophia* and in Latin
*Sapientia*). Several books of the Bible speak about her, some of
which, however, are not found at all or only in an appendix in
Protestant versions of the Bible.[20] Divine Wisdom-Sophia-
Sapientia plays a significant role in Greek Orthodox theology
but less so in modern Western Protestant theology.

In biblical as well as in contemporary religious discourses the

---

19. I am quoting from the text of the Revised Standard Version (RSV) of
the Bible but have changed masculine language for G*d and humans.

20. The following books that are called by Protestants 'apocryphal' or
'deuterocanonical' are usually printed in Protestant Bible editions in an
appendix placed after the Christian Testament. They are found in the
Roman Catholic, Greek, and Slavonic canon: Tobit, Judith, Wisdom of
Solomon, Ecclesiasticus, also called the Wisdom of Jesu Ben Sirach,
Baruch, 1 and 2 Maccabees, 3 Maccabees (only in Greek and Slavonic
Bibles), 4 Maccabees (only in an Appendix to Greek Bible), 1 Esdras (in
Greek Bible; = 2 Esdras in the Slavonic Bible), Prayer of Manasseh (in
Greek and Slavonic Bibles; as appendix in the Vulgate, the Latin transla-
tion of the Catholic Bible), Psalm 151 (following Psalm 150 in Greek
Bible), and additions to the books of Daniel and Esther.

word 'wisdom' has a double meaning. It can either refer to a quality of life and of a people and/or it can refer to a figuration of the Divine. Wisdom in both senses of the word is not just a characteristic of the biblical traditions but it is found in the imagination and writings of all known religions. It is trans-cultural, international and inter-religious. It is practical knowledge gained through experience and daily living as well as the contemplation of creation and human nature. Both word meanings, that of capability (wisdom) and that of female personification (Wisdom), are crucial for articulating a feminist Christian theology and global spirituality.

Wisdom in distinction to intelligence is not something with which a person is born. It only comes from living, from making mistakes and trying again and from listening to others who have made mistakes and tried to learn from them. It is a perception of wholeness that does not lose sight of particularity, relativity and the intricacies of relationships. Wisdom understands complexity and seeks integrity in relationships. It is usually seen as integrating the left and right brain in a union of logic and poetry, as bringing together self-awareness and self-esteem with the awareness and appreciation of the world and the other. Wisdom is neither a specialised discipline nor a discrete field of study. It is a radical democratic concept insofar as it does not require extensive schooling and formal education. Unschooled people can acquire wisdom and highly educated people might lack it.

Wisdom, however, is most fascinating to feminist theologians as a representation of the Divine in female 'Gestalt' or form. She is a Divine female figure who in extra-biblical traditions is represented by a variety of Goddesses and Goddess traditions. The biblical texts about Divine Wisdom-Chokmah-Sophia-Sapientia retain the subjugated knowledges and the submerged language of the G*ddess within Christian tradition, just as the figure of the Divine Shekhinah-Presence does within Judaism. Although the feminist scholarly search for the footprints of Divine Wisdom-Sophia in biblical writings encounters a host of historical-theological problems, it is nevertheless commonly accepted that the biblical image of Wisdom-Chokmah-Sophia-Sapientia has integrated G*ddess language and traditions.

Whereas the biblical wisdom literature generally has been seen as kyriocentric literature written by and for elite educated, propertied men, more recent feminist studies have argued that post-exilic wo/men in Israel and Hellenistic Jewish wo/men in Egypt have conceived of Divine Wisdom as prefigured in the language and image of Egyptian (Maat, Isis) or Greek (Athena or Dike) Goddesses. According to a very well known-prayer, all the different nations and people use divine titles derived from their own local mythologies when they call on the Goddess, Isis. They do so in the full knowledge that Isis is one, but encompasses all. Like the Goddess Isis, so Divine Wisdom is using the 'I am' proclamation style for announcing her universal message of salvation:

> Wisdom speaks her own praises, in the midst of people she glories in herself ...
> I have grown tall as a cedar in Lebanon, as a cypress on Mount Hermon;
> I have grown tall as a palm in Engedi, as the rose bushes of Jericho;
> As a fine olive in the plain, as a plane tree I have grown tall ...
> I am like a vine putting out graceful shoots,
> My blossoms bear the fruit of glory and wealth.
> Approach me, you who desire me, and take your fill of my fruits,
> For memories of me are sweeter than honey,
> Inheriting me is sweeter than the honeycomb.
> They who eat me will hunger for more
> They who drink me will thirst for more.
> (Sir 24:1, 13-14, 17-21)

Or consider this:

> I, Wisdom, am mistress of discretion, the inventor of lucidity of thought.
> Good advice and sound judgment belong to me, perception to me, strength to me.
> I hate pride and arrogance, wicked behaviour and lying mouth.
> I love those who love me, those who seek me eagerly shall find me.
> By me monarchs rule and princes issue just laws; by me rulers govern
> And the great impose justice on the world.
> With me are riches and honour, lasting wealth and justice.
> The fruit I give is better than gold, even the finest,

The return I make is better than pure silver.
I walk in the way of virtue, in the path of justice,
Enriching those who love me, filling their treasuries.
(Prov 8:12-21)

In the same way as the widespread Isis cult and mythology, so also the variegated wisdom discourses of post-exilic Palestinian sages elaborate the image and figure of Divine Chokmah-Sophia-Wisdom as the 'other name' of G*d. Her ways are ways of justice and well-being. In the figure of Chokmah-Sophia-Wisdom, ancient Jewish scriptures seek to hold together belief in the 'one' G*d of Israel and the language and metaphors of a female Divine being. Hence the texts struggle to subordinate Wisdom to YHWH and at the same time express her Divine character:

From everlasting I was firmly set,
From the beginning before earth came into being.
The deep was not, when I came into existence,
There were no springs to gush with water ...
When G*d fixed the heavens firm, I was there ...
When G*d assigned the sea its boundaries
– and the waters will not invade the shore –
When G*d laid down the foundations of the earth,
I was by G*d's side, a master craftswoman, delighting G*d day after day,
Ever at play in G*d's presence, at play everywhere in the world,
Delighting to be with the children of humanity.
(Prov 8:23-24, 27, 29-31)

Scholarship and texts about Divine Chokmah-Sophia-Wisdom have received intensive feminist attention because of the female gender of Chokmah-Sophia-Wisdom.[21] Feminists in the churches have translated the results of biblical scholarship on early Jewish and Christian wisdom discourses into the idiom of song, poem,

21. For the most recent discussion and literature see the contributions of Marie-Theres Wacker, 'Von Göttinnen, Müttern, und dem einzigen Gott. Zum Stand der feministisch-exegetischen Diskussion um die Göttin/nen im Alten Israel,' and Angelika Strotmann, 'Die Entdeckung der personifizierten Weisheit im Ersten Testament durch die feministische Theologie,' in Andreas Hölscher and Rainer Kampling (eds), *Die Tochter Gottes ist die Weisheit. Bibelauslegung durch Frauen* (Münster: LIT Verlag, 2003), 7-34,34-68.

story, art and ritual.[22] This practical and creative feminist attention to the divine female figure of Wisdom has brought the results of scholarship on biblical wisdom literature to public attention and has raised public objections.

For instance, in 1993 Protestant feminists sponsored a conference in Minneapolis that not only featured lectures on Divine
Wisdom-Sophia but also invoked and celebrated her in prayer
and liturgy. This Re-Imagining Conference was allegedly the
most controversial ecumenical event in decades. Conservatives
claimed that it challenged the very foundations of mainline
Protestantism in the USA. The reaction of the Christian Right to
this conference was so violent that one high-ranking woman lost
her church job and others have run into grave difficulties.[23] This
struggle indicates the significance and power of Divine
Chokhmah-Sophia-Sapientia-Wisdom for contemporary Christian self-understanding.

Some feminist theologians have raised serious historical and
theological objections against attempts at recovering the Wisdom-
Sophia discourses in order to valorise 'Lady Wisdom.'[24] They
have argued that feminists must reject the figure of Divine Lady
Wisdom as an elite male creation that serves both misogynist
and elitist interests. The fascination of feminist theologians with
Wisdom-Sophia is misplaced, they insist. Wisdom speculation is
at home in Israel's elite male circles and bespeaks their interests.
They also point to the possible theological dangers inherent in
such biblical language and imagination. The spirituality of the
Divine Feminine that extols the romantic ideal of the 'Lady' and
the 'Eternal Feminine' has a long ideological tradition in biblical
religions and is still pervasive in malestream and even some
feminist spirituality.

The Eternal Feminine or the Cult of True Womanhood which
I have dubbed the discourse of the 'White Lady' was developed
in tandem with Western colonisation and romanticism that celebrated Christian white elite European-American women/ladies

---

22. See e.g. Susan Cady/Marian Ronan/Hal Taussig, *Sophia> the Future
of Feminist Spirituality* (San Francisco: Harper & Row, 1986).
23. See Nancy J. Berneking and Pamela Carter Joern (eds), *Re-
Membering and Re-Imaging* (Cleveland: Pilgrim Press, 1995).
24. For this discussion and extensive documentation see my book *Jesus:
Miriam's Child and Sophia's Prophet. Critical Issues in Feminist Christology*
(New York: Continuum, 1994).

as paradigms of civilised motherhood and cultured woman-hood. This ideology has the function to legitimate both the exclusion of elite wo/men from positions of power in society and church and at the same time makes us colonial representatives who mediate Euro-American culture and civilisation to the so-called 'savages'.

A similar ideal for the Japanese Christian wo/man is for example articulated by the Japanese writer Junichi Natori:

> Mrs Hosokawa was a self-sacrificing wo/man whose chastity and affection for her husband was really unique. Her life was one of suffering but she lived solely for the faith ... When I read about her life, I was struck by admiration for her chastity, her self-sacrifice, her gentleness and her strong faith which was felt by anyone who came in contact with her ... her obedience to her husband's wishes are still remembered in the nations' memory as a perfect example of a model Japanese woman.[25]

However, it must not be overlooked that this image of the genteel femininity and sacrificing motherhood is a projection of elite, (western), educated gentlemen and clerics who stress the complementary nature of wo/men to that of men in order to maintain a special sphere and place for upper class 'cultured' ladies. This construct of Christian femininity does not have the liberation of every wo/man as its goal but seeks to release the repressed feminine in order to make men whole. Associated with this cult of the White Lady was and is a feminine spirituality of self-alienation, submission, service, self-abnegation, sentimentality, dependence, manipulating power, backbiting, powerlessness, beauty, body regimen, duplicity and helplessness – 'feminine' behaviours which are inculcated in and through cultural socialisation, spiritual direction, and secular 'ascetic' disciplines such as dieting and cosmetic surgery. In and through traditional biblical spirituality wo/men either internalise that they are not made in the Divine image because G*d is not She but He, Lord/Slave-Master/Father/Male (Greek *kyrios*). Or wo/men are told that if they fulfill their religious and cultural calling to supplement and complement the Divine Other, they

---

25. Junichi Natori, *The Life of Gracia Tama Hosokawa* (Tokyo: Hokuseido Press, 1955), 35. I owe this quote to Elisabeth Gössmann, 'Gracia Hosokawa Tama (1563-1600),' in Elisabeth Gössmann (ed), *Japan – Ein Land der Frauen?*, 56-80; 62, note12.

will embody the Divine Feminine. In both cases cultural and religious structures of self-alienation and domination are kept in
place in and through biblical wisdom spirituality and the theological articulation of the Divine as Father-Lord.

Feminist objections to the feminine valorisation of the biblical
wisdom tradition also point out that this tradition is permanently
suspect not only as an elite male tradition but also as one that, in
a dualistic fashion, plays the 'good' woman against the 'evil'
woman.[26] Such a misogynist tradition cannot be concerned with
justice at all. However, other scholars specialising in wisdom literature have rightly objected to such a negative evaluation of the
wisdom traditions.[27] They have pointed out not only that wisdom discourses are permeated with the teachings of justice,[28] but
also agree that in the first century, prophetic-apocalyptic and
sapiential (wisdom) traditions were intertwined, integrated and
changed. They espouse a cosmopolitan ethos that can respect
local particularities without giving up claims to universality.

In addition, the advocates of Divine Wisdom-Sophia argue
that the wisdom traditions had long been democratised and that
much of the sapiential traditions of the gospels reflect folk wisdom which very well could have been articulated by and for
wo/men. Finally, they point out that feminist exegetical-histori-
cal objections against the feminist regeneration of Divine
Chokmah-Sophia-Wisdom may also be due to different confessional locations and indebtedness of some feminist theology to
Neo-orthodox theology.[29]

---

26. However, in fairness to the Wisdom traditions it must be pointed
out that the prophetic or apocalyptic traditions are equally suspect be-
cause they are also permeated by kyriocentric bias.
27. See especially Silvia Schroer, 'Weise Frauen und Ratgeberinnen in
Israel: Vorbilder der personifizierten Chokma,' in Verena Wodtke (ed),
*Auf den Spuren der Weisheit: Sophia – Wegweiserin für ein neues Gottesbild*
(Freiburg: Herder, 1991), 9-23. Cf also Silvia Schroer, 'Die göttliche
Weisheit und der nachexilische Monotheismus,' in Marie-Theres
Wacker and Erich Zenger (eds), *Der eine Gott und die Göttin:
Gottesvorstellungen des biblischen Israel im Horizont feministischer Theologie*
(Freiburg Herder, 1991),151-183.
28. See also Claudia V. Camp, *Wisdom and the Feminine in the Book of
Proverbs* (BLS 14; Sheffield: Almond, 1985).
29. Cf Silvia Schroer, 'The Justice of Sophia: Biblical Wisdom Traditions
and Feminist Discourses, ' in Maria Pilar Aquino and Elisabeth
Schüssler Fiorenza, *In the Power of Wisdom* (London: SCM Press, 2000),
67-77.

Moreover, a closer look at the biblical Wisdom-Sophia traditions reveals that these traditions do not so much portray Divine Wisdom in terms of the Lady and the cultural Feminine. Wisdom is a cosmic figure delighting in the dance of creation, a 'master' crafts wo/man and teacher of justice. She is a leader of her people and accompanies them on their way through history. Very unladylike she raises her voice in public places and calls everyone who would hear her. She transgresses boundaries, celebrates life, and nourishes those who will become her friends. Her cosmic house is without walls and her table is set for all.

Furthermore, biblical discourses on Divine Wisdom are still significant today not only because they are a rich resource of female language for G*d but also because they provide a framework for developing a feminist ecological and interreligious Christian theology of creation and a biblical spirituality of nourishment and struggle. Moreover, they embody a religious ethos that is not exclusive of other religious visions but can be understood as a part of them, since wisdom/Wisdom is celebrated in all of them. The earliest Sophia-traditions that still can be traced in the margins of early Christian works intimate a perspective that combines Jewish prophetic, wisdom and *basileia* (which means the political realm of G*d or G*d's vision of a transformed creation and world) traditions as central to a political, open-ended and cosmopolitan religious vision of struggle and well-being for everyone. In short, biblical wisdom spirituality is a spirituality of roads and journeys, public places and open borders, nourishment and celebration. It seeks for sustenance in the struggles for justice and cultivates creation and life in fullness.

In sum: Divine Wisdom-Sophia, the Presence of G*d the Creator and Liberator, is not exclusive of other religious traditions but is at work among all peoples, cultures, and religions. She teaches justice, prudence and well-being. She is present as the crafty trickster, the guide of the people, and the wise woman of the ancients and indigenous peoples. She embraces creation in its living beauty and manifold variety and delights in its wonders. Divine Wisdom encompasses and sustains everything and every one. While in its worship practices, the Eastern Orthodox Christian tradition has always retained the memory of her as Hagia Sophia, she has been virtually forgotten in Western christocentric theology. In Catholicism traces of her splendour have been reflected in Mary, but mariology has relegated Divine

Wisdom-Sophia to a subordinated feminine figure or completely erased her from the religious consciousness of the people. At the same time it has made her a 'second class citizen' in the symbolic space of the Divine.

## NAMING G*D

It is clear that in all cultures and religions the desire and longing for a female deity among wo/men is strong and has found many different expressions. I have focused here on two such Divine female figures: Kuan Yin-Kannon and Wisdom-Sophia. However, I have also argued that feminist theology cannot simply and un-critically take over the cultural feminine language about Kuan-Yin-Kannon or Wisdom-Sophia if we do not want to re-inscribe into the Divine the the kyriarchal sex-gender system[30] that sus-tains wo/men's second class citizenship in society and religion. Feminist theology must question the cultural and religious femi-nine while at the same time insisting that wo/men are the image of G*d and as such can represent and embody the Divine.

Theological discourses on G*d always have named the Divine in interaction with their respective societies. The imperial structures of Rome and of medieval feudal society celebrated G*d, the Father, as an all-powerful king and omniscient ruler of the universe.[31] The absolute power of G*d legitimated the power of princes and overlords, of bishops and popes, of fathers and males. According to Jürgen Moltmann, monotheistic monar-chism not only justified the power of a few over the many but also provided a unifying ideology for such imperial power.

> One God – one Logos – one humanity, and in the Roman
> Empire it was bound to be seen as a persuasive solution for
> any problems of a multi-national, multi-religious society.

30. Cf Elisabeth Schüssler Fiorenza, 'Gender', in R. Wuthnow (ed), *The Encyclopedia of Politics and Religion* (Washington, DC: Congressional Quarterly Books, 1998), 290–94

31. Brian Wren, *What Language Shall I Borrow? God-Talk in Worship: A Male Response to Feminist Theology* (New York: Crossroad, 1989), 119, has argued that the metaphorical system which undergirds Christian imag-ination, worship, prayer, and theology is that of 'KINGAFAP – the King-God-Almighty-Father-All-Powerful-Protector.' In this frame of reference G*d is worshipped as a powerful king enthroned in splen-dour who receives homage and atonement for offences against his majesty, rules by word of command, and legitimates the cosmic kyriar-chal order.

The universal ruler in Rome had only to be the image and correspondence of the universal ruler in heaven.[32]

Among others, Susan Brooks Thistlethwaite has pointed out that a radical break in this monotheistic-monarchic conceptualisation of divinity occurred in the Renaissance and the Reformation but that the emphasis on authoritative unity nevertheless continued.

> ... that watershed period is characterized by the modern emphasis on God as Absolute Subject ... Thus the experiencing self is the starting point for modern white, Western theological reflection. But the emphasis on unity remains. Subject can only be considered an identical self, acting in different ways. This is the modern bourgeois concept of personality.[33]

It is against this absolutised and universalised subject of modernity that the postmodern critique of the subject is advanced. Postmodern theory insists that to posit an I or a subject forecloses the investigation into its production. How then does one engage in the naming of G*d as 'Absolute Subject' without ruling out in advance a critical reflection on the socio-political rules and cultural practices 'that govern the invocation of that subject and regulate its agency?'[34] How does one speak of G*d without reducing the Divine to a being like other beings, to a symbol for the dominant cultural ethos, or to an object like other objects?

While believers may share the conviction that G*d is a reality beyond Being and claim that they have experienced this reality, just like non-believers they have no adequate language to express that conviction. To say that G*d is a 'Being beyond Being' linguistically concedes this lack of a proper name while at the same time occluding that no adequate language untainted by socio-political theoretical frameworks and interests can be had. Hence, it is the task of *the*legein* – in the original sense of the word – to subject all language about G*d to a radical critical ethics of naming.

If language and images for G*d say more about those who

32. Jürgen Moltmann, *The Trinity and the Kingdom* (San Francisco: Harper & Row, 1981), 129ff.

33. Susan Thistlethwaite, *Sex, Race, and God. Christian Feminism in Black and White* (New York: Crossroad, 1989), 122.

34. Judith Butler, *Gender Trouble. Feminism and the Subversion of Identity* (New York: Routledge, 1990),144.

use them and the society and church in which they live and en-
vision the Divine than about Divinity itself, then thea/o-logy's
proper task is to engage in a persistent critical analysis of all discourses about G*d. The task of *the*legein* in the proper sense is
best positioned, I argue, not in the sphere of metaphysics and
ontology but in that of ethics and communicative praxis. To say
that all language about G*d and all knowledge of the Divine is
rhetorical means to assert that all discourses about the Divine
are articulated in specific socio-political situations, by particular
people, with certain interests in mind, and for a certain audience
with whom they share cultural codes and religious traditions.
G*d-discourses are not just rhetorical, i.e. persuasive address,
but they are also ideological communication enmeshed in
power relations Accordingly, the*logy must focus on the rhetor-
icality of all language about G*d, whether it pertains to her
place, his reign, or its name.

Rhetorical analysis assumes that language not just produces
meaning but also affects reality.[35] Moreover, all communication
circulates between a speaker and an audience who are both historically and socially determined. For that reason, feminist
rhetorical analysis must first of all investigate the structures of
domination that have produced the exclusion and marginalisation of wo/men from the Divine. In other words: emancipatory-
rhetorical analysis is not so much interested in exploring the
modern question as to whether G*d exists but the liberation
theological question as to how philosophers or theologians
speak about the transcendent Divine and what kind of G*d believers confess and proclaim. Do we proclaim a G*d of injustice
and dehumanisation or a G*d of liberation and well-being, a G*d
of domination or of salvation? Do we speak about a G*d who
sides with the poor who are wo/men and children dependent
on wo/men, or about one who is aligned with those who wield
oppressive power?

What is G*d's proper name if we all name G*d not only differently but also often in pernicious and violent ways? How is
our language about the Divine shaped by and in turn shapes the
social location of our G*d-talk? Who is the subject of such nam-

---

35. See Jane Tompkins, 'The Reader in History: The Changing Shape of
Literary Response,' in *Reader-Response Criticism: From Formalism to
Poststructuralism* (Baltimore: The John Hopkins University Press, 1980),
201-232.

ing and in whose interest does it take place? These questions are intensified by the experience of multiculturalism and growing inter-religious awareness.

For these reasons feminist G*d-talk must carefully avoid surrendering to a 'romantic' notion of femininity[36] which re-inscribes the cultural kyriocentric gender binary that either devalues women and femininity or idealises them as representing superior transcendent and salvific qualities. In extolling the Divine Feminine in the figure of Wisdom-Sophia or of KuanYin-Kannon, such a feminist binary-gender approach cannot but re-inscribe cultural kyriarchal systems of domination in theological terms, insofar as it divinises the hegemonic gender ideology of cultural femininity that is shaped after the image and likeness of the 'White Lady'. Whenever thea/o-logy is positioned within a framework of essential gender dualism, it cannot but reproduce this ideological frame.[37]

In order to avoid this pitfall, I have argued, one must explicitly read against the grain of the cultural feminine framework and shift the discussion of a divine female figure from the ontological-metaphysical level to a linguistic symbolic rhetorical level of reflection. Such a shift is justified insofar as divine female as well as divine father language are not unified theological discourses about the essence and true being of G*d, but rather rhetorical discourses embodying a variegated 'reflective mythology'.[38] The grammatically masculine language adopted for instance by ancient wisdom discourses and modern biblical interpretation has a difficult time to speak adequately of Divine Wisdom in the 'preconstructed' frame of Jewish and Christian kyriocentric i.e. Lord, Slave-Master, Father centred monotheism. Insofar as this language struggles to avoid turning Divine Wisdom into a sec-

---

36. See the roundtable discussion Catherine Madsen *et al*, 'If God is God. She Is Not Nice,' *Journal of Feminist Studies in Religion* 5/1 (1989), 103-118.

37. See e.g. Christa Mulack, *Jesus der Gesalbte der Frauen* (Stuttgart: Kreuz Verlag, 1987).

38. For this expression see my article 'Wisdom Mythology and the Christological Hymns of the New Testament', in Robert L. Wilken (ed), *Aspects of Wisdom in Judaism and Early Christianity* (Notre Dame: Notre Dame, 1975), 17-42. I became fascinated with the wisdom tradition in the Christian Testament in the context of the 1973 Rosenstil seminar on Wisdom in Early Judaism and Christianity sponsored by the Department of Theology at the University of Notre Dame.

ond feminine deity who is subordinate to the masculine deity, it also struggles against the theological reification of monotheism in terms of western cultural elite male hegemony.

When speaking about the biblical G*d, scriptural discourses and Christian liturgies as well as malestream theologies have mostly succumbed to this danger insofar as they have used predominantly masculine language, metaphors and images for speaking of the Divine. Biblical interpretation re-inscribes such kyriocentric G*d language as G*d-given or divinely revealed when it understands female images for G*d in metaphorical terms but understands the language about G*d, the Father, King, and Lord, as descriptive theological language that adequately expresses G*d's nature and being.

In short, I argue, it is neither patriarchal God nor matriarchal Goddess, neither the Masculine nor the Feminine, neither Divine Fatherhood nor complementary Motherhood that redeems and saves. Rather all kyriarchal symbols – masculinity and femininity, pale and dark skin, domination and subordination, wealth and exploitation, nationalism and colonialism – must be carefully tested out in an ongoing feminist ideology critique. Such a feminist ideology critique takes its cues neither from established dogmatics nor from cultural systems of domination. Rather it attempts to name and to reflect critically on the negative as well as on the positive G*d experiences of wo/men. For doing so, it needs to sustain a permanent critical self-reflexivity which is able to reject language about G*d that promotes hierarchical masculinity or an ideal feminine and thereby projects the cultural sex-gender system into heaven.

At the same time feminist theology must continue to protest against naming the heavenly world and the Divine in purely masculine language and kyriarchal images that are exclusive of wo/men. In order to sustain such a persistent critical impetus thea/o-logical reflection, I argue, must transform the traditional rules for speaking about G*d in ontological-metaphysical terms rather than simply complement or replace male G*d language with female/feminine language. It further needs to develop them into a critical method that understands these traditional rules for speaking about G*d as rhetorical strategies of affirmation, negation, proliferation and transformation.

Although G*d is 'beyond' gender, race, class, age, or colonial oppression, her revelatory presence can be experienced in the midst of the struggles against dehumanisation and injustice. Hence, the Divine must be re-named again and again in and through such experiences of struggling for the change and transformation of oppressive structures and dehumanising ideologies. G*d is to be named as active power of justice and wellbeing in our midst. It is s/he who accompanies us in our struggles against injustice and for liberation, just as s/he has accompanied the Israelites on their desert journey from slavery to freedom.[39]

---

39. See Wis 10:1-21.

# CHAPTER TEN

## The Future of Christianity in Europe

### Werner G. Jeanrond

The Tsunami in South-East Asia on St Stephen's Day 2004 motivated many people in Europe to go to church. Anybody participating in the various national mourning services or following
the broadcasts of these services on television might therefore be
inclined to conclude that Christian faith and worship in Europe
are in excellent condition just now. In the shadow of this tragic
event national governments, presidents and royalty, church
leaders and impressive crowds gathered in many churches
throughout Europe in order to relate to God, to each other, and
in solidarity with all the victims of this catastrophe in Asia and
beyond. Of course, the fact that many Western tourists were
killed by the Tsunami brought this tragedy closely home to a
number of European countries. A sense of 'It could have been
me' helped many Europeans to reflect anew upon their own
mortality, vulnerability and possible relatedness to a power
higher than nature and science. In times of crisis, God tends to
become a closer friend again. Although it is quite possible that
Christian practice in Europe may have been affected more permanently by this tragedy, it would appear premature to specul-
ate about a sudden revival of Christian faith in Europe.

The death and funeral of Pope John Paul II and the election of
Pope Benedict XVI in April 2005 caused huge crowds to gather
in Rome and worldwide around television screens. Especially
the great number of youth present on St Peter's Square at these
occasions was interpreted by some commentators as yet another
sign of a revival of Christian faith in Europe. However, no indications have emerged that ordinary parish life in Europe has
been permanently affected or renewed as a result of these papal
events in Rome.

If we wish to consider the future of Christianity in Europe beyond the mere moment we must reflect in greater depth on the
larger patterns and contexts of Christian belief and praxis in the

Europe of today. There are two immediate challenges to European Christianity at present. First, there is the uncertain role of Christianity in the process of European integration. Is Christian faith to deliver the glue that guarantees future European cohesion? Secondly, there is the question of the nature of the relationship between Christianity and the increasing religious pluralism within Europe – especially in view of the growth of Islam in Europe.

In this article, I shall first discuss current challenges to Christianity in Europe. Secondly, I shall reflect upon the relationship between religion, politics and ethics in an integrating Europe. And thirdly, I shall suggest a reconsideration of the potential of Christian love for the development of a Christian voice in Europe.

### I CURRENT CHALLENGES TO CHRISTIANITY IN EUROPE

For some years there has been a debate in Europe on the soul of Europe. A number of politicians, among them the former head of the European Commission Romano Prodi, have called for a gathering of spiritual energies in Europe. In order to discuss this search for Europe's soul in some more depth, I wish to illustrate the role of religion in European integration politics by focusing on two developments, namely the debate on the place of religion in the proposed Constitution for the European Union and the debate on religion that arose in 2004 around the composition of the latest European Commission.

With regard to the proposed Constitution for the European Union a number of Christian forces, especially from Roman Catholic countries, had been lobbying for an explicit reference to God in the opening paragraphs of this document. Their hope was that such a reference would safeguard a clear emphasis on those religious values that have been underlying and inspiring the process of European integration ever since its beginnings after the Second World War. However, a combination of Northern European states, France and Belgium have rejected such a reference and instead favoured the very general mentioning of the significance of the cultural, religious and humanist heritage of Europe as the basis for the development of universal values.[1] Hence, neither God nor Jesus Christ is named in the

---

1. See the opening words of the constitution *Traité établissant une constitution pour l'Europe* (Brussels, 2004), 3 .

proposed European constitution. The constitutional framework for the future Europe has been kept neutral with respect to religion. This is not to say that religion has not been or will no longer be a force to be reckoned with in Europe. Rather this means that the constitutional process of European integration is considered to be neutral with respect to any specific religious tradition.

The heated debate in 2004 on the suitability of some of the politicians nominated for the new European Commission has further illustrated the uneasiness about the public role of religion in the process of European integration. The Roman Catholic philosopher Rocco Buttiglione, who was the nominee of the Italian government for the new European Commission and who was proposed by José Manuel Barroso, then incumbent President of the Commission, to head the portfolio for justice, freedom and security, had made some remarks on the sinfulness of homosexual acts and the domestic role of women that were interpreted as compromising for such an office holder. Not only in Sweden, where issues of social justice are treated with high intensity, Buttiglione's remarks were ruled out of order and the candidate was rejected as unsuitable for the proposed office. The European Parliament subsequently forced Barroso to drop Buttiglione from his list and to reorganise his proposed Commission in order to keep it free from explicit religious particularity.

What was Buttiglione's crime? Surely not that he was known to be a Roman Catholic and not that he personally held particular religious convictions. In that respect he is not unique in European politics. But as a public representative of the European Union he was judged unable to distinguish sufficiently between his personal religious convictions and European social politics, although he himself had insisted that his religious convictions would not conflict with his tenure of such a high office. European integration, it was argued, was not a matter of religious conviction, but of legal concord. However one evaluates this episode, one could draw the conclusion that it further helped to clarify that the project of European integration is first of all to be understood in terms of a legally defined project, and not in terms of a religiously defined project. The European Union constitutes a community of law, and not a community of views of life.

Both of these examples strengthen the impression that Europe does not have such a thing as a soul. Rather Europe offers a constitutional space to all of its citizens and legal protection for the development of their respective religious or humanist convictions.

This is of great significance for the perhaps most dramatic challenge to Christian faith in Europe, namely the permanent establishment and flourishing of Islam in Europe. The arrival of Islam in Europe has as such nothing to do with the desire of the Turkish State to join the European Union; negotiations to that effect have already started. But the combination of both the Turkish intention to join the process of European integration and the existence and continuing development of large numbers of Muslim communities in many European societies demonstrates the challenge to any aspiration of defining the Europe of today in predominantly Christian terms. Hence, the future of Christianity in Europe will be a future characterised by religious plurality. Jews, Christians, Muslims and an increasing number of other religious movements and traditions will together shape the religious fabric of an integrated Europe. The religious future of Europe is thus radically pluralistic. The myth of a Christian Europe has been exposed as a dangerous project. However, this is not to say that this myth is no longer a powerful force in European culture and politics.

In the perception of many, Europe has been a Christian continent during the greater part of the last two thousand years. In spite of the fragmentation of the Christian church into a Western and an Eastern church, in spite of the separation of the Western church into Catholic and Protestant denominations, in spite of the secularisation process following the Enlightenment critique of church and religion, many continue to think of Europe in terms of a common Christian heritage.

There can be no doubt that Christianity has been one of the major ingredients in the European concern for a distinct identity over against other traditions. The myth of a Christian Europe has been put forward against Islam, against Judaism, against Communism, against secularism, in short against all movements deemed to be 'other' and therefore potentially dangerous. In that sense Christianity has been employed by defenders of an integrated Europe in order to give the European project a strong internal identity. At times, this myth has suited church leaders, at times it has suited the political rulers of Europe.[2]

However, Christianity has not always had this function of providing internal coherence to various European unification projects. Rather, when the Christian faith emerged within the Roman Empire, it was at first experienced as a dividing force. The Roman authorities acted against the spread of the Christian faith because of the danger it was considered to present to the social coherence of Roman society. By approaching and offering its religious options to individual persons, Christian faith had split families and households. Christians were seen to be dubious citizens; their allegiance was oriented towards another realm. Their monotheistic faith challenged the order and cohesion of the Roman state. They were politically dangerous.[3]

Only after the Roman emperors following Constantine found it useful to adopt the Christian religion as a state ideology did Christianity assume the role of a culturally and politically unifying factor. One kingdom, one religion and one people were the framework into which Christianity was integrated from now on. Since the collapse of the West Roman Empire, Christianity performed this service of religious harmonisation in changing parts of Europe. A number of Western European rulers, such as Charlemagne, Charles V, Gustav Vasa in Sweden, Henry VIII in England and others, found the Christian missionary project congenial for their political purposes: Christianity defended mission both *ad extra*, in the crusades and the religious wars against either the infidel or opposing Christian trends and denominations, and *ad intra*, in both the fight against all forms of deviation in terms of religious orientation and the development of an explicitly hostile attitude towards Jews, Muslims and travelling people.

The foundation myth of a Christian Europe not only survived the different fragmentations of the church since 1054 and 1517, but benefited enormously from them. Reformation and Counter-Reformation only increased the drive for a large scale

---

2. See Werner G. Jeanrond, 'European Perspectives on Ethics and Religion', in Göran Bexell and Dan-Erik Andersson (eds), *Universal Ethics: Perspectives and Proposals from Scandinavian Scholars* (The Hague: Martinus Nijhoff, 2002), 129-139.
3. Cf Norbert Brox, *Kirchengeschichte des Altertums* (2nd ed; Düsseldorf: Patmos, 1986), 44.

Christianisation of Europe. Moreover, until 1917 the foundation myth worked even in Eastern Europe where Moscow considered itself to be the legitimate heir to the first and second Rome, i.e. Rome and Constantinople, and employed Orthodox Christianity in order to support its own colonial system in Siberia and elsewhere. Recent events in the Ukraine have exposed the continued clash between different versions of the myth of a Christian Europe.

In 1799 both the theologian and philosopher Friedrich Schleiermacher (1768-1834) and the Romantic writer Novalis [Friedrich von Hardenberg] (1772-1801) defended the vocation of Christianity to be the highest religion on earth. In his famous *Speeches on Religion*, Schleiermacher attempted to demonstrate the superiority of Christian religion over all other religious traditions.[4] Novalis applied the Christian vocation in particular to Europe: 'Only religion is capable of awakening Europe and of offering security to the peoples, and of visibly installing Christianity with new splendour on earth to its traditional, peace-making office.'[5] Moreover: 'The other parts of the world are waiting for Europe's reconciliation and resurrection in order to join [Europe] and to become fellow citizens in the kingdom of heaven.'[6] Christianity, Novalis argued, must form a visible church without regard to national boundaries. The universal vocation of Christianity thus means that it will sooner or later bypass all other religions on earth. Novalis considered religion to be necessary for Europe: 'Where there are no gods, only demons rule.'[7] And, like Schleiermacher, he quickly identified Christianity as the one true religion.

A few years later, in 1815, the Holy Alliance concluded the Congress of Vienna by grounding the alliance of European nations on the Christian concept of the indivisible Trinity's name. Orthodox Russia, Protestant Prussia and Roman Catholic Austria considered themselves to be members of one and the

---

4. Friedrich Schleiermacher, *On Religion: Speeches to Its Cultured Despisers* [1799], trs Richard Crouter (Cambridge: Cambridge University Press, 1988), 189-223.

5. Novalis, 'Die Christenheit oder Europa' [1799], in *Monolog, Die Lehrlinge zu Sais et al.* (Rowohlts Klassiker der Literatur und Wissenschaft: Deutsche Literatur, Bd. 11; Reinbek bei Hamburg: Rowohlt, 1963), 35-52, here 50 (my translation).

6. *Ibid.*, 51 (my translation).

7. *Ibid.*, 48 (my translation).

same nation and agreed to promote *fraternité* – though not *liberté* and *égalité*. Hence, their universal project, to which they also invited the ruler of Britain, was firmly grounded on the principles of Christian religion: to build one single family of all the Christian peoples and through such action under the Almighty's providence and protection work for their happiness, security, the blessings of peace and eternally indissoluble brotherliness. Christian conviction here formed the ground rules for international contact, co-operation and relationship.

Both Novalis' essay and the self-understanding of the Christian rulers (against Napoleon and the French Revolution) appeal to the integrationist power of Christianity to help build a Christian Europe. The price of such an integrationist Christian Europe has, of course, been the exclusion of others, of other religions, of other interpretations of Christianity, and of secularised forces as they became visible during and after the French Revolution. As we all know today, the project of enforced Christian harmony and uniformity across Europe has proven to be a costly project for all those *others*. Moreover, this project attempted to lock the faithful into a monist system of one ruler, one religion and one people, a system which in its secularised form even inspired Hitler's political vision for Germany and beyond.

Although nostalgia for a monist Christian Europe still moves some Europeans, the majority of people in Europe recognises that today Europe is a pluralist area even in religious terms. There is a great diversity within Christianity, even within the different Christian denominations. In spite of the Nazi attempt to 'free Europe from Jews', Europe again has a number of lively Jewish congregations – manifesting a significant diversity with regard to religious observation and practice. Europe has also, as already noted above, a large Muslim population that in itself also displays a rich diversity. Hence, today Europeans know and, for the most part, affirm more religious diversity than ever before in Europe's history. This new religious situation in Europe calls for active measures of promoting inter-religious coexistence, dialogue and co-operation.

The myth of a Christian Europe has been exposed as dangerous for Europe, for Christians in Europe, for non-Christians in Europe and elsewhere, and for the world. Europe is not a Christian property. It is neither an exclusively Christian space, nor is its future the exclusive concern of Christian believers. Since the problematic nature of nationalist ideologies has been recognised and fought, any attempt now to embrace a religious or pseudo-religious myth in order to give Europe some form of cohesion seems utterly misguided. Christianity must not be instrumentalised once more in order to fill the vacuum after the fall of ideologies since 1989.

Europe does not have a soul. Rather, Europe is a space where people of different religious and secular orientations and backgrounds attempt to live together in closer co-operation. As distinct from the United States of America, European integration on the whole has not developed any form of civic religion. Hence, the unmasking of the myth of a Christian Europe and the absence of any surrogate form of religious cohesion make it necessary in Europe to reconsider the role of religion in general and of Christianity in particular for the future of an integrated Europe, a Europe significantly affected by the ever increasing process of globalisation.

## II RELIGION, POLITICS, AND ETHICS IN AN INTEGRATING EUROPE

In a reflection upon the proposed Constitution of the European Union, the Belgian born Yale philosopher of religion, Louis Dupré, expresses his critique of the absence of explicit references to the contribution of religion to 'Europe's spiritual identity'.[8] Agreeing that none of the past models of organising the religious fabric of Europe seems suitable for the future, he concludes: 'The foundation of the new Europe needs a more inclusive base. Yet if Europe's spiritual identity is to be preserved, it must remain firmly attached to the principal values of its tradition.'[9] Among those values he lists most prominently the age old European belief in the primacy of reason together with a common faith. Yet Dupré admits immediately that '[a]s for the common Christian faith that forged such a strong bond among Europe's peoples, many Europeans have lost it and most recent immigrants never had it.'[10] But he wonders whether this means that 'Europe must be satisfied with a merely political, technical, scientific, and economic integration?'[11] No, he argues:

8. Louis Dupré, 'The ties that bind us', *The Tablet*, 24 April 2004, 6-7, here 6.
9. *Ibid.*, 7.
10. *Ibid.*
11. *Ibid.*

Europe's political and economic unification must be accompanied by a strong awareness of a distinctive cultural and spiritual identity. This is the reason why the dispute over Europe's Christian heritage is so important. In writing the preamble to the EU Constitution, the most significant element in the European tradition must not be erased.

Today Europe needs a strong spiritual reintegration as well as a political-economic one. The former requires that it assimilate essential parts of its spiritual heritage: the Greek sense of order and measure, the Roman respect for law, the biblical and Christian care for the other person, the *humanitas* of Renaissance humanism, the ideals of political equality and individual rights of the Enlightenment.[12]

Dupré refers to this European heritage in terms of a single cultural body with different facets, and he detects here a 'unity of spirit in a variety of expressions' which he wants to see explicitly mentioned in the EU's Constitution.[13]

Dupré's choice of terminology is not necessarily helpful in this regard. Speaking of a European identity rather than of a pluralistic and ambiguous religious, cultural and intellectual heritage seems to me to narrow the focus unnecessarily. Although Dupré is fully aware of the need for a more inclusive cultural base for the new Europe and the desirability of a variety of expressions, he still wishes to defend some sort of spiritual identity. References to 'identity' are always problematic in that they often carry some claim to unity and uniformity. I do not wish to read European religious, intellectual and cultural history with respect to a presumed spiritual identity; rather I propose to consider that history with respect to the tensions and conflicts which emerged from the many efforts to forge some kind of spiritual unity. Thus, although I agree with Dupré's list of European achievements, I would not like to construct a unitary or evolutionary bond between them. Rather I see the need to argue again and again in word and action for these achievements in order to protect them in a future Europe.

There seems to be some sort of common misconception about the relationship between religion and identity according to which religion could function as a primary provider of personal

---

12. *Ibid.*
13. *Ibid.*

and social identity. Religious reality, however, is much more complex. The prophetic traditions within Judaism, Christianity and Islam offer sharp challenges to all human efforts to define personal, religious or social identities. The prophets question all forms of identity which are built on human projection, wishful thinking, and, even worse, idols. The prophets admonish people to give up their wrong ways of living and turn to the worship of the one and true God of the universe. Also the contemplative traditions within Buddhism, Hinduism, and even within the Abrahamic religions challenge all images of God or ultimate reality and invite deeper levels of contemplation upon the divine mystery. Different expressions and forms of so-called negative theology radically question all human efforts at grasping the divine mystery. Hence, rather than being concerned with any firm identity, religions are first and foremost concerned with ultimate mystery and the difficult ways of approaching God and of relating to the mysterious nature of the divine. All other human relations spring from this concern. Thus, in their different ways, religious traditions contain an element of unrest, of instability, of challenge and of search. Religions cultivate a sense of radical *otherness* and of the fragmentary nature of ultimate knowledge.[14] In this sense religions are also potential cultivators of resistance to all forms of idols and of false and static identities.

This 'negative' or critical dimension of religious traditions is of great importance for any evaluation of the potential of religious contributions both to the shaping of ethical values, virtues, norms and codes and to political developments. However, there is more to the relationship between religion and ethics, on the one hand, and the relationship between religion and politics, on the other hand, than the potential of religious movements to exercise critique and resistance.

It appears that all religions, however differently, inspire and shape specific forms of human community. In all three Abrahamic religions the call to form communities is an essential part of their faith in God. Moreover, there is an eschatological dimension operative in each of these religions: the messianic expectation within Judaism, the expectation of Christ's second

---

14. Cf David Tracy, 'Form and Fragment: The Recovery of the Hidden and Incomprehensible God', in Werner G. Jeanrond and Aasulv Lande (eds), *The Concept of God in Global Dialogue* (Maryknoll: Orbis, 2005), 98-114.

coming within Christianity, and the vocation to restore the entire world to the worship of Allah within Islam. These eschatological expectations also contribute to the shaping of the present
situation, and therefore are of political significance. Moreover,
all three religions, though at times in different ways, reckon
with God's active presence in this world. The spectrum of references to God's presence is large; it reaches from references to
God's direct and unmediated involvement to God's total respect
for the laws of nature and for human freedom and action. In
spite of differences between them and internal to them, each of
these three religions expresses belief in the work of God as creator
and in God as sustainer of creation.

In Europe all three religions have been operative in terms of
inspiring political visions, developing political philosophies and
creating ethical systems, although in Europe's past Christianity
was clearly the most important religious force in this respect.
These religions have offered the foundations for particular ethical decision making processes and choices.

However, religious traditions have lost some of their attraction to contemporary Europeans so that many people today do
not avail themselves any longer of explicitly religious principles
in order to structure their world and develop political visions
and ethical strategies. For Christianity this means that the
medieval Christian aspiration of a consensus in ethical matters
supported and facilitated by a detailed canon law and intricate
forms of excluding deviant or non-Christian traditions has long
broken down. Moreover, religious authority has been weakened
by painful disclosures of instances of political, sexual and spiritual misuse of power. Christianity's record as a religion that promotes peace, love and understanding in Europe is ambiguous
indeed. Every Christian church has added its own list of ambiguities, conflicts and problems to this overall record.

The ongoing shift from belonging to a religious tradition to
soliciting religious services when needed has radically altered
the religious landscape in Europe. Once firmly established religious community structures are being reinterpreted by many
European contemporaries now in terms of spiritual service centres. When the postmodern consumer needs religion, she or he
gets it wherever it appeals to her or his expectations. Formal religious traditions are less sought after. Instead looser forms of individually based spiritualities emerge and challenge traditional

forms of church life. Accordingly, Christian churches are approached more through the perspective of religious needs rather than through the perspective of a strong sacramental ecclesiology.[15]

Troubled church leaders in Europe react at times by trying to sharpen the boundaries of their respective denominations and thus attempt to increase loyalty to their particular ecclesial tradition. However, a concentration on the formal shape of a particular tradition without proper attention to the theological centre of that tradition may only further increase the suspicion of many genuinely searching contemporaries that what is undertaken is not reform, but an intensification of what Simone Weil once labelled 'church patriotism'.[16] Such a strengthening of the church's formal identity structure will not convince those contemporaries in Europe who base their existential decisions more on individual insight and openly syncretistic selections from all available religious traditions than on well defined laws and a unified body of doctrines handed down from religious authorities above.

The one thing that seems evident already today about the future of Christianity in Europe is that it will be more colourful, more diffuse, more pluralistic than its past. But will it be better?

III THE FUTURE OF CHRISTIANITY IN EUROPE:<br>TOWARDS A PRAXIS OF LOVE

Nobody knows how the future of Christianity in Europe will unfold. But we do know that it will differ from the past. A constitutional framework has been proposed now on the accord that the new European political space should not be monopolised by any one religious tradition or movement.

Of course, people convinced that the modes of authentic Christian existence can only be found in the past will continue to compete about which Christian century might offer the best model for church and society. But those reflecting on the potential of Christian faith to help shape the future of Europe will want to consider a mutually critical correlation between an honest interpretation of the present European religious context and an appropriate interpretation of the prophetic and contempla-

---

15. See Reiner Preul, *So wahr mir Gott helfe! Religion in der modernen Gesellschaft* (Darmstadt: Wissenschaftliche Buchgesellschaft, 2003).
16. Simone Weil, *Waiting for God*, trs Emma Craufurd (New York: Harper & Row, 1973), 53.

tive traditions and resources of Christian faith. The process of European integration thus presents an urgent challenge to the Christian church and its theologians to state their faith, hope, and eschatological convictions publicly, constructively and self-critically. Christian visions of how to organise a pluralistic society and how to develop political structures for European integration must be discussed both internally and within the larger conversation with other religious and humanist visions. What is needed specifically here is a discussion of models of unity that do not aim at uniformity.

Louis Dupré referred to the significance of the biblical and Christian care for the other person in this respect (see above). Nobody doubts the central place of love of God, of neighbour, of God's creation, and of self in Christian faith. However, everybody appreciates how difficult it is to grasp the mystery of love in the midst of the ambiguous nature of the many love discourses of today. It is impossible here to develop a comprehensive theology of love.[17] But I would like to present at least some thoughts on the larger significance of a renewed appreciation of the model of love for the future of Christianity in a radically pluralistic Europe.

The overall record of the Christian churches in terms of meeting religious and non-religious others is not good. The same may be said about Christian theology throughout the ages. One only needs to recall that the 12th century Cistercian leader Bernard of Clairvaux was at the same time one of the most brilliant exponents of a Christian theology of love and one of the most militant promoters of the crusades. This reminder should warn us against any hope that a simple theology of love might pave the way for either a Christian recognition of religious pluralism or a much improved Christian conduct in a pluralistic Europe. Rather Christian thinkers have often reflected happily upon love within the horizon of the Christian church without ever problematising the restricted nature of this very horizon. Moreover, the tragic history of demonisation of the religious other still throws its long shadow over the churches today.

---

17. I am presently working on a theology of love. See Werner G. Jeanrond, 'Biblical Challenges to a Theology of Love', *Biblical Interpretation* 11 (2003), 640-653; and 'Thinking about God Today', in Jeanrond and Lande (eds), *The Concept of God in Global Dialogue*, 89-97.

Martin Luther had nothing much good to say about either Judaism or Islam. The inherent belief in the superiority of Christian religion is deeply rooted in all Christian churches in spite of recent efforts by many churches to change the consequences of this belief. The widespread inability of many Christian churches to come to terms with their internal pluralism does not increase the hope for a rapid change in mentality towards the religious others.

In spite of the ambiguities surrounding any theology of love I wish to approach the question of how women, men and children who belong to different religious traditions or none can live together in a democratic Europe from the perspective of love. Love is neither a Christian invention nor possession. But it is generally considered to be the central aspect of Christian religion. Christians go so far as to identify God as love (1 Jn 4:8, 16). Although there are many different approaches and conceptions of love already within the New Testament itself, there seems to be some agreement that all forms of love have to do with relating to human otherness and God's radical otherness. The double love command to love God and the neighbour as oneself is more than a kind invitation to explore and enjoy the other's otherness, it is a *commandment*.

> 'You shall love the Lord your God with all your heart, and with all your soul, and with all your mind.' This is the greatest and first commandment. And a second is like it: 'You shall love your neighbour as yourself.' On these two commandments hang all the law and the prophets. (Mt 22: 37-40)

The Danish philosopher Søren Kierkegaard put great emphasis on this obligatory nature of Christian love. For him love is not left to a mere game of emotions, sensations and longings, rather love is a divine command. A Christian is confronted with the moral obligation to love God and the neighbour as herself or himself.[18] While Kierkegaard forcefully demonstrated the obligatory nature of relating to the otherness of the other, he undervalued the element of desire in this relational activity. He separated the erotic tradition of love from the moral tradition of love and thus truncated human relationality and reduced its transformative potential. Is not all love erotic in the sense that it seeks to relate to the other holistically, i.e. not only through acts of

---

18. Søren Kierkegaard, *Works of Love* [1847], ed and trs Howard V. Hong and Edna H. Hong (Princeton: Princeton University Press, 1995), 17-90.

will, but through a comprehensive outreach that desires and allows the formation of larger 'bodies'?

It is interesting to note that up to the 1970s few, if any, Christian theologies of love treated of the body or bodies of love. A love devoid of both longing and body never can hope to reach the other as other and to relate to the other in a personal, social, religious, developmental and mutual way.[19]

Unlike Kierkegaard, Augustine of Hippo did include longing and desire in his theology of love. But he considered God to be the only agent really capable of loving. Hence, a human being that loves God or another human being does not actually love herself or himself, but allows God to love through him or her. Here, love becomes totally divine and thus beyond the limits of human agency.[20] Augustine's theology of love was developed in the tradition of the Johannine approach to love.[21] It was this New Testament tradition that produced the famous dictum that God is love, and it was this tradition that significantly reduced the Christian horizon of love.

While Luke's gospel considers every human being and God to be worthy of human love – the story of the Good Samaritan highlights this universal horizon of love – the Johannine community reduces the scope of love to inner-Christian proportions. Christians ought to remain in God's love and treat each other in this love. Moreover, the Johannine tradition combines this inner-Christian focus on love with the issue of Christian unity, thus allowing the unholy alliance between Christian love, unity and uniformity to emerge that still throws its long shadow over much of the Christian discourse of love. Is love a way of producing and protecting unity – even uniformity – in view of potential conflicts and experiences of otherness or is it a way of handling conflict, as Paul suggests in 1 Corinthians 13? For John love is a way of protecting the church from otherness, conflict and division, whereas for Paul love is the 'more excellent way' of hand-

19. For a new approach to the concept of 'body' in Christian thinking see Regina Ammicht Quinn, *Körper – Religion – Sexualität: Theologische Reflexionen zur Ethik der Geschlechter* (Mainz: Grünewald, 1999).

20. See Hannah Arendt, *Love and Saint Augustine* [1929], ed Joanna Vecchiarelli Scott and Judith Chelius Stark (Chicago: University of Chicago Press, 1996).

21. Cf Augustine, 'Ten Homilies on the First Epistle General of St John', in *Augustine: Later Works*, trs John Burnaby (The Library of Christian Classics; Philadelphia: Westminster Press, 1955), 251-348.

ling otherness, conflict, and division (1 Cor 12: 31). However, Paul harbours no illusions about how demanding his understanding of love is. 'Love is patient; love is kind; love is not envious or boastful or arrogant or rude ... Love never ends' (1 Cor 13: 4-8).

It is interesting that this Pauline passage is often read at Christian marriage ceremonies, although the context addressed by Paul was the conflict on matters of religion in the Christian community of Corinth. Thus, the original occasion for this text is confessional conflict. Love is presented here as a means of handling conflict, and not as the opposite of conflict. The opposite of love is ignorance, not conflict. Love rejoices in the truth and not in evil. Hence, for Paul love clearly includes a cognitive dimension, not only an emotional one.

This all too brief reference to some Christian theologies of love has not only revealed tendencies of using love in order to promote inner-Christian identity projects, but also the potential of love to face divine and human otherness. The horizon of love thus can shift in Christian communities from purely local and immanent concerns to universal concerns with otherness, respect and attention. Hence, it appears to me very promising to develop a theology of love that affirms this universal horizon and that further explores the potential of love to deal with religious and political conflict. Of course, such a theology of love would need to build on a holistic appreciation of human relationality, thus it must acknowledge the erotic nature of love (including difference, body and desire) and the capacity of love to promote the establishment of always new or renewed 'bodies'.

Many other issues, questions and problems would need to be considered in a more fully developed theology of love. But I hope it has already become clear that a Christian praxis of love could contribute to the development of a religious, cultural, social and political climate in which the inner-Christian other, the non-Christian religious other, and the non-religious other could be respected, listened to and attended to. Such a praxis of love could open new ways of engaging with others and of facing internal Christian otherness, change and conflict. Underlying this praxis is the theological insight that love as divine gift or grace is *one* and that therefore the exploration of God's radical otherness will necessarily lead to an exploration of all forms of human otherness and *vice versa*. Moreover, the loving formation of the church as the body of Christ ought never to be developed at the expense of others. Belonging to the body of Christ would not include ultimate possession of truth, but it would mean a commitment to develop a body of love in response to God's invitation in Jesus Christ. But, theologically speaking, any body of love needs to be concerned with all other emerging bodies in this world. In other words, a loving body, however intimate in form and initial development, will always be drawn into greater awareness of radical transcendence. Hence body is not the framework for a consideration of love, but love appears ultimately to be the most appropriate framework for the consideration of any body and for any further search of truth.

Christians committed to the praxis of love within the contemporary context of religious and political conflict will not be able to accept religious, moral or political relativism. The praxis of love is always concerned with particular others and their concrete needs, visions and concerns. This radical particularity of love always seeks to reopen channels for attending to the other, follows the eros of meeting the other, and affirms the commandment to love every other – however difficult that may prove to be. Loving the other, respecting the other, and longing to be in contact with the other does not mean simply accepting every manifestation of otherness or condoning it. Otherness has to be discerned and considered in love. Respect does not necessarily mean approval. Love always contains cognitive, moral and emotional considerations. Thus, true love calls for judgment about what is good and what is evil. True love always seeks the truth.

Participating in the democratic process in today's pluralist Europe through the praxis of love leads at best to 'a weak praxis', a term introduced by Gianni Vattimo in a different context.[22] The praxis of love is weak because it always seeks to concentrate on the need to listen, to consider and reconsider otherness in all its manifestations, and to approach its deliberations with great attention, self-critique, critique and care. The weak praxis of love, however, will not shy away from challenging all forces in religion and society that do not show respect for otherness. Love not only means critique and self-critique, it also calls for acts of

---

22. See Gianni Vattimo, *Beyond Interpretation: The Meaning of Hermeneutics for Philosophy*, trs David Webb (Cambridge: Polity Press, 1997).

resistance both to those forces in society that promote terror, racism, triumphalism, and to oppressive forms of leadership, religious authority and government. Love wishes to help build a culture in which new and more dynamic forms of relationality can emerge. Love is also a political force. Hence, the praxis of love could become a great asset for the democratic process and constitutional development in a pluralist Europe.

The potential of love includes the concerns for God, for the individual other, the corporate other, the emerging self, but also for the approach to nature and to God's universe. The horizon of Christian love is universal. Hence, ecological concerns as well as concerns arising from the process of globalisation are part of this horizon. Overcoming partisanship within Europe must never lead to a new European partisanship against the rest of the world. Rather love demands not only an open pursuit of truth, but also a passionate concern for justice.

## IV CONCLUSION

The future of Christianity will ultimately depend on the willingness of women, men and children to respond to God's call in Christ to help transform this world into God's reign. In Europe this act of transformation takes place not against efforts towards mutual understanding, but in the context of the intensifying process of political, social, cultural and religious co-operation on this continent. Moreover, European integration is part and parcel of the ongoing globalisation of all of our lives in this world.

Against the voices that call for a strong preservation of Christian achievements in Europe, I consider a weak praxis of love to be a more appropriate response to Christ's call to discipleship. Neither church patriotism nor national patriotism seem adequate approaches to the possible contribution of Christian faith to a better future of Europe and the world. Christianity will never succeed in unifying and pacifying the world on its own. Rather it confesses that God saves the world in Jesus Christ, but also that God in Christ has called on all his followers to engage in a critical, self-critical and constructive praxis of love.

The myth of a Christian Europe is dangerous. A call to develop a Christian praxis of love in Europe, both theologically and practically, will not produce any kind of spiritual identity, but in the spirit of the prophets will put into question any identity project that is developed against all the others. If, however, following

Paul Ricoeur, one wishes to understand identity in terms of a way toward developing one's true self in relation to others and not against them, then the project of a Christian identity in a radically pluralist world could very well be a meaningful endeavour for women, men and children in and beyond Europe.[23]

---

23. Paul Riceour, *Oneself as Another*, trs Kathleen Blamey (Chicago: University of Chicago Press, 1992), 2-3.

CHAPTER ELEVEN

# Interreligious Dialogue and Global Ethic in an Age of Globalisation

## Karl-Josef Kuschel

What I try to do in the following essay belongs neither to comparative religious studies nor to theology of religions. I am not going to talk about ethical principles in the different religions of the world: religions of Indian, Chinese or Near Eastern origin. I am also not going to answer the question, why a confessing Christian, Jew, Hindu, Muslim or Confucian should enter into interreligious dialogue and what the limits of interreligious communications are. What I try to do is to deal with one crucial question: what factors in contemporary world politics make it necessary to talk about 'common ethical standards' and what role can religion play in the search for a global order.

### I THE NEW RELIGIOUS SITUATIONS IN GLOBAL SOCIETY

On November 8th and 9th 2001 the General Assembly of the United Nations in New York met in order to talk about principles of dialogue between different cultures after the tragedy of September 11th. Members of a 'group of eminent persons', called together by the General Secretary of the United Nations, Kofi Annan, handed over on that occasion to the General Assembly a copy of the report 'Crossing the Divide. Dialogue among Civilizations'. In a following resolution the General Assembly demanded a 'Global Agenda for Dialogue among Civilizations'. This agenda should include the following steps:

– Promotion of confidence-building at local, national, regional and international levels;
– Enhancing mutual understanding and knowledge among different social groups, cultures and civilisations in various areas, including culture, religion, education, information, science and technology;
– Addressing threats to peace and security;
– Promotion and protection of human rights;
– Elaboration of common ethical standards.

In the report 'Crossing the Divide' one can read that new global challenges need an answer from the side of global ethic:

As never before in history, the emerging world community beckons us to seek a new understanding of the global situation. In the midst of a magnificent diversity of cultures, we are one human family with a common destiny. As our world becomes increasingly interdependent, we identify ourselves with the whole global community as well as with our local communities. We are both stakeholders of our own respective countries and of one world in which the local, national, regional and global are intricately linked. A shared vision of common values can provide and sustain an ethical foundation for a dialogue among civilizations.[1]

The present crisis in world politics in the aftermath of the second Gulf war makes it even more urgent to reflect about possibilities and limits of global interfaith and intercultural dialogue. Even in secular societies (especially in Western Europe) there is a growing awareness that religion can no longer be ignored as one important factor in the future of the world society. I mention as one example the most highly regarded contemporary German philosopher Jürgen Habermas. In his programmatic speech after the September 11th event, Habermas recommended that secular societies (especially in Western Europe) adjust to the 'continued existence of religious communities', and thus count on a 'post-secular society'.[2]

If that is true, one should draw the consequences: world religions with their influence on hundreds and millions of people around the world have to be taken seriously as an important factor in world politics and economics. As many contemporary sociologists of religion suggest, the traditional categories and theories of secularisation have to be revised. The question of religion has to be discussed in a new global context with new categories. Two consequences follow:

1. interfaith communication between members of different world religions becomes an urgent need in the interest of world peace and world justice;

---

1. Picco, Giandomenico (*et al.*), *Crossing the Divide. Dialogue among Civilizations* (New Jersey: Seton Hall University, 2001), 70.
2. J. Habermas, 'Was bedeutet der Denkmalsturz?', *Frankfurter Allgemeine Zeitung* of 17 April 2003.

2. gaining competence in interfaith communication is an urgent need for learning institutions.

### II CHANGES IN THE GEO-STRATEGIC GLOBAL SITUATION

Interreligious dialogue is taking place today on the threshold of the third millennium in an age of globalisation and is thus in the framework of political, social and economic stages of change that we have been able to observe *worldwide* in recent decades. At the beginning of the 21st century, we are more clearly aware of the worldwide role and significance of world religions than at the beginning of the 20th century. Geo-strategists and influential political scientists are indeed signaling a return – which can be called sensational – of the analysis of world religions to the geopolitical scenarios. Again and again (especially after September 11) one is referred to the study of the director of the Institute for Strategic Studies at Harvard University, Samuel P. Huntington, whose essay, 'Clash of Civilizations?', in the influential magazine *Foreign Affairs*, was later expanded into an extensive book with the title *The Clash of Civilizations* (without the questionmark!).[3]

The crucial point is: Unlike in the 20th century, the central debates of world politics in the 21st century will no longer proceed along the ideological dividing lines of the East-West conflict, but will instead be conducted between ancient culturally and religiously defined civilisations. The age of the cold war is over, and to Huntington it seems to be a temporary historical anomaly. Due to the military and economic superiority of the superpowers, the power of cultures and religions in international politics could be quickly driven into the background. The East-West conflict worked like a huge clamp which forced things together that didn't belong together. With the collapse of the Soviet Union, this state of affairs changed instantly.

But for Huntington there is a feeling of belonging together in ancient civilisations of cultural groups. Above all, three will determine the conflicts in world politics of the 21st century: the Western-Christian, the Oriental-Islamic and the Asian-Confucian. However, in addition to these three, the political scientist identifies further civilisations that are also shaped by religion in their deep cultural dimensions: a Japanese cultural group, a

---

3. S. P. Huntington, *The Clash of Civilizations and the Remaking of World Order* (London: Simon & Schuster, 1997).

Hindu cultural group with India in the centre, an orthodox cultural group with Russia as the core country, a Latin American
cultural group and an African one. The 'fault lines' between these
eight civilisations will be the central conflict lines of the future.

Huntington's analyses of world politics have been met with
an almost unprecedented response. These analyses evidently
touch on something which is either latent or openly present in
fears and visions. In the foreword to his book, Huntington himself speaks about his article in *Foreign Affairs* as being the most
internationally discussed geo-political analysis since George
Kennan's world famous article from the 1950s about the 'Policy
of Containment' towards Stalinist communism.

Here I cannot summarise the fierce discussion set off in the
media and among scholars by Huntington's theses.[4] Huntington
himself denied that the current crisis (around the Iraqi conflict)
confirms this theory: the present situation has to do with the col-
lision of civilisations (to which the great world religions also belong) and an antimodern, religious fanaticism. However, the debate on Huntington's theses brought something crucial to light
even before September 11: while global reports in the past,
begun by the futurologist Kahn in the 1960s, up to the Brandt-
Palme-Report in the 1970s and the Global 2000 Report by Jimmy
Carter in the 1980s, and other prognosis scenarios of world politics, notoriously excluded the dimension of world religions, we
now have a case of a political scientist doing the opposite.
Unlike all the superficial political theories which, as a rule, leave
out the influence of world religions based on an ideological bias
that is critical of religion, *world religions will be allotted a fundamental role in world politics in the future*. Even today active politicians admit that, in this regard, there have been fateful fallacies
and erroneous decisions in world politics. In numerous conflict
scenarios, the religious dimension behind the conflicts has been
completely ignored. Therefore religion could, in an uncontrolled
manner, play a negative role, or the potential of religion to inspire, organise and sponsor political peace settlements was not
utilised. The examples in Lebanon, Iran, Bosnia-Herzegovina

---

4. Cf D. Senghaas (ed), *Frieden machen* (Frankfurt/M., 1997); *id*,
*Zivilisierung wider Willen. Der Konflikt der Kulturen mit sich selbst*
(Frankfurt/M: Suhrkamp, 1998); V. Rittberger & A. Hasenclever,
'Religionen in Konflikten', in H. Küng & K.-J. Kuschel (eds),
*Wissenschaft und Weltethos* (München: Piper, 1998), 161-200.

and Kosovo are convincing enough. The most flagrant case of the failure of global-political analysis in the last twenty years is actually the case of the Iranian Revolution of 1979 and Islam's resulting ability, which became evident to the whole world, to revitalise itself as a religion and to play a new role as a factor in world politics.

Certainly the role of world religions is profoundly ambivalent in world politics – as it is everywhere. Catchwords like rousing fanaticism combined with violence, absolute claims to the exclusivity of salvation, fundamentalist dualism in viewing the world, anti-modernistic regression with regard to human rights, especially women's rights, are the identifying catchwords of a generally negative picture of religions. This development has less to do with a religious revitalisation than it does with a political instrumentalisation of religion in the context of the intensification of social and ethnic conflicts in many countries under Muslim influence. Sociologists talk about worldwide, global and social fragmentation which has an enormous effect in many countries – from Algeria to Pakistan and Afganistan.

For an analysis of the world situation in terms of world religions, it can be inferred that:

(1) In many countries of the world (from Algeria and Turkey to Indonesia) rebellion against social fragmentation is no longer clad in the ideological garments of the East-West conflict (Marxism-capitalism), but instead in religious garments. The protest of the losers in modernisation and globalisation is now expressed – particularly in the Islamic world – in religious language. Such language is often the single remaining medium for making the cry for justice audible. It also already lies ready as potential in many Muslim countries. Even Marx knew that religion was not merely an expression of misery, but that it could also be a 'protest against misery'. In this way, a special responsibility falls upon the representatives of religions not to fanaticise the existing social and ethnic conflicts, but rather to civilise their religious dimension.

(2) In spite of all the economic globalisation, religions are certainly not merging together as a single unified religion for the service of a humane unified society. On the contrary, it is realistic to assume that the religions are holding mutually exclusive claims to truth against each other. Huntington put this into the

useful and coherent formula: 'A person can be half-French and half-Arabic, and be citizens of two countries simultaneously. However, it is difficult to be half-Catholic and half-Muslim.'[5] From which it follows: The conflicting claims of religions to the truth are making interreligious dialogue a task for peace ethics.

### III CHANGES IN THE GLOBAL ECONOMIC SITUATION

The necessity of interreligious dialogue is not only made clearer by the analysis of crisis scenarios in world politics; today interreligious dialogue must also be re-thought and re-justified in a global situation which is referred to as globalisation. After all, interreligious communication requires the ability to take part in global dialogue and is more necessary than ever during a time when intensive discussion has begun about a global civilisation, cosmopolitan democracy, community of global risks and global state. We plainly experienced the deep ambivalence of global economic processes at the end of the 20th century. The current world economic crisis and the striking brittleness of international finance markets pose, according to experts, the most dangerous threat to global prosperity since the oil crisis of 1973.

Above all, that is related to the unprecedented acceleration of capital movements in eclectronically interlinked financial markets and the actual independence of finance cycles with an inherent dynamism separate from the real economy. Very few people have understood what these technological and economic thrusts in innovation mean for their life. Measures of nation states have lost their effectiveness. Economic globalisation seems like a rising river that undermines and washes away previous control of borders. Long ago, control shifted from the dimension of space to the dimension of time: if it was the case earlier that economic success depended on which territory one controlled, the most important factor today is who is the first on the market – regardless of the country.

Therefore, increasingly more politicians and economists realise that exactly those who think the globalisation process is irreversible must insist that the market attain a basic structure globally. For globalisation is not fate, but, in spite of everything, a controllable process. Yet controllability requires a political conception, and this is also based on preliminary ethical decisions,

---

5. S. P. Huntington, 'The Clash of Civilizations?', *Foreign Affairs* 72 (1993), No 3, 27.

on moral energy for the benefit of the people. The influential theorist of an ethos of humanity, Tübingen theologian Hans Küng, referred to that emphatically and categorically: the global market demands an answer from the realm of global ethic.[6] This is for three reasons:

(1) For the sake of social responsibility. Unless we want globalisation to be accompanied by processes of fragmentation – that is, processes, as a consequence of which entire regions of the single world community 'break away' economically and politically, and become marginalised – the process must be kept in check in an ethical manner. And this is a matter of properly understood self-interest: it is in the promotion of world justice that world peace is to be found. Without world justice, there will be no world peace. If we don't want world terrorism to continue drawing energy in a demonic way from the appalling social opposites in the world community, we must analyse the deeper causes and help overcome them. The protests against the International Monetary Fund as well as the World Economic Forum in Davos show that the losers in the development of globalisation are beginning to become a political factor.

(2) For reasons of consistency. In the age of worldwide communication networks, the world community can least afford to have regions with absolutely different ethics or with ethics inconsistent in central points. What good are ethically sound prohibitions in one country if they can be evaded in other countries? Those who speak out for the controllability of economic globalisation, in the interest of millions of affected people in many countries of the world, need to acquire competence in the process of intercultural and interreligious ethical self-commitment. Also in the areas of management levels in globally active economic enterprises and financial institutions, one should know what the fundamental elements of Jewish, Muslim, Hindu or Buddhist ethics are. One should know how people are shaped in their basic attitudes, their outlooks, their ways of reacting and their preferences by those cultures, often thousands of years old, in which religious convictions play a large role.

(3) For reasons of integration. Globalisation of the world economy does not necessarily mean globalisation of world cultures and world religions. Expectations that, under the control of

---

6. Cf H. Küng, *Global Ethic for Global Politics and Economics* (New York: Oxford University Press,1997).

the globalisation of markets, there would also emerge, to a certain extent automatically, a globalisation of consciousness, more understanding for the other, the 'stranger', or even more planetary solidarity, remain unfulfilled so far. On the contrary: in no way has a worldwide removal of interreligious communication barriers corresponded to the worldwide removal of economic barriers. However, this worldwide removal of barriers is urgently necessary, since intercultural and interreligious non-communication represents a destabilising factor for the world economy, as well. Therefore, it must also be in the interests of people trading in the world economy that not only economic factors be considered in a global analysis. Globalisation of markets that does not also include globalisation of consciousness, globalisation of cultural exchange and interreligious dialogue, is reductive. Globalisation as a phenomenon is not problematic, but its economic one-sidedness is. Thus, in the age of globalisation, global thinking is also required in the areas of culture, ethos and religion.

### IV THE CONTRIBUTION OF RELIGIONS: CENTRAL MESSAGES

In view of the absolute necessity of interreligious dialogue as a task in the promotion of world peace and world justice, the question arises as to what extent this consciousness exists in the realm of churches and religions. Are representatives of churches and religions prepared for the new worldwide developments? There is no question about it: dialogue contacts are often restricted to just academically educated elites, or they are systematically destroyed by fundamentalist groups. Fundamentalism, loaded with antimodernistic sentiment, is a global phenomenon not only dispersed throughout Judaism, Christianity and Islam, but also recently in the sphere of influence of Hinduism. Within Abrahamic religions in particular, a conflict of principles concerning attitudes to the 'other', to the 'outsider', is becoming visible: dialogue or mission; restriction, self-restriction or global dispersal; self-questioning or aggressive self-assertion. This conflict of principles is often laid out in the respective 'holy writings' themselves and leads to problematic reinterpretations. The following developments seem to be characteristic for our time:

(1) Since the middle of the 20th century, a new situation has been emerging in many European countries. Some 100,000 Jews are again living in Germany (organised in eighty-three communities); but there are also 3 million Muslims in Germany, 10-12

million in Europe. Historically, there has never been a presence of such strong religious minorities in Germany. Judaism, which had been the largest religious and cultural minority in Germany, included about 600,000 people at the beginning of the 1930s. There have never been religious minorities of the present size, and the religious minority has never been Islam.

That brings new challenges to all European societies. Religious pluralism is a worry for both the denominational and secular-humanist *status quo*. The separation of many western societies into a religious and a secular part, which had been amicably accepted, is now getting muddled by a new religious factor. This factor calls into question the representatives of established Christianity as well as those of established secularism. The social responses are ambivalent.

– Many experience religious pluralism as a threat. It is joined by the experience of fragmentation: by mental separation, refusal of dialogue, self-ghettoisation and cultural resistance.

– Others experience pluralism as an enrichment. There are meetings which used to be unthinkable and which still have the freshness of the 'first time': never before in history has there been, as there is today, a German-speaking Muslim theology (the names of Abdoljavad Falaturi, Fuad Kandil and Mohammed Salim Abdullah stand for many others); never before was there a consensus among all relevant parties and churches in Germany that 'Islam' be taught as a regular school subject; in Germany's history there was never so much dialogue and co-operation between Christians and Muslims, yet also between Jews, Christians and Muslims regarding many questions of societal practice, in prayers for peace, peace campaigns and weeks of fraternity. On May 24, 2001, my faculty for Catholic theology at the University of Tübingen conferred an honorary doctorate in theology upon a Muslim for the first time in the history of German universities: upon the Jordanian Prince Hassan bin Talal.[7]

(2) The signals inside the Catholic Church are contradictory. In September of 2000 Pope John Paul II had his Congregation for the Doctrine of the Faith publish a declaration under the title *Dominus Jesus*. Not only Protestant fellow Christians – only a few months after the signing of the joint document in Augsburg regarding the doctrine of 'justification' – interpreted this declar-

---

7. Documents of this event can be found in: *Theologische Quartalsschrift* 181 (2001), No 4.

ation as a new attempt at a self-absolutisation on the part of the
Catholic Church, as if it alone were being claimed as the true
church of Christ. With respect to the dialogue among world religions, too, this declaration amounted to a jolt. For here it is confirmed to non-Christians that they find themselves 'objectively
in a serious deficit situation' compared to those who are claimed
to possess, 'in the church, the fullness of the means to salvation'.
The interreligious dialogue is not, according to this declaration,
an expression of respect for the path of the other, but instead a
means of converting non-Christians. Just as before, the 'conversion to Jesus Christ and belonging to the church' are declared as
necessary for salvation. Non-Christians are once again threatened with disaster! And many have anxiously asked themselves: should the goal of the interreligious dialogue, in the official Catholic view, really be that Jews stop being Jews and that
Muslims stop being Muslims?

In May of 2001 all this sounded totally different from the
mouth of the Pope himself. John Paul II is the first pope in the
history of the Catholic Church to enter a mosque. We keep track
of the date: May 6, 2001, a date just as important as the first synagogue visit by a pope in 1984, also by John Paul II, and just as
important as the peace prayer meeting of the religions in Assisi
1986 and 2001. In Damascus the Pope directed an address to his
'Muslim friends':

> I sincerely hope that our meeting today in the Omajaden
> Mosque expresses our determination to bring the interreli-
> gious dialogue between the Catholic church and Islam a step
> further. This dialogue got underway in recent decades, and
> today we can be thankful for the long way that we have come
> together ... It is important that Muslims and Christians con-
> tinue to explore philosophical and theological questions to-
> gether, in order to gain more objective and comprehensive
> knowledge of each other's faith. On a practical level, better
> mutual understanding will doubtlessly help us refrain from
> portraying our two religions as being in opposition to each
> other, as has happened all too often in the past. Instead this
> understanding will portray our religions in a partnership for
> the good of the human family.[8]

8. Text in: *L'Osservatore Romano. Wochenausgabe in deutscher Sprache* of 25
May 2001, 6. Cf also F. Gioia (ed), *Interreligious Dialogue. The Official
Teaching of the Catholic Church* (1963-1995) (Boston: Pauline Books, 1997).
B. L. Sherwin & H. Kasimow (eds), *John Paul II and Interreligious
Dialogue* (New York: Orbis Books, 1999).

These are conflicting signals, without question. I say that completely unpolemically, since it is important for me to expound on an issue that we are intensively working on in the field of theology of world religions, an issue that has not been resolved in a consensual manner by Catholic or Protestant theology: the relationship between interreligious dialogue and mission.

(3) It is also a fact that interreligious communication and cooperation are global phenomena today. Since World War II the dialogue between Judaism and Christianity has been placed on new foundations, as has the dialogue between Christianity and Buddhism.[9] Since the Islamic Revolution in Iran (1979) at the latest, the Christian-Islamic dialogue, and even the 'trialogue' between Judaism, Christianity and Islam, have experienced a historically unprecedented upswing. These processes have neither been sufficiently scientifically documented or reviewed, nor have they become part of public consciousness.

The changed global circumstances have also led to changes in the area of churches. The worldwide representative organ of Protestantism, the World Council of Churches (founded in 1948), as well as the Second Vatican Council for the Catholic Church, no longer identify the relationship between Christianity and the non-Christian world in exclusively missionary form, but instead they have defined it in religious dialogue form. In three areas, this paradigm change has become concrete for the churches:
 – in a new attitude toward human rights;
 – in a new attitude toward freedom of religion;
 – in a new attitude toward interreligious dialogue.

(4) An important element in the process of global interreligious communication is the 'Global Ethic Project', which was given worldwide significance by a declaration of the Parliament of the World's Religions in Chicago in 1993. This project is the crystallisation point of complex global, interreligious dialogue efforts and research in religious studies and comparative religion. It is publicly signalled here that representatives of religions – regardless of 'claims to the truth' still maintained against each other – based on their own religious beliefs, feel able to take part in shaping the ambivalent process of economic globalisation with recourse to the 'spiritual and moral' resources of religions.

The effects of the global ethic debate have become recognis-

---

9. Cf M. von Brück & W. Lai, *Buddhism and Christianity: History, Confrontation, Dialogue* (Munich: Beck, 1997).

able in the realm of science, as well as in the realm of practical politics, as shown in the outline of a 'Declaration of Human Responsibilities', by the Inter-Action Council, an assembly of former heads of states and governments, in 1997.[10] In 1999 a second assembly of the Parliament of the World's Religions took place in Cape Town (South Africa), during which the Global Ethic Declaration of Chicago was updated and implemented.

Global ethic is not intended to mean a purer humane ethic outside of all religions. It is not a matter of overcoming the religions with all of their supposedly rigid traditions, contradictory teachings and incompatible practices, and replacing them with a few universal and binding humane norms. By Global Ethic is not meant a unified world ethic above all religions, or even a dissolution of the religious into the ethical. The canonical fundamental texts of each of the world religions contain infinitely more for the ethos of the individual faith-communities than for that which can constitute consensus among them. Therefore, the Torah of the Jews, the Sermon on the Mount of the Christians, the Koran of the Muslims, the Bhagavad-Gita of the Hindus, the Speeches of the Buddha and the Sayings of Confucius remain as a basis for living and dying for hundreds of millions of people.

By Global Ethic is meant quite fundamentally a basic consensus regarding binding values, unalterable standards and fundamental personal attitudes that can be practised by people of all religions; a basic consensus that does not have to be found first or imposed on the religions, but rather one that is found in the sources of the religions themselves. The Global Ethic Project wants to bring out what all religions (not only Jews, Christians and Muslims) of the world, in spite of all the differences in theology and anthropology, already have in common – with regard to human behavior, ethical values and basic moral convictions. At the same time, it invites all people, religious and non-religious, to adopt this ethos and to act accordingly.

The Global Ethic Declaration of the Parliament of the World's Religions in Chicago, passed in 1993 and put in more concrete terms at the second Parliament of the World's Religions in Cape Town in 1999, is an important milestone on the way to a 'global ethic', an 'ethique planetaire', an 'etica mundial', an ethos of humanity. The text starts from the basic insight that the religions

10. Text in H. Küng & H. Schmidt (eds), *A Global Ethic and Global Responsibilities. Two Declarations* (London: SCM Press,1998).

have spiritual and wisdom resources that, for the good of all humanity, must be more strongly activated than in the past.

The Global Ethic Declaration has identified two basic values which underlie all other values: humanity (*ren* in Chinese) and reciprocity (*shu*). The principle of humanity means that 'every human being – man or woman, white or coloured, rich or poor, young or old – must be treated humanely'. The principle of 'reciprocity' is the Golden Rule which can be found already in the *Analects* of Confucius, but also in the biblical, Islamic and other traditions: 'What you do not wish done to yourself, do not do to others.'

In addition to that, in comparing the religious traditions of humanity, 'four unalterable directives' can be named that are approved of, in principle, in all religions of the world:

1. obligation to a culture of non-violence and of reverence for all life (the ancient directive: 'Thou shalt not kill' or 'Have reverence for life!')
2. obligation to a culture of solidarity and a just economic system (the ancient directive: 'Thou shalt not steal' or 'Act justly and fairly!').
3. obligation to a culture of tolerance and a life of truthfulness (the ancient directive: 'Thou shalt not lie' or 'Speak and act honestly!').
4. obligation to a culture of equality and the partnership of man and woman (the ancient directive: 'Thou shalt not commit adultery' or 'Respect and love each other!').

These are elementary precepts of humanity, without which a common social life among human beings cannot be guaranteed. Only in this way can human dignity and human rights be guaranteed.

The documents of the Parliament of the World Religions (Chicago 1993, Capetown 1999, Barcelona 2004) are guided by the conviction: religious energies can be used even more than in the past for carrying out the global tasks of mankind in a positive manner. The spiritual strength of the religions would benefit all humanity in this way, because the strength of the religions is their ability to literally transcend the realm of laws, instructions and institutions. Religions can appeal to people at completely different levels, not merely at the level of rational calculation, operations, and strategies, but at the level of the heart, feelings and 'soul'. Herein lies the deep difference between religion and ethic.

(5) The dialogue on global ethic is only fruitful if such a dia-

logue itself is a global phenomenon. This is indeed the case. Among various activities in the context of Islam and Hinduism I only want to mention one example, which proved to be very fruitful: the communication process with China. In 1997 and 2001 two international symposia took place in Peking on the topic 'Global Ethic and Traditional Chinese Ethic'. Both conferences took as their basis the principles of the Chicago Declaration, in order to find parallels in the classical Chinese ethical traditions (especially in the tradition of Confucianism and Taoism). At the end of this essay I want to quote from the declaration of the first conference in 1997:

> The participants explored how traditional Chinese ethics could play its part in the concept of a 'global ethic'. Traditional Chinese ethics has always put a premium on 'harmony in diversity' and 'the value of harmony', and this quest for harmony is the very basis for China's participation in the building of a 'global ethic'.

> The participants recognised that it is necessary fully to understand and respect the different civilisations, ethnic groups, communities and even individuals with their diversity and distinctiveness; the essential feature of a 'global ethic' is the acceptance of a reasonable pluralism as its premise, so as to treat with equality individuals and communities which are different from ourselves. As expressed in the code of conduct, this is expressed in the basic laws like 'do not kill', 'do not steal', 'do not commit adultery', etc., which have been handed down as unchanging core values of any culture or ethical tradition, and have been formulated in remarkably identical ways in different classical ethics or religious scriptures.[11]

Along this agenda it is worthwile to engage in a scholarly and personal way in interreligious dialogue and global-ethic-activities in an age of globalisation.

11. Hans Küng & Helmut Schmidt, *A Global Ethic and Global Responsibilities. Two Declarations*, 127.
In addition to works already mentioned, the following may be regarded as basic literature on the subject of this essay: H. Küng & K.-J. Kuschel (eds), *A Global Ethic. The Declaration of the Parliament of the World's Religions* (New York and London: Continuum, 1993); K.-J. Kuschel, *Abraham. Sign of Hope for Jews, Christians and Muslims* (New York and London: Continuum, 1995); K.-J. Kuschel & D. Mieth, *In Search of Universal Values* (Concilium 2001/4; London: SCM Press 2001).

# CHAPTER TWELVE

# Theatre, Tragedy and Theology

## Enda McDonagh

Seán Freyne and I come from a famine county, the 'snipe-grass' country of Irish writer and journalist John Healy. Born and nurtured within a few miles of each other, we followed much the same educational trajectory, local national school, St Jarlath's College, Tuam, and Maynooth with various postgraduate outings in Rome and Germany. Despite our subsequent worldly wanderings we have maintained an affection for and commitment to our native county and villages, even if that has not yielded very much in practical benefit for them. As a remarkable athlete and footballer as well as an outstanding academic Seán Freyne has kept the pride of Mayo alive and well from Tooreen to Jerusalem and Athens and from Trinity College Dublin to Sydney, Australia and all parts in between. His transformation of theology in TCD and the consequent influence on theology in Ireland is saluted by peers and students alike, although that cannot be the focus of this essay. The bonds of Mayo origins and of lifelong friendship, as they affected our shared engagement with theology, have found many and diverse expressions over the decades. In continuity with some of these this effort will seek to connect his early classical and theological education, his biblical/theological concerns in all their prophetic, poetic and dramatic interpretations of Yahweh/God's interaction with humanity and the cosmos, with current dramatic and poetic interpretation of our present world and particularly of our Irish world. The remarkable literary achievements of the biblical writers so familiar to biblical scholar Freyne could throw fresh light on the recent achievements of Irish dramatists, also remarkable in their very different ways.

A little further historical and biographical background may help set the scene for this perhaps curious conjunction of biblical/theological and Irish secular drama. In the impoverished Mayo of our overlapping youth, apart from directly church activities

the two notable sources of cultural involvement were the local
GAA club and the local drama group. Not that the GAA club
was without its drama and really high drama in Croke Park, in
which Seán himself figured, while the drama club quickly extended its repertoire from John Murphy's Charlestown to
Arthur Miller's Salem, Mass. For the future seminarians and
would-be priests this was no bad preparation. The interclass
football and hurling dramas on High Field, Maynooth were frequently exhilarating and the main theatre productions in
Maynooth at November, Shrove and St Patrick's Day, under the
direction of Abbey actors including former Maynooth student/
seminarian Ray Mac Anally, proved a rich cultural experience
for participants and audience which often bore fruit in their
parish assignments, as promoters and sometimes directors of
dramatic and musical productions. It must be admitted that no
real connection was made in these student days between biblical
studies and theatrical productions. Given this year after the
Abbey Theatre centenary and the extraordinary dramatic richness apparent among recent as well as more established Irish
dramatists during decades that have seen such a decline in Irish
religious participation, attempting to explore a couple of major
Irish plays, in this instance of tragic mode, might be illuminating
for, as well as illuminated by, biblical and Christian tradition
without impugning the integrity of either dramatic or faith traditions.

The focus on plays of tragic mode (a less definitive term than
tragedy) has personal and social as well as dramatic reasons.
Many of the best Irish plays of what might be called the Abbey
century are dominantly tragic in character. From Synge's *Riders
to the Sea*, premiered on the Abbey's opening night in 1904,
through plays by Yeats, O Casey, Beckett, Molloy, Murphy,
Friel, Kilroy, Keane, Mc Guinness, Parker, Barry, Carr, Jones, Mc
Pherson and Mc Donagh, (the list could go on and on), playwright, director and cast have exposed audiences to the specific
sufferings of a range of characters and situations that have been
all too true to the human condition but seldom resolved in
human peace or happiness. Not that many of these plays were
lacking in moments of rich comedy but the laughter only reinforced the overall tone of revealing lamentation.

In personal terms it proved impossible to escape from the
shadow of a countryside devastated by emigration and neglected

by successive British and Irish governments. Mayo was no country for young men. Poet John F. Deane's Achill 'egg-woman' and
mother knew that world; 'Sons, to boys, to men; she cried / each
time they left to build / / Birmingham and Liverpool, they , too,
/ obedient to the laws of the world's orbit. Kyrie/ eleison'...
Seán Freyne had the further personal pain of losing his father
when he himself was just five years of age.

How far increasing exposure to poverty, and now the plague
of HIV and AIDS in the developing world, has influenced this
author's preoccupation with tragedy on stage is not easily as-
sessed and one can never rule out the influence of individual
temperament based on nurture or nature in such preferences,
even when such influences are no longer accessible to the conscious mind. All one can say is that tragedy on stage is one of the
great transforming experiences available.

In the recent, if rather superficial, debate about the end of
history, there seemed to be at least a suggestion for people in the
West, of an end of tragedy as well. Such a delusion was only
effectively eliminated for these people by the horrors of
September 11, 2001. The people in deprived worlds, personal
and social, have lived with tragedy for so long that they may
also become immune to it. To compound the problems the privileged who saw themselves as protected from tragedy and even
death are now tempted in their fresh terror to see the deprived
as all terrorists. Today one may well adapt Seamus Heaney's famous line to 'history and tragedy rhyme' once again as he himself hints in his own recent Abbey play adapted from Iphegenia,
*The Graves at Thebes*.

To return to Seán Freyne, sportsman and classical scholar as
well as theologian, one might reflect on a recent comment by
classical scholar, Simon Goldhill:

Theatre and the gladiatorial games, these archetypal enter-
tainments of Greece and Rome, are very much still inside us,
either through the artistic tradition or in the popular imagination. Partly because of this, they turn out to be a particularly
valuable route in reflecting critically on what we do. They
give us a necessary vantage point to see ourselves. If you
want to know what you think you are doing, the theatre and
the games are a good place to do that thinking from.

ATHENS AND JERUSALEM ONCE MORE

The western tradition of theatre and tragedy has its classical source in the Athens of the fifth century BCE. More particularly in the Dionysian festival at which dramatists competed with one another, presenting a trio of tragedies each over a number of days. Out of these competitions emerged the great dramatists, Aeschylus, Sophocles and Euripides with such powerful and still influential works as *Oedipus Rex, Antigone* and *Medea*. How the gods, fate, human blindness and self-destructiveness combined to inflict such futile human suffering and dying may vary from play to play. They all revealed to their male citizen audiences the inner tensions and weaknesses of god, city and citizen, particularly of leading or royal citizens including women like Medea. Women were not citizens or among the actors or audience. The complex and, in that religious and cultural context, plausible plot, the characters, language and verse offered what Aristotle in his *Poetics* described as catharsis, an intellectual and emotional resolution which entered into the soul of the audience member to the point of personal transformation. At least such experiences are available to the modern audience member at a contemporary production such as that of Fiona Shaw's *Medea* in a relatively recent production at the Abbey Theatre, Dublin.

The setting of the religious festival of Dionysius with its surprising emphasis on tragedy, the intervention of the gods and the confrontation of some of humanity's deepest needs and frustrations, put Greek tragedy firmly in the context of religion. Even at this secular time, authentic productions and adaptations carry that context with them however implicitly or disguisedly. A review of western theatre and tragedy in the post-medieval period, something well beyond the scope of this essay and the competence of the essayist, would probably find that the religious context had receded if not disappeared, certainly in the case of somebody like Shakespeare. This may be partly due to the cultural presence of Jerusalem through the medieval period and its increasing absence thereafter. For many believers, artists and critics the events of Jerusalem excluded the possibility of real tragedy. Hope had replaced despair; the life of the risen Christ the prospect of futile killing and death. The supreme literary artist of the period entitled his classic work, *The Divine Comedy*.

Such a simplistic and crude review of the recurrence of great tragedy could not possibly do justice to the interaction of Athens and Jerusalem over two millennia. Yet in the modern and even post-modern times a very different approach may be necessary for the Christian believer or theologian who finds modern drama and particularly its tragedies so disturbing and enriching in human but also in faith terms. To track that disturbance and enrichment while respecting the integrity of a particular play and the particular Christian faith of the theologian is the difficult, perhaps the impossible, task of this essay.

The two Irish plays chosen for this study were selected primarily on the basis of their disturbing and enriching impact on this theologian-playgoer, although they have both received much critical acclaim as significant modern tragedies. In the modern Irish theatrical canon, John Millington Synge and Brian Friel are two of the great names. Synge's *Riders to the Sea*, first produced at the official opening of the Abbey Theatre in December 1904, has long entered the canon of world theatre as one of the great modern tragedies. Friel's *Faith Healer*, although first produced on Broadway, New York in 1979 with James Mason in the lead, may not have attained that status as yet but in this author's opinion must eventually do so. As some commentators have noted, Synge was one of the first tragedians to attend to the tragic lot of lower-class, working people as opposed to gods and heroes, warriors, kings and queens. Of course this has become commonplace in the twentieth century, from Miller's *Death of a Salesman* to a range of works by such compatriots of Synge and Friel as O Casey, Murphy, Mc Guinness, Barry, Carr *et multi alii*. Despite Chesterton's quip, not all Irish songs are sad, but many of their best theatrical works certainly are, as the two examined here will illustrate, except that 'sad' is much too feeble a word for their achievement and impact.

RIDERS TO THE SEA

The two major protagonists in *Riders to the Sea* are Maurya and the sea; the Atlantic Ocean and the frail old island woman, presumed to be of Aran, who has lost her five sons, their father and his father to that insatiable sea. As the curtain rises her two daughters are examining some clothes that may belong to Michael, the latest son to go missing and whose body has not been recovered. Maurya is resting off-stage, exhausted by the grieving for Michael. The only surviving son, Bartley, is about to set out for the horse-fair in Galway although his mother begs him not to go. When he persists she follows him to give him some newly baked bread and her blessing. She returns completely inconsolable because of the 'fearfullest thing' she has just seen, Bartley on his horse leading his pony and on the pony the last lost son Michael rides, 'with fine clothes on him, and new shoes on his feet'. The girls explain it can't be Michael as they have meantime identified the clothes found in the far north as his. Maurya's lament and its search for closure is interrupted by the entry of the keening women and the return of Bartley's body wrapped in a wet sail like that of an earlier drowned brother. 'The gray pony knocked him into the sea, and he was washed out where there is a great surf on the white rocks', one of the women reports. Maurya's closing lamentation has echoes of both Athens and Jerusalem and indeed of many traditions of grieving, but it is a magnificent personal and poetic cry in the face of natural and inevitable catastrophe. Such crude summary is utterly inadequate to the living play as presented on stage around the world. It also misses completely the high poetry of the language itself and of its shaping by playwright to the pain and dignity of one of theatre's finest final facing of mortality.

In this essay one must be satisfied to let the language, particularly that spoken by Maurya, echo around the mind and on to the page. Without simply repeating the whole text, which is a sore temptation when one is talking about this play, it is very difficult to convey power of *persona*, word and action. Quoting from some of Maurya's more poignant passages seems the only way forward.

As her daughter Cathleen tells her that Michael's 'body is after being found in the far north, and he's got a clean burial by the grace of God', the death of Bartley is almost taken for granted and Cathleen begins to keen. Nora the second daughter tries to console them: 'Didn't the young priest say the Almighty God won't leave her destitute with no son living?'

Maurya: 'It's little the like of him knows of the sea … Bartley will be lost now, and let you call in Eamon and make me a good coffin out of the white boards, for I won't live after them. I've had a husband, and a husband's father, and six sons in this house – six fine men, though it was a hard birth I had with every one of them and they coming to the world – and some of them were found and some of them were not found, but they're gone now the lot of them … There were

Stephen and Shawn were lost in the great wind, and found after in the Bay of Gregory of the Golden Mouth, and carried up the two on them on the one plank, and in by that door … There was Sheamus and his father, and his own father again were lost in a dark night, and not a stick or sign was seen of them when the sun went up. There was Patch after was drowned out of a curragh that turned over. I was sitting here with Bartley, and he a baby, lying on my two knees, and I seen two women, and three women and four women coming in, and they crossing themselves, and not saying a word. I looked out then, and there were men coming after them, and they holding a thing in the half of a red sail and water dripping out of it – it was a dry day, Nora – and leaving a track to the door.'

As the women begin to come in again and men carry in the body of Bartley with a bit of sail over it and lay it on the table, Maurya says: 'They're all gone now, and there isn't anything more the sea can do to me … I'll have no call now to be up crying and praying when the wind breaks from the south, and you can hear the surf is in the east, and the surf is in the west, making a great stir with the two noises, and they hitting one on the other. I'll have no call now to be going down and getting Holy Water in the dark nights after Samhain, and I won't care what way the sea is when the other women will be keening … Give me the Holy Water, Nora, there's a small sup still on the dresser.'

After dropping Michael's clothes over Bartley's feet, she sprinkles the Holy Water over him, and then: 'It isn't that I haven't prayed for you, Bartley, to the Almighty God. It isn't that I haven't said prayers in the dark night till you wouldn't know what I'd be saying; but it's a great rest I'll have now, and it's time surely. It's a great rest I'll have now, and great sleeping in the long nights after Samhain, if it's only a bit of wet flour we do have to eat, and maybe a fish that would be stinking.' After arrangements for making the coffin are made by the daughters and neighbours, Maurya sprinkles the last of the Holy Water on Michael's clothes. She lays her hands on Bartley's feet and says:

'They're all together this time and the end is come. May the Almighty God have mercy on Bartley's soul and on Michael's soul, and on the souls of Sheamus and Patch, and Stephen and Shawn; and may he have mercy on my soul, Nora, and on the soul of everyone is left living in the world.' … 'Michael has a clean burial in the far north, by the grace of the Almighty God. Bartley will have a fine coffin out of the white boards, and a deep grave surely. What more can we want than that? No man at all can be living for ever, and we must be satisfied.'

The special language of Synge's plays and his musical deployment of it were based on his own study of the Irish Gaelic language but above all on his acute listening to the language of the local people who became his friends and neighbours in Aran, Mayo, Kerry and Wicklow. Adopting or translating as the occasion required he forged a new language of the theatre which enabled him for example to express the keening thoughts and feelings of Maurya in the mastering cadences of her speeches throughout the play. But Synge was no simple language-master. The dramatics of the play, which can only exist on stage, are finely wrought. And behind and beyond all that are the human depth and tragic glory of Maurya, her family and her story.

At the time of writing, Synge had abandoned the rather rigid Protestant Christianity of his mother. This may be why some critics are inclined to dismiss the overt piety of Maurya or reinterpret it as part of an ancient pagan inheritance in the references to Samhain or as influenced by the Greek tragic tradition, with Maurya becoming *moira*, the Greek word for fate. There is no doubt something to both these suggestions. Irish Christianity always maintained a certain connection with its pagan and Celtic antecedents and Synge was schooled in the great Greek tragedies. The action in his play as in the Athenian works takes place off stage, his keeners are reminiscent of the Greek chorus, and the unrelenting force of the sea is indeed akin to the force of fate, of *moira*, even if it is force of nature rather than of the gods, closer to tsunami than to Dionysius,

Synge's fidelity to his Aran islanders and other local peoples led him to respect their piety as well as their language. And at least in the play Maurya's religious beliefs and practices are given their due. Her very name, despite its unusual spelling, almost certainly derives from Mary, the Mother of Jesus, as the Almighty God she invokes is in her mind the God and Father of Jesus Christ. At the back of her praying and keening lie such New Testament stories and images as Rachel bewailing her children after the slaughter of the innocents by Herod, Simeon's words to Mary on the presentation of her Son in the temple, Mary at the foot of the Cross, and the endless images of the Pieta. Synge would not, perhaps could not, be consciously aware of all this, but faithful to the grieving mother he created he would not exclude it either, at least not for Maurya's co-religionists as they responded to her prayerful lament in ways different from their response to the piercing wail of Medea on the death of her sons.

All this is not to turn the play into any kind of religious tract. It is merely to draw attention to how any work of art has varying meanings for different or even for the same observer. For the Christian theological observer more important than making explicit any implicit religious references is the art work's capacity to draw the theologian into the creative process itself, and still further into creation, in this instance, of a remarkable human being and her remarkable experiences of suffering and loss and her ways of dealing with them. Allowing oneself to be inhabited by Maurya and her encounter with life and death has expanding and even transforming effects of the kind Aristotle suggested, and of the kind the Christian doctrines of creation and incarnation also affirm. Without entering the darkness of such experience the theologian remains less human and so less capable of understanding and living the Christian message. The appeal to being 'satisfied' by Maurya at the end of the play may not echo the despair of some Greek counterparts but its pain is unmistakable and its hope as far from established as it was for Mary and the others on Calvary.

### FAITH HEALER

If *Riders to the Sea* is dominated by the conflict between (wo)man and nature, Brian Friel's *Faith Healer* is dominated by a man basically in conflict with himself, but the healer/artist is also in conflict with his gift/craft, his companions and clients. His wife/mistress Grace describes him to her psychiatrist as an artist and many reviewers and critics draw a close parallel between 'The Fantastic Francis Hardy, Faith Healer, One Night Only' and the artist/writer. Hardy himself puzzles over a 'craft without an apprenticeship, a ministry without responsibility, a vocation without a ministry'. It (occasionally) works for him, which is why he got involved he says, and 'the questions that undermined my life then became meaningless' – for a few hours.

In the four monologues which constitute the play, with Hardy delivering the first and fourth, Grace the second and his manager Teddy (the Cockney) the third, the splits and contradictions within and between characters and narratives abound. Even such a central event as the still birth of Frank's and Grace's son 'in Kinlochbervie in the far north of Scotland, almost as far north as you can go', differs in significant detail in the accounts of Grace and Teddy while Frank simply 'erases' it as he explains that 'Grace was barren' although he would have liked a son. The 'erasion' of Grace in her view always occurs when he is preparing 'to perform'. Their return to Ireland and to Ballybeg, which climaxes in Frank's death, differs in important detail in the three accounts. These accounts converge most closely perhaps in the great triumph of Glamorganshire when Frank cures ten people of various diseases and disabilities. However, it was failure and death that dominated and divided them.

Friel like Synge is a master of language and the style here is a kind of prose-poetry if not quite the verse which Eliot thinks appropriate to tragedy. The opening incantation of place-names from Wales and Scotland, presumably the names of the towns and villages which the trio visited on their 'healing' journeys had the effect of 'sedation' on Frank on his way to a 'performance'. The repetition in the course of their monologues by all three gives it the force of lamentation, of Synge's keening women as well as of the Jewish tradition of lamentation expressed in the Hebrew scriptures, and kept alive to this day at the Wailing Wall in Jerusalem. As the play opens Frank's 'incantation' comes out of the darkness and the lights go up at the second line while he continues:

> Aberarder, Aberayron, Llangranog, Llangurig, Abergorlech, Abergynolwyn, Llandefeilog, Llanerchymedd, Aberhosan, Aberporth. All those dying Welsh villages ... I'd get so tense before a performance, d'you know what I used to do? As we drove along these narrow, winding roads I'd recite the names to myself just for the mesmerism, the sedation, of the incantation – Kinlochbervie, Inverbervie, Inverdruie, Invergordon ... Welsh-Scottish – over the years they became indistinguishable ....

And the settings for the performances, their kirks or meeting houses or schools, indistinguishably dirty and derelict. In all three accounts the story is of decline in Frank's performance and *persona* with the rarer results unable to still the internal questioning, the whiskey losing its effectiveness and the relationship with Grace becoming more bitter.

The undermining questions focused on his status as faith healer, authentic gift or just that of a con-man, and endless questions in between about faith in what or whom; and the desperation of those who came to him, knowing he could not help and would only reinforce their desperation except on the very odd occasion, as 'in that old Methodist hall in the village of Llanbethian in Glamorganshire in Wales (when) every single person was cured'.

In the darkened secular sanctuary of the Abbey Theatre, Frank Hardy as played by Donal Mc Cann was overwhelming, demanding and mysterious. And the mystery remains as it should in relation to any major stage figure, and of course in relation to any living human being. As Frank dismissed those he failed to cure, by Grace's account, we are all tempted to dismiss the personally unattractive or the socially (to us) insignificant. In that Abbey auditorium in the city of Dublin, it was impossible to dismiss Frank Hardy, hours, even weeks and months after the play had ended: Teddy's tattered poster, rescued from a dump on his way back from identifying Grace in the morgue: 'The Fantastic Francis Hardy, Faith Healer: One Night Only' – 'A lifetime in the business and that's the only memento I've kept'. And one night only was so disturbing, yet one felt compelled to go back to theatre and to text to wrestle with Frank's own questions and still more with that climactic event of his death so knowingly, deliberately and freely accepted at the hands of the wedding guests, as he failed to cure, as he knew he would, their crippled friend McGarvey. As Frank McGuinness observes, we are in this play listening to the voices of ghosts at least in the *personae* of Frank and Grace Hardy. Their stories of the final confrontation and death differ in important detail as nearly all their stories do. But the conclusions tally, Frank in attempting to cure McGarvey is killed for his failure. However it is Frank's telling that brings the play to its powerful, tragic and, yet in speech and on stage, serene conclusion.

The yard was a perfect square enclosed by the back of the building and three high walls. And the wall facing me as I walked out was breached by an arched entrance.

Almost in the centre of the square but a little to my left was a tractor and a trailer. In the back of the trailer were four implements: there was an axe and there was a crowbar and there was a mallet and there was a hay-fork. They were resting against the side of the trailer ...

And I walked across that yard, over those worn cobbles, towards the arched entrance, because framed in it, you would think, posed symmetrically, were the four wedding guests; and in front of them, in his wheelchair, McGarvey ...

And although I knew nothing was going to happen, nothing at all, I walked across the yard towards them. And as I walked I became possessed of a strange and trembling intimation: that the whole corporeal world – the cobbles, the trees, the sky, those four malign implements – somehow they had shed their physical reality and had become mere imaginings, and that in all existence there was only myself and the wedding guests. And that intimation in turn gave way to a stronger sense: that even we had ceased to be physical and existed only in spirit, only in the need we had for each other ...

And as I moved across that yard and offered myself to them, then for the first time I had a simple and genuine sense of home-coming. Then for the first time there was no atrophying terror; and the maddening questions were silent. At long last I was renouncing chance.

On stage this closing speech invaded the audience who offered themselves to it and to Frank; no, invade is not the right word because it is an aggressive word. Frank and his speech inhabited the surrendering audience. They too were 'awed and elated' and for a moment 'existed only in spirit'.

For the theologian in the audience, even as reader but more as transcriber, the whole play and particularly its closure is resonant with religious reference. Not that it is a religious play in any conventional sense. *Faith Healer* has much closer and overt connection with the fictions and factions of art than with the salvific/healing claims of Christian word and sacrament. But readers or theatre-goers, however captive to the play, can never completely shed their cultural endowment including its religious dimension. So while respecting the integrity of play and playwright they inevitably draw on their own resources in responses, positively receptive and negatively critical as they may be. Living with *Faith Healer* over many years, and more intensely over recent weeks, I have in reading and transcription of some sections, in reflection and even prayer made my own theological and biblical connections with Frank, and through him in diminished fashion naturally with Grace and Teddy.[1]

As I remarked earlier, the recurring incantation of the Welsh and Scottish placenames has the effect of biblical and Greek lamentation. The play for all the leavening of Teddy's humour might constitute one long lament were it not for final lyrical presentation of the tragic and fatal healing of Frank himself. His return to Ireland and Ballybeg had echoes of Jesus setting his face to Jerusalem. The Glamorgan healing of the ten and the short-lived transfiguration of the relationship between Frank and Grace has its own gospel echoes. Indeed the four quite differing accounts of the odyssey of the central character and his retinue may not be very close parallels to the four gospels of Jesus Christ or carry much in the way of 'good news'. Yet the figure four had at least symbolic significance for one member of the audience and there was the intimation of a healing, a new life of sorts, analogous perhaps to resurrection in those closing sentences. A new life free of the terror and the questioning through death freely and knowingly accepted at the hands of his enemies.

This is not intended as a rewriting or a restaging of Brian Friel's remarkable play. *Quod scripsit, scripsit*. And so it will be for actor and audience. But for one reader/audience member, the transformative experience opened him up to dimensions of human suffering, failure and mortality which connected with and deepened his personal convictions. As a kind of bonus there was also a healing of his human and Christian faith.

Synge and Friel, in these two plays at least provide not only for Irish audiences but also for world audiences the sense of tragedy in the human condition which is essential to a healthy psyche and society. The shopping and other addictions which turn so many citizens into consumers only and so many of their leaders into morally indifferent power-seekers, need to be confronted by the Mauryas and Franks of the developed and developing worlds if their sense of their own humanity is to be restored, through care and attention to the healing presence of the

---

1. I leave aside here the connections with the ancient Irish legend of Deirdre and the Sons of Ushna to which some critics refer, and the subject coincidentally of Synge's last and unfinished play. I do this not because the connections seem to me unfounded but because they are not relevant to my task.

suffering individuals and masses, from local suicide to distant tsunami.

*Seán Freyne*
It may all now seem a long way from Tooreen, Seán Freyne's native village in County Mayo. Yet Aran and Ballybeg in the far west of Europe, almost as far west as you can go, are clearly akin to Tooreen. And he too passed through Athens and Jerusalem on his way home. His original degree, as indicated earlier, was in Ancient Classics, Latin and Greek language and literature, before he started the study of theology and then specialised in biblical studies. And since his retirement, such as it is, he has become head of a new Centre for Mediteranean Studies at Trinity College, Dublin. The scholarly circle is complete in a sense, although Seán's enthusiasm for work and play will keep him moving between Jerusalem, Athens and Mayo as long as the life cycle continues.

CHAPTER THIRTEEN

# The Galileans of the South
# The Untouchables at the Margins

*Felix Wilfred*

At the time of Jesus, Galilee was a region viewed as bordering on impurity because of the presence of numerous Gentiles who were by definition polluted, and deserved rejection. Seán Freyne's abiding interest in the study of Galilee is a symbol of his passionate concern for those who are despised and marginalised. While thinking of an essay to honour Seán and his remarkable biblical and theological contributions, the plight of the untouchables of India flashed on my mind. The untouchables are considered as polluted, and they suffer alienation and social exclusion, and live on the fringes of a highly stratified society. Though their life is carried on in a completely different cultural and historic setting, the untouchables share at least some of the traits of the Gentile Galileans of Jesus' time. On the other hand the untouchables' experience of extreme marginality could serve as a lens to see and understand better Galilee and the Galileans.

In the first part of this essay I shall try to briefly describe and characterise the marginality and exclusion of the untouchables and some of the theories trying to explain their social and cultural position. The second part will examine critically the various attempts undertaken in favour of their emancipation, and highlight their own struggles to overcome the situation of exclusion and marginality. The third and final part will reflect on Galileans of the South in relation to Christianity.

## I AN EXCLUDED PEOPLE

The idea of margins may conjure up the thought that we are dealing with a small group of people or a minority group. The fact is that the untouchables of India are no small group at all. They constitute 14.6% of the Indian population, that is about 150 million people. Very few countries in the world will have this much of population. To realise the magnitude of the people about whose marginality we speak, we need to put together the population of a few large countries of the European Union.

*Outcaste and Untouchable*

It is important to direct our attention briefly to the inhumanity to which the untouchables have been subjected.[1] Worst of all is the ascription of untouchability they inherit at their very birth on the basis of the principle of *purity and pollution*. This is at the root of the social marginalisation and discrimination they suffer in every day life.

The untouchables are the ones who are outside the pale of the Hindu caste hierarchy. They have no place in the traditional order of society which is constituted of four castes – the *Brahmins* (the priestly caste), the *Kshatryas* (royal and warrior castes), the *Vaishyas* (the trading and artisan castes) and the *Shudras* (the serving castes). The untouchables belong to none of these groups, and therefore they are truly *out*-castes, and socially outcasts. This social marginalisation is glaring in the very physical set-up of their hamlets at the periphery of the village, scornfully referred to as '*Cheri*'. It stands in contrast to the place of inhabitation by the upper caste people, called '*uur*'.[2] The untouchables are to carry out in the strictest fashion the most impure works – cleaning human excreta, removing the carcasses of animals, washing clothes, working with leather, beating drums to ward off the evil spirits, and so on.

In the religious realm, untouchability disqualifies anyone from entering into the temple. This is true even today, in spite of abolition of untouchability through the Indian Constitution. It may be observed here that the struggle for temple entry of the untouchables is an important page in the social history of India.

---

1. The untouchables of India refuse to accept names imposed on them. They define themselves as '*Dalits*', which signifies their condition of 'brokenness' as a people, as a community. However, since Westerners are more familiar with the word 'Untouchables', I am employing throughout the essay this term. The significance of the transition from one nomenclature to the other is well brought out in an important contribution by E. Zelliot, *From Untouchable to Dalit: Essays on Ambedkar Movement* (Delhi: Manohar, 1992). For want of space I am restricting to bare minimum my references in this essay.

2. Here I am using the terminology as in vogue in Tamilandu, South India. In other parts of India, there are other local names. However, the pattern of differentiation is the same.

*An Economically Exploited People*
The social and educational marginalisation of the untouchables is compounded by their condition of abject poverty and the resultant powerlessness. It suits the interests of the upper castes to keep the untouchables subjugated with the stigma of untouchability, because the labour of the untouchables is indispensable for their (upper caste) growth and prosperity.

Most of the untouchables – about 90% – live in villages, and the rest in the slums of the burgeoning Indian cities and towns. Economically they belong to the lowest strata of the society. If 40% of the Indian population lives below poverty line, 80% of the untouchables belong to this category. In villages and countryside, the overwhelming majority of them are landless agricultural labourers, ruthlessly exploited by the land-owning castes and classes who hold many of them as bonded labourers. The condition of these bonded-labourers is not very different from that of slaves. In the cities, they struggle to survive in the midst of the odds placed in their way. While the powerful are engaged in violently controlling more and more space, the untouchables are increasingly forced to overcrowded slums or to eke out their existence at side-walks and pavements.

Through their hard labour, blood and sweat the untouchables have contributed to build up the land more than any other segment of the population. And yet they are the ones most vulnerable to all kinds of physical illness owing to malnutrition, lack of proper hygienic living conditions and medical care.

*How About Globalisation?*
Has not the globalisation of today helped the untouchables to move ahead and improve their lot? Contrary to the general impression and imagination, globalisation is a new actor that has aggravated the economic condition of the untouchables, instead of helping them. This is the simple truth. Experience shows that globalisation is not anything indifferent; it creates winners and losers in every part of the world, and this is true as much of India.[3] To put it simply, the untouchables belong to the losers, to the victims, whereas the upper castes – their traditional oppressors – belong to the winners. In effect it means that globalisation

---

3. J. Sobrino & F. Wilfred (eds), 'Globalisation and Its Victims', *Concilium* 2001/5.

has empowered the oppressors, which results in greater suffering and deprivation for the untouchables.

Let me illustrate what all this means concretely. Globalisation offers opportunities for fast communication, trade, specialised education, etc. But these are availed of by the upper castes whereas it is the untouchables who constitute the physical labour force in a country which is still by and large agrarian and has the overwhelming majority of its population living in countryside and villages. Every bit of power enjoyed by the higher castes, with their integration into the global market, goes against the untouchables at home. These Indian acolytes at the altar of globalisation in fact exploit the resources of the poor untouchables to derive advantages for themselves in the market. The elites in the country, identified with Brahmins and the upper commercial castes, are the avid supporters of privatisation. This however goes diametrically against the interests of the untouchables who are very much dependent on state interventions and state enterprises. In fact, the opportunities offered within the state-run enterprises and establishments have been an important avenue at least for a small segment of the untouchables to improve their living conditions and gain dignity and respectability. To this we must add the reduction, if not abolition of state subsidies (which corresponds to social security and welfare measures in the West) for education and health care. Abolition of state intervention and its subsidies may promote privatisation of which the upper castes are the enthusiastic supporters, whereas for the untouchables it spells hunger, starvation and lack of protection from illness.

*Violence Against a Defenceless People*
All along the history, the untouchables were subjected to violence whenever they dared to defy or challenge the caste-rules and injunctions which degraded them and kept them in continuous bondage. The fury of the upper caste was most violent whenever an untouchable boy dared to love a girl from the upper caste. In not a few cases death was the punishment. Citing such a violent case in which the people killed brutally both the lovers, Robert Deliege comments:

> It is easy for us in the West to see nothing but pure savagery in such revolting violence, and condemn it accordingly. Yet those who committed these atrocious acts were not profes-

sional killers, but no doubt peaceable farmers who were normally no more violent than any of us. No doubt too, they
were upstanding men, good husbands and most certainly
devoted fathers, who were hard-working and not out to
make trouble. Moreover, most of them probably never had
any previous dealings with the law. And if, in this case, they
behaved with such cruelty, it was because, from their point
of view, they had good reason for doing so.[4]

What is important is to note the extent to which the prejudices
and discriminations against the untouchables have got entrenched in the minds of ordinary people so as to think of violence against the untouchables as a matter of course.

Instances of atrocities done to the untouchables are on the increase. This is also due to the new consciousness on the part of
the untouchables about their dignity and their efforts to forge a
new identity for themselves. For example, if they were denied
lands in the past and were forced to be simply landless agricultural labourers, today in many parts of the country, the untouchables are determined to claim some land of their own. Many of
the atrocities are connected with the agricultural issues. They
dare to defy today the age-old taboos and interdictions in the
process of their self-assertion as a people with dignity and
rights. As many studies on ethnic violence show, in the case of
the outcasts too, the anger of the upper castes against the untouchables is expressed by humiliating and raping their women.
The women untouchables are then the most affected in all respects, and they bear the brunt of violence too.

*Theoretical Explanations*
What the experience of the untouchables and the violence they
undergo tell us is that they are victims of a deeply entrenched
system of caste, which could be named as 'casteism'. There may
be few subjects so debated in the field of anthropology and sociology in Asia as the origin of the unique caste-system with its mil-
lennial history. Going into those theories will lead us too far
afield. We are concerned here more directly with the various
theoretical interpretations of the plight of the untouchables.

---

4. Robert Deliège, *The Untouchables of India* (New York: Berg Publishers,
1999), 1; *id, The World of the Untouchables: Paraiyars of Tamil Nadu*
(Delhi:Oxford University Press, 1997).

There are two major sets of theories. The first set of theories views the untouchables as an integral part of a system of mutual dependence. The society is so organised that it needs the mutual dependence of the Brahmins on the one extreme and the untouchables on the other extreme to perform their respective duties. The fulcrum of this hierarchically organised and mutually dependent society is the principle of *purity and pollution*, which determines also the relative position of castes within the hierarchy. The major exponent of this theoretical orientation is Louis Dumont, who is followed by Michael Moffat and others.[5] Basically this theory of explanation espouses the view of the Brahmins and other upper castes who would like to see the untouchables in the most inferior position, nevertheless *integrated within the system*. To put it differently, this set of theories assumes that there is a tacit *consensus* on the part of the untouchables to the system and acceptance of their role within it.[6] This is something important to note, especially in differentiating caste from class. The relationship, in the integralist view of caste, is not *competition* as in the case of classes, but *co-operation* so as to create an integral whole inspired by the principle of hierarchy.

A second set of theories views the untouchables as *excluded* from the system but availed of for the functioning of the system. In other words, these theories reflect the actual reality of the untouchables and their experience which is not of integration but exclusion. The explanation of untouchability within the scheme of integration fails to see that the situation of the outcasts is not a matter of ritual pollution alone but has also to do with economic and political power. The ritual status almost inevitably leads to economic and political marginalisation.

How the untouchables are viewed – in terms of integration or exclusion – has its serious practical consequences. Basically, we are confronted with the question of identity. The theories

---

5. Louis Dumont advanced this position in his classical work *Homo Hierarchicus. Caste System and Its Implications* (London: Weidenfeld and Nicholson, 1970); see also Michael Moffat, *An Untouchable Community in South India: Structure and Consensus* (Princeton: Princeton University Press, 1979).

6. One piece of evidence adduced in support of integration explanation is to say that the untouchables replicate among themselves the hierarchical system, in such a way that there is a whole sub-system of discrimination and hierarchy. But in fact, this may not be interpreted as consensus to the system.

which interpret their position in terms of integration would acknowledge no separate *identity* for the untouchables, since they are part and parcel of one single homogenous cultural and social world. On the other hand, to interpret the plight of the untouchables as the excluded is to claim a separate identity for them. In plain words, the untouchables have their own culture, their own religious world, distinct from the world of the upper castes who have marginalised them ritually and socially.

A very important consequence is in the area of religion and its manifold expressions. It is obvious that the untouchables have a different kind of religious worship and a different type of religious experience, as numerous micro studies and researches have shown.[7] Now the theorists who see the untouchables as integral part of the system, see also their religious expressions as part of a single Hindu religious universe. But with greater affirmation of the social and cultural identity of the untouchables, there is a growing tendency on the part of the untouchables to claim a separate religious identity too.[8]

Recognition of the distinct identity of the untouchables is crucial today, for it serves as a very important means in their struggle against upper castes and in their search for human dignity and rights. In fact, the carving out of an identity of their own has cemented the unity among the untouchables who are dispersed – a dispersal that has immobilised in the past any possible protest or revolt against the oppressive caste system. The affirmation of a separate identity has been the beginning of their unfinished journey towards liberation.

---

7. On the subaltern religious experience, see Felix Wilfred, *The Sling of Utopia. The Struggles for a Different Society* (Delhi: ISPCK, 2005), 137-163.

8. There have been several studies investigating the religious world of the untouchables and other lower castes. To cite two unpublished dissertations written under my direction, A. L. Sebastian has gone into the study of Parayiar [a particular group of untouchables in Tamilnadu, India] religiosity, and James Ponniah into the study of the popular cutalaimatan cult in the district of Tirunelveli. A. L. Sebastian, *Indian Culture and Christianity. An Interpretative Study of the Cultural Continuity in the Life of the Christian Converts of Uthiramerur Taluk, Kancheepurm District, Tamilnadu* (unpublished dissertation; University of Madras, 2004); K. James Ponniah, *Folk Religion and Ritual Power in Society. A Study on Cutalaimatan Cult* (unpublished dissertation; University of Madras, 2005).

## II WAYS OF EMANCIPATION

What we have seen about the appalling condition of the untouchables becomes all the more serious when we note what it has done to their psychological make-up. It has been deeply impaired through the infusion of a sense of imposed shame. The spirit of the untouchables has been bruised and mortified, and their self-confidence has been deeply eroded. The words of a modern poet from the untouchable community reflects the deep inner pain in the face of poverty, destitution and the humiliation he and his like suffer. He writes, 'God, make me a beast or a bird but not a Mahar [untouchable] at all'.[9]

Who will really come to the aid of the outcasts thrown into the abyss of misery? How could the untouchables themselves work out their own emancipation?

### Initiatives from the Outside

The struggles of the untouchables have been taking place for the past two centuries with growing momentum, and often under pressure. Certain measures have been taken up in favour of the untouchables, but they fall short of the real aspirations of this oppressed community. Let us briefly examine some of these initiatives.

### Integration within a Reformed Hinduism

Religiously inspired reformers saw untouchablility as an aberration or deviation from genuine Hinduism and its vision of society.[10] Historically seen, the efforts of reform movements to accord the untouchables a place within Hinduism was also a pragmatic strategy to arrest the mass exodus of the outcasts from Hinduism to other religions – Buddhism, Christianity and Islam.

Symbolic of the reformist and integrative approach was the new name *Harijan* (children of God) given to the untouchables by Gandhi. It was intended to elevate their religious and social position and give them the sense of a new identity. For many,

---

9. These are words of Kisan Phagu Bansode. See Ghansyam Sha, 'Dalit Movement and the Search for Identity', in *Social Action* 40 (1990), 321.

10. There came into existence many associations and societies with the idea of promoting the welfare of the untouchables. Such was the case, for example, with India Sudhhi Sabha and Depressed Class Mission which appeared at the turn of the twentieth century. A few decades later the Harijan Sevak Sangh came into existence.

like Gandhi, to opt for the poor meant recognising and accepting the untouchables as an integral part of the Hindu society. Unfortunately, the option, though well meant, has left unchallenged the deep rooted caste-structure which even Gandhi accepted as the foundational Hindu social order.

Here precisely is one of the points of conflict between Gandhi and his younger contemporary Ambedkar, the foremost leader of the untouchable community. If the efforts of Gandhi to integrate the untouchables within a reformed Hinduism were well-meant, Ambedkar saw in this a paternalist attitude that inhibited their legitimate self-assertion. Besides, efforts like integrating the outcasts within Hinduism or appealing to the upper castes to mend their way, as Gandhi did, could not bring about any lasting solution to the plight of the untouchables. While Gandhi saw in the radical movement of the untouchables the threat of a diversion in his struggle against the British colonial rulers, for Ambedkar the social agenda in terms of radical reformation of Indian society by achieving justice and equality for the untouchables was of primary importance. The movement of the untouchables spearheaded by Ambedkar delivered the blunt message to Gandhi that his concern and strategies do not take the cause of the untouchables far, since it is a position that fails to recognise that the first and most insidious enemy of the untouchables is within, namely the elites and the upper caste of the country.

*Upward Social Mobility*

A fundamental reason that accounts for the powerlessness and inequality suffered by the untouchables is the very structure of the social order: it did not permit any social mobility. The lowliest status and the occupational roles were fixed by birth. But in recent decades '*Sanskritization*' was introduced as a theory explaining the process of social change among the untouchables and other lower castes. According to the anthropologist, M. N. Srinivas, who coined this theory,

> Sanskritization is the process by which a 'low' Hindu caste, or tribal or other group, changes its customs, rituals, ideology and way of life in the direction of a high, and frequently 'twice-born' caste. Generally such changes are followed by claim to a higher position in the caste hierarchy than that traditionally conceded to the claimant caste by the local community.

What is to be noted is that 'sanskritization' is not a free and spontaneous move on the part of the untouchables, but an induced process. The values, ideals and ways of life of the upper castes are projected as the ideals which are then internalised by the lower castes and the untouchables. They are led to believe that if they follow the ways of the upper castes, they would reach a higher status. As a social process, sanskritization may account to some extent for change in Indian society. However, viewed in itself, this process is nothing but another variation within the walls of the caste-prison. It alienates the untouchables from their authentic self, and leads them to assume a false identity. The stigma of untouchability is so deep that any upward mobility achieved through sanskritization is incapable of eradicating it; at the most it can temporarily cover it up.[11]

*Marxism and the Untouchables*
Since the ideals and vision of Marxism and socialism resolutely move around the axis of justice, equality and the liberation of the downtrodden, we shall examine to what extent they have been able to respond to the aspirations of the untouchables.

In spite of the sharp social consciousness it has brought about among the oppressed, Marxism has tended to interpret caste in terms of class, and therefore primarily in economic terms. It may be added here that Marx's own analysis of Indian society was a biased one, as it based itself on the British colonial picture of India as a static society. Indian society and its caste were approached with a pre-conceived theoretical framework of Western class, and consequently, Marxist interpretation could not come to grips with the situation of the poorest of the poor of India – the untouchables – arising out of the caste reality peculiar to India and South Asia.

The heart of the question is to view caste as a socio-religious and cultural reality with serious economic implications, and not to explain it as something secondary and derivative from the material base of economic relations. Ambedkar, while confessing his faith in the egalitarian ideal professed by socialism, nevertheless took pains to underline the necessity of considering the

---

11. The humiliation and shame to which the untouchables are exposed in public is such that a section of them, especially in the urban areas, vexingly conceal their identity and pretend to belong to a higher caste.

caste reality in itself. There can be no revolution in India, according to him, without doing away with caste. As he observed:

> [I]f the Socialists wish to make Socialism a definite reality then they must recognise that the problem of social reform is fundamental and that for them there is no escape from it. That the social order prevalent in India is a matter which a Socialist must deal with ... He will be compelled to take account of caste after revolution if he does not take account of it before revolution. This is only another way of saying that, turn in any direction you like, caste is the monster that crosses your path. You cannot have political reform, you cannot have economic reform, unless you kill this monster.[12]

In India, without relating to the caste-matrix, the formation of class itself remains unexplainable. Analysis in terms of economic processes could not come to terms with the reality of the untouchables whose poverty is inextricably bound up with social marginalisation and untouchability in a system governed by caste. The extraction of labour, the appropriation of surplus value, accumulation of wealth and the ideological justification of all these invariably relate to the ideology of caste and its functioning. Further, the Marxists have, by and large, concentrated their attention on the industrial working class, and have found themselves in a rather unfamiliar terrain with regard to the untouchables who are mostly rural poor and belonging to an unorganised sector of workers. All this is confirmed by experience. In fact, attempts to organise the untouchables on the basis of class and along with upper castes of the same class have not yielded any appreciable results.

### Measures Adopted in Favour of the Untouchables

Modern constitutional and legal means are yet another way open to remove the stigma of untouchability and eradicate the situation of discrimination and inequality connected with it. That is precisely what the Indian Constitution did through its Article 17, which declared: 'Untouchability is abolished and its practice in any form is forbidden.' This and other subsequent laws abolishing untouchability have remained, by and large, a

---

12. Ambedkar, 'Annihilation of Caste', in *Dr Babasaheb Ambedkar Writings and Speeches*, vol I (Bombay: Education Department, Government of Maharashtra, 1989), 47.

revolution on paper. In short, the package of modern constitutional and legal instruments, unfortunately, have not delivered
the goods. Caste has survived with its extraordinary capacity to
adapt itself to re-appear in ever new avatars.

Caste has endured over the ages to its great resilience: like
the proverbial cat, it has nine lives. In fact no scheme of social
organisation can survive for long unless it keeps adjusting
with changes in society and is able to produce effective answers to the contemporary problems. It was its basic resilience that enabled the caste system to survive the challenges of Buddhism and Islam, the shock of the alien British
culture and administration, and crusades of Gandhi, Ambedkar and Lohia.[13]

More practical measures were adopted for the uplift of the untouchables. Among these we must include what is known as
reservation policy in India, and elsewhere known as affirmative
action or protective discrimination. The Indian Constitution admitted the necessity of the principle of reservation. For, in an un-
equal society, it is not enough that one acknowledge the general
principle of equal rights. Effective social justice can be realised
only through protective discrimination or preferential option for
the powerless. It is a small step towards balancing of power,
particularly in a hierarchical society.

The Agency of the Untouchables
All the above measures are a far cry from the new sign of hope
that is emerging: the untouchables are taking into their hands
the project of their own liberation, and are becoming the agents
and actors of their own future. When we look at the complexity
of the problem and the millions involved, this can be characterised only as a small beginning. Yet in its import and transformative power, it simply surpasses all the ideologies and measures
adopted from the outside in their favour.

The basic ambiguity characteristic of the life of the untouchables tells us also about the difficulty in the emergence of the
subjecthood of the untouchables. What is this ambiguity? The
need for survival and a sense of pragmatism force them to con-

---

13. *Reservations for Backward Classes. Mandal Commission Report of the
Backward Classes Commission, 1980* (Delhi: Akalank Publications,1991),
23.

form to a system of hierarchy and discrimination. They are not able to extricate themselves from a system that has chained them for many centuries and generations. On the other hand, they resist the system and are not prepared to accept hierarchy and inequality as the natural order of things. The various expressions of life among the untouchables are characterised by the interplay of these two poles. This ambiguity could also, perhaps, explain the absence of armed revolt, revolution and violence on the part of the untouchables in spite of the oppression they have suffered for millennia.

The resistance today begins with the refusal of a constructed identity imposed on them by the upper castes.[14] As many studies in the dynamics of oppression, specially feminist studies show, the obstacle for liberation is the internalisation of a given and imposed identity. In the case of the untouchables, they have never accepted such an image and identity-construal by the upper castes. They see their own position in a very different way. Often they attribute their present plight to sheer accident, as illustrated by many myths they narrate about their origins. Today with greater activation of their agency and the urge for liberation, they challenge the very caste ideology which creates such an identity for them.

The awakening of the untouchables in the nineteenth century took on a political form and found social and cultural expressions. They refused to form part of any political process that denied them identity and agency. This was exemplified in the conflict between Gandhi and Ambedkar. Thanks to Ambedkar, for the first time in history, the untouchables could rally together to struggle against their oppression. Disillusioned with reforms Gandhi and others wanted to create for them, they carved out for themselves a path of struggle which continues even today. The radical movement of the untouchables is the greatest challenge the caste-system has ever faced, surpassing even the one posed by Gautama Buddha more than two thousand five hundred years ago.

The untouchables realise the importance of education in their contemporary struggle against their oppression. During three

---

14. What this means is expressed by Steven M. Parish after a study among the Newars in the Kathmandu valley of Nepal. See Steven M. Parish, *Hierarchy and Its Discontents. Culture and the Politics of Consciousness in Caste Society* (Delhi: Oxford University Press,1997).

millennia they were deprived of the right to knowledge and education. The illiteracy among the untouchables, specially among untouchable women, is appallingly high, compared to the national average. The empowerment education can play in their liberation was realised by them when the modern educational system was introduced.

Their struggle is supported also by other factors and forces. Since they have been denied any history of their own, and since whatever history is there has been distorted in favour of the upper castes, the untouchables today try to rewrite their history, reversing in the processes the interpretations of the upper castes. To this we must add also the growing body of writings by the untouchables which reflect their suffering, pain and anguish, and their hopes and dreams for a different order of society. The untouchables' literature has acquired a profile of its own.[15]

Modernity is one of the most important forces that has triggered the liberation process of the untouchables. This is understandable against the background we have seen above. The advent of modernity, in general, represented a threat to the traditional system of control by the Brahmins and other upper castes, whereas it was a force of liberation for the untouchables. It helped them break loose of the traditional strangleholds of casteism. Ambedkar and other leaders of the untouchables are known for their love for modernity in contrast to the traditional Brahminical ways. Besides education, and freedom from tradition, modernity also brought a new legal system which helped the untouchables challenge the traditional legal practices of the caste-system as laid down by Manu, the Hindu law-giver.[16]

---

15. We could form some of idea of the literature by going through a brief anthology by Arjun Dangle (ed), *Poisoned Bread (Translation from Modern Dalit Literature)* (Bombay: Orient Longman,1994).

16. It may be interesting to draw a parallel between the relationship of modernity in India in the case of the untouchables and the experience of modernity in East Asia – China, Korea and Japan. The untouchables of India welcomed modernity for its liberating potential, but did not necessarily relate modernity to Christianity. In the case of East Asia, Christianity was welcomed back (after rejection and persecution) when it was perceived to provide the entry-point to modernity. See Felix Wilfred, 'Asian Christianity and Modernity: Forty Years after Vatican II', *East Asian Pastoral Review*, 42 (2005), 1 / 2.

### III CHRISTIAN THEOLOGY AND THE UNTOUCHABLES

It may appear as most obvious that Christianity, which stands for the dignity of every human person and for equality of all, is diametrically opposed to untouchability and caste. Unfortunately, the reality is different. The matter has been much more complex in practice than expectations on the basis of principles. The missionaries and the Indian Christian communities have been divided on this issue, and this is true of the situation even today. The question has been raised to what extent really the Christian message has been able to influence the society by infusing the value of equality so very essential for overcoming the plight of millions of the untouchables in the country. There has been certainly some influence, but not to the extent one may tend to imagine. We will be led to a sombre realisation about the extent of the influence, if we note a curious irony: more than perhaps the Christian message affecting and changing the situation of untouchability, Christian communities of India have been infected by caste and by the practice of some kind of untouchability.

What may be of interest here is to note that the approach and attitude to untouchability, and caste in general, has been coloured by the difference in theologies.[17]

At the risk of oversimplifying a very complex issue, let me present three basic theological orientations that have shaped the Christian attitude and praxis towards untouchability.

### 1. A Theology of Accommodation

The missionaries were puzzled by the unique system of caste in Indian society. In trying to make sense of it some of them concluded that this is something that is part of the social reality. One should not interfere with it, also because it endangers the possibility of saving more souls. In other words, one should work for the salvation and redemption of the people without disturbing the caste-system that creates untouchability. This theology of accommodation went to such an extent that some missionaries like Roberto de Nobili (1577-1656) who worked exclusively among the Brahmins and upper castes, refused to mingle with the untouchables and other lower caste people, fearing that he would not find acceptance among the Brahmins and other upper castes. Such a theology and accommodative methodology has its conse-

---

17. Cf Felix Wilfred, *On the Banks of Ganges. Doing Contextual Theology* (Delhi: ISPCK, 2002),113-137.

quences till our day. Many Christian communities are divided on caste-basis and the untouchables are refused equal rights in the Christian churches. Till recently in many places the untouchable Christians could not mingle with Christians of higher caste, but were segregated and assigned separate sitting-places during church services.

## 2. A Theology of Equality

The approach to untouchability on the basis of a theology of accommodation did not go unchallenged. From the very beginning there were other missionaries and Christians who found untouchability diametrically opposed to the gospel, and found it contradicting Christian belief in the dignity of human persons. In fact, it is this kind of theology which accepted the untouchables as equals. This openness attracted them in large numbers, and created mass movements of conversion to Christianity starting from the nineteenth century. This theology of equality, besides finding its basis in the gospels and the practice of Jesus of Galilee, was supported by the European Enlightenment ideals of freedom, equality and fraternity, and by the movement of the social gospel. The theology of equality was inspired by evangelical spirit. That explains why the missionaries who stood for equality were also the ones who argued against caste because it is an expression of Hinduism, which is a pagan religion, and therefore unacceptable. Without generalising, it may be stated that the ideal of dignity and equality to the untouchables was strongly upheld by missionaries who hailed from the northern parts of Europe, more strongly under the influence of the Enlightenment, than their counterparts (mostly Roman Catholics) from the southern parts of Europe.

## 3. A Prophetic Theology by the Untouchables

Thanks to the many forces that have been at work, the untouchables are becoming themselves the actors of their own liberation. The growing agency of the untouchables in the political, cultural and social fields has found expression also in the area of theology. The untouchables are developing a theology of their own, which is called 'Dalit Theology'. It is a theology that is developed from the perspective and experiences of the untouchables. It reflects the experiences of their suffering and humiliation. I may point out here that one of my students, an untouchable himself, has written an excellent doctoral dissertation working exegetically on the text of the passion narrative in the gospel (Mk 15:1-47), reading it from the perspective of the experience of the suffering and humiliation being undergone collectively by the untouchables.[18] This prophetic theology of the untouchables distinguished itself from other types of theologies done for their cause, also because of its great transfromative character. What is perhaps most characteristic of the theology of the untouchables is the political dimension it brings into theology. In short, it is a theology whose purpose is not primarily to explain, but to transform prophetically the order of things, for which it is highly important to be political.

It is instructive to note that certain of the themes which liberation theology would take up in the 1970s were already gone into by some of the Christian untouchables reflecting upon their situation of oppression in 1930s. The social and political consciousness with which the prophetic theology of the untouchables vibrated was a challenge to the theology of missionaries centred on the theme of redemption and salvation from sin and interpretation of Jesus' death on the cross from this perspective. By way of example let me cite here from the address of John Subhah speaking to the leaders of the untouchables at the All-Religions Conference at Lucknow in 1936, wherein he gives a fresh interpretation of the cross of Jesus.

> For this is what the death of Jesus on the Cross reveals: it reveals the Love of God who suffers because of the suffering of humanity. It reveals God identifying Himself with men and women who are suffering under the tyranny and oppression of the so-called upper classes in society … He reveals the very heart of God bleeding for suffering men and women. He from the Cross is proclaiming that He is on the side of those who are oppressed, the victims of the tyrannies of an unjust social system. Christ on the Cross is God's answer to the question 'Does God care for the out caste … who are under the cruel and humiliating domination of the so-called high class people'.[19]

---

18. Maria Arul Raja, *Dalit Encounter with Their Suffering: An Emancipatory Interpretation of Mark 15: 1-47 from a Dalit Perspective* (unpublished doctoral dissertation; University of Madras, 2000).

19. As quoted in John C. B. Webster, *The Dalit Christians. A History* (Delhi: ISPCK, 1994), 221.

The political consciousness with which this theology of the untouchables is imbued provides its cutting edge. It is therefore important for this theology to be closely associated with the new movements of the untouchables fighting for their dignity and rights.

The character of this prophetic theology of the untouchables stands out in bold relief when it is contrasted with other types of theologies developed in India. The most common form of Indian theology, in the name of inculturation, tried to employ and interpret Christian faith through cultural and religious categories of classical Hinduism. This is something the untouchables reject: here Christianity is getting closer to the culture and tradition of upper caste Hinduism which, in the view of most untouchables, has been the cause of their oppression, and hence they could not agree to the kind of theology of inculturation followed by the upper castes and classes within the Christian community. They would like to draw from the marginal and subaltern religious and cultural tradition which speaks to their aspirations and hopes, rather than from the dominant culture and tradition. The theology of the untouchables is developing its own hermeneutics and approach to the reading of the Bible.[20]

The prophetic theology of the untouchables tends to be more political and radical than other types of theologies. This is important in view of the fact that the Christian untouchables share the same condition of oppression and humiliation with the rest of the untouchables. If the Christian untouchables are to contribute theologically, this should come about in the context of a political process in which the masses of the dalit people across religious differences are involved. A theology responding to this situation of a common engagement across religious affiliation, as the theology of untouchables seeks to be, will also be credible and more effective. This theology is a prophetic and radical critique of the Christian community which is challenged to mould itself after the gospel and the vision of Jesus. It helps us to rethink theology close to the vision of Jesus. The critique relates to the continued discrimination of the untouchables in the Christian community and the refusal by the upper caste Christians to allow them equal participation. In fact it took a long time before

---

20. Maria Arul Raja, 'Some Reflections on a Dalit Reading of the Bible', in V. Devashayam (ed), *Frontiers of Dalit Theology* (ISPCK/Gurukul, 1997), 336-345.

it was accepted that an untouchable could be ordained a priest or a minister in the church.[21]

The Gospel of the Galilean
The developing theology of the untouchables finds in the gospels and in the practice of Jesus the source and inspiration. Speaking from his experience as a pastor and now a bishop, V. Devashayam, himself an untouchable, observes:

> In most Dalits [untouchables'] homes in the villages, the only valuable thing is the Bible, which they cherish and value greatly. They are familiar with the narrative sections of the Bible. It has been our experience, that given this devotion to the Bible, theologising through Bible studies will facilitate understanding and acceptance of even new ideas.[22]

It is the attraction of the good news of the Galilean Jesus that brought about mass conversions of the untouchables to Christianity. They embraced this path as the one that will lead

---

21. Many missionaries – both in the Catholic church and in Protestant churches – were not willing to ordain the untouchables for fear of the violent reaction and threat from the upper castes. There are numerous instances. To cite only one instance, Rajanaiken, an untouchable who was very actively collaborating with the Danish mission at Tranquebar in 18th century, though in every way qualified for ordination, was refused simply because he was an outcaste; instead another catechist by name Diogo was ordained. This is what the missionaries wrote to the principal at Halle, in Germany. It reads like a lesson in diplomacy! 'Not you only, but several of us desired to ordain Rajanaiken to the office of priest. This might be done if he were to confine his labour to the pariahs [untouchables]. It is true there are several honest and respectable persons among them, like Rajanaiken himself; still, from the low character of those people, the Christians of higher caste avoid coming in contact with any of them. We take great pains to lessen these prejudices among our Christians, still to a certain degree they must be taken into consideration. Rajanaiken is very useful and successful in his labour as a catechist in his four districts. But we should greatly hesitate to have the Lord's Supper administered by him, lest it should diminish the regard of Christians of higher caste for that sacrament itself.' As quoted in James Massey, 'History and Dalit Theology', in V. Devashayam (ed), *op. cit.*, 162-163.
22. V. Devashayam, *Doing Dalit Theology in Biblical Key* (Madras: Department of Research and Publications, Gurukul Lutheran Theological College and Research Institute,1997), 4.

them to dignity and personhood. In fact, it is no exaggeration to say that the majority of Indian Christians belong to the untouchables. They were not only the ones who responded most generously to the call of the gospel, but have been also important actors in making the gospel known to others. This is a point which has been neglected in the writing of the history of Indian Christianity. There are numerous untouchable Christians – some of them known, and many of them unknown or forgotten – who have been very active in the work of mission. But for them, many missionaries practically could not have functioned.

The theology of the outcasts draws inspiration from the gospel to overcome the stigma of untouchability. Finding himself in a geographical location in which there was mixing and mingling of many cultures and ways of life, Jesus could not subscribe to an ideology that divided people on the basis of purity and pollution. There are numerous passages in the gospels wherein Jesus comes down heavily with his critique on purity pollution which is divisive and which undermines the dignity of men and women. He highlights Naaman the leper, the Samaritan and the Syro-Phoenician woman – all considered impure. What Jesus did was to unmask and challenge the socially constructed purity-pollution practices, and recognise the dignity of the victims of this social construction.

Another important aspect which the untouchables find in the message of Jesus is *hope*. It is in a way an extension of the self-respect and dignity they find in the good news. The negation of dignity and respect meant for the untouchables that they were never thought of in terms of their future. This was of no interest to the upper castes for whom the untouchables were important in terms of the 'impure' jobs they have to perform and the hard labour they were expected to do. The untouchables were not entitled to a future. The sense of hope the gospel of the Galilean inspires is an important source of empowerment.

Yet another question is the way the untouchables understand and interpret their own sufferings in a different light. It is a universal practice that the victims are blamed for their situation of suffering – be it the poor, women or the untouchables. For the untouchables the explanation of their abysmal poverty, humiliation, suffering and pain had an immobilising effect on their spirit. The suffering they undergo has been viewed in a new light by the untouchables in the light of the suffering of the Galilean Jesus and his cross.

*Conclusion*

The plight of the untouchables is a unique story of oppression. But their continuing struggle for liberation has much wider connotation and significance. From a global perspective it could be viewed as a new social movement for justice and equality, or as a human rights movement with unique characteristics. Seen from the context of India, the liberation movement of the untouchables is a radical anti-caste movement, and as such it is an important process in the struggle for democracy. If every society has its own historic path to democratic ideals, a very crucial instrument of the democratisation of Indian society is being carried out by the movement of the untouchables for their emancipation. It is the same movement of the untouchables which is bringing about a secular character to the Indian society – a very different path from what the West has followed. From a Christian perspective, this movement embodies some of the most important ideals, values and vision which are associated with the image of the 'Kingdom of God' – the message of Jesus of Galilee. 'After John had been arrested, Jesus went into Galilee. There he proclaimed the gospel from God saying, "The time is fulfilled, and the kingdom of God is close at hand"' (Mk 1:14).

Obviously theology does not solve all human problems. But it can contribute to strengthening the forces and movements that work towards total liberation of human beings. This is true of the theology of the untouchables. What is most significant is the dignity and self-worth and the sense of hope the gospel of the Galilean Jesus can offer to a people who have been degraded and humiliated for too long. It is this conviction that underlies the theology of the untouchables, and hence its importance compared to all other forms of theology being pursued in India.

This theology poses challenges to the Christian community itself. However much the church community may try to sympathise with the plight of the untouchables, increase their opportunities in life, and engage itself in developmental, educational, health-care works in their favour, it may not respond adequately to the aspirations of the untouchables. There are two important things to be fulfilled for the liberation of the untouchables. First, a proper environment needs to be created in which the active agency of the untouchables comes to expression. This is true also of the Christian community, its leadership, and of theology. For a people who have been dependent on others generation after generation, liberation begins to appear on their horizon when they strengthen their own subjecthood and agency. Part of this process is the highlighting of the cultural and symbolic resources of the untouchables.

The second condition is the sharpening of political consciousness. This is what is often found wanting in the initiatives on the part of the Christian community.[23] This is also the reason why not a few among the untouchables look with scepticism at the contribution of the church community, in spite of all that it has done to highlight their plight and try to elevate them through education and other means.[24] The more the prophetic theology of the untouchables is imbued with political consciousness and is in relationship with various movements initiated by the untouchables themselves at various levels, the more this theology will acquire transformative power and radical character. It will be a theology of the marginalised in the spirit of the Galilean Jesus.

23. A dissertation written under my guidance comes to this conclusion, after a field study among the Madigas (an untouchable community in the Indian state of Andhra Pradesh). See Jose Maliekal, *Political Economy and Religion in the Encounter of the Dalit Madigas of Konaseema with Catholicism* (Unpublished dissertation; University of Madras). The same conclusion is arrived at in another study conducted in the district of Kancheepuram; see the dissertation of A. L. Sebastian, referred to above.

24. Ambedkar (in *op. cit.* [n.12], vol V, 475) faulted the Christian community for its lack of political consciousness. It is worth recalling his words here: 'The Indian Christians are living in sheltered waters. They are, at any rate a large majority of them, living in the laps of the missionaries. For their education, for their medical care, for religious ministration and for most of their petty needs they do not look to the government. They look to the Missions. If they were dependent upon government they would be required to mobilise, to agitate, educate and organise their masses for effective political action. For without such organisation, no government would care to attend to their needs and their requirements. They are not in the current and not being in the current, they care not for public life, and therefore have no recognised place in the public.'

# CHAPTER FOURTEEN

# Specifying the Meaning:
# Jesus, the New Testament, and Violence

## Nigel Biggar

Meaning depends on context. The meaning of a text depends on its historical context – or, rather, on two historical contexts: that of the author and that of the reader. What the author originally meant when he put pen to paper and what a reader learns from his text will not be exactly the same. The reader's situation, and the concerns and questions that it presents, will not quite match the author's. This is not to say, of course, that their respective meanings will be entirely different; for insofar as the reader regards the author as writing the truth, what the former takes will have much in common with what the latter gives.

The meaning of an historiographical text is more complex yet. For in addition to the meaning that the author gives and the meaning that the reader takes, there is also the historical subject-matter to which the author refers – and, if he is responsible, defers. The sense that the author makes of the past – the meaning he gives it – is one thing; the sense or the meaning that the past gives itself is another. If the author is writing history and not fiction, then his meaning is accountable to the past. It is constrained by it. Some things happened there, others did not. Some things were said, others not. Some things were intended, others not. For sure, the historian is bound to interpret the past, and not merely repeat it. He must do a new thing. He must invent an interpretation. But a responsible historian will invent strictly within bounds – bounds set by respect for the integrity of the past.

What applies to texts in general, applies to the New Testament in particular. Here is a collection of texts that all refer, directly or indirectly, to events in the past associated with a certain Jesus of Nazareth. They purport, therefore, to be historiographical. But they are not historiographical in the desiccated sense of positivistic history writing; for they claim to find in the history of Jesus existential and moral meaning of a theological

character and of universal import – that is, they find it 'revelatory'.
This meaning they are busy developing and elaborating – interpreting – in their own rather different historical and cultural
contexts. Taken in their own terms, however, their existential
and moral interpretations are accountable to the history of Jesus:
they do, after all, claim to be interpretations *of* that history.

Scholars of the New Testament take as one of their specific
tasks that of illuminating the relevant historical contexts in
order to help determine the meaning of the text. Some, doubting
the possibility of reaching behind the text to grasp the history of
Jesus, confine themselves to delineating the situation of the New
Testament authors – intellectual, religious, cultural, social, economic, and political. Rudolf Bultmann, for example, upheld
such doubt but downplayed its significance, arguing the improbable case that the New Testament authors had no interest in
the historical Jesus and that their religious faith did not depend
on him. On both these counts, Seán Freyne has long begged to
differ. Confident that the search for the historical Jesus is no lost
cause, he has devoted most of his career to unearthing the history
of first century Galilee and to locating Jesus in it. But his interest
in history is hermeneutical and not merely antiquarian for,
aligning himself with those who 'accept that the early followers
of Jesus had some interest in and memory of the historical figure
of Jesus as they began to proclaim the good news about him',[1] he
holds that the history of Jesus is relevant to what the New
Testament authors meant by their texts. Moreover, he has not
confined himself to the task of addressing the question of what
the texts meant to their authors: on several occasions he has ven-
tured upon the moral theological task of asking what the New
Testament texts should mean for the beliefs and conduct of their
readers today.[2]

It is here, between the historical hinterland of the New
Testament, the New Testament texts themselves, and the foreground of contemporary Christian ethics, that what follows will

---

1. Seán Freyne, Jesus, *A Jewish Galilean: A New Reading of the Jesus Story*
(London and New York: T. & T. Clark, 2004), 4.
2. E.g., 'The Ethic of Jesus: The Sermon on the Mount Then and Now', in
S. Freyne (ed), *Ethics and the Christian* (Blackrock: Columba, 1991), 41-
57; 'Jesus, Prayer, and Politics', in Linda Hogan and Barbara FitzGerald
(eds), *Between Poetry and Politics: Essays in Honour of Enda McDonough*
(Blackrock: Columba, 2003), 67-85.

operate. As hinterland, we will take for granted Seán Freyne's reading of the historical Jesus as one who refused the option of violent nationalism.[3] This is controversial. Richard Horsley, for one, has argued that, excepting 'the terrorism of the Sicarii directed against their own high priests', Jewish resistance to Roman rule during Jesus' lifetime was 'fundamentally non-violent'.[4] *Pace* those interpreters who see the 'Zealots' as a continuous movement or 'party' straddling the first seven decades of the 1st century AD and make of them 'a convenient foil over against which to portray Jesus of Nazareth as a sober prophet of a pacific love of one's enemies', Horsley holds that they did not come into existence until the winter of 66-67 AD.[5] Against this it is reasonable to argue that the absence from Jesus' context of the 'Zealots' as a definite 'party' may not be taken to mean the absence of militant nationalism *tout court*. That had irrupted in 4 BC and it was to irrupt again in 66 AD. While it is possible that the failure of the earlier revolt had completely discredited violent nationalism during the intervening period – and so during Jesus' lifetime – it is *prima facie* unlikely. While crushed revolts may confirm some – typically the middle-aged, married, and propertied – in their conviction that armed resistance is futile and counter-productive, they tend to provide others – typically gangs of young bachelors – with heroes, an activist ideal, and a

---

3. Freyne, *Jesus*: Jesus' 'attitudes towards people of other ethnic backgrounds ... could not be interpreted in the light of the conquest narratives which called for their removal, conversion, or annihilation, as the Maccabean heroes had attempted. If the suggestion is correct that his image of God was inspired more by the Genesis than the Exodus account, then we must ascribe to him a broader horizon for understanding Israel's role among the nations than one of hostility, leading to an aggressive militancy in reclaiming Israel's political freedom. Likewise, it appeared that ... Jesus refused to endorse the triumphant Zion ideology which viewed the nations as Israel's servants, and which was to provide a rallying call for some of Jesus' near-contemporaries in their struggle against Roman imperialism' (135); 'Jesus was not prepared to share the violent response to such conditions [of oppressive imperial rule], espoused by many Jews throughout the first century, which eventually plunged the nation into a disastrous revolt' (149).
4. Richard Horsley, *Jesus and the Spiral of Violence: Popular Jewish Resistance in Roman Palestine* (San Francisco: Harper and Row, 1987), 117.
5. *Ibid.*, x-xi.

lust for revenge.[6] What is more, even if Horsley is correct in claiming that the violence of the Sicarii was directed only at 'their own high priests', the rule of this religious elite can hardly be considered something entirely separate from Roman hegemony.

So, taking for granted the hinterland as Freyne describes it, we shall proceed to address the question of what the New Testament has to say to contemporary Christians about the use of violence. More exactly, our question is whether the New Testament may be read as enjoining on Christians the unconditional repudiation of any kind of violence anywhere – including politically motivated violence – or whether it should be read as only repudiating the use of certain kinds of violence in certain circumstances. Among the latter is the use of armed force against Roman occupation for religiously inspired Jewish nationalist purposes. The larger aim of this operation is to test the grounds that contemporary Christian pacifism claims to find in the New Testament, and to explore the possibility that the New Testament data might be better comprehended by the Christian doctrine of just war. (Let me declare my hand here: I come to this hermeneutical task as a proponent of that doctrine.) In order to make this exercise manageable within the compass of a single essay, we shall focus our question upon an egregious instance of contemporary Christian pacifism, which is to be found in Richard Hays' *The Moral Vision of the New Testament*.[7]

### RICHARD HAYS' PACIFIST READING OF THE NEW TESTAMENT

Widely showered with superlatives on its first publication in 1996,[8] and yet to be bettered as an attempt to build the frame-

6. I confess that I am transposing the pattern evident in the membership and reception of the IRA in County Cork during the period 1916-23 (see Peter Hart, *The I.R.A. and its Enemies: Violence and Community in Cork, 1916-1923* [Oxford: Oxford University Press, 1998]) back onto 1st century Palestine. Still, I take it to be common, universal sense that human beings who are old enough to have developed commitments to spouses and families and adequate livelihoods are likely to be less keen than herds of young unattached males to run the risks and unleash the unbiddable forces of violent revolution.

7. Richard B. Hays, *The Moral Vision of the New Testament: A Contemporary Introduction to New Testament Ethics* (Edinburgh: T. & T. Clark, 1996).

8. Among the pre-publication plaudits to be found on the back cover and opening page are these: 'Hays's ... book ... has neither peer nor

work of a contemporary Christian ethic out of the New Testament, *The Moral Vision* devotes its fourteenth chapter to mounting an incomparably full and sophisticated justification of Christian pacifism. The foundation of Hays' argument, predictably, is the Sermon on the Mount in the gospel of Matthew (chs 5-7). This he sees as Jesus' 'basic training on the life of discipleship', his 'programmatic disclosure of the kingdom of God and of the life to which the community of disciples is called', and 'a definitive charter for the life of the new covenant community'.[9] While not taking the form of 'a comprehensive new legal code', this 'charter' 'suggests by way of a few examples the character of this new community'. And what is this character? *Inter alia*, one in which 'anger is overcome through reconciliation (5:21-26), ... retaliation is renounced (5:38-42), and enemy-love replaces hate (5:43-48)'.[10] In sum, 'the transcendence of violence through loving the enemy is the most salient feature of this new model *polis*'.[11]

Lest it be supposed that this vision of a non-violent Christian community is confined to the Sermon on the Mount, Hays proceeds to argue that it finds confirmation in Matthew's 'overall portrayal of Jesus'. In the temptation narrative (4:1-11), for example, Jesus renounces the option of 'wielding power' over the kingdoms of the world; and (following John Howard Yoder's interpretation) his deflection of the temptation to refuse the cup of suffering amounts to a renunciation of the resort to armed resistance.[12]

---

rival' (Leander Keck, Yale Divinity School); 'Hays has pulled off, with a success for which I can think of no contemporary parallel, one of the most difficult tasks in theological and biblical writing today' (James Dunn, University of Durham); '[Hays's] description of the variegated ethical vision of the early church is state-of-the-art, and the application of that vision to contemporary issues is hermeneutically skillful ...' (George Lindbeck, Yale Divinity School); 'A gem that sparkles on every page' (Graham Stanton, University of London); ' ... an extraordinary accomplishment' (Allen Verhey, Hope College); 'Hays's method and proposals will ... prove a benchmark for future scholarship' (L. Gregory Jones); ' ... a rare and fine book' (John Riches, University of Glasgow).

9. Hays, *The Moral Vision*, 321.

10. *Ibid.*

11. *Ibid.*, 322.

12. *Ibid.*

Hays' next move is to tackle 'various ingenious interpretations that mitigate the normative claim of this text [Mt 5:38-48]'.[13] Among these are interpretations holding that the only violence prohibited is that in self-defence (and that violence in defence of third parties is implicitly permitted). Against these, Hays invokes the 'larger paradigm of Jesus' own conduct in Matthew's gospel', which 'indicates a deliberate renunciation of violence as an instrument of God's will'.[14] He substantiates this by appeal to the temptation narrative, where Jesus 'does not seek to defend the interests of the poor and oppressed in Palestine by organising armed resistance against the Romans or against the privileged Jewish collaborators with Roman authority'. He also appeals to the narrative of Jesus' arrest, where the disciple who draws his sword in defence of his master receives a severe dominical rebuke (Mt 26:47-52). This he takes to be 'an explicit refutation' of the justifiability of the use of violence in defence of a third party.[15]

A second set of interpretations that Hays seeks to discredit are those that would limit the meaning of the prohibitions of violence in terms of their social and political context. One of these readings is offered by Robert Guelich, who argues that the scope of Mt 5:39a ('But I say to you, Do not resist one who is evil') should be limited to a courtroom context, specifying its meaning as an injunction against seeking judicial redress against a false accuser.[16] Hays concedes that one of the illustrative injunctions in Mt 5:38-48 does have a specifically judicial meaning (v. 40: 'and if anyone would sue you and take your coat, let him have your cloak as well'), but he denies that the others (e.g. v. 39b: 'But if one strikes you on the right cheek, turn to him the other also') can be confined to a forensic context, pointing out that Guelich himself admits that verses 41 and 42 ('and if any one forces you to go one mile, go with him two miles. Give to him who begs from you, and do not refuse him who would borrow from you') cannot be so constrained.[17] Hays' case here seems cogent.

---

13. *Ibid.*, 320.

14. *Ibid.*, 323.

15. *Ibid.*, 324.

16. Robert A. Guelich, *The Sermon on the Mount: A Foundation for Understanding* (Waco, Texas: Word, 1982).

17. Hays, *The Moral Vision*, 325-26.

Another restrictive interpretation that Hays seeks to discredit is Horsley's. Horsley argues that in the original historical setting, the 'enemies' whom Jesus exhorted his disciples to love (Mt 5:44) referred only to 'personal enemies' – other members of small Palestinian villages who found themselves competing against one another for scarce economic resources – rather than foreign or military ones; and that Jesus' primary concern was to get the peasants to stop squabbling with each other so as to cooperate for mutual economic benefit.[18] Hays' first counter-argument is that such a reading commands no lexicographical support: the Greek word *echthroi* in Mt 5:44, translated as 'enemies', is a generic term and is often used in biblical Greek of national or military enemies, not just of personal or local ones.[19] His second point is that nothing in the gospel of Matthew suggests such a precisely local social situation, and that Horsley himself acknowledges that the Matthaean context actually requires the more general interpretation of enemies as 'outsiders and persecutors'.[20] (Given that we hold that militant nationalism was an option for Jesus and his contemporaries, we agree with Hays that *echthroi* should be read broadly to include political and foreign oppressors.) But Hays' main complaint is methodological, namely that Horsley makes his reconstruction of the history behind the text normative, and uses it to trump the intended meaning of the Matthaean text itself. On the contrary, according to Hays, 'the canonical narrative context governs the normative theological use of the text; the historical reconstruction remains speculative'.[21]

After his defence of a pacifist reading of the gospel of Matthew, Hays proceeds to show that the non-violent stance of this gospel is echoed throughout the canonical New Testament as a whole. The gospels, he finds, are unanimous in portraying Jesus as a Messiah who subverts all prior expectations by assuming the vocation of suffering 'rather than conquering Israel's enemies'.[22] The Acts of the Apostles present the martyr Stephen, praying for the forgiveness of his enemies (Acts 7:60), as the model of a Christian response to violence.[23] In his epistles, Paul

18. Horsley, *Jesus and the Spiral of Violence*, 255-73.
19. Hays, *The Moral Vision*, 328.
20. *Ibid*.
21. *Ibid*., 324 (cp 328).
22. *Ibid*., 329.
23. *Ibid*., 330.

presents God himself as responding to his enemies, not by
killing them, but by seeking reconciliation through the 'self giving' of his Son.[24] And while Paul writes that the governing authority bears the sword to execute God's wrath (Rom 13:4), that,
according to Hays, is not the role of believers. Those who are
members of the one body in Christ (12:5) are never to take
vengeance (12:19); they are to bless their persecutors and minister to their enemies, returning good for evil'.[25] Likewise, the
Epistle to the Hebrews and the catholic epistles offer 'a consistent portrayal of the community as called to suffer without anger
or retaliation'.[26] Finally, the Apocalypse 'seeks to inculcate in its
readers precisely the same character qualities that we have seen
extolled through the rest of the New Testament canon: faithful
endurance in suffering, trust in God's eschatological vindication
of his people, and a response to adversity modeled on the paradigm of "the Lamb who was slaughtered".'[27]

The concluding move that Hays makes in his argument is to
deal with certain particular texts that 'seem to stand in tension
with the central witness of the New Testament concerning violence'.[28] Prominent among these are the passages where soldiers
make an appearance. In Lk 3:14-15 John the Baptist does not ex-
hort them to abandon their profession, but merely to pursue it
honestly without exploiting the civilian population. In Mt 8:5-13
and Lk 7:1-10 Jesus marvels at the faith of the centurion whose
servant he has healed, but raises no questions about his military
profession. In Mk 15:39 it is a centurion at the foot of the cross
who is the first human character in the gospel to recognise Jesus
as the Son of God. And in Acts 10:1-11:18 the centurion
Cornelius, described as 'an upright and God-fearing man', converts to the Christian faith, but there is no indication that this is
supposed to involve his renunciation of military service.[29] Hays'
response to these awkward texts is to argue that they have a
particular literary role, that is, 'to dramatise the power of the
Word of God to reach even the unlikeliest people'.[30] In Lk 3:12-13,

---

24. *Ibid.*
25. *Ibid.*, 331.
26. *Ibid.*
27. *Ibid.*, 332.
28. *Ibid.*
29. *Ibid.*, 335.
30. *Ibid.*

for example, soldiers appear alongside tax collectors as examples of how John's preaching reached even the most 'unsavory characters'.[31] Moreover, when measured against 'a synthetic statement of the New Testament's witness', the examples of individual 'good soldiers' in the New Testament 'weigh negligibly': in the light of the vocation of the Christian community to the work of reconciliation and to suffer in the face of great injustice, 'the place of the soldier within the church can only be seen as anomalous'.[32]

There we have Hay's argument. Now let us scrutinise it.

### HAYS' PACIFIST READING: A CRITIQUE

Hays is commendably frank about the location of the weakest link in his armour: 'these narratives about soldiers provide the one possible legitimate basis for arguing that Christian discipleship does not necessarily preclude the exercise of violence in defence of social order or justice'.[33] He attempts to tame these passages by arguing that they are intended to play a particular literary role, namely, to illustrate the rashly generous capaciousness of Jesus' version of the kingdom of God – its capacity to embrace even 'sinners' such as tax collectors and soldiers. However, sinners who do become Christian disciples are usually portrayed as renouncing their sinful practices; and Hays himself notes that, whereas the Acts of the Apostles takes care to mention that the Ephesian magicians who became 'believers' publicly burned their magic books (Acts 19:18-20), it does not say that the centurion Cornelius surrendered his military profession (Acts 10:1-11:18).[34] Likewise, Hays could also have mentioned that whereas the gospel of Luke makes a point of showing that a tax collector's salvation involves the public mending of his extortionate ways (Lk 19:1-10), on no occasion does it suggest that a soldier's salvation involves the renunciation of military service as such. In the end, Hays finds himself forced to concede that the New Testament's treatment of soldiers simply does not fit his pacifist reading – it is 'anomalous'.[35] From this it follows that the witness

31. *Ibid.*
32. *Ibid.*, 337.
33. *Ibid.*, 335-36.
34. *Ibid.*, 335.
35. *Ibid.*, 337.

of the New Testament canon is not, as he claims, 'unambiguous'.[36]

Hays' response to the ambiguity is to suppress the intractable material, claiming rather desperately that it is 'outweighed' by 'a synthetic statement' of the New Testament's witness. Quite what is the nature of this outweighing he does not make clear. Is it simply that the examples of 'good soldiers' are so few? But surely they are quite sufficient in number to point a robust finger of doubt at a pacifist reading? For if the New Testament witness were unambiguously committed to the repudiation of all violence, surely its authors would have taken care to tell us that soldiers who became Christian disciples renounced military service? After all, a soldier's profession is not only *more* violent than that of a tax-collector or magician; alone among them it is *intrinsically* violent. Rather than brush the awkward finger aside, then, we intend to let it guide us and to look for a non-pacifist reading that does better justice to *all* of the relevant material in the New Testament.

If the New Testament does not appear to regard military service as incompatible with Christian discipleship, what may we take that to imply? One straightforward inference is that neither the historical Jesus nor the authors of the New Testament had any objection *in principle* to the publicly authorised use of lethal force. Indeed, St Paul says as much in his Epistle to the Romans when he writes that '[he who is in governing authority] does not bear the sword in vain; he is the servant of God to execute his wrath on the wrongdoer' (13:4). It is true that Paul also enjoins members of the body of Christ not to take revenge themselves but to leave vengeance to the wrath of God (12:19). Instead, they should bless their persecutors (12:14) and minister to their enemies (12:20), repaying no one evil for evil (12:17). Hays reads this along classic Anabaptist lines: the governing authority's use of force to punish the wicked is ordained by God, but 'that is not the role of believers'.[37] This interpretation gathers its exegetical

---

36. *Ibid.*, 341.

37. *Ibid.*, 331. The 1527 Schleitheim Confession, the classic statement of Anabaptist faith, puts the point thus in its sixth article: 'The sword is ordained of God outside the perfection of Christ.... [I]t is not appropriate for a Christian to serve as a magistrate ...' (in John Leith, [ed], *Creeds of the Churches: A Reader in Christian Doctrine from the Bible to the Present*, rev. ed. [Atlanta: John Knox, 1973], 287, 289).

force from the fact that what the governing authority is instituted by God to do – namely, execute God's wrath on the wrongdoer (13:4) – is precisely what Christians are forbidden to do (12:19). Nevertheless, one need not take this to imply the awkward position that Christians are forbidden to assume a public role that God himself has ordained. Instead, we should recognise of Paul's Epistle what Hays recognises of the Sermon on the Mount: that it was addressed to 'a marginal community outside the circle of power'.[38] The possibility of Christians assuming public responsibility was nowhere on the horizon either for Paul or for the Christian community in Rome. Therefore the question of whether or not they should avail themselves of the opportunity simply did not arise. What did arise was the question of whether or not Christians should respond to their persecutors by taking the law into their own hands – avenging themselves – thus making themselves into a threat to public order. Paul's answer is that rather than do this, they should bear injustice patiently and charitably, trusting the public authorities to do their job. We may not take this to imply that Paul held that all private use of violent force in defence or promotion of justice is forbidden to Christians. We may only infer that Paul considered public order to be a sufficiently precious good that Christians should bear some injustice – and try and turn it to good – rather than conjure up an anarchy of private vendettas and provoke the brutality of public repression.

As we read it so far, then, the New Testament does not object in principle to the publicly authorised use of violence. As for its private use, we may say at least that St Paul has very strong reservations. The remedying of injustice is the proper, divinely instituted task of public authorities; and even where the authorities fail to complete their task – as they are bound to do from time to time – private (Christian) persons should bear injustice and respond to it constructively rather then take the law into their own hands and risk all the attendant evils of so doing.

St Paul's concern about the evils of private violence finds a strong echo in Jesus' teaching and practice. Hays argues that Jesus and the gospels repudiate the use of violence, not just in self-defence, but also in defence of justice. As witness he calls the temptation narrative in the gospel of Matthew (4:1-11), where Jesus refuses 'to defend the interests of the poor and oppressed

---

38. Hays, *The Moral Vision*, 342.

in Palestine by organising armed resistance against the Romans or against the privileged Jewish collaborators with Roman authority'.[39] He also appeals to the narrative of Jesus' arrest in the Garden of Gethsemane, where a disciple draws his sword in defence of his master, but Jesus, perceiving the same temptation, rebukes him (Mt 26:47-52).[40] This Hays takes to be 'an explicit refutation' of the justifiability of the use of violence in defence of a third party.[41] Here as elsewhere, however, he generalises beyond the evidence. The option historically available to Jesus was not merely an abstract 'violence in defence of third parties against injustice', but specifically private violence motivated by a conviction that Israel is *the* divinely chosen nation and by a corresponding hatred of her Gentile imperial masters. What the temptation and Gethsemane narratives permit us to say, then, is only that Jesus declined to participate in violence that was not publicly authorised and that was inspired by religious nationalism. Why he should have done so, the text does not make explicit. We do know, however, that in Jesus' view the boundaries of the kingdom of God were defined less by ethno-national identity than by 'faith' – that is one clear implication of his response to the centurion at Capernaum (Mt 8:5-13 and Lk 7:1-10). He therefore had a theological reason to distance himself from religious nationalism. It is also conceivable – although I can think of no textual evidence for this – that he had a moral-prudential one. After all, the insurrections of 4BC had not merely failed, but had in the process provoked ruthless repression – as would the revolt of 66-70AD.[42] And insofar as nationalist revolts lack the unanimous support of the people they purport to represent (and they usually do), they are quite as much civil wars as 'wars for independence'. Of all kinds of war, civil wars are arguably the most vicious and inflict the most long-term damage on civil society. As the Latin American 'liberation' theologian, Juan Luis Segundo, has observed, prolonged guerilla war destroys the social ecology. It 'undermines … basic rules of human and social existence', because it raises doubts about the non-combatant

---

39. *Ibid.*, 324.
40. Hays himself reads the disciple's offer of defence as another instance of the temptation that Jesus had earlier refused (*ibid.*, 324: '… the temptation that Jesus rejects in the wilderness and again at Gethsemane').
41. *Ibid.*
42. See Horsley, *Jesus and the Spiral of Violence*, 50-58.

status of civilians (are they clandestine 'terrorists' or treacherous 'informers'?), proliferates suspicion, and dissolves the cement of trust between citizens.[43] Further, civil war also lends itself to a downward spiral of atrocity and reprisal as each side tries to terrorise the civilian population into compliance and to demoralise the enemy by attacking their families.[44] We might also add that among the most ruthless and uncompromising kinds of civil war is that precipitated by a nationalism that operates in religious terms, divinising the nation and sanctifying hatred of its enemies.

Whatever his reasons, Jesus declined the option of an uprising inspired by religious nationalism. Logically, this represents a specification of St Paul's caution against pursuing justice by taking the law into one's own hands. Beyond these reservations about its private, unauthorised use, does the New Testament evidence any more general concerns about violence? It certainly does. As Hays points out, it forbids anger and hatred (and therefore the violence that issues from them), as well as 'retaliation'.[45] However, we should not assume, as Hays does, that all violence is angry, hateful, and retaliatory. It is not.

Regarding anger, a distinction may be made. On the one hand, there is the 'resentment' that is both appropriate and proportionate. It is appropriate because it is the human emotion by which we take injustice seriously, recognising it for what it is; and it is proportionate because it is tempered by a resolve not to compound injustice in return and, as far as possible, to seek reconciliation. On the other hand, there is the 'anger' that, driven by rage and indignation, intemperately answers injustice with injustice. This distinction may be made, and the Anglican moral philosopher, Joseph Butler, made it.[46] But, as Butler pointed out,

---

43. Juan Luis Segundo, *Faith and Ideologies* (Maryknoll, NY: Orbis, 1984), 287.

44. Again, I am generalising here from the experience of County Cork during the IRA's campaign against the Royal Irish Constabulary, the British Army, and then the Free State forces during the period 1919-22 (see Hart, *The I.R.A. and its Enemies*).

45. Hays, *The Moral Vision*, 321, 322,

46. Butler argues that resentment is a 'natural passion' that may take either virtuous or vicious form according to circumstances. For biblical support, he appeals explicitly to St Paul in Eph 4:26 (Joseph Butler, 'Upon Resentment', *Fifteen Sermons*, W. R. Matthews [ed] [London: G. Bell & Sons, 1953], 123 [Section 3]).

so does the New Testament. St Paul, for example, distinguishes a restrained form of anger that is not sinful, when he exhorts Christians at Ephesus, 'Be angry, but do not sin; do not let the sun go down on your anger ...' (Eph 4:26). And if we read the Sermon on the Mount in this light, we notice that the anger that Jesus prohibits is qualified by abuse: 'But I say to you that every one who is angry with his brother shall be liable to judgment; whoever *insults* his brother shall be liable to the council ...' (Mt 5:22 – my emphasis). In these terms, then, violence against injustice is bound to be resentful, but it need not be angry.

Anger can be driven by several possible motives. Impatience is one. Disappointment is another. Hatred is a third. If the use of violence need not be angry, then by the same token it need not be hateful. This is not merely a theoretical truth, but an empirical one. It is widely recognised, for example, that soldiers in battle are often motivated by loyalty to their comrades rather than hatred for the enemy.[47]

One of the defining characteristics of anger is its lack of control by any sense of proportion or of moral duty: it hits back instinctively, no matter how trivial the injury; and even if its retaliation is designed to deter and not merely to inflict suffering, it defends the self without any regard for what it owes the aggressor. In this light, it is noteworthy that none of the injuries with which Jesus illustrates his injunction not to retaliate are very serious ones. If we should understand being struck on the right cheek (Mt 5:39) by the back of someone's left hand as a calculated insult,[48] then that is merely a verbal, and therefore arguably a trivial, injury; and as a purely physical injury being struck on one's cheek hardly rates highly. Losing one's coat to a creditor (Mt 5:40) and being coerced into carrying military equipment for a mile (Mt 5:41) are more serious forms of oppression, but still less than grave ones. What the text allows us to say, then, is that the Sermon on the Mount urges Christians not to hit back (and

47. See, for example, Joanna Bourke, *An Intimate History of Killing: Face-to-Face Killing in Twentieth Century Warfare* (London: Granta, 1999), ch 5, 'Love and Hate', especially 141-48.

48. This is David Daube's interpretation in *The New Testament and Rabbinic Judaism* (London: Athlone, 1956), 260-63, which Robert Guelich follows (*Sermon on the Mount*, 222) but Hays does not (*The Moral Vision*, 326).

presumably start a fight) in response to tolerable injuries to one-self. As Hays rightly says, Jesus' disciples are to relinquish the 'tit-for-tat ethic of the *lex talionis*'.[49]

Clearly, there is a definite bias here away from instinctive retaliation and towards more generous, conciliatory, and constructive responses. Nevertheless, the text does not allow us to infer – as Hays does – an absolute prohibition of violent retaliation of any kind under any circumstances. Specifically, it does not forbid retaliation that is not motivated by anger or hatred, that observes its moral obligations to the aggressor, that aspires to achieve a just reconciliation, and that *therefore* takes seriously and registers the fact of a serious injustice. As we should distinguish between appropriate 'resentment' and immoderate 'anger', so we should distinguish between on the one hand retaliation governed by a certain care for the aggressor and a desire for genuine peace, and on the other hand retaliation that is driven by a self-regarding indignation. Or, to put the matter more succinctly, we should distinguish between retaliation that is directed by 'love' and that which is not.

Notwithstanding this, it might be protested that 'loving' retaliation cannot be violent, and *a fortiori* it cannot be lethally violent. Thus Hays: the practice of loving enemies is, *pace* Augustine and Reinhold Niebuhr, 'incompatible with killing them'.[50] This is not so. I may (intend to) kill an aggressor, not because I hate him, nor because I reckon his life worth less than anyone else's, but because, tragically, I know of no other way to prevent him from perpetrating a serious injury on an innocent neighbour. My intentional killing is 'loving', therefore, in two respects: first, its overriding aim is to protect the innocent from serious harm; and second, it acknowledges the aggressor's equal dignity, it wishes him no evil, and it would gladly spare him if it could.

The main thrust of my complaint against Richard Hays' pacifist reading of the New Testament is that it over-generalises. The New Testament does forbid certain kinds of violence, namely, that which is inappropriate and disproportionate because motivated by anger or hatred rather than love. It also refuses the private resort to violence against certain kinds of injustice – and especially that resort which is inspired by religious nationalism. But its prohibition of violence is specific, not absolute. This spec-

---

49. Hays, *The Moral Vision*, 326.
50. *Ibid.*, 329.

ification or delimitation of the violence forbidden by the New Testament implies a corresponding delimitation of the patient suffering that it recommends as morally normative for Christian life and ethics. We should demur from saying, as Hays does, that all four evangelists present Jesus' choice of messianic career, epitomised in the symbol of the Cross, as involving 'the vocation of suffering' rather than conquering Israel's enemies;[51] and that the Epistle to the Hebrews and the catholic epistles prescribe the suffering of violence as the pattern of Christian life.[52] To talk of 'the vocation of suffering' is to make the negative practice of suffering in general the central and defining feature of Jesus' life and teaching. But surely Jesus' vocation would be better, more fully, and more positively characterised as that of wooing sinners and enemies and Gentiles into a generous, compassionate, if not undemanding kingdom of God? Such a vocation did entail the abjuring of hatred, unloving anger and retaliation, easy recourse to private violence in self-defence, and religious nationalism. And it therefore entailed a patient endurance of the *correlative* suffering. It follows, however, that the character or pattern of Christian life should not be defined primarily in terms of suffering, and not at all in terms of *suffering-in-general*.

The final element of Hays' interpretation of the New Testament with which we take issue is his reading of St Paul's theology of the atonement in the Epistle to the Romans. As Hays presents it, Paul infers from the death of Christ that God-in-Christ deals with his enemies, not by killing them, but by seeking peace through 'self-giving' or 'self-emptying service'; and that those whose lives are reshaped in Christ must treat their

---

51. *Ibid.*
52. *Ibid.*, 331-32: ' … in Hebrews and the catholic Epistles we encounter a consistent portrayal of the community as called to suffer without anger or retaliation…. [T]he author of 1 Peter holds up the suffering of Christ as a paradigm for Christian faithfulness'. To his credit, Hays reports the qualifications that these texts make on the suffering to which Christians are called – the suffering of Christ, and suffering without anger or retaliation – as he reports the qualification that the gospels make on the suffering to which Jesus himself was called – suffering rather than the conquest of Israel's enemies. His mistake, however, is that he does not pause to consider whether these qualifications might only require the enduring of some kinds of violence under certain circumstances, rather than all kinds of violence everywhere.

enemies likewise.[53] In textual substantiation of this interpretation Hays quotes Rom 5:8-10,[54] which clearly affirms that God regards sinners with love, that he has taken gracious initiative toward sparing them his 'wrath' by being reconciled with them, and that this initiative has expressed itself in the death of his Son, Jesus Christ. What ethical implications may Christians draw out from this theology? Certainly, that they should respond with love to those who do them wrong, that they should therefore desire reconciliation above punishment (or 'wrath'), and that this predominant desire should express itself in the taking of appropriate initiatives. Can we go further and, with Hays, infer an absolute prohibition of the use of lethal force? I think not. While the text clearly implies that God wants to save sinners from his wrath, and that those who are 'in Christ' will be saved, it does not imply that all sinners will be. It follows that, if (with Hays) we take death to be the effect of divine wrath on sinners, then, notwithstanding God's active desire that they should be saved, he nevertheless ends up 'killing' those who do not participate 'in Christ'.

This brings us to a second point, namely, the metaphorical nature of theological language. If we follow John Calvin in picturing God as dealing with sin in the way that a king or magistrate deals with grave crime, then we may find ourselves thinking of God as authorising capital punishment – as killing. But since this is a metaphorical way of speaking, it should not be taken as literally true – or, more exactly, not as literally true *throughout*. A metaphor relates to that to which it refers analogically: at certain points what is true of the metaphor is also true (literally, if eminently) of its referent, but at other points it is not. A metaphor contains both similarity and dissimilarity. With regard to the metaphor of God dealing with sinners by condemning them to death, then, which points do we take to be true and which points not? One uncontroversial point of corresponding truth is that, like grave crime, sin is a seriously destructive force.

---

53. *Ibid.*, 330.

54. Rom 5:8-10: 'God proves his love for us in that while we were still sinners Christ died for us. Much more surely then, now that we have been justified by his blood, will we be saved through him from the wrath of God. For if while we were enemies, we were reconciled to God through the death of his Son, much more surely, having been reconciled, will we be saved by his life' (NRSV).

Another is that, like a magistrate who acts against crime for the sake of the good of the community, the divine Creator acts against sin for the sake of the good of creation. It is hard to imagine that either of these points should prove objectionable to Christians.

What does prove objectionable to some Christians, however, is the notion that as a magistrate authorises the infliction of capital punishment, so God 'kills' faithless and impenitent sinners. But why baulk at this? Why decide that this a point of similarity too far? Two reasons present themselves. The first carries little weight: namely, the fact that in the predominantly liberal cultures of western societies (excepting that of the USA) – and in those many Christian circles that assume that whatever is liberal must also be Christian – capital punishment is widely regarded as a pre-modern, 'medieval' barbarity. There is ground for this view, of course, in the (to us) shocking and brutal liberality with which regimes in previous centuries meted out the death penalty for (to us) trivial crimes. On the other hand, there is ample room for 21st century liberals to become more mindful of the extent to which they enjoy the luxury of historically unprecedented public order and social peace; of the horrors and terrors into which a society can very quickly plunge when that order breaks down; and of the immense difficulty of hauling that society back into a condition of civilisation. There is an argument – and to my mind it is a good one – that the infliction of capital punishment may be warranted *in extremis*, when a society has no other means of containing violent crime.[55] The death penalty is always severe and terrible; but it need not be cruel.

A second, more cogent reason for declining to think of God killing sinners as magistrates kill capital criminals is that magistrates are warranted in so doing by exigencies of history, and that almighty God is presumably not subject to these. The rationale for capital punishment that we have just articulated is that it might be the only effective way for a society to contain grave violence: that is, it might be warranted *in extremis socialibus*.[56] While it might be justified, the death penalty is nevertheless

---

55. See Oliver O'Donovan, *Measure for Measure: Justice in Punishment and the Sentence of Death*, Grove Booklet on Ethics no. 19 (Bramcote: Grove Books, 1977), 21-22.

56. This, of course, is a non-Kantian rationale, for it is not the intrinsic nature of the criminal's crime alone that makes him worthy of the death

tragic. It involves causing at least two evils – the cutting off of the possibility of a criminal human being's (earthly) repentance and reformation and reconciliation, as well as his physical death. Were there an alternative way of securing innocent neighbours against the threat of violence, the execution of the criminal would not be justified; but sometimes history constrains us into a tragic set of circumstances where we cannot do our primary duty to our innocent neighbours without bringing grave evil (albeit justifiably) upon the heads of those who threaten them. Presumably in his dealings with sinners and their moral and spiritual wrongdoing, almighty God is never so constrained.

On the contrary, he might be. Whatever the radically different conditions of the Next World, the ultimate well-being of creation will require the eradication of sin and the threat it poses; and if some sinners should persist in cordial commitment to their sin, then the ultimate well-being of creation would require their destruction too. It might prove to be the case that God's love is sufficiently powerful to woo every last sinner away from their sin – that his Yes will exhaust all our Noes. But with Karl Barth, we can only hope and pray so; we cannot know so for sure.[57] As the dignity of free will makes possible the voluntary growth of human beings into virtuous maturity, so it necessarily also makes possible the voluntary degeneration of human beings into terminal corruption. We must entertain the possibility, then, that the ultimate salvation of creation will require the permanent removal of some sinners along with the sin to which they are inextricably attached; and unless we can conceive of a form of permanent removal short of final destruction that secures creation against the threat of sin, then we must entertain the

---

penalty, but also the capacity of his society to contain violence. The consideration here is prudential, but it does not render our rationale utilitarian: the death penalty may only be inflicted on someone who has committed a crime by a public body that has a duty to protect citizens from criminal violence. It may not be inflicted on an innocent by a public body that aspires to achieve the greatest happiness of the greatest number of people.

57. See, for example, Karl Barth, *Church Dogmatics*, Vol II, Part 2, 'The Doctrine of God' , ed G. W. Bromiley and T. F. Torrance (Edinburgh: T. & T. Clark, 1957), 417-18; and Vol IV, Part 3.1, 'The Doctrine of Reconciliation', ed G. W. Bromiley and T. F. Torrance (Edinburgh: T. & T. Clark, 1962), 477.

possibility that ultimate death will be the destiny of some sinners.

Paul Fiddes recommends that we think of the ultimate death of sinners in naturalistic, rather than judicial, terms: as the natural, automatic consequence of persistent spiritual alienation from God, rather than the result of an act that God decides to perform.[58] This has the rhetorical advantage of distancing God from the brutality that is commonly (if mistakenly) assumed to be associated with the death penalty. However, insofar as it is designed to dissociate God from all responsibility for the death of sinners, it both fails and misleads. It fails because God, being responsible for creating the world as it is, remains indirectly responsible for death being the natural end of intractable sinners. Therefore, the ultimate death of sinners remains the foreseeable result of a decision of God.

This naturalistic conception of the death of sinners also misleads, in that it assumes that if God is responsible for the death of sinners, then he must be culpable. But God's responsibility here is not that of one who malevolently wants the sinner dead (which would be morally culpable). Rather, it is the responsibility of one who, for the sake of the possibility of the voluntary growth of virtuous persons into human fulfilment, is willing to risk the possibility of the voluntary degeneration of vicious persons to the point of ultimate death. Some argue that taking such a risk would have been culpably rash (if God had existed to make it). But, frankly, what human being has the competence to say so for sure? Who among us can judge that the terrible annihilation of incorrigible sinners (and how exactly is the ultimate bringing to nought of a Hitler or Stalin or Pol Pot 'terrible'?) outweighs the shining beauty of fulfilled humanity? How do we begin to compare the relative 'weights' of annihilation and fulfilment? Who has the numbers and proportions of saved and damned to hand? It is not unreasonable to trust that a world in which some sinners might perish beyond hope is worth a world where other sinners might grow into glory. Nor is it unreasonable, therefore, to trust that God was not being culpably rash when he made it so.

Where has this extended discussion brought us? How does it help us to answer the question whether Richard Hays is correct

58. Paul S. Fiddes, *Past Event and Present Salvation: The Christian Idea of Atonement* (London: Darton, Longman and Todd, 1989), 91-93.

to claim that St Paul's theology of the atonement conceives of God responding to sinners by serving rather than killing them; and that therefore Christians are forbidden to kill their enemies. First, Paul does not say that all sinners will escape God's wrath. Second, it is not inappropriate for Christians to think of God dealing with incorrigible sinners as magistrates deal *in extremis* with criminals who continue to pose a grave threat – since the execution of the death penalty need not be malicious, cruel or barbarous; since the dignity of freedom requires that sinners be allowed to become inextricably attached to their sin; since the ultimate fulfilment of creation requires the permanent removal of sin; and since in the case of incorrigible sinners, this amounts to their death.

There are nevertheless two lingering reasons for hesitating to think of God as a magistrate authorising the capital punishment of sinners. One is rhetorical: that in Western Europe the death penalty so connotes cruelty that such theology would foster misunderstanding of God. To this one response would be that 'Western Europe' here really denotes liberal political elites rather than the majority of citizens, and that it is time for the relevant assumptions of those elites to be challenged. The second reason for demurring from the judicial metaphor is that it attributes to God *an intention to kill*, whereas the naturalistic metaphor only attributes *a reluctant acceptance of death*. Actually, this is not so. A judge who metes out capital punishment certainly causes the death of a criminal, and does so deliberately. But it would be misleading to say that the judge therefore 'intends to kill' the criminal, insofar as this implies a positive desire to see the criminal dead. The condemning judge might have no such desire. What he desires is the safety of innocent citizens; and if this could be secured by any means other than the tragic death of criminal, he would gladly choose it. But because there is no alternative, he reluctantly accepts the death of the criminal as an unavoidable and proportionate side-effect of ensuring public security.

We conclude, then, that it is appropriate to think of God as being prepared to respond to incorrigible sinners (should there be any) by authorising their deaths, not at all because he wants them dead, but because he wants to secure the fulfilment of creation, and because he cannot have the latter without the former. In this sense, and with all these qualifications, we may say that

God 'kills' incorrigible sinners. And we may say so without in any way detracting from God's driving desire to save sinners from their sin, and from the costly initiatives that he has taken to do so. Accordingly, we think Hays mistaken to infer from St Paul's theology of the atonement that Christians may never kill their 'enemies'.

## CONCLUSION

We have tested Richard Hays' pacifist reading of the New Testament against what the text itself says. What we have taken the text to say has been determined partly by what it consistently and significantly fails to say (e.g. that soldiers should abandon their immoral profession); partly with reference to relevant features of the social hinterland of its main subject, Jesus (e.g. the option of revolutionary violence inspired by religious nationalism); partly with reference to relevant features of the social hinterland of its readership (e.g. the lack of any prospect of Roman Christians holding public office in the mid-1st century AD); and partly by the logical limits of what we may take the text to imply (e.g. the prohibition of anger and hatred, and the injunction of love for one's enemies, do not in themselves amount to an absolute prohibition of the use of lethal violence; and St Paul's theology of the atonement does not permit us to infer that Christians may never kill their 'enemies'). According to our interpretation of the text, we may say that the New Testament abjures hatred, unloving anger and retaliation, easy recourse to private violence in self-defence, and violence inspired by religious nationalism. We may say that it enjoins whatever suffering forbearance from these involves. We may say that, beyond the passive suffering of frustration, insult, and tolerable injustice, it also enjoins the active, generous, and enterprising desire for reconciliation. From this, however, it does not follow that the New Testament absolutely forbids the publicly authorised use of lethal violence by Christians, nor even their use of private violence *in extremis*. Our concluding verdict, therefore, is that the New Testament does not bear Richard Hays' pacifist interpretation.

What is more, Hays is wrong to claim that '[i]t is not possible to use the just war tradition as a hermeneutical device for illuminating the New Testament, …'[59] It is not only possible, but preferable; for the doctrine of just war can make better sense than paci-

---

59. Hays, *The Moral Vision*, 341.

fism of all that the New Testament text does and does not say. On the one hand, of course, this doctrine does not prohibit the publicly authorised use of force by police or soldiers. On the other hand, it insists that recourse to lethal violence is only ever justified when its undoubted evils are made risk-worthy by the serious prospect of ending grave and intolerable injustice. By implication injustices that are less than grave must be suffered (creatively) rather than used as a pretext for premature violence. Further, given the horrors of anarchy, this requirement sets down a strong presumption against the private use of violence. And *a fortiori* given the severe and long-term social damage that is characteristic of civil war fought by guerrilla tactics, it places a very large question mark against the launching of insurrection. Finally, the doctrine of just war also insists that lethal violence may be used only with the intention of securing a just peace (reconciliation). This intention is not compatible with motives such as hatred or unloving anger. And it is all the more incompatible with a religious nationalist view of the enemy, which sees them as infidels to be ruthlessly destroyed by the righteous, and not just as one set of sinners whose evil actions must, alas, be curtailed by another set.

CHAPTER FIFTEEN

# The Quest for Freedom in a Culture of Choice

## Stephen J. Duffy

### INTRODUCTION

Freedom reigns supreme among Western values. But freedom is one of those core words in the language of human experience for which, like being, goodness, truth, beauty, we can find no universally acceptable definition. Because freedom is at the heart of our distinctive being as humans, different perceptions of what a human being is lead to rival views concerning the meaning of freedom.[1] Christianity has offered its own understanding of freedom, and in advancing its view it merges at some points with other views. Where it diverges it may offer worthwhile correctives. I want, therefore, to reflect on the meaning of freedom in the Christian theological tradition.

To clear the way for our reflections, at the outset I postulate the existence of freedom. Freedom assumes myriad forms, but beneath them all resides the basic freedom of the person, transcendental, essential or inner freedom. This essential freedom is not a thing with empirically describable properties. Rather, it is the condition grounding the possibility of the phenomena of our experience that render us distinctive as humans. Usually, and with some truth, freedom is defined in negative terms as freedom *from*. Though this, as we shall see, is not completely adequate, freedom is first of all a negation, an absence of restraints, a distancing from nature and the world of persons and things; we are beings not wholly subject to nature's or society's compulsions. This transcendence is freedom's beginning. In a way, freedom is the empty space, the room left us for maneuvering within these determinisms.

---

1. On rival views of freedom see P. Hodgson, *A New Birth of Freedom: A Theology of Bondage and Liberation* (Philadelphia: Fortress, 1976), 42-112. On Catholicism's confrontation with modernity's views of freedom in the nineteenth and twentieth centuries see W. Kasper, *The Christian Understanding of Freedom and the History of Freedom in the Modern Era* (Milwaukee: Marquette University Press, 1988).

On the other hand, because freedom is not a thing, and therefore not empirically accessible for observation and verification, some espouse a determinism of some kind, in terms of which any postulation of freedom is considered unscientific, even antiscientific. This is wrongheaded. Although there is no way to study freedom as an empirical object, it is freedom that makes science possible. All science thrives on judgments of what is true or false, probable or improbable. Such judgments are reached on rational grounds. But if determinism has it right, rational discrimination, and science with it, becomes impossible. We are wrong to think we are reasoning. We are simply being manipulated by our physical and social environments. Beliefs and judgments, including the belief in universal determinism, become unalterably determined products of chains of natural causes beyond our control, not the conclusions of any truly rational process in humans.

Our physical and social environments are important factors, but to make them the whole story undercuts true science, to say nothing of our juridical systems and our responsibility as moral agents, since we become mere spectators of our lives. What is questionable is not the validity of studies of brain chemistry or sociological correlations, but the paradigm that is operative when causal relations are thought to exhaustively define human behaviour. At a certain level the paradigm of causality is valid. However, it overlooks human beings' experience of themselves. Because that experience cannot be quantified, it does not fall into the causal network. Though we cannot prove that we are free, which would demand a misguided objectivisation of freedom, we have to postulate it to ground rational discrimination and moral agency.

It is mistaken, however, at the other extreme, to deny that human behaviour is determined by external and internal factors. Nor is such a denial required to defend freedom against fatalism. We are not so autonomous as to be wholly independent of the determinations of our physical and social environments. We are not angelic intellects inhabiting physical vehicles that have no effect upon our motivations. These are not creations *ex nihilo* of our freedom. We are born into worlds of culture and language and subject to the necessities of our biology. Skinner, therefore, correctly drew attention to the conditioned character of our behavior.[2] Behaviourist theories are right about the involuntary elements at work in our lives. But we must distinguish between determinisms setting limits and strict causality. Motives for an action are not independent of the decision that invokes and shapes them, all the while itself being shaped by them. These involuntary elements cease being extrinsic elements once they enter the circle of the voluntary. Motives acquire significance from the will they dispose and solicit. The will determines them by its choice, adopts them in its consent. Motives determine the will only insofar as the will determines itself. Motives incline, they do not compel. Passivity and activity lie at the heart of decision.[3]

Today, the image of the scientist, able to understand and manipulate the determining elements of destiny, promises a more extravagant freedom than any previous mythic image. This modern myth portrays the people in white coats as free, able to exercise control according to their creative purposes and the person on the table as an object of inquiry. However, the one on the table can always look back at the investigator-controller, even cheat on the objective test. As Langdon Gilkey has remarked, since both the controller and the controlled can be instances of the same things, freedom and determinism, the myth self-destructs. A myth promising freedom from destiny's necessities on the basis of humanity's complete subservience to necessitating determinisms is even less intelligible than paradoxical theological accounts of the conundrum of grace and freedom.[4]

### FREEDOM AS GIFT, TASK AND GOAL
### IN THE JUDEO-CHRISTIAN TRADITION

What can the Judeo-Christian tradition contribute to our understanding of freedom? In this tradition freedom, like everything

2. B. F. Skinner, *Beyond Freedom and Dignity* (New York: Knopf, 1971). See P. Ricoeur, 'A Critique of B. F. Skinner's Beyond Freedom and Dignity,' *Philosophy Today* 17 (1973), 166-175.

3. P. Ricoeur, *Freedom and Nature: the Voluntary and the Involuntary* (Evanston, IL: Northwestern University Press, 1966). See also E. Farley, 'Toward a Contemporary Theology of Human Being,' in J. Angell and E. Banks (eds), *Images of Man: Studies in Religion and Anthropology* (Macon, GA: Mercer University Press, 1984), 55-78.

4. See L. Gilkey, *Religion and the Scientific Future: Reflections on Myth, Science and Theology* (New York: Harper & Row, 1970), especially ch 3.

else, is considered in relation to God. The starting point is creation. The human person is created free, an assertion that tows in its wake several implications.[5] First, freedom is not something humans seize from God; rather, it belongs to humans as a gift of creation. It is the distinctive mark of a being created in the image of the free God. But second, the gift entails a charge, a vocation. Freedom is a dynamic, not a static endowment. 'You were called to freedom,' says Paul (Gal 5:13). Created in the image of God (Gen 1:26), humans must become more and more conformed to that image, as the Christ was. Freedom is gift and acquisition, privilege and responsibility, goal and task. As Irenaeus of Lyon (130-200 AD) has it, humans are made in the image of God but must grow into likeness to God, i.e. be conformed to the Christ.[6]

Third, humans are called to creativity; they are created to be, with God, co-creators. The gift is a task, an adventure we must embark upon. Images of a creative God, humans are creators of a world. God has perfectly made an imperfect world that humans might perfect it. Freedom is more adventure than possession; it is given to us to explore the unknown, the undreamed of, to fashion the new by our free initiatives. Confronting the old, freedom becomes negation, but freedom cannot live as negation, purely as freedom *from*. It flourishes on affirmation, as freedom *for* God's inbreaking future.

Fourth, far from setting out on a purely private or humanistic adventure, we are by reason of our freedom summoned to assume a role in the Creator's plan. We are challenged to construct not just an earthly city but the kingdom of God. The Christian prayer 'Thy kingdom come' signals awareness that we are participants in a drama far vaster than the private pursuits of our small biographies. Paul steers us away from overly anthropo-

---

5. For this sketch of the Judeo-Christian vision of freedom I am indebted to A. Gesché, 'L'invention chrétienne de la liberté,' *Revue Theologique de Louvain* 28 (1997), 3-27. See also H. Schleier, 'Eleutheria,' in G. Kittel (ed), *Theological Dictionary of the New Testament* (Grand Rapids, MI: Eerdmans, 1964), II, 487-502. I do not imply that biblical notions of freedom are posed in the philosophical terms of modernity. Vatican II opened a new chapter in Christian understanding of freedom as it initiated a new openness to modernity. One catalyst was twentieth-century totalitarianism. But Vatican II did not integrate the idea of religious freedom (*Dignitatis Humanae*) into a comprehensive theology of freedom. See W. Kasper, *The Christian Understanding of Freedom*.
6. *Against Heresies*, v. vi, 1; xxxviii, 2 and 3; xxxix, 1.

centric views and casts our freedom into a cosmological perspective: 'Creation awaits with eager longing for the revealing
of the children of God ... that creation itself will be set free from
its bondage to decay and will obtain the freedom of the glory of
the children of God' (Rom 8:19, 21). Paul detects a mysterious
affinity between humans and God's total creation, of which humans are part, and with which humans are meant to share the
call to freedom. This flies in the face of the dualisms bedevilling
the Hellenistic world that saw only incongruity between human
freedom and the physical world.

Finally, the biblical tradition alerts us to the fragility of freedom and views fallible humanity as ravaged by fault, which results from freedom's abuse, for freedom implies the capacity to
unmake what God has made. Evil, in the Judeo-Christian tradition, is neither woven into our being nor predestined by the
gods or fate, but enters God's creation through the door of
human choice. The defeat of evil is the theme of the liberation of
freedom (*eleutheria*) that Paul so often sounds. Authentic freedom is won not by overcoming a jealous God, but by throwing
off the chains of our own self-imposed bondage. 'For freedom
Christ has set you free. Stand firm and do not submit again to a
yoke of slavery,' says Paul (Gal 5:1). Thus Augustine's frequent
distinction between *liberum arbitrium*, free will, the capacity for
choice, and *libertas*, true feedom, the capacity to use free will as it
should be used, a capacity now in bondage and in need of freeing by God's grace. The flawed doctrine of original sin was an
attempt to articulate our dark underside, an uncomfortable
truth for our secularised cultures where 'evil' and 'sin' have all
but vanished from the vocabulary, as have the symbols once
helpful in giving expression to our experience of evil. If the doctrine of original sin was shelter from naïve optimism about
humanity, it was shelter also from an excessively brutal view of
humanity and despair, because it told the human story not only
in terms of fallibility but in terms of redeemability as well.[7]

These are, then, the distinctive characteristics of freedom in
the Christian tradition. In sum, the tradition affirms that God is
not an overpowering God, the blinding incandescence of whose
presence incinerates human freedom. God has placed a discrete
distance between Godself and creatures so as to allow us room

---

7. See S. Duffy, 'Our Hearts of Darkness: Original Sin Revisited,'
*Theological Studies* 49 (1988), 597-622.

and space. This God of the possible, according to the tradition, wants humans to freely make actual the possible, not to be marionettes acting out a pre-scripted story. Aquinas marvelled that human freedom was woven into the plan of divine providence.[8] When theology denigrates humanity, that is an indication of probable error. Not that we should negate divine transcendence so as to aggrandise humanity and its freedom. But can a theology of God be adequate if based upon denigration of God's creation? Often, inadequate theologies are rooted in inadequate anthropologies, which lead to false gods, false because falsifying the image of God, they falsify God. Fragile humanity is fallen, but no lower than God descended in the Christ. Anthropology is the touchstone of theology.

FREEDOM AS CHOICE

One of the markers setting off modernity from previous historical periods is choice. In the secularised consciousness of the West, freedom means the ability to make choices on one's own without outside influences or constraints. Modernity privileges choice as the apex of human aspiration. In this mindset, freedom increases as one's options increase. The greater the multiplicity of models, flavours, styles, brands, the freer we believe ourselves to be. There is a kernel of truth in this. Freedom is the capacity to act on one's own independent initiative. Negation of this is negation of responsibility, of juridical and ethical accountability. But that said, there remains need for nuance.

The reduction of freedom to arbitrary choice creates the illusion that life is a kind of shopping mall and choice a kind of economic transaction based on a cost-benefit analysis. This commodification of life risks the trivialisation of freedom by consumerist culture. The phrase 'standard of living,' viz. that in accord with which people can live humanly, has imperceptibly come to be measured by our growing capacity to consume. This makes economic advance, irrespective of the nature of the advance, a socio-political priority. In many ways we choosers have become a generation of surfers moving from choice to choice. A dizzying multiplicity of options may leave us restless, drained of energy and discernment needed for truly serious decisions, where our options are limited, if indeed there are options at all. For the array of options varies inversely with the importance of

---

8. *S.T.* I, q. 22, a. 2, ad 4.

the decision to be made. Yet endless options about things basically the same erode the ability to distinguish the significant
from the trivial as all choices become the same. This cult of
choice fits well with modern individualism and flight from social
consciousness and responsibility. In our atomised societies, private pursuits of personal happiness and special interest groups'
pursuit of their own selfish ends trump the common pursuit of
the good society. Where freedom reduces to arbitrary choice,
others fast become hindrances to my freedom, objects of resentment.[9] But do we want to be creatures of the global market or
creators of a more humane global community?

In connection with freedom as choice, most would also view
freedom as the capacity to choose between good and evil, to sin
or not. This is true: what and how we choose is as important as
that we freely choose. To assume that all that matters is that I
choose freely, no matter what I choose, is narcissistic choice for
the sake of choice, and again, the trivialisation of choice. Not all
options are equally worthwhile just because freely chosen.
Choice does not of itself confer value. This line of thinking about
freedom as the capacity to choose either good or evil goes awry,
however, when it assumes that we stand in a posture of indifference before good and evil. First, the ability to choose between
good and evil seems not to be of the essence of freedom. God,
whose image we are, is pre-eminently free, yet cannot choose
evil. The unjustified sinner, according to the Christian tradition,
cannot not sin (*non posse non peccare*); the just are able not to sin
(*posse non peccare*); and the *beati*, confirmed in good, cannot any
longer sin (*non posse peccare*), absorbed as they are in the
supreme good, an absorption already seen in the predictability
of the virtuous person. Is the predictable virtuous person less
free than the unpredictable libertine?

Second, the will is not neutral, straddling the fence between
good and evil. Far from being neutral, we are, prior to any
choice, already determined to the good, to universal good. The

9. See S. Freud, *Civilization and Its Discontents* (New York: Norton, 1961).
Despite the cult of choice and the pursuit of pleasure, discontent dogs
many Americans who are overworked and overspent. See the studies
of L. Calder, *Financing the American Dream: A Cultural History of
Consumer Credit* (Princeton, NJ: Princeton University Press, 1999) and J.
Schor, *The Overworked American: the Unexpected Decline of Leisure* (New
York: Basic Books, 1991).

will, the heart itself, is insatiable hunger for the comprehensive good. Even when one does evil, it is behind a facade of seeking what is good. Freedom is freedom to seek and do the good. To bring about evil, the absence of due good, is to fail the good, to abuse freedom and refuse to be what we are. This is unfreedom, a moral vacuum. Sartre, in *Being and Nothingness*, describes this as 'bad faith,' choosing what runs counter to authentic humanity while at the same time viewing such choices as life-promoting and of value.[10] The tragic irony is that evil choices in the guise of good are parasitic. They draw energy from the heart's dynamic eros for the good. We cannot gauge the worth of anything without affirming the all-encompassing good, source of all worth. To make any lesser good our master does not free us but debases our attachment to and dependence upon the all-inclusive good. Allegiance to a pretender cannot be 'instead of' but only 'in addition to,' which places us in self-contradiction. The self becomes a house divided, and divided selves lead to divided societies, which, in a vicious cycle, foster divided selves. Socio-political and economic divisions reflect deeper religious problems within divided selves living together. In sum, negation of the unlimited good that is the horizon of all our choices is a travesty of self-determination, and in reality, self-negation.

The real opposition, then, is not between freedom and necessity or determinacy, but between freedom and sin, the negation of the heart's eros. Freedom and necessity as such are not opposed, but freedom and an inner servitude that compels one to act contrary to one's authentic nature. Aquinas speaks of the will's inbuilt finality, its determinacy to the comprehensive good as a natural and necessitating appetite, the *voluntas ut natura*, the will as nature, which asserts its grounding presence in all affective and voluntary movements.[11] Augustine is more existential: 'Thou hast made us for Thyself, O Lord, and our hearts are

---

10. J.-P, Sartre, *Being and Nothingness: An Essay in Phenomenological Ontology* (New York: Philosophical Library, 1956). See also Aquinas, *De Malo* 6.7 and *S.T.* I-II, q. 10, a. 2; F. Gamwell, 'The House Divided,' *Criterion* (Spring 2001), 18-22.

11. *De Veritate*, q. 22, a. 1; q. 25, a. 1; S.T. I, q. 60, a. 5; q. 108, a. 8; I-II, q. 1, a. 2. The ambiguity of the term 'will as nature' reflects the ambiguity of the term 'nature,' which has metaphysical, physical, and social meanings. See also S. Duffy, *The Dynamics of Grace: Perspectives in theological Anthropology* (Collegeville, MN: Glazier-Liturgical, 1993), 148-149, 158-160.

restless until they rest in Thee.'[12] For Thomas, the *voluntas ut natura*, the natural desire for the good, orients, sustains, and arouses the *voluntas ut ratio*, or the will of decision or choice, the willing of concrete, relative goods and the means to secure them. All too easily, particular goods transmute into the absolute good that they manifest and participate in. When that happens, they become demonic, their devotees enslaved and unfree, and the heart's eros stifled. No finite good can sate the heart because the heart's hunger is always already beyond every finite good as it forever thrusts toward the transcendent good, the lure of which is the ground of freedom and self-transcendence, and of our ceaseless restlessness for being, life, truth, goodness.

To put this another way, freedom is not sheer randomness, undirectedness, or unpredictability. What freedom requires is not unpredictability but something more positive, spontaneity. What matters is not that my acts are predictable but that they are my own. When magnanimous persons spontaneously act magnanimously, our reaction is not, 'How predictable'. Rather, we see these individuals as more free than those who are unpredictable because the latter are, for whatever reason, swept up in passions of the moment. So a directedness is scripted into us. We are not blank pages. Being determined to universal good is as necessary to freedom as light to seeing or sound to hearing. This determination is the condition of the possibility of freedom, not its antithesis. Unless there is something definite we want from the beginning, we will not be able to start choosing. Admittedly, given the plodding pace of human cognitional and moral development and of personal integration, we often lack sufficient knowledge to discern the authentic good. And even when we do, we may be unable to will it because our freedom is in self-imposed bondage.[13] A culture where diversions afforded by myriad choices overshadow meaning and value further aggravates matters. The distinction between fun and happiness, the pleasant and the good, blurs. Emotional elation is feeling good. Ethical happiness is doing and being good by pursuing the absolute good in and through all relative goods. This is not to deny room for what Thomas, following Aristotle, called the *bonum delectabile*, sheer pleasure, as distinct from the *bonum honestum*,

---

12. *Confessions*, Book 1.
13. Augustine's inability to will the conversion he desired is a classic example. See *Confessions*, Book 8.

an intrinsic good (e.g. health), and the *bonum utile*, a means to the intrinsic good (e.g. surgery).[14] But being ethically good, far from bringing emotional happiness, may be no fun and may cost one's life. Fun comes and goes; happiness is a steady state. In the end, freedom is authentic fulfilment, not just a capacity for choice, which at best bears the fruit of fulfilment and at worst is the manifestation of egoism and dissipation.

### FREEDOM AS SELF-CONSTITUTION

If we probe beneath the surface, where freedom is flattened out and narrowed into choice, we may at a deeper level see freedom for what it truly is, self-constitution. The self determines its course of action, freely chooses to act or not to act in a particular way, to pursue or not pursue particular goods. But freedom is not only about choosing this or that, but about defining oneself, what kind of self one wants to be. By its choices the self often unconsciously determines its stance toward life, its way of being in the world. In its depth, freedom is not about choosing this or that, but choosing in and through all the 'thises' and 'thats' the person I will be, someone open or closed to the mystery that draws us. The point here is not merely to exist, but to live a life so that its course and what we become are not just fated but freely plotted, insofar as possible. Choices about friends, work, family, civic life derive from the all-embracing decision that determines for us what gives value to our lives and loves, captures our heart and is our ultimate concern.

Of course, we can renege on self-creation, drift with no inner spiritual gyroscope, become shadow persons of no substance. To recognise that the significance of my life comes from its being chosen, however, requires that that significance and my choices depend on awareness that independent of me there is something worthwhile in shaping my life, that some life-options are more significant than others. Self-choice cannot be made in isolation. Defining myself is dependent on a horizon of values, on issues that matter, e.g. the needs of others, the duties of intelligent citizenship, the demands of truth, love of God. What makes me to be me is neither trivia, nor self-centred quests for fulfilment that

---

14. See e.g. Aristotle's *Nich. Eth.* 1, 2, 5 and 6; *S.T.* I, q. 5, a. 6; II-II, q. 145, a. 3. Though distinct, the three goods are not necessarily separate, but ideally integrated, e.g. better to do justice with pleasure than reluctance.

are oblivious to the collective wisdom of the past or opposed to the demands of social life. To turn a deaf ear to demands arising from beyond the self forfeits the possibility of significant self-constitution. In place of a self there is only a roiling stream of choices, suited to the moment. And all this has social consequences. There are no purely private choices and actions. Our choices and actions make us the kinds of persons we are, and in turn make society the kind of society it is.

What kind of person I am determines what I do with my freedom; what I do with my freedom determines what kind of person I am. This needs qualification, and we must turn to that below. For each human life is an intricate pattern of choosing, doing, but also of being done to, of activity and receptivity, of the voluntary and the involuntary. But even passivity can open the way to new levels of doing and becoming. We are not condemned to vanish without remainder into the circumstances of our lives, our genes, or our culture.

The Christian tradition adds to all this that choices are not only about self-definition, deciding who I shall be. They are also acceptance or rejection of a call inscribed in my being, an invitation that summons me in and through all the goods and all the dreams that entice desire. I am choosing not only who I shall be; I am also choosing myself in relation to and assuming a posture toward the absolute good, the mystery that is the horizon of all my decisions. Choosing this or that, choosing my self, and choosing or rejecting the holy mystery are not separate decisions. The three coinhere.

### FREEDOM AS SITUATED

We have contended that we do not stand before good and evil in a condition of neutrality and indifference, because a natural appetite determines us to the good prior to any choice, while evil is negation of that appetite and, therefore, of what we are. I want to suggest additional dimensions of our humanity that eliminate the possibility of neutrality in choosing between good and evil. These factors lead us to see that freedom is never absolute, but always relative, hemmed in, a situated freedom. Biological, psychological, social, and historical givens condition freedom. I am the sum of my choices, but I am to a large extent what others have bequeathed to and chosen for me.

First, disproportion is part and parcel of our humanity, for we are torn between finitude and infinitude. As Hamlet put it: 'O God, I could be bounded in a nutshell yet count myself a king of infinite space, were it not that I have bad dreams.' We are exocentric beings open to the beyond. We reach for the stars yet are earthbound, tethered to nature and history, of which we are part. We crave the universal, but must settle for the particular. We are tortured by failure to achieve our full possibilities, to do better than we have, to be more than we have become. Integration of these polarities, openness to the infinite with loving acceptance of our finitude, is difficult, because from the parentage of the two, angst is born. Frustration at the ambiguity in our being flows from this tragic dimension of our existence. And the always-latent threat of non-being, of having to die prods anxiety. In Kierkegaard's words, 'Anxiety is the dizziness of freedom when freedom gazes down into its own possibility grasping at finiteness to secure itself.'[15] Unable to tolerate the angst, we may overweight freedom, and veer toward destructive hubris and, in defiance of our finitude, toward a Nietzschean will to power. Or we may overweight our limitations, exchange our freedom for the bread of a false security and veer toward acedia, sloth, lack of self-assertion, even despair at our finitude. Shrinking from freedom and resting content with the 'good enough' of mediocrity can parade as simplicity and selflessness, when in fact, it may be the failure ever to become a self. For many, freedom's incessant possibilities are dreadfully frightening, a phenomenon Dostoevsky portrays in his story of the Grand Inquisitor in *The Brothers Karamazov*. We desire freedom yet flee its dizzying responsibility to seek illusory security in something finite. Angst, however, is not in itself evil. Without it we would never build a home, found a city, or seek a cure for illness. Nevertheless, angst remains a non-necessitating precondition for sin. Here, then, is a basic ontological phenomenon conditioning our freedom.

Second, there is our evolutionary heritage, that reservoir of unconscious libidinal energies and cravings that spontaneously

15. On the disproportion in human being and angst see S. Kierkegaard, *The Concept of Anxiety* (Princeton, NJ: Princeton University Press, 1980); M. Heidegger, *Being and Time* (New York: Harper & Row, 1962) 228-235; P. Ricoeur, *Fallible Man* (Chicago: Henry Regnery, 1965); W. Pannenberg, *Anthropology in Theological Perspective* (Philadelphia: Westminster, 1985) 96-107; S. Hiltner and K. Menninger (*eds*), *Constructive Aspects of Anxiety* (Nashville: Abingdon, 1963).

erupt and, controlled by the pleasure principle, clamour for satisfaction, what Freud called the id, 'a cauldron of seething excitement,' and somewhat akin to what Augustine called concupiscence and Paul called *epithumia*, covetous desire (Romans 7).
Try as it may to govern these unruly energies, the ego, the censor
aligned with the reality principle, is not always master in its own
house. Here again we experience a rift in our being, a psychic
dualism: the conscious and the unconscious, the voluntary and
the involuntary, the active and passive dimensions of our being.
As with angst, the id, or concupiscence, is not evil in itself.[16] It is
part of God's good creation, though in humans no longer exactly
what it is in other animals. The pleasures of bed and board are
blessings of our finitude. Nonetheless, gone awry, the psychic
tension makes of us divided selves to the point of bondage. Our
task is not suppression of these libidinal stirrings, for where
would civilisation be without the passion that creates poetry,
music, and the family? Rather, our task is integration of the
will's appetite for the good with these libidinal appetites so that
we become unified selves. Inner tension though there be, to
overspiritualise our being at the expense of what are wrongly
termed the 'lower' appetites, is to make of ourselves half-per-
sons. The id remains a constitutive ontological dimension conditioning freedom.

Closely linked with id and ego is that other component of our
personalities that may limit our freedom, the superego. If our
parents' first legacy is our genes, the superego is the second and
it shapes us psychically. Unconsciously, we internalise the values and disvalues of our parents, and their legacy lingers in the
sediment of the unconscious. Thus the superego is another involuntary given and a powerful, pre-reflexive, pre-volitional
moral orientation for good or ill. Yet while the superego is a natural facticity, we may through the history of our choices connive
with it and thereby reinforce it. Facticity meets with complicity,
much as the Greek tragic hero, finding himself in a situation not
of his making, effects his own undoing by the exercise of his
freedom. We are forever in a dynamic process of exchange between unconscious representations and conscious perceptions,
between an active sedimented past that conditions freedom and

---

16. See K. Rahner's revisionist essay on concupiscence, 'The Theological
Concept of Concupiscentia,' *Theological Investigations*, I (Baltimore:
Helicon, 1961), 347-382.

the calls that summon us from our present world and the approaching future.

Third, evil is not a private and static phenomenon; it has social and historical dimensions. Evil becomes incarnate in our culture's institutions and symbols, spreads like a contagion infecting each and all. There is the serpent within, but the serpent without as well, the already-thereness of evil lying in wait for us when we enter the world.[17] As Paul expresses it, sin is a demonic power, it enters the world, inhabits us; it abounds, it reigns (Romans 5). Paul's language is mythic, struggling to say what is unsayable in rational, discursive discourse. Through social, political, economic, and ecclesiastical institutions, with which we are complicit, evil becomes systemic and sin becomes social sin, organised sin, the sin we do together, and more than the sum of our individual sins. And it arises less from conscious choice than from blindness, lies, and self-deception. With globalisation, evil spirals. We now live in a world where transnational corporations have become the pivotal institutions, masters of our world, and we cannot vote them out or storm the palaces of the oligarchy, with whom we are complicit. There are corporations with vast potential for good, but also with a pitch-dark underside sustained by corporate cant and greed. The good turns demonic when institutions with vast potential for good and weighty social responsibility are driven by lust for power and profit.[18]

The point is that while consciousness precedes structure, structures in turn determine consciousness. We make a culture, the culture makes us and becomes a collective superego whose values and disvalues orient our freedom, endowing us with a powerful pre-volitional slant by teaching us what to love. In Augustine's physics of the heart, 'My weight is my love.' I choose what I love, indeed, I become what I love.[19] Our identity and the goods we love are inextricably linked. Before making any choices we have been shaped interiorly by culture and our

---

17. On the varied symbolism of the serpent in the Adamic myth see P. Ricoeur, *The Symbolism of Evil* (New York: Harper & Row, 1967), 252-259.

18. A telling case exemplifying our interrelatedness in evil appeared in 'Labor Progress Clashes with Global Reality,' *New York Times*, April 24, 2001, A1.

19. *Confessions*, Book 13, 9; Ep Jo, 2, 14.

communal past. If the siren call of social sin had its way it would become the all-encompassing horizon of our lives, for its logic is totalistic. The idolatry of hubris and the flight of acedia infect every social world. All human societies are at best ambiguous amalgams of community and alienation, freedom and oppression.

A fourth component of our humanity that conditions our freedom derives from our biological history. A long evolutionary process has physiologically encoded in our being a proclivity to selfishness which, if not properly ordered, tilts us toward diverse forms of aggression that render us clever savages capable of harming others and ourselves. This proclivity, in itself not evil, is the kernel of savagery surviving in us as the legacy of our evolutionary past and one more involuntary given that freedom must contend with and integrate with its desire for the good. Fifth, and finally, we stand at an epistemic distance from God, the supreme good, veiled in incomprehensibility. All God-talk reaches a breaking point and cannot bridge the abyss that yawns between infinity and the finite. Theologies fail us. Our world offers ambiguous evidence of God. We live *etsi Deus non daretur*, in a night of faith and hope. Meanwhile, the alluring loves of our life-world call to us, engross us, and nudge into oblivion the transcendent good.

Considering these five factors, we see the conditioned character of our vaunted freedom and, hence, our ethical impotence. There is a structural instability or fallibility in the human, who exists at the intersection of spirit and nature, consciousness and body, the personal and the social. Seduced by dark psychic powers within, ensnared in a history of evil without, we are unable wholeheartedly to pursue the good that beckons. Like middle-aged Augustine, after Paul (Rom 7:14-19), we feel the awful distance between 'I ought' and 'I can'. As Augustine said: 'Our hearts are not in our power.'[20] Small wonder that for Aquinas the re-creation of persons by grace is God's greatest work, greater than creation *ex nihilo*, for the stubborn contrarieties of the voluntary and the involuntary within us offer a resistance that nothingness cannot.[21] The poet Auden caught this well: 'We would rather be ruined than changed/ We would rather die in

---

20. *On the Gift of Perseverance*, 13; see also *Against Julian*, 3, 57.
21. *S.T.* I-II, q.113, a. 9.

our dread/ Than climb the cross of the moment/ And let our illusions die.'

To summarise, my existential or actual freedom is in process and has yet to coincide, if ever, with my essential freedom. Augustine was right to view us as 'convalescents' in whom two loves, *caritas* and *cupiditas* are at war. Luther, too, was right in seeing us as *simul iustus et peccator*. I shape my effective freedom by my choices, but involuntary elements shape it too. Herein lies the truth of the Greek tragic vision. No one's history can be understood in terms of pure freedom. There is choice but also heritage, room for blame and lament. Freedom and destiny play upon one another. In the end, we cannot speak adequately of human agency and freedom without resorting to this paradoxical double discourse. Christianity's profoundly realistic grasp of human fragility and redeemability moves beyond today's facile optimism and deadening despair.

## FREEDOM AS GRACED

Considering the reciprocity of voluntary and involuntary, we now have to ask what prevents the voluntary from being swamped by the involuntary.[22] How does community survive in a world of alienation and stifling, oppressive institutions? The will is ridden with instability. How, then, can it sustain itself in the face of the forces of its physical and social environments? The freedom the heart desires cannot be had, as Marx proclaimed, simply by a revolution in socio-economic and political structures, for the powers that bind us are primarily internal rather than external. Nor can freedom be won simply by freeing the psyche, as Stoicism, Freud, and some existentialists thought, for bondage perdures in the social order even as the individual psyche is liberated. Worst of all, cunning self-deception and bias blind us. Masters of deception, we deceive ourselves in deceiving others and the bondage of deception is objectified and reinforced in the institutions of our social existence.

Yet, we cannot release ourselves from our self-imposed captivity. Freedom is possible only if we remain open to a liberating power that transcends us and our physical and social environments. Such openness seems a structural component of human being. We cannot liberate ourselves because we ourselves are

---

22. For the framing of this question I am indebted to P. Hodgson's elaboration of it in *A New Birth of Freedom*, 151-166.

the captors. Thus Cassius to Brutus: 'The fault, dear Brutus, is not in our stars but in ourselves that we are underlings.' Because of our openness to the beyond, the *desideratum* not to be confused with our finite reality, our restlessness cannot be stilled by the ambiguous fulfilments history offers. We look for liberation from a power of deliverance that occurs in history from beyond history yet does not abandon it but draws it toward its goal, a kingdom of freedom.[23] 'Where sin increased, grace abounded all the more' (Rom 5:21). Open to our world, and in and through it to the beyond, we are forever looking past every experience. Thrusting to the beyond, the *desideratum* half-guessed in every finite good, our desires are endlessly unfulfillable. The infinite beyond is experienced by us as the power of the future.[24] What grounds and constitutes the power of the future lies beyond the range of philosophical anthropology. But the future's transforming power is experienced as redemptive, for the future holds hope of release from the past's dead weight and the present's bondage by bringing new possibilities within our horizon. Above the cacophony of tragedy we hear the music of redemption. Yet this leaves unanswered the question of the nature and origin of the redemptive event. Nonetheless, humans appear structurally open to being set free by a redeeming power not reducible to ourselves or our world. Are the redemption and liberation we seek and need realities or possibilities or, worse, illusions? Though we may be redeemable, are we in fact redeemed?

Arriving at this threshold we have to turn to a faith community and its symbols of bondage and liberation. That humans say yes to life, despite its cruelties, that they plan and play, love and hope seems to signal that redeemability is scripted into our being and detectable even before we turn to the symbols of a tradition. Humans continue to affirm life, anticipate, and sometimes experience liberation as a gift; they go on seeking an integration of freedom and the determinisms of nature through art, music, poetry, sport, and love. They live as though a kingdom of freedom is in the making. But, again, who is and what is the nature of the redeemer? To answer these questions each faith com-

---

23. G. W. F. Hegel, *The Phenomenology of Mind* (2 ed; London: George Allen & Unwin, 1949), 269-271.

24. This theme runs through W. Pannenberg's *Anthropology in Theological Perspective*, and his shorter work, *What is Man?* (Philadelphia: Fortress, 1970).

munity delves into its own symbolics of freedom. Christians who explore their own symbols would then have to engage in a hermeneutical theology that appropriates and translates their symbols, rendering them intelligible and meaningful to contemporary consciousness.[25] Providing an intelligible framework that enables Christianity to contribute to a new birth of freedom is the task of systematic theologians and ethicists, something more than I can do here, though I shall offer a glimpse of what we find in the Christian tradition.

Christians have long dealt with the questions raised above, at least from the time of Augustine. To compress our questions: what can one do to move beyond the limits of one's present horizon and the freedom it allows? Christianity's great doctors, Augustine, Thomas, Luther, and Calvin, answer: Alone, I can do nothing. They assert that this is a truth founded in Christian scriptures and experience. Were I able to move myself beyond the limits of my present freedom, I would not now be confined within those limits. Something, someone must act on me from without and within to free my freedom, enable me to break out; something, someone has to draw the heart, liberate my powers of self-realisation awaiting release. For Paul, the love of God, the universal good that Augustine and Thomas see as the heart's desire, has to be 'poured into our hearts through the Holy Spirit that has been given to us' (Rom 5:5). The tradition came to speak of this empowering gift as grace. In Augustine's view, despite our sinfulness, we retain freedom of choice (*liberum arbitrium*), but not freedom in its deepest reality (*libertas*), the ability to be what we are meant to be, lovers of the supreme good above all else and of all else in and for the supreme good. To the extent that we fall short of this, our lives and loves are disordered. Grace reorients us, brings a new spontaneity, a new disposition and horizon, a qualitative change in our mode of being. Christ mediates the Spirit of freedom: 'If the Son makes you free, you will be free indeed' (Jn 8:36). Yet despite our re-creation by grace, always we fall short. Our entanglement in sin is never completely voluntary, because sin becomes habit and cultural *modus vivendi*, and because the enduring power of the involuntary renders commitment to good or evil less than wholehearted. Disposal of the self in basic freedom is never total, but can grow in depth and intensity and has to be sustained in choices made

25. See, e.g. P. Hodgson, *New Birth of Freedom*, chs 5, 6 and 7.

in myriad situations in face of the involuntary. But total self-determination goes unrealised. Ambiguity dogs human agency. Thus our sin, while ours, is also something suffered. It is moral evil, but it is nature as well; it begs forgiveness, but also liberation. Because sin, personal and social, is born of the entwinement of the voluntary and the involuntary, grace is not restricted to the realm of conscious, deliberate action. In its depths, where hidden roots stretch forth from a preconscious matrix of psychic and social forces, sin must be met by a correlative depth of grace. Sin thrives, but grace all the more in heights and depths of our being unsuspected.

The relationship of grace and freedom leads to a thicket of difficulties, as the history of theology and philosophy attest. But perhaps we find analogies in everyday experience. We know that relationships with others are a function of our self-concept, of our self-love.[26] To arrive at awareness of our own worth and an ordered love of self, however, we have to be graced by someone's gift of love. One becomes a self only in relationship to significant others. To be is to-be-to-another. Being loved by the other frees us, makes us lovable and capable of loving. Yet the other's love comes only as gift, as grace. It cannot be coerced, earned, or bought. We experience this in the nurturing, freeing love of parents for children; in the caring teacher who draws out and makes free the student snared in fear and blind to her own capacities, in the therapist who assists persons in freeing themselves from their inner demons. Paradoxically, freedom grows with dependence. We have to be drawn to freedom by another's gracious caring. And because God's gracing presence is always incarnated, these others are mediations of that presence. But a stumbling block is met here in squaring freedom with the idea of its 'being caused,' for freedom appears to be *causa sui*, self-causing rather than caused by another. Yet, while there are forms of causality that affect us as objects, love 'causes' in a manner quite different from mechanical modes of causality. Love nourishes our being and autonomy as persons. Freedom and being influenced as a person are not incompatible, but live in reciprocity. One who draws, encourages, empowers, and sustains us does not devour us, but frees us. Our identity is shaped by the people who love us and whom we love. They are forever embedded in

---

26. On the importance of love of self see Aquinas, *S.T.* II-II, q. 26. a.'s 3, 4, and 5.

our identity. The creation and sustaining of our identity remains throughout our lives inescapably dialogical.

Although the flourishing of freedom is from start to finish, Christians claim, the work of God, it does not follow that free human agency is negated. However, philosophers and theologians have not and cannot articulate the compatibility of divine and human agency to the satisfaction of most, Christians included, most of whom are Pelagians of some stripe. The problem, better yet, the mystery, remains a neuralgic point among Christians, with some, especially Catholics, stressing humans' free co-operation with grace; others, especially Lutherans, stressing the primacy of divine initiative. Neither denies both divine and human agency. All is grace, yet the human agent does not do nothing when choosing the good with the help of grace. Freedom is gift and choice. A new birth of freedom is the work of God and of humans, though on infinitely different levels, hence neither a divine monergism nor a synergism of two equal, independent agents. A human is exactly that, a human, image of the free God, not a stone or a cabbage. The turn to the good, while due to divine initiative, must be a human turning, thus a free turning.

There is no threat to God's sovereignty and universal causality in allowing creatures the fullest measure of free agency. It is a measure of God's creative power that it can raise up creatures who participate in the divine being to such a degree that they are, in their turn, creative and sustaining. In the words of Aquinas, 'To detract from the perfection of creatures is to detract from the perfection of divine power.'[27] God is primary cause, ground of all being and action; creatures are secondary causes, moved movers receiving from God power to freely act. These diverse causalities, divine and human, are not two species of a genus. The former is cause of all causes; the latter participates in the power of the former. God does not act in the world apart from secondary causes, nor beside them, nor as complementary to them, each contributing distinct elements to the outcome. God, transcendent creator, is necessarily immanent and does not from time to time insert Godself into the series of finite causes, but empowers and sustains each member of the finite series of causes and the series itself. God acts in and through finite agents, the one effect issuing simultaneously from the primary

---

27. *S. C. G.* 3, 69, 15.

and secondary causal agents, each standing, as Aquinas says, in a different relationship to the outcome.[28] Against any simplistic determinism of grace, therefore, the Christian tradition forged a more complex anthropology involving humanity's total dependence upon a gracious God in receiving the gift of freedom and its liberation, enabling it to freely co-operate in its own ongoing regeneration. Grace and freedom are not at war; the former is the condition of the latter's possibility. The issue is not whether grace and freedom are compatible, but whether freedom is even possible without the divine empowering presence. Grace, God's healing, liberating, self-communicating presence, does not negate human freedom, but presupposes and perfects it. 'Gratia non tollit naturam, sed praesupponit et perficit.'[29] That which fulfills freedom cannot be something less than freedom itself.

CONCLUSION: FREEDOM AS CRUCIFORM

The Enlightenment and its child, modernity, as noted, glorify autonomy, freedom as choice, self-determination. Christianity does not rest easy with that, for choice and self-determination are ambiguous. They can be sources of authentic selfhood, but also of folly and evil. No emancipation can immunise individuals or society to the re-emergence of idolatry and injustice. Freeing freedom intellectually, socially, and politically frees for truth, reconciliation, and justice, but for wrongdoing as well. This, however, is not reason to abandon efforts at reform, but simply a *caveat* against naïve optimism. Recall that free, enlightened moderns made the twentieth century a slaughterbench. Of ourselves we cannot resolve the mystery of our tragic existence, our misuse of freedom. A Christian reading of history differs from secular readings, not merely because it asserts that God is ground and goal of all processes of liberation, but more so because it affirms the ongoing need for forgiving, healing, reconciling grace, and the new possibilities that God alone, the absolute future, can provide for the relentless perversity of even liberated humans. As tensive theological symbols, 'freedom' and 'liberation' are more far-ranging than as political or eco-

---

28. *Ibid.*, 3, 70.
29. *S. T.* I, q. 1, a. 8, ad 2; q. 19, a. 5. On the history of this axiom see J. Alfaro, 'Gratia Supponit Naturam,' in J. Hofer and K. Rahner (eds), *Lexicon für Theologie und Kirche* (2 ed; Freiburg: Herder, 1957-1968), IV, 1169-1171.

nomic categories. They surely include these two spheres as integral to a new birth of freedom and to salvation, yet move beyond them, for the roadblock on the way to the kingdom of the free is sin, the root of all injustice and oppression.

Sometimes, modernity's rhetoric about freedom rings more Kantian and Enlightenment-inspired than Christian. Kant saw enlightenment as release from self-imposed intellectual tutelage and from the incapacity to resort to one's own understanding. The problem was, he said, not lack of reason but of courage to cast off self-incurred bondage. Others after Kant urged casting off social, political, and economic bonds. The measure of this noble vision and its positive impulses, however, must be taken by the Christian vision; while certainly more sober, it does not demand rejection out of hand of all Enlightenment ideals, for they greatly enhance humanity, *pace* Pius IX. Nevertheless, Christianity adds qualifiers. The hope of Christians is well expressed by Chesterton: to sing both the *Marseillaise* and the *Magnificat*.[30] In many ways, modernity is less defection from its Judeo-Christian roots than a flowering of their secular possibilities. Still, the Christian vision modifies the meaning of autonomy. What Christianity envisions, following the one who 'emptied himself, taking the form of a servant' (Phil 2:7), is not a life free of suffering and servanthood, but a life that freely takes on servanthood to the point of voluntarily taking on suffering as an action in behalf of the other. The Christian seeks less to be free than to be of service. Paradoxically, freedom is realised in service. The first Adam lost freedom in attempting to seize it; the second Adam won freedom in surrendering it. Christian freedom is not a privatistic autonomy, free from all claims but those it pleases us to take on. Freedom is not sheer autonomy, but response-ability. Freedom comes when we allow the summons of the other to challenge the egoism of our autonomy.

Iris Murdoch suggests, not with complete fairness, perhaps, that we live in 'the age of Kantian man,' or 'Kantian man-god,'

---

30. With Vatican II's *Dignitatis Humanae* Catholicism accepted, after much foot dragging, some concerns of the Enlightenment. Nonetheless, church leaders have yet to arrive at a middle ground between two one-sided reactions, outright rejection or endorsement of modernity's views of freedom. Church leadership in the modern era has been more authoritarian and imposing of uniformity than the medieval church. See W. Kasper, *The Christian Understanding of Freedom.*

portrayed in the *Grundlegung*, the man who turns away even
from Christ to ponder his own conscience, listen for the still,
quiet voice of his own reason; the man who is free, independent,
rational, strong, perhaps lonely, but courageous; the hero strid-
ing through numerous films and novels. Conscious of estrange-
ment from the material world, he probes it, tries to control it.
But, Murdoch notes, it is a short step from Kant to Nietzsche. In
fact, Kantian man, Murdoch notes, nearly a century earlier, had
been incarnated in Milton's work; his name, Lucifer.[31] Where
each one's aim is to become sole, uncompromising agent of
one's own destiny, society's atomisation waxes and solidarity
wanes. Not that self-determination is inherently incompatible
with solidarity in community, but the tension between them is
constant and integration no easy task, indeed, impossible left to
our own meagre resources.

The struggle for freedom is not incidental to Christian life,
but integral to it. 'For freedom Christ has set us free; stand fast
therefore, and do not submit again to a yoke of slavery,' charges
Paul (Gal 5:1). But the freedom Christians are called to is of a distinct kind. The meaning of freedom for Christianity is found in
the crucified and risen one. This freedom lives by the law of the
cross. Not only a freedom *from* but a freedom *for*, it responds to
the need of the vulnerable other. 'You were called to freedom,'
Paul continues, 'only do not use your freedom as the opportunity
for the flesh, but through love be servants of one another' (Gal
5:13-15). Christian freedom is, ideally, service, even to the point
of willingness to suffer and die for the other. One is called to
reach the point where one aims not simply to become master of
one's own destiny but where, as John's Jesus says, 'You will
stretch out your hands and another will gird you and carry you
where you do not wish to go' (Jn 21:18). Many find this unrealis-
tic. No doubt, few approach this ideal. But it is the standard to be
aspired to in one's small acre of the world. The cruciform freedom to which Christians are called may not be reduced to the
liberation desired and struggled for in so many post-
Enlightenment contexts. It includes but transcends them. But
neither does a cruciform freedom imply supine passivity, obse-
quious subservience, much less the *acedia* noted earlier, an absence of self-realisation. Pure heteronomy is as destructive of

---

31. *The Sovereignty of the Good* (New York: Schocken, 1971), 80.

personhood as pure autonomy. Rather, Christian freedom is self-involving freedom that willingly engages in service, even suffering, as an action for the well being of others. It may involve strenuous effort, consuming struggle to achieve healing, reconciliation, justice. Authenticity, for theonomous personhood, is arrived at only through ecstasis towards others. For Christianity, there is a cross erected over history. Freedom comes by embracing it.

CHAPTER SIXTEEN

# Virtues and the God Who Makes Everything New

## Maureen Junker-Kenny

At a time when disciplinary boundaries are shifting, new affinities are being discovered, and immediate interaction takes place between, e.g. New Testament Studies and Christian Ethics, it is worthwhile to probe some of the assumptions behind the new flourishing of such co-operations.[1] The reality of such joint ventures may be a sign that historical enquiries can meet with contemporary concerns; history is not just antiquarian and ethics not merely ruled by the urgent demands of today's world. The 'ugly ditches' between history, truths of reason and theological appropriations may have actually been filled in and made passable through the hermeneutical awareness that all sciences, be they secular or biblical and theological, start from presuppositions they have to lay open and justify. Thus, the assessment of historical processes depends on one's horizon of expectation and cannot be passed off as 'objective' without giving account of how a scholar construes the relationship between the present, the past and the future.[2]

1. See, e.g., M. Welker and F. Schweitzer (eds), *Reconsidering the Boundaries between Theological Disciplines. Zur Neubestimmung der Grenzen zwischen den theologischen Disziplinen* (Münster: LIT-Verlag, 2004).
2. Cf P. Ricoeur, *Hermeneutics and the Human Sciences. Essays on Language, Action, and Interpretation* (ed and trs by J. Thompson) (Cambridge: CUP, 1981), 63-100. In *Memory, History, Forgetting* (trs K. Blamey, D. Pellauer) (Chicago: University of Chicago Press, 2004), 333-342), he distinguishes between the historian's task of 'representation' over against 'interpretation' as a 'second order reflection on the entire course of this operation' (333). A parallel to this critical philosophical insight into historical reconstruction can be found in the distinctions offered by Halvor Moxnes, *Putting Jesus in his Place. A Radical Vision of Household and Kingdom* (Louisville and London: J. Knox Press, 2003) which Seán Freyne quotes in *Jesus, a Jewish Galilean* (London: T& T Clark, 2004), 18: Instead of taking location positivistically as a geographical given, the concept of 'place' needs to be reconstructed in

But the directness of the new links sought between historical and practical disciplines across a previously gaping precipice may also betray a problematic loss of the willingness to engage in systematic perspectives;[3] 'systematic' in the sense of seeking a coherent thought form in which the ongoing significance of the biblical heritage is outlined with regard to contemporary self-understandings. Yet it is true that such coherence has not even been achieved in Systematic Theology. The following observation of the simultaneous use of alternative paradigms shows that it still remains very much a project:

> The *ad hoc* use of arbitrary means of thought is not an adequate method; e.g. to conceive of the celebration of the mysteries of faith with Platonic, of the Eucharistic presence of Jesus Christ with Aristotelian categories, to go on to grasp the unity of divinity and humanity in his being in Neo-Chalcedonian or in Hegelian-speculative terms, and at the same time apply some thought forms from a theory of freedom to the proceedings of revelation, tradition and grace. Since in changing from one thought form to another also the content of what is thought changes, this manner of proceeding either overlooks the objective interference of the content of the themes treated, or the incompatibility of the thought forms used.[4]

three dimensions: 'the experience of place, namely, how it is managed and controlled; the legitimation of place, i.e. the ideological underpinning of the dominant controlling view; and the imagination of place or the way in which an alternative vision of place can be developed'. The ethical relevance of such critical hermeneutical reconstruction of the present in the light of past legitimations and alternative futures is evident. The theological question about the 'the imaginative resources available to Jesus' for 'his version of Galilee' (18-19) leads to the creation and prophetic traditions in the Hebrew Bible. How their interplay is traced by Seán Freyne will give clues further below as to how the concept of Christian community can and cannot be defined.

3. For a parallel concern from the discipline of philosophy when its genuine task and method of reflecting on the genesis and validity claims of products of the human spirit gets levelled down in the comparatistic perspective of 'cultural studies,' see especially Birgit Recki's contributions to the discussion on 'Die kulturwissenschaftliche Wende' with Thomas Goeller, Ralf Konersmann and Oswald Schwemmer in *Information Philosophie* 33 (2005) 20-32.

4. Th. Pröpper, 'Zur vielfältigen Rede von der Gegenwart Gottes und Jesu Christi,' in *Evangelium und freie Vernunft* (Freiburg: Herder, 2001), 245-265, 245-46. All translations from German titles are my own.

In view of this analysis of irreconcilable methods, can Christian Ethics be blamed for not wanting to get bogged down in the quagmire of never-ending systematic quarrels? What is wrong about reaching for uplifting biblical concepts and images such as 'covenant' or 'city on the mountain' to inspire the types of practice and disposition Christian Ethics is held to reflect on? The accompanying move away from a mainly prohibitive style of Moral Theology towards a Christian Ethics of capability, from 'ought' to 'can do,' may have sound theological reasons behind it. Yet on the other hand, counter-movements to what is perceived as the ruling modern orthodoxies may not be free from ideology themselves. There could be just as much cultural drivenness behind the position that sees modernity solely in terms of decline as in the opposite desire to be fresh, innovative, and daring in aiming to create a discipline as fetching in its own way as contemporary appeals to market attraction and fun. Can a balance be struck between the aims of rehabilitating understandings of ethics that have been sidelined unjustly and to the detriment of contemporary moral experience, and the urge of Christian Ethics to be cutting-edge or at least not behind the times?

Praxis-oriented disciplines such as Ethics cannot wait for all conceptual disputes to be resolved before they venture what may turn out to be premature and wrong conclusions. Yet, by eclipsing systematic theological reflection one runs the risk of short-circuiting Christian ethical argumentation by jumping from the ancient world straight into the postmodern: from pre-secular to post-secular, Patristic to post-liberal, from early Christian to late modern ecclesial communities, or from antique philosophical to (early and modern) Christian virtue ethics. In what follows I am going to investigate the claim that Christian Ethics should take the form of virtue ethics by comparing the classical philosophical tradition of virtues and its theoretical underpinnings to exegetical accounts of the Jesus who proclaimed a Creator who makes everything new. Here, Theological Ethics can learn from systematic theological enquiries into the gradual change of Greek philosophical concepts of God effected by the biblical testimony to a God of liberation, faithfulness and of the unique power to begin. By illustrating the need to go back to such issues of systematic reflection, I am hoping to upset the easy alliance between the decidedly non-speculative self-understandings that historical and practical disciplines sport of themselves.[5]

My enquiry into current attempts to recast Christian Ethics as a whole in the antique 'virtue' mode will take the following steps: In order to clarify in what the distinctiveness of Christian Ethics consists (1), and starting from the discontents expressed with modern, i.e. 'liberal' approaches to deliver on this (2), I will discuss the charges of individualism versus community (a), and of rule-definition versus character-orientation (b). The position resulting from these options will be examined in the light of the status that ethics receives in a hermeneutical-contextual framework over against a critical deontological one (c).

---

5. 'Systematicians beware!' is how Seán Freyne ended a public lecture on 'The Bible and Christian Theology: Inspiration, Projection, Critique?' In his 'Introduction: Understanding the Issues of Unity and Diversity of Scripture Today' to the Concilium issue *The Many Voices of the Bible*, S. Freyne and E. Van Wolde (eds) (London: SCM Press, 2002), 7-8, its diversity and conflicting voices are explored 'as a challenge to a monistic understanding that is often imposed on the Bible in the name of canonical orthodoxy.' His warning in the lecture was issued against the tendency to downplay 'differences and disputes,' such as those between Paul and the Judaisers of Galatia and within the Johannine community, and to 'seek to establish agreement between them in the name of a pure biblical theology.' Seán Freyne's invitation, instead, is to see ambiguity 'as a blessing rather than a curse. Questions need to be asked as to the theological significance of such diversity in terms of an understanding of God and of Jesus Christ, and what these different understandings might mean for Christian praxis in the community and in the world.' I agree to the definition he gives of the task at hand: An 'adequate Christian theology rooted in the Bible... would involve exploring the larger world of the text, not simply as a way of providing a background, but rather as a theological necessity... Such a contextual approach helps to avoid modernising and individualistic readings, and clarifies the distinctive point of view and critical stance that the biblical writers adopted in terms of their own worlds and the value-systems that they encountered and challenged.' The only qualification I would want to add is that the advantage of a consistent systematic theological approach is to be able to pinpoint where tacit projectionist readings from one's own contemporary concerns creep in even under the guise of reconstructing the Ancient Near Eastern and Mediterranean context of beliefs and practices. The programmatic attempt to regain the 'unsystematic' perspective of a virtue ethics as the only adequate framework for contemporary Christian Ethics is one such case.

I DEFINING THE DISTINCTIVENESS OF CHRISTIAN ETHICS

It is remarkable how differently the distinctiveness of Christian Ethics can be configured with regard to its historical origins. The feature familiar to all hermeneutically conscious reconstructions that the terms used are inevitably predetermined and loaded, will be exemplified by comparing two definitions. Such basic descriptions influence the way in which the conceptual and hermeneutical difficulties are portrayed that arise when guidance is sought from the New Testament for contemporary ethical problems.

> What was distinctive about the approach of the people of the Bible to morality? How did faith determine and enlighten its conduct; how much better off is it than its neighbours in discovering how one should lead the good life and in what that good life consists? Such a use of the Bible in theology seems to me best to take account of its historical and time-conditioned nature, on the one hand, and yet accept its normative value as God's word for the church of every age, on the other... One could answer what is distinctive about biblical morality by briefly saying that it regards man's behaviour as the direct and immediate response to God's revealed will.[6]

From the background of subsequent decades of debate in Christian Ethics, two features are distinctive in this short formula offered at the end of the 1960s by Seán Freyne: What is specific for biblical, including Christian, particularity, is sought in the approach to morality, not first of all in a totally different content from the surrounding cultures. It is a specific way of dealing with the moral element in the human constitution, not necessarily a different set of instructions.

This approach typical for Jewish and Christian monotheism is marked, secondly, as a human response to the prior self-expression of God, and more precisely, of God's will. The voluntaristic turn thus introduced into antique thought structures will merit further attention.

Leaving aside the article's subsequent development of differences in content and motivation from the specific eras and sources of biblical morality, I want to turn to a more recent basic

---

6. S. Freyne, 'The Bible and Christian Morality' (1969), repr in R. P. Hamel and K. R. Himes (eds), *Introduction to Christian Ethics. A Reader* (Mahwah, NJ: Paulist Press, 1989), 9-32, 9-10.

description which shows the traces of the last quarter-century's debate between liberalism and communitarianism. The Belgian moral theologian Jef Van Gerwen concludes his overview of the origins of Christian Ethics as follows, anchoring the understanding of morality following from the person and practice of Jesus firmly in the tradition of virtue ethics:

> Early Christians all agreed that morality was a matter of training in the basic virtues, rather than just the application of a universal set of rules or rational principles. These approaches stress the particular features of moral education in a concrete sociohistorical community. Morality depends on the training of character, and seeing and imitating concrete examples, such as Jesus Christ, the saints, or the ordinary faithful.[7]

The beginning of the article makes it quite clear that there is more continuity with antique understandings of ethics than with modern ones. The fact that these later interpretations were developed in the history of reception of Christianity does not invite closer attention to their content.

> (E)thics for early Christians was a matter of attitudes or habits, rather than just rules and commandments. Although the Jewish Law (especially the Ten Commandments) played a central role in it, Christian morality was primarily based on the practice of a number of virtues, such as love, hope, justice, forgiveness, and patience ... Consequently, it was committed to fight vices such as hate, envy, lust, sloth, and anger. Early Christian Ethics resembles more closely other antique schools of ethics, such as Aristotelianism or Stoicism, than our modern Kantian and utilitarian paradigms. (204)

Jesus' practice and proclamation is seen as continuing the 'virtues' chosen by the prophets:

> The ethical teaching of Jesus of Nazareth fits perfectly into the tradition of prophetic and early rabbinical representatives of Jewish ethics. In the line of the prophets, Jesus stresses the importance of the virtues of justice and mercy over the ritualistic ethics of purity and cult offerings that had been developed in the Jewish Law (the books of Leviticus and

---

7. J. Van Gerwen, 'Origins of Christian Ethics', Schweiker, W. (ed), *The Blackwell Companion to Religious Ethics* (Oxford: Blackwell, 2005), 204-213, 213. Further page numbers are included in the text.

Deuteronomy). In his interpretation of the Mosaic Law (Mt 5-7) he focuses on the purity of intention of the agent, rather than on the mere act of trespassing a rule of law. (205)

What stands out in this position are the alternatives against which the Christian moral view is constructed as belonging to the virtue tradition. As in similar attempts, the deficiencies to be overcome always include individualism (a), the understanding of ethics as legislation centred on acts (b), and 'abstract' or 'universal' criteria, i.e. standards of evaluation that are independent of the context and 'situatedness' of agents and communities (c).

## II VIRTUES AS AN ALTERNATIVE TO AUTONOMY

In contrast to other rehabilitation projects that seek to integrate Aristotelian elements such as striving for the good life, or the rationality of virtuous practices, into a comprehensive understanding of ethics,[8] it is clear that it is not a matter of complementing but of challenging the modern foundation of ethics on the autonomy of the subject. The programmatic embrace of premodern ethics as a way out of current impasses raises the questions whether such a return is philosophically desirable and possible, and whether it is theologically appropriate for Christian Ethics. While not all sympathy for the virtue mode of ethics (e.g. Dietmar Mieth's) and not all communitarian leanings (e.g.

---

8. P. Ricoeur combines a theory of self with an ethics that proceeds from the first level of spontaneous striving 'to live with and for others in just institutions' to the moral awareness of the human reality of violence. Thus, it is the limit that the other poses to each person's self-expansion that calls for the second, deontological level of ethics. The third, 'practical wisdom,' applies both in a judgment that balances moral rule and each person's singularity. Cf *Oneself as Another* (Chicago: University of Chicago Press, 1992), chs 7-9, 169-296.

O. Höffe marks his reintegration of eudaimonistic insights into a full understanding of the ethical life clearly as complementary and not as an alternative to modern autonomous ethics. His critique of Kant for his near-exclusive focus on morality and disregard of the rational guidance available in eudaimonistic reflections on the limits of human fulfilment is matched by an equal dismissal of the arbitrariness of Political Liberalism in making goals of life a totally private and unaccountable affair, and of the over-dramatised contrast some Neo-Aristotelians draw between the antique tradition and the Enlighenment. Otfried Höffe, 'Zur Rehabilitierung einer eudämonistischen Ethik' in *Moral als Preis der Moderne* (Frankfurt: Suhrkamp, 1993), 137-150.

Charles Taylor's) are dismissive of modernity's principle of freedom, the folio against which the renaissance of virtue is called for most often is modern liberalism.

### a) Community orientation versus liberal individualism

In societies marked by structural differentiation and individualisation, it will be part of the service of self-enlightenment that philosophy can offer to reassess models of linking individual and political life. When each person is forced to become the stage manager of their own life under market conditions, where community ties are subordinated to demands of mobility and the local is devalued as peripheral to the centre, a counter-move is necessary to do justice to requirements of human existence that can only be fulfilled in an intersubjective, communicative way.[9] Education, cultural self-expression, political participation and religious practice need a community that is valued not just as a conduit to a next 'higher' stage.

If the current revival of virtue ethics was just a matter of balance and of critiquing the degeneration of the moral subject to a bearer of rights but not of equal original obligation to others, this dissatisfaction would find resonance in Kantian objections to the liberal emptying of the moral concept of autonomy to mere choice. Virtue ethicists and deontologists could agree on the need to foster 'virtues' in the sense of intersubjectively shared proposals of attractive human models of being and would thus have convincing alternatives to offer to a public culture in danger of reducing itself to a cult of celebrities. However, even then it will be necessary to clarify in *philosophical* terms the two constitutive poles of the individual and the community, or of human reflexivity and sociability, and explain the model pursued in relating them (1). When it comes to the *theological* appropriation of the philosophical turn to 'community,' it is even more urgent to come clear on one's implicit claims. If the Aristotelian bent towards the existing ethos that Hegel named *'Sittlichkeit'* is already problematic as a foundation for ethics, it does not help if ecclesial communitarians claim this ground for

9. Ulrich Beck's sociological analyses in *Risk Society. Towards a New Modernity* (London: Sage, 1992), especially ch 5, depict the double face of modernisation that Jürgen Habermas criticises as the colonisation of the life-world by system imperatives. The triumph of purposive rationality can only be counter-acted by developing the resources of communicative action in civil society.

the Christian church as the seat of salvation. The three dangers Theological Ethics should avoid are to reduce the kingdom of God to the visible church, thus denying its universal claim and the legitimacy of relating to civil society; to downplay the role of individual conscience over against dispositions acquired within a supportive ethos; and to dismiss the ongoing role of an autonomous morality of respect for human dignity in critiquing in-group ideologies, be they ecclesial or issuing from other politics of identity that claim exceptions for themselves from the rule of mutual recognition (2).

*(1) Two poles: reflexivity and sociability*
The current emphasis on community in social ethics has evident advantages: life stages other than full autonomy are recognised, attention is paid to the genesis and renewal of values, and the political element in human nature is emphasised as part of its fulfillment. Yet, there are two significant draw-backs in communitarian analysis:
– Without an equal consideration of the pole of human reflexivity, it remains one-sided and in danger of promoting social conformity with no regard for individual conscience.
– And by conceiving all social relations in terms of community, it ignores the 'most important *non*-Aristotelian element in our modern ethos: the concept of legality.'[10]

There is no need to cry 'atomism' when a transcendental analysis of human freedom distinguishes its formal unconditionality from its concrete, embodied, intersubjectively nurtured existence. Without this distinction of levels, there could not even be any specific appropriation of a surrounding ethos, but only an unquestioning connectedness, a seamless belonging or primary embeddedness that could never be regained as, in Paul Ricoeur's words, a second *naiveté*. As little as it is necessary to devalue the ethos in which one was socialised as a preliminary stage to be left behind for a 'post-conventional' identity,[11] as unconvincing is the identification of the goal of self-determination with that of self-invention or even self-production. The ability to

---

10. H. Schnädelbach, 'Was ist Neoaristotelismus?' in *Zur Rehabilitierung des animal rationale* (Frankfurt: Suhrkamp,1992), 205-230, 228.
11. See Hille Haker's critique of Habermas's previous stance that goes far beyond Kant's test of universalisability, in her *Moralische Identität* (Tübingen: Francke, 1999), 67.

distance oneself from the community's ethos is a condition also for its conscious and critical appropriation.

The second shortfall in communitarianism is the lack of regard for mere 'legality.' Arising from the Kantian turn to subjectivity, respect for personally espoused convictions, developed in the interaction of individual reflexivity with culturally transmitted values, has the consequence that 'legality' denoting not substantive communal, but formal legal relations, becomes a valued condition of personal freedom.[12] The reverse side of 'legality' within a neutral *state* is religious freedom within *society*.[13] The familiarity and social bondedness that are lost in this transition can be transferred to a different register; one can work at being

12. Herbert Schnädelbach points out how legality is the condition under which modern citizens can be reconciled with the ethos of their societies. 'Legality concerns the conditions of freedom in the *exterior* relationships of people to each other. Exactly this element of exteriority bemoaned by the traditionalist we experience subjectively as *the basic condition of our individual freedom in the modern life-world* (228) ... A lifeworld in which universal principles that guarantee individual freedom are institutionalised, embodies not only a historical-contingent but a rational-universalist ethos... with which an individual who insists on his rational autonomy can be "reconciled"'(227).
On the basis of this clear appreciation of the universalism inherent in a modern-day ethos, I find the hostility overdrawn that he presumes between Kant's understanding of freedom as self-determination and any existing ethos as denoting heteronomy. The enemy against which autonomy is defined as self-obligation is not an ethos, or conventions, as in Discourse Ethics up to the 1980s, but inclination. 'The controversy between morality and *Sittlichkeit* can only be resolved if one comes to an agreement on the concept of freedom. When freedom is grasped as subjective self-determination as in Kant, ethos and *Sittlichkeit* can only appear as heteronomy; when freedom is understood with Hegel as being with oneself in being with the other (*Beisichsein im Anderssein*), subjective autonomy is a misleading goal.' This sounds as if Kant had no idea of interaction between free subjects, despite his conceptions of a '*Commercium der Freiheit*' and the 'kingdom of ends.' Ricoeur's critique of the unbridgeable contrast between morality and convention in Discourse Ethics also applies to Schnädelbach's alternative between self-determination and ethos.
13. W. Huber, 'Die jüdisch-christliche Tradition,' in H. Joas and K. Wiegand (eds), *Die kulturellen Werte Europas* (Frankfurt: Fischer, 2005), 69-92, 91: 'The secular state thus saves society from having to be secular. Rather, society is the space in which a guaranteed freedom can flourish equally as a freedom for religion as it can as a freedom from religion.'

willing to live together with anonymous others even without an
already given social vision of the good. The end of the *polis* does
not have to spell barbarism, as for Alasdair MacIntyre in the last
pages of *After Virtue*; it is also possible that a diverse civil society
without pre-established alliances is born. Then, it is the matter of
the resources of each conviction whether mutual respect can be
created. In a pluralist culture one feature of Christian religious
convictions may even come out stronger: that their claim is not
simply directed to members of an in-group ethos but to 'all people of good will.' This key expression, familiar to all hearers of
the nativity stories and oratorios, contains a second significant
difference that an anti-modern project of virtue ethics cannot appreciate: the change from a cognitive, intellect-oriented model of
ethics to a will-based one.

### (2) Consequences of the communitarian vision
### for the concept of church

The Aristotelian and Hegelian starting-point of the existing
ethos over against a deontology of imperatives that can never be
fulfilled completely, results in a focus on the church as the
framework of the ethical life of the faithful. This setting has several advantages: it avoids the interpretive practice of 'norm
hunting' in the New Testament[14] by focusing on the shared self-
understanding of the community 'prior to legislation'. It aban-
dons 'quandary ethics' and has an interest in formation, socialisation, spiritual and ethical growth.[15] Its subject is not simply a
deliberating individual, but a participant and contributor to a
shared enterprise of faithful hope. The main dangers to be
avoided, however, are an apotheosis of the church, a denial of its
internal differences, and a corresponding loss of interest in contributing to the spheres outside the *communio*. A further consequence, to be treated in Section c), is the reduction of the status
of ethics to a hermeneutics, in this case of church life.

Setting up the church as the counter-model to a liberal soci-

---

14. T. Deidun, 'The Bible and Christian Ethics,' in B. Hoose (ed),
*Christian Ethics. An Introduction* (London: Cassell, 1998), 3-46, 22.
15. C. Deane-Drummond admits that 'virtue theory requires some
modification in order to be compatible with Christian thought. For example, concepts such as reconciliation, forgiveness and the need for
God's grace are essential components of a Christian ethic.' *The Ethics of
Nature* (Oxford: Blackwell, 2004), 22.

ety seen as consumerist, permissive and aggressive in defending its wasteful lifestyle, risks sacralising it and isolating it from the 'world'. The price of this contrasting of ideal types is that, the more the church becomes a fortress against moral degeneration, the more its instrumental character for the kingdom of God disappears. The unity of faith gets stressed to an extent that faithful practical and theoretical conscientious dissent from what has been defined as orthodoxy and orthopraxy is hardly conceivable. And the possibilities of mutual learning and critique, instead of constant correction of secular society, as well as the chance for the world to repent are no longer held open.

Seán Freyne's account of the dispute about the proper content of 'Zion' gives helpful biblical pointers on how to conceive the service of the church beyond its own confines.In his discussion of 'Jesus' Disciples as the Servant Community' he shows how Jesus aligned himself with the 'servants of Yahweh' understanding of Zion that Isaiah raised as a challenge to the triumphalist view held by the circle that dominated the cult. For Isaiah, a 'genuinely inclusive universalism' of both Israel and the nations was the proper goal.

> The catalyst for this understanding of what Mother Zion could mean was a changed understanding of Yahweh and the nature of his demands. The 'servants of Yahweh' group certainly did not espouse a notion of tolerant syncretism in which Yahweh would merely be one of the many different names for God. Ironically, that was the position of the dominant group, while at the same time exploiting the Zion symbol to regard the nations as their servants. For the 'servants of Yahweh', on the other hand, Yahweh alone was God, but this one God was concerned for all because he had created all … Isaiah's Yahweh and Jesus' God is no tribal warrior, but one whose 'eternal covenant' was with all the children of Noah, as well as with the earth.[16]

The line of demarcation does not run between those in the community and those outside, but between those who answer the needs of the vulnerable and those who do not:

> The beatitudes are cut from the same cloth as Yahweh's oracle to the temple authorities, declaring that it was the poor and

---

16. S. Freyne, *Jesus, a Jewish Galilean* (London/New York: T & T Clark, 2004), 116-121, 117. Further page numbers in the text.

those who are broken in spirit and not they, who will eat,
drink, and rejoice. (118)

No-one's openness is discounted:

> The Queen of the South (Sheba) coming to hear Solomon's
> wisdom, and the Ninevites repenting at Jonah's preaching
> are adduced as evidence of 'outsiders' seeking wisdom and
> taking the prophetic warning seriously (Mt 12...40-42; Lk
> 11...30-32) ... Wisdom is available to all and repentance is a
> possibility for non-Jews. (118-20)

Isaiah's and the synoptics' critiques of those who 'do not understand the universal scope of their own tradition' are a telling
precedent in an on-going interpretative struggle. Emphasis on
the resources of one's particular religious *communio* should not
blind one to its own shortcomings. The implicit repristination of
the *extra ecclesiam nulla salus* model cannot be supported, however justified current prophetic critiques of market-bred
lifestyles and the cognitive marginalisation of religion in liberal
states may be. But if the claim of the community on a member's
allegiance is not tempered by the distinction of legality from
legitimacy achieved by Kant, then communitarianism can de-
generate into totalitarianism. The dignity of a believer's own
personal assent can only be safeguarded if exterior conformity
to the rules of the law that is obligatory for all is distinguished
from interior appropriation which will always be particular, se-
lective, contextual, and developing. The possibility of legitimate
interior dissent is the pass to an un-suffocating sense of ecclesial
belonging. This reminder of the singularly individual character
of religious response runs counter to the virtue ethicists' interest
in minimising the difference between the person's and the community's ethical life. A holistic bent is also visible in their wish to
relate 'acts' back to 'character' and to avoid the external authority
of 'rules' in favour of habits that arise organically from virtuous
dispositions.

*b) From rules to 'character'*

The move away from an ethics totally centred on acts to the
being behind the agency lifts several impasses at once. An
overemphasis on agency risks ignoring receptivity and facticity
as constitutive features of human existence, dissects the moral
life into a series of isolated acts regardless of any over-arching

intention and vision, and neglects the issue of conditions for developing stable identities that put values into practice in a reliable instead of a once-off way. If the counter-model of a 'character' ethics is to fill these *lacunae* of act-centred moral theories, it is a helpful correction. But is the concept of 'character' or 'being' from which agency follows[17] sufficient to serve these different tasks? Or does the opposition of 'character versus decision' and 'being versus legislation' need to be related dialectically and embedded in a more comprehensive approach? Within the perceived alternatives, 'character' stands for steadiness over against disjoint decisions, and for the Hegelian shift from an ethics of obligation to one of confidence in people's own powers, competence, and ability to be good. The *philosophical* question here is whether 'character' is only one pole and has to be complemented by another element in a full theory of subjectivity. In P. Ricoeur's account of the ethical self, the *'idem'* element of recognisable sameness through time has to be related to the *'ipse,'* the responsible and spontaneous centre of creativity. 'Character' as the *'idem'* pole is not a complete description of ethical selfhood; the *idem* does not exhaust the *ipse*, it is a basis that has to be made one's own. The task of shaping the open future out of the past is to be captured as the *'ipse'* aspect of the self.

The need for the subtle distinctions Ricoeur offers can also be shown from a theological perspective. Their relevance for a theological anthropology comes out most clearly when virtue ethics' antipathy to the 'legislation' mode of Kant's approach is analysed. If it only amounted to broadening ethics to include the narrative dimension of tracing a person's particular moral insights to his biographical identity, it could easily be compatible with a Christian appreciation of life as a journey in faith towards

---

17. J. Keenan explains the appeal of A. MacIntyre's critique of the 'depersonalisation' present in contemporary action ethics to Christian circles by applying the scholastic axiom of *agere sequitur esse* to Jesus' call to become disciples. 'If action follows being (*agere sequitur esse*), where was being? ... Who more than Jesus beckons us to consider the question about the people we can become? In scripture, Jesus invites us to become his disciples, children of God, and heirs of the kingdom.' (24) Virtue Ethics is thus seen to provide a 'method for building bridges between Scripture and Moral Theology', which the book *Jesus and Virtue Ethics* (Lanham, MD/Chicago: Sheed & Ward, 2002), co-authored with the New Testament scholar Daniel Harrington, constructs from both sides.

God. The perspective to which virtue ethics is committed, to include into the moral task also the level of affects and to sympathetically shape one's emotions within an over-arching vision of an authentic life, rather than denounce them as mere inclinations, can be seen as opening up a spiritual dimension. But the emphasis on 'growth' that they find missing in act-centred ethics, is in danger of being contaminated by the residual legacy of a natural entelechy. We don't need 'rules' because we are already striving for the good life. This Aristotelian assertion is less harmless when it comes as Hegel's critique of Kant, as a triumphalism of reason against the evidence of human brokenness and disposition towards violence. Theologically, the issue in need of assertion is not that 'being' is more than 'acting,' but that the person is more than the sum of her acts and that God distinguishes between our deeds and our selves in need of redemption.[18] Jesus' emphasis on God's forgiveness that creates a new beginning for us cannot be captured in the terms of a natural entelechy, of organic development, and growth without conversion. Here, John Barton's doubt whether a scheme of virtues and vices can be a suitable model for a biblically inspired ethics that turns on 'conversion' points in the right direction.[19] 'Conversion' denotes a re-orientation of the will which cannot be grasped in categories of striving. That exterior actions arise from an interior source does not tie us to the conceptual framework of virtuous dispositions. The Aristotelian cast of virtue ethics can hide the decisive difference between this antique philosophical and Christian ethics: the shift from ends towards which we strive naturally to an emphasis on the will. It results in repositioning the good from the cognitive sphere of insight to the quality of the will. Its volatility poses other limits than a mere lack of understanding did.

---

18. In his discussion of H. Arendt's claim that forgiveness is a natural condition of action, Paul Ricoeur insists on its origin 'from elsewhere' and the need for it to be given, not just presupposed. See the 'Epilogue: Difficult Forgiveness' in *Memory, History, Forgetting* (457-506) and his lecture 'The Difficulty to Forgive' in P. Kenny and M. Junker-Kenny (eds), *Memory, Narrativity, Self, and the Challenge to Think God. The Reception within Theology of the Recent Work of Paul Ricoeur* (Münster: LIT-Verlag, 2004), 6-16.

19. J. Barton, 'Virtue in the Bible,' *Studies in Christian Ethics* 12 (1999), 12-22.

*c) The status of ethics*

My final point starts with reclaiming the modern, Kantian measure of the 'good will' as the origin, in contrast to the utilitarian outcome, of acts, as founded on a new anthropology arising from the Jewish and Christian religious heritages. Concluding with a comparison of the status of ethics in a hermeneutical to a deontological framework, I want to show that context-independent criteria are needed at a time when a previously existing moral consensus on the inviolability of human life, itself the fruit of historical struggles, is represented as an outmoded and indefensible taboo.

What MacIntyre sees as the deplorable emphasis of modernity, the voluntarist bent of ethics, can also be deciphered as a paradigm shift in Greek thinking resulting from the encounter with the religious experience of a saving God and free creator. While not offering any views on the roots of this change, Otfried Höffe analyses the new ground that is broken by the idea that striving can acquire a distance from itself (*Idee einer Distanz des Strebens in sich selbst*) introduced by the concept of the will. Without it, change in patterns of action that are deemed ethical could only be explained as arising from outside, e.g. from modifications in needs, or of the means of satisfying them. Value change and critique for moral reasons, radical reform, or the proclamation of a 'new law' such as that of the New Testament would be unthinkable. The

> concept of striving lives off an unproblematised presupposition: the (individual-spontaneous) finality of human agency. Interpreted as striving, human praxis is always already assigned a goal ... In phenomena such as moral criticism out of morality or ethical-political protests, in the giving of a 'New Law' (cf New Testament), in constitutional reforms, political revolutions or in an explicit renewal of personal and political value priorities aims are no longer pursued in the framework of a lived ethos. Rather, the ethical-political basic framework itself is up for decision. An inherited system of institutions and patterns of behaviour and the activities of striving that correspond to them is put up for disposition with regard to the principles themselves. Such a process can no longer be conceptualised as agency due to internalised basic orientations, as a spontaneous affirmation and pursuance of ends, i.e. as an act of striving. It is rather a case of a distance of

striving within itself, i.e. an act of the will ... due to which
ends are not only pursued but first of all posited.[20]

The human dignity of agency in the sense of 'positing' goals can
only be captured in the modern idea of self-determination, as a
'strictly non-necessary movement.' Virtue as an acquired disposition of character may presuppose some appreciation of freedom besides reason,[21] but it is caught in the framework of
Aristotle's metaphysics of movement which does not allow for a
clear distinction between the quality of action authored by
human beings and that of every other part of the universe. The
constraints of a model of continuity between the natural world
and the sphere of human reason become clear when compared
to the image of the human person arising in biblical monotheism. As a 'summoned self' (P. Ricoeur) she stands in a counterpart relationship with a personal God to whom she is responsible. In this anthropology, failure is not first of all weakness of
insight but a denial of response, an act of the will, not a lack of
reason. In his comparison of a 'Greek ethics of insight' with a
'biblical ethics of command' the New Testament scholar Gerd
Theissen characterises the main difference as that between
founding ethical judgments on the nature of things as opposed
to vocation by God. 'It is said: "You shall love your neighbour
like yourself; I am Lord." Israel shaped human behaviour not
through rational insight into the world, but through disciplining
the will through God's will.' What is decisive for the subsequent
development of ethics is where human frailty and goodness are
located: in the power of the will.

> Important for the biblical ethics of command is a difference
> in the view of the human person: One can oppose a com-
> mand – also against good insight. The human person has an
> independent will that can be good or bad. Wrong behaviour
> does not originate from an incorrect judgment, but from an
> evil will. This ethics is voluntarist.[22]

One interesting conclusion from this contrast is that what
sounds more authoritarian than liberating to modern ears, the

---

20. O. Höffe, *Ethik und Politik* (Frankfurt: Suhrkamp, 1979), 329-332.
21. J. Rohls, *Geschichte der Ethik* (Tübingen: Mohr, 1991), 68.
22. G. Theissen, 'Urchristliches Ethos. Eine Synthese aus biblischer und
griechischer Tradition.' The only version published up to now is in
Swedish, under the title 'Urkristet etos – en syntes av biblisk och
grekisk tradition' *Svensk Teologisk Kvartalsskrift* 79 (2003), 1-12.

emphasis on God's command and discipline, allowed a break-through in the understanding of the interior dynamics of being human. Just as the idea of creation out of nothing (that the Christian apologists defended against the Greek conviction that matter was as eternal as God) underlined God's absolute power to begin, and thus the origin of the world in God's free motivation of love, so is the human person seen as endowed with the power to posit, not just to follow the given goals of nature. There is more tension, but also more freedom in seeing the human person as the addressee of God's call than governed by the anonymous laws of the cosmos that human reason seeks to explore and live by.

Höffe's reference to 'principles' by which existing social arrangements and personal orientations can be judged and discontinued, rather than only ever evolved and adjusted, gives an important clue to the new understanding of the status of ethics. Are context-independent principles possible, or is all that reflective reason can achieve the self-exploration of the internal logic of one's ethos? Is moral judgment always a situated, *a posteriori* elucidation of the self-understanding of a community and its agents, or is an evaluation led by independent criteria possible? That is the point of debate between universalist and hermeneutical approaches. Schnädelbach's critique of what he calls the 'phronesis ideology' of contemporary Neo-Aristotelianism shows the danger of emphasising the contingent, singular nature of human action so much that no general evaluation according to recognised criteria is possible. Contingency, skepticism and an ethics favouring the *status quo* are intellectual neighbours.

> If it is no longer possible to attach strong normative claims to an idea, a radical critique can also no longer be founded. Theoretical skepticism always favours the power of what is established; thus, it is not by chance that Descartes is the inventor of a provisional morality. The historically enlightened Neo-Aristotelian can in fact only be a skeptic ..., leaving praxis – in equal distance both to a Kantian ethics of obligation and to platonising ethics of value – to practical cleverness, and unburdening himself and us from normative challenges as far as possible.[23]

For Schnädelbach, the advantage in Aristotle's admission that the realm of praxis does not allow for standards of exactness

23. Schnädelbach, *Rehabilitierung*, 214.

similar to theoretical *episteme* is that common sense is allowed a chance against the expert knowledge of elites and of 'the philosopher kings and their dictatorship of theory'(212). But the price of disallowing any relevance of 'theory' (which also includes principles) for praxis is an embedded *phronesis* that can never go beyond the confines of the community ethos. An entirely hermeneutical model of ethics thus resigns itself to the *polis*'s internal limits to moral growth and is hermetic to radical outside questioning. But is it really a choice between dictatorial *a priori* normativists and insular ethos interpreters?

The context-sensitivity of *phronesis* could be safeguarded without the cost of minimalising ethics to a normatively and prescriptively powerless explication of the existing self-understandings of agents in a community if one follows a model that seeks to combine the strong points of each approach. Ricoeur's use of the term 'practical wisdom' does not denote a return behind Kant, but intensifies the unconditionality of his concept of respect for each person as an end in himself by focusing on singularity. The deontological unconditional norm is independent of the context and 'situatedness' of agents and communities, but it is possible to make exceptions from the 'rule' precisely to honour the concrete person as an end in herself. The 'ought' is maintained, but its potential rigorism softened, while the tacit background assumption of a virtue ethics, the primacy of the given ethos with the weak and context-dependent justifications it implies, is avoided.[24]

---

24 In *Oneself as Another*, Ricoeur thinks through the famous humanistic formula of the Categorical Imperative and discovers a conflict between a 'universalist' and a 'pluralist' reading of the norm to treat 'humanity in one's own person and in the person of others' as an end in itself. Under the headings, '2. Respect and Conflict' (262-73) and '3. Autonomy and Conflict' (273-296), he analyses 'the *caesura* so carefully concealed by Kant between respect for the rule and respect for persons. This *caesura*, which will become a gaping tear in the case of the conflicts we shall mention, was probably not able to appear along the path where we subsumed actions under maxims and maxims under rules. The tear cannot help but attract attention, however, once we take the return path from the maxim, sanctioned by rules, to concrete situations,' (268) such as what telling the truth to a fatally ill patient can mean. Once the possible split between 'respect for the law and respect for persons' has been admitted, the task for 'practical wisdom may consist in giving priority to the respect for persons, in the name of the solicitude that is

Wayne Meeks' advice to understand ethics as an 'interpretative exercise'[25] can be theologically defended insofar as it points to the givenness of salvation which was not created by human reason. It is attractive and especially apt to portray the church as testifying to this givenness, and constituting its social tradition. However, 'interpretive' can also mean an exclusive focus on its own resources. But can these be separated so clearly from its history of reception and secular conversion? A touchstone for any group ethics is the question as to whether any relationship is to be conceived between its own legal system, in this case church law, and human rights. While it is true both that the proliferation of 'rights' talk constitutes a problem and undermines the core application of the term, and that there is, e.g. no 'right' to be ordained, even if there should be a right to have one's vocation tested, a church distancing itself completely from the standards it establishes would be suspicious. The fate of the concept of conscience in Hegel's ethics should be a warning.[26] His view of 'conscience' as mere subjectivity and as an almost terrorist singularity against the established mores of a community is not the example a Christian ecclesial ethics should follow. Yet, if Christian Ethics is to be seen not only as an interpretive, in-house exercise, its internal relation to the discovery and ongoing determination of who counts as a subject, and what constitutes a violation of human rights will be part of its brief.

To come clean on this part of the secular heritage of Christianity is all the more urgent in view of the ethical debates arising under the pressures of global market conditions. Are virtues enough to stem the tide from Shanghai to Cambridge that is swallowing every moral standard achieved in long processes of historical struggle inspired by the Jewish and

---

addressed to persons in their irreplaceable singularity (262) ... Practical wisdom consists in inventing conduct that will best satisfy the exception required by solicitude, yet betraying the rule to the smallest extent possible ... Practical wisdom consists here in inventing just behavior suited to the singular nature of the case. But it is not, for all that, simply arbitrary ... Never can practical wisdom consent to transforming into a rule the exception to the rule.' (269)

25. W. A. Meeks, 'The Christian Beginnings and Christian Ethics: The Hermeneutical Challenge,' in *Bulletin European Theology* 9 (1998) 171-181.

26. Here, Schnädelbach's quotations (222-3) from paragraphs 139-141 of Hegel's *Philosophy of Law* are apposite.

Christian values of justice and compassion for the vulnerable? Is 'Europe just a suburb of Shanghai?'[27]

If 'Shanghai' stands for the willingness to compromise principles for the goal of the successful competition of one's own *polis*, it is just on our doorstep. Aubrey de Grey, a biomedical gerontologist at the University of Cambridge, admits:

> I don't have much time for the Hippocratic Oath myself. I think it's something that made a lot of sense when the understanding of medicine was primitive and people could spontaneously recover from illnesses for reasons that the doctor could not identify. That's where the 'do no harm' idea comes from. That becomes less reasonable as we become more knowledgeable about how to intervene in the body's metabolism. One also has to remember that around the world there are very different versions of medical ethics. There's good reason to believe that many of these therapies will be first developed in countries where they are more forward-looking about cost-benefit ratio.[28]

## CONCLUSIONS

I have tried to show that Christian ethical interpretations of the message of Jesus in terms of virtue are in danger of downplaying the shift to an emerging new paradigm of thinking that broke with many plausibilities especially of Greek high culture. To encompass such revolutions of attitude in the framework of a virtue ethic that in its inherited form only knew one context, the existing *polis*, risks short-changing the message of Jesus on two counts:

(1) The emphasis on the will that the call to conversion im-

---

27. This is the question with which the ex-European commissioner Mario Monti is quoted by Josef Joffe in his lead article in *Die Zeit* No 26, 23/6/05, p 1.

28. EMBO, 'Interview: Curing Aging and the consequences', EMBO Reports 6 (3) (2005), on line, p 4 of 7, quoted in C. Deane-Drummond, 'Future Perfect? God, the Trans Human Future and the Quest for Immortality,' in Deane-Drummond, C. (ed), *Fabulous Humans* (London: T & T Clark, forthcoming 2006). Her critical conclusion is that 'in order to foster a technology that will ultimately benefit Western societies the most … Grey makes the remarkable suggestion that those who are less squeamish about ethical objections in other parts of the world will subject inhabitants of less regulated countries to medical experimentation for First World "rejuvenation treatment."'

plies is smoothed into a new set of personal habitual practices, which are held to express the person's 'character'. The challenge to forge one's personal identity out of the dialectic of *idem* and *ipse*, i.e. to unite the recognisable, familiar traits of character and life story with the internal working out of selfhood is reduced to just one pole. The idea of personal 'growth', however, so dear to the new advocates of virtue ethics in theology, asks for categories that go beyond natural striving.The shift towards an interiority engaged by God is better expressed in terms of reflexivity and personal calling than in those of an ethos-ethic.

(2) The new social framework of the church in which Christian (ascetic) virtues are to be exercised is deemed the only existing one; the result is that any emphasis on the autonomy of the world and the recognition of civil society as a proper setting beside the church for living the Christian calling seems to be misplaced. Ecclesial virtue ethicists such as Stanley Hauerwas transpose previously secular virtues completely into religious ones, thus breaking with the classical tradition of practical reason. The route taken by Thomas Aquinas, however, does not sanction this denial of reason. Modern virtue ethicists who accept both world and church as equally important vineyards to plough, have already tacitly extracted virtues from the grip of their ancient civic setting to be able to relate them to the dimension of faith in a saving God that transcends local alliances.

The task that remains, to determine the relationship between ethical and theological virtues, can be accomplished with greater promise, if the shift in thought forms engendered by Christianity to categories of freedom is taken as the matrix of reconstruction. Once the entelechy of nature in human and other creatures is changed into a human-specific teleology of the quest for meaning, the orientation of nature towards grace can be assumed without resulting in a contradiction for the creator, that to withhold grace would leave the creature incomplete.[29] If God's offer is addressed to human freedom, the superabundant shape that it takes may disappoint a strict regard for the virtue of egalitarian justice but engage the imagination to come up with different measures for justice than a meritocratic one. It opens up the possibility of new self-interpretations and projects that are 'out of character.'

---

29. Th. Pröpper, *Erlösungsglaube und Freiheitsgeschichte* (München: Kösel, 3rd. ed 1991), 279.

The turn to the reliable and more or less verifiable guide of virtues at a time when all other measures of goodness seem to be controversial is to be welcomed. It trusts in the evidence of personal authenticity, opts for prevention rather than repair,[30] reinvests in the building of long-term basic attitudes over against individual decision-testing, and in steady personal responsibility over against the anonymous forces of unrelated systems. But it takes moves for granted that virtue ethics on its own could never have achieved: the prophetic, in many ways anti-communitarian break with practised modes of living, the discovery of individual irreplaceability in one's own singular response to God's personal calling, the foundation of ethics on the good will of the autonomous morality of each human being, not on the striving for a happiness congruent with the typical features of human nature.

Do these distinctions underestimate the power for innovation and change inherent in the traditions of Homer, Antigone, Socrates, and the idea of a good life governed by justice? We cannot know how antique traditions would have evolved without Jesus' faith in a God who makes everything new. It is likely that the *virtù* which Nietzsche admired in the Renaissance would not have had to suffer the interception of the 'slave morality' of the Beatitudes. Would the ability to understand oneself in a new framework once the old one had collapsed in irresolvable conflicts of compatibility, as in Antigone, have arisen? Or would the last word have been Zarathustra's 'deep midnight' of the human mode of being coming to an end, as not worth saving? The promise of a 'new heaven and a new earth,' instead, is for a humanity redeemed, invited to a new mode of self-understanding, and not abandoned.

---

30. D. Mieth, *Moral und Erfahrung II* (Fribourg/Freiburg: Universitätsverlag/ Herder, 1998), 127.

CHAPTER SEVENTEEN

# The Role and Backgrounds of Religious, Ethical, Legal and Social Issues in the Progress of Science

## Dietmar Mieth

One has to distinguish between religious and secular ethics. This distinction does not mean a total separation. The concept of secular or autonomous ethics may also be seen as a product of the development of Christianity. The religious understanding of ethics may support the secular or rational character of ethics. Religion may be seen as a motivation and an abiding motive within ethics, as a motive to discover ethical problems, as a motive to understand the ethical failure of humans and as a practical motive to implement ethics: not only to think morally but also to live morally. But religion delivers no specific argumentation for the foundation of right norms. Academic representatives of religious ethics may differ in their positions depending on the rational philosophy which they adapt.

This concept of secular ethics may be seen as a companion of the development of modern science, of the development of ethics in the sciences and of ethics as an academic discipline. It may be that European societies see their religious heritage more as an historical fact than as a commitment. In the secular city secular ethics lost its relation to religion and often even the memory of it. Therefore it may happen that science itself, promising a better future, replaces religion, and scientists promote their options and their hopes with quasi-religious feelings.

On the other hand, the distinction between religious and secular ethics is not self-evident for all societies. We have learnt in the past few months that for example a great part of US society will not follow this distinction between religion, ethics and even politics. But this concept of a covenant between secular ethics and science remains also a part of the American culture.

In my analysis I will trace the distinction between religious and ethical issues.

## I RELIGIOUS ISSUES

There are specific religious rules for the behaviour of believers, like norms about food or fasting. In this case the task of a tolerant society is only to make it possible for religious communities to follow these rules. There are specific religious ideas or motives which can influence the way of ethical thinking even if they cannot decide the ethical argumentation in itself. There is for example the 'sanctity of life'. The religious understanding used for instance by Hans Jonas is related to three issues: to a spirituality of sanctification of the believer's own life, to the integrity of reproductive life, and to the unconditional acceptance of human life in its mere existence.

Spiritual values and virtues which are not exclusively related to religion but which are enforced by religious motives are for example: finiteness and humility in the expectation of scientific progress, and calmness/tranquillity in questions of personal decisions, underlining the possibility not to know, not to decide oneself (for example about one's own death) and to refrain from doing something even if doing it is possible and ethically allowed.

Science replacing religion may also be an issue. Because it is impossible to prove in advance the scientific option (for example embryonic stem cells as healing diseases), scientists need a kind of faith, not only for themselves but also in public.

## II ETHICAL ISSUES

Ethics in this context can be seen as a normative theory of reflection about moral behaviour. The question is: what is good or evil and what is right or wrong? This question has a more personal answer in the so-called 'ethics of a good life', and an institutional answer in normative ethics which may be transformed, if necessary for society, into legal rules.

Ethical issues are not only different in the face of the different fields of applied ethics. They often differ more fundamentally. In Central Europe the principle of human dignity as the highest point of reference may prevail over the principle of autonomy; in Western Europe on the contrary ethics will put more emphasis on a libertarian concept of autonomy as self-determination. Those who understand autonomy with I. Kant, take it not as self-determination but as self-obligation: there is no autonomy without social responsibility. Deontologists and utilitarians also differ in principles and in the application of them. Principle based pragmatism in medical ethics (autonomy, non-malefi-cience, beneficience, justice) is widespread but often in tension with deeper foundations of criteria in moral philosophy. Discourse Ethics tries to establish a right discourse for an indi-rect solution of the new challenges of science.

But even if the ethical theories and therefore the methods of the academic approaches are different, there may be criteria which are accepted from different points of view, because there are 'arguments of convergence' between different ethical theo-ries which strengthen for example the criterion of 'informed consent' in biomedicine. (Other well accepted criteria are: re-spect for the right to privacy, confidentiality of personal data, non-discrimination, non-exploitation, non-commercialisation of the human body, proportionality of risks and benefits, special protection of vulnerable persons, equal access to benefits and equal protection of risks ...) In a more 'inductive' method not for the foundation but for the implementation of ethics in the sci-ences (as for example in our Centre for Ethics in the Sciences and Humanities in Tübingen) 'arguments of convergence' will also be formed by the joint undertaking / significance of scientific and ethical arguments in technology assessments.

### III LEGAL ISSUES

Legal issues may be either more dogmatic or more casuistic. In a casuistic approach, an extreme case may be the reason why the interpretation of the law is changed. The intention is to integrate the case into the law. With the solution of a new case, the system of regulations may receive a new interpretation. Case law seems to be more flexible.

A strict logical deduction from the highest principles of the law makes the legal issue into an ally of the deontological ap-proach in ethics. This logical deduction may start with the prin-ciple of human dignity, or with a principle of constitutional just-ice, or with a principle of mutual recognition and with human rights derived from it, understanding society as a 'community of rights'.

Legal issues may also be more pragmatic: searching for the 'overlapping consensus' (Rawls). The ethics of discourse (Habermas) applied to legal issues try to find a consensus by in-troducing a public discussion and by insisting on the independence of discourse and on the participation of everyone who may be concerned, himself or through an advocate.

IV SOCIAL ISSUES

Social issues may be more descriptive. The interest for example may be to know whether a new scientific experiment (like human cloning in vitro) or the application of new technologies (for example in human reproduction) will be accepted by a majority of a particular society or not. The interest may be prognostic in technology assessments which try to find out about future benefits and risks. The interest may also be to know more about the values in question, for example the values of special communities and of greater or smaller groups of the population. In this case also religious communities become interesting for descriptive research.

On the other hand, social issues can be combined with normative questions. The interest is then not what will be accepted or rejected, so-called social acceptance. Social acceptance does not give a sufficient indication about the question of good or evil and of right or wrong. The interest is insofar normative as it follows some criteria, which help us to distinguish what may be a benefit and what may be a risk or harm for society. Often this will be not self-evident and therefore needs a normative, well reflected foundation. Social issues then become issues of social ethics for the 'community of rights' or more traditional for the 'common good'.

Such a normative approach can for example follow the 'principle of precaution'. Hans Jonas proposed that if we have different scenarios for the future after the application of new scientific methods and new technologies, we have to follow the worst prognosis.[1] Others insist that we have also 'to expect the unexpected'. I propose for this principle as a rule of problem-solving 'not to solve a problem in a way that the problems which arise by this solution will be greater than the problems solved'.[2]

Other principles of normative approaches to social questions in technology assessment are the principles of 'compatibility' and 'sustainability'; compatibility with social and cultural val-

1. See Hans Jonas, *Das Prinzip Verantwortung. Versuch einer Ethik für die technologische Zivilisation* (Frankfurt a. M., 1976).
2. See Dietmar Mieth, *Was wollen wir können? Ethik im Zeitalter der Biotechnik* (Freiburg-Basel-Wien, 2002), 9.

ues, with democratic institutions, with good ecological perspectives, with the choice of good life styles, with gender perspectives ... In searching for a 'new covenant' between science and society not only descriptive but also normative discussions are irreplaceable.

### V TWO PROPOSALS FOR EUROPEAN RESEARCH IN 'RELSIFICATION'
*(Religious, ethical, legal and social issues as methods of testing what is right or wrong)*

a) Participating in EU programmes: We as ethicists often have the impression that the interest of these programmes is more about descriptive research and less about normative approaches. Often a misunderstanding exists: that normative problems can be resolved by descriptive knowledge. In ethics this is well-known as the 'is-ought-fallacy'. Arguments on technology assessment on contexts and consequences are often very important, but their interpretation and evaluation depends on the ethical approaches.

b) If religion is to take its role in the investigation of the 'Images of Science' (in general fields of progress and in concrete developments) this cannot be only a question of 'sociology of religion' or corresponding fields of descriptive academic approaches to the various religions. Religion depends on an academic self-reflection on faith, on 'theology'. In the European Union there is no academic programme for which theology as such is required for participation. Most of the participations are indirect: by competence in philosophical ethics and through sociology of religion.

The reason for this situation is clear: on the one hand the widespread prejudice that religious questions in a laicistic political society are seen as more peripheral, as a *'quantité négligeable'*. On the other hand it seems that theology depends on the authority of the churches. So it is better to speak directly with church authorities. But theology is not so closed. Not even in Catholic theology is this the case: there is more academic freedom than is perceived in public. Theologies today find themselves in/work towards a coherent discussion between Christian denominations and also between different religions. The global ethic approach of Hans Küng is one example.[3]

---

3. See Hans Küng, *Projekt Weltethos* (München, 1990).

## VI THEOLOGICAL ARGUMENTS IN (BIO)ETHICS

Theological Ethics in Europe prefers, as already noted, the independence of rational ethical reflections and argumentations. No normative argument is available which cannot be validated by communicability and reason. The added value of religion in ethics (and through ethics in legal and social approaches) is the set of irreplaceable motives from values and of irreplaceable motivations towards values. These motives and motivations cannot replace or cancel out secular ethics; but surely secular ethics will profit from the existence of communities and traditions of value. Secular philosophers have recognised in the past few years that societal values can only exist if they are kept alive in communities, if they are being practised. Democratic discourse on social and legal decision-making needs sources of values, especially for new interactions between science and society.

If one accepts the concept of an autonomous morality in the context of Christian ethics, as do many German-speaking moral theologians (A. Auer, F. Böckle, J. Fuchs *et al*),[4] then this does not yet mean a decision in favour of a particular philosophical way of thinking in ethics, but only the insight that the basis for judgments is achieved by philosophical means. Assigned to theology the context of the discovery of ethical values and obligations contributes significantly to ethical motivation, that is, to the motivation for ethics. Finally, theologically handling ethics – one just has to look at the doctrine of grace and justification – has a very specific function. Theology is relevant to the discovery of ethical problems, to moral sensitising, to moral motivation and to the limits of morally judging persons. In contrast to Kant, the epitome of being human is not moral capacity but rather the need for salvation, the 'feeling of absolute dependency', to complement Kant's anthropology with Schleiermacher's. Happiness, freedom, and God are not philosophical postulates, but rather specific religious experiences.

Given this, it is not to be expected that theology will replace, circumvent, or change the ethical arguments in the biomedical and biotechnological debate in general or in the debate about human genetics in particular. This is to be illustrated by an ex-

---

4. See Alfons Auer, *Autonome Moral und christlicher Glaube* (Düsseldorf, 1971); Franz Böckle, *Fundamentalmoral* (München, 1977); Josef Fuchs, *Für eine menschliche Moral. Grundfragen der theologischen Ethik* (Freiburg i. Br. u. a., 1988-1997).

ample. In the debate about the protection of embryos, documents of the Catholic church emphasise that from the beginning humans are the image of God, and thus carriers of dignity before God, that is, of personhood (person and human dignity are interchangeable in church documents). However, does not this doctrine spare us from the need for philosophical reflection in which we must first explain which living entity is meant when speaking of God's image? We may not attempt to replace this reflection either with false biblicism or with false positivism of doctrine – the first is the Protestant, the second the Catholic temptation.[5] This could cause abstruse speculations to come into being. In line with biblicism, for example, the words of the Psalmist, 'Thou art he who took me from the womb ... and since my mother bore me thou hast been my God' (22: 9-10) would mean that being the image of God should be understood as beginning at birth. Or the words of Ps 51:5, 'in sin did my mother conceive me', could be understood to mean that personhood begins at conception. The Bible cannot be applied to answer questions which did not exist in biblical times. It is more likely that the way of discourse can serve as a model for solving controversial problems.

A tutiorism that regards the fertilised egg as a person only for reasons of caution would not help either. It could, however, be reinforced by philosophical arguments about the continuity of the human from the very beginning.[6]

If ethical rightness or rather its anthropological conditioning does not belong to the theological deposit (except possibly in that tautological form which prohibits murder, where murder is by definition unethical), then the theological argument can

---

5. See Adrian Holderegger, 'Die Beseelung' als Menschwerdung. Stadien der theologischen Lehrentwicklung. Bleibende Unsicherheit?', in Dietmar Mieth & Rene Pahud de Mortanges (eds), *Recht – Ethik – Religion* (Luzern: Edition Exodus, 2002), 167-183.
6. See Deryck Beyleveld, 'The moral status of the human embryo and fetus', Hille Haker & Deryck Beyleveldt (eds), *The ethics of genetics in human procreation* (Vermont: Aldershot & Brookfiel, 2000), 59-100 (with comments); Elisabeth Hildt & Dietmar Mieth (eds), *In Vitro Fertilisation in the 1990s* (Vermont: Aldershot & Brookfield, 1998), Part 7: The status of the embryo, 237-278, Maureen Junker-Kenny, 'Embryos in vitro, Personhood, and Rights', in Maureen Junker-Kenny, *Designing Life? Genetics, Procreation and Ethics* (Vermont: Aldershot & Brookfield, 1999), 130-158.

'only' address ethical insights contextually. It is ethically relevant without making philosophical methods irrelevant. By this,
the significance of theology is in no way played down or diminished. The significance of such contextual arguments can be that
they change the whole scenery of ethics and, with that, they can
significantly influence the relative importance of ethical arguments. In the following I want to illustrate this.

Asked whether there is a relevant theological argument
against the cloning of human beings, I have indicated, without
neglecting the previous explanations, that the diversity of humanity is a commandment of creation. This is Ellen van Wolde's
conclusion in the examination of Genesis 11.[7] The many languages imposed by God are not an answer to human hubris, since
towers that reached up to heaven were in no way interpreted as
storming heaven. (This has been better known among oriental-
ists than among preachers!) It was the urban centralisation of
humanity, their inclination to uniformity in culture (and religion?) that displeased God. Therefore he reminded them of the
commandment of creation to fill the whole earth, and he spread
out humanity by the confusion of tongues. Something similar
was repeated at Pentecost: the gospel, communicable despite the
many languages, was spread throughout the world. Of course,
diversity, not repetition of the same, can only be applied as a
theological motive if we have good ethical arguments in its
favour. Just as the argument about the person being the image of
God and the argument about dignity are only inspirational in
ethics, but are not substitutes, the thought about diversity is also
a theological stimulation but not a substitute for arguments.

The stimulating effects of such theological impulses transcend the problem itself. This can be shown by a second theolo-
goumenon of ethical relevance: finitude, that is to say, contingency. Obviously, contingency is also a philosophical concept.
Of course, this concept is rather removed from theology when it
is combined with 'coincidence', as in Richard Rorty's post-modern interpretation. In classical philosophy, on the other hand,
contingency rather has the meaning: the dependence of being,
being time dependent, finite in the sense of ending at death, capable of mistakes, the imperfection of all that is human. This is
exactly what is meant by the theological theorem of the creature-

---

7. See Ellen van Wolde, *Worlds Become Worlds. Semantic Studies of Genesis
1-11* (Leiden, 1994).

liness of humanity – of not being like God. Seen theologically as well as philosophically – both ways are united in Pascal, for example – trying to transcend its own finiteness humanity would gamble away the quality which makes up its being human. Theology expresses this narratively in the story of the Fall. Philosophy draws attention to the fact that it is precisely in the corporeality of being human where both fulfilment and deprivation or scarcity are located (according to Merleau-Ponty), that finiteness is the form of the possibility of happiness.

Finiteness could be a concept of convergence between theology and philosophy. It is relevant in ethics because it interprets the following as missing the point of what it means to be human: the expectation of humanity's perfectibility, of the principal feasibility of achieving anything, and of still being able to correct all problems that are created by problem-solving. This interpretation considerably changes the context of the biomedical and biotechnical debate. It is, for example, a stimulation for the ethical rule of problem-solving: one should not solve problems in such a way that the problems which arise through the solution are greater than the problems which are solved. I do not believe that the paradigm of progress in modern biotechnology, including human genetics, keeps to this contextual insight. In bio-politics I have observed that in this regard continental Europeans, even if they are agnostics, can be convinced of this insight more easily than US Americans, even if they consider themselves to be Christians. How is this possible?

A third theological argument, which I often painfully experience as a missing context of reflection: the vulnerability of humanity. Analogously to the theological 'option for the poor' in our context (bio-technology, human genetics), it is possible to formulate an option for the priority of vulnerable persons. Here one easily runs into a lack of understanding in the secular context. Certainly, the average pragmatist who does ethics in political advisory groups will acknowledge that one must respect disabled persons and incompetent persons, even (more or less) foetuses and embryos. But he or she will face a theological theorem such as 'the prophecy of disabled persons' with little understanding. And yet, it is still easy to explain to him what it means: being explicitly disabled reminds us that we are all disabled in some way. It reminds us of our finiteness.

In the practice of finding ethical judgments in an accelerated world of suspended doubt one often meets the readiness to represent persons who are not able to realise their interests and opinions by themselves, that is, who cannot articulate themselves, by extrapolating their presumed intention via analogous deduction. The fiction of 'informed consent' is stretched to include them. Curiously, exactly by this they tend to be instrumentalised. When, for example, the Human Rights Convention of the European Council on Biomedicine tried to formulate the conditions under which research for the benefit of others can be carried out on those incapable of consent, it forgot to secure in the document the ability to withdraw proxy consent. A whole mindset can be recognised in this forgetfulness!

There is an aura of vulnerability around persons who cannot represent themselves, the lustre of the butterfly that may not be touched. The poetic expressiveness is meant to illustrate that we are dealing here with the need for greater sensitivity. Sensitivity can be easily declaimed. We then carry the burden of proof that it is not present. Our time lives with the ideal of the person as young and strong, an ideal for which Paul already admonished the Corinthians. It is not just a matter of developing a culture of perception and feeling (although also of this). It is a matter of the role of taboos which have grown out of historical experiences, such as the Nuremberg code which simply forbids experimentation on those not capable of self-determination. Taboos can only be ethically justified if they are understood as cautionary fences. They do not belong in an ethical justification but in its context which modifies the importance of the justification. Or stated differently: situations of vulnerability demand caution. I keep asking myself why the Bioethics Convention of the European Council did not allow advocates for the affected groups themselves to formulate the norms regulating non-therapeutic research on those incapable of granting consent. Here, a sense of superiority of the experts is expressed which seems to me embarrassing and not democratic.

A fourth argument: Today we suffer from our incapacity to accept other beings without reservation. What previously was, often enough, comprehended as *personal* guilt has today become *structural* sin: the loss of unconditional acceptance. This is just as visible in our relationships as in the expression '(Un-) Zumutbarkeit', translatable as un-acceptability or un-reasonableness, which has become a central term for immunity from criminal prosecution, for example, in the case of abortion. Of course, to force acceptability via prosecution would be wrong, from the moral viewpoint as well. But to utilise individual unacceptability in order to avoid societal problems is cynical. The structural sin lies in this cynical variant of reason which replaces solidarity and assistance with the assignment of guilt to the individuals. Their psychic suffering elevates the economic society with its deficiencies in solidarity to the sovereign over the norms of constitutional society, which actually should make human life acceptable, inviolable, and reasonable.

The loss of unconditional acceptance is at the same time a cultural amnesia, a structural sin, and a distortion of God. For God has allowed his history with humankind to be written as a history of acceptance, a progressive purification of the image of God, until God and the human being were bonded together in this faith of acceptance (here we could compare the Pauline lines on love). God is not thinkable without this longing, taken from yet exceeding human powers; the human being is not thinkable without this human image of acceptance and without its base in God. Together with the amnesia of acceptance the advocatory discourse to the benefit of those who cannot themselves decide and are vulnerable has lost its cultural *Sitz im Leben*. This discourse, not personal commitment, has been ousted. The advocacy is attributable as a result of the segmentation of the human. Not the advocate but those to be represented by him or her are 'appointed': as human beings, pre-human beings, or 'no longer human beings'. Personalised through the loss of its structural roots in the unity of the human being and human dignity, forced to revert to the competition of attributions, the advocatory element loses momentum through segmentation. (Then not even affected handicapped or disabled persons are necessary members of a national ethics commission.)

Cultural amnesia exists on the basis of a false choice between remembering and forgetting. Our technological advances are drummed into our heads day in and day out, by the media and by the constant training of our capacity for knowledge; consciousness of our failure with respect to the laboriously achieved values is only occasionally present. Ignoring memory produces the normative power of the fictive, as if the promised – whoever promises a cure is right fom the very beginning – were the true reality. A capitalist teleology replaces the communist one.

Facticity becomes bearable through the prognosis and the fiction of its presence. And when fictions are redeemed, the world immediately divides itself into those who participate and those who are excluded. Fiction as a teleology leading to a better world is only encountered with scepticism by followers of a different faith. The unbelieving belief watches while the believing unbelief expands. Idolatry is based on a new affirmative culture of the fictive. This culture has long become a part of the structures of knowledge, learning, working, and pleasure. Fantasy and cyberspace allow the memory of history only as a citation of robes and weaponry. If history is also based on narratives, these are recollecting and not exclusively drafting narratives. In conjuring the imperfect tense the imperfect has a chance, too.

The problem of human genetic engineering does not only concern respect for human beings as regards their genotypes and phenotypes. It also concerns the issue of human contingency, which may not be ignored in science and modern technology (human fallibility and finitude). We should be aware that by reducing fundamental problems to technical ones and by isolating them, we might solve technical problems by technical means. However, this may cause new problems as regards the adequateness of problem-solving strategies – other dimensions related to the technical problems easily move out of sight: for instance social problems of individual decisions, ecological problems, anthropological problems etc. Therefore, in continuing the research we have to keep in our minds that progress in one dimension will not guarantee progress for human destiny in general.[8]

We can identify the common structural trait of the cultural assessment of losses also as forgotten finitude. It is probable that we will experience finitude as a dictate of the real future. Chernobyl has been one such experience, 11 September 2001 is another. If the 'perfect world' once again becomes a world of the imperfect, we will learn to better deal with the possibilities and limitations of human freedom.

---

8. See Mieth, *Was wollen wir können?*, 436-453, Otfried Höffe, Ludger Honnefelder, Josef Isensee, Paul Kirchhof, *Gentechnik und Menschenwürde* (Köln, 2002); Ludger Honnefelder *et al.* (eds), *Das genetische Wissen und die Zukunft des Menschen* (Berlin, 2003).

VII A FINAL REMARK ON PLURALISM AND TOLERANCE
AS LEADING VALUES

In the Opinion of the European Group on Ethics (EGE) no 12, on Ethical aspects of Embryo research, published on 23 November 1998, we can read about the diversity of ethical views:

1.23 'The diversity of views regarding the question whether or not research on human embryos in vitro is morally acceptable, depends on differences in ethical approaches, theories and traditions, which are deeply rooted in European culture ...'

1.25 'The diversity in policies and regulations concerning embryo research in the Member States of the EU reflects fundamentally differing views ... and it is difficult to see how, at these extremes (cf embryo as human life or as human being), the differences can be reconciled.'[9]

This kind of introduction of an opinion leads often to the result that a substantial restriction will not be acceptable. The reason for this liberal approach is called 'mutual respect'. This 'mutual respect' is also mentioned in the EGE-Opinion:

1.27 'Pluralism may be seen as a characteristic of the European Union, mirroring the richness of its tradition and asking for mutual respect and tolerance.' (cf 2.5)

In other papers 'the mutual respect' is precisely focused on 'moral choices'. Therefore the more liberal positions always have a political advantage. They can ot be dominated because, if they are, respect for different approaches and moral choices is not granted. This is what in critical ethics we call 'repressive tolerance'. You always can suppress substantial restrictions but not a substantial liberalisation.

The ethical discourse on pluralism, tolerance, compromise seems to be very underdeveloped. Most of the members of bioethical committees speak of these attitudes but the words remain without clarification. If pluralism is not *'laisser faire'*, as EGE said, what is the meaning? If pluralism is not the same as

---

9 See Ludger Honnefelder & Christian Streffer (eds), *Jahrbuch für Wissenschaft und Ethik* (Bd 7, Berlin, 2002) (with a documentation of international and national regulations and ethical advices about embryonic stem cell engineering); Deutscher Bundestag, Referat Öffentlichkeitsarbeit (ed), *Enquete-Kommission Recht und Ethik der modernen Medizin: 'Stammzellforschung und die Debatte des Deutschen Bundestages zum Import von menschlichen embryonalen Stammzellen'* (Zur Sache 1 / 2002).

the lowest restrictive level, how can it be precisely defined? If pluralism has a tendency to compromise, what is the distinction to be made between a practical compromise and an ethical judgment? I am speaking from a concrete experience, which I had as a member of a European Project on Pluralism. The ethical paradox of the result was that if you take pluralism as the 'norma normans', you need no more ethics because all restricting argumentation can be stopped by the norm of pluralism. And if there are no limits for pluralism, then the so called position (reclaiming pluralism) is nothing else than a new kind of fundamentalism. This may be a paradox, but it is as the French expression has it: 'les extrèmes se touchent'.

If we try to have a moral discourse with the goal of consensus, we must begin for example with doubt on our own moral position and with reflection on the conditions which are necessary not to be dominated by the power of definition, by the politics of language or by repressive tolerance. We must also understand that a moral conflict is not against respect for persons. If ethicists have to learn something about scientific specialities and the scientific use of language, the same is necessary for scientists in the public debate. In both cases there is a danger of too little education of public opinion for the conditions of a moral discourse.

As an ethicist, when dealing with the high hopes and great promises of biomedical advances, I cannot help wondering about the break-through mentality that will not take into account essential factors of the human constitution. Humans are prone to error. Often we attempt to rationalise our motives and ignore the danger of instrumentalising others. We can only postpone but not abolish our abiding finitude.

# CHAPTER EIGHTEEN

# 'It is part of a process. It is part of a pilgrimage':[1] Text in Context and Conflict

## Elaine M. Wainwright

Text in context is not a new theme for biblical scholars as is indicated by the title Seán Freyne has given to a recent collection of his essays, *Texts, Contexts and Cultures*. The place of this theme in his own scholarly journey is highlighted in his account of this journey that forms an introduction to the above collection,[2] and it is evidenced by his long-term engagement with the study of Galilee as context for the gospels and the life of Jesus.[3] Perhaps less evident in, although not absent from, his scholarly career is the theme of the biblical text in conflict, that is functioning in contemporary conflicts over ethical or moral questions in churches or Christian communities for whom the Bible is a foundational document of faith and life. It is this aspect of text in contemporary context and more particularly contexts of conflict that I wish to explore in this essay, which seeks to honour Seán's scholarly career, and to acknowledge with gratitude his engagement with and support of students and colleagues who have, as

---

1. These words are taken from the foreword to *The Windsor Report* 2004 (London: Anglican Communion Office, 2004), 6, written by Robin Eames. http://www.anglicancommunion.org/windsor2004/downloads/index.cfm, accessed 5 October, 2005. The phrases are used there in relation to *The Windsor Report* itself. In this essay, however, they are evoked as an apt description of the way the Bible journeys with communities of faith through history, being brought into dialogue with contemporary issues in differing ages and differing contexts.
2. Seán Freyne, *Texts, Contexts and Cultures* (Dublin: Veritas, 2002), 13-20.
3. Freyne, *Galilee: From Alexander the Great to Hadrian 323 BCE to 135 CE: A Study of Second Temple Judaism* (Paperback Edition; Edinburgh: T & T Clark, 1998); *idem, Galilee and Gospel: Collected Essays* (Tübingen: Mohr Siebeck, 2000); and *idem, Jesus A Jewish Galilean: A New Reading of the Jesus-story* (London: T & T Clark International, 2004).

a result of gender, contextual or other locations, been deeply im-
mersed in texts in conflict as well as context.[4]

One of the current issues under debate or causing conflict in
churches in many parts of the world today is homosexuality and
the related question of same-sex unions. The recent *Windsor
Report* was commissioned to address ways in which the
Anglican church could preserve its very unity as an international
communion in the face of these and other issues which threaten
schism.[5] The Catholic Church is poised, toward the end of 2005,
to issue a document on homosexuality in relation to prospective
candidates for seminary formation and ordained ministry.[6] And
in Australia, the Uniting Church has grappled with questions relating to homosexuality and church membership and ordination
over a number of years without resolution.[7] In this essay, I do
not propose to engage in interpretation of the small number of
biblical texts that are deemed to address homosexuality and
homosexual relationships. Rather, the current controversies provide a context in which to explore the process of biblical interpretation in which the churches engage on their pilgrimage

---

4. See *Texts, Contexts and Cultures*, 17, where Freyne acknowledges the
challenges of 'voices of Liberation, Feminist and Asian Theologies.' I
would like to personally acknowledge Seán's presence in my scholarly
journey, first as teacher during his very 'brief stint' as he calls it [16] in
the Department of Studies in Religion at the University of Queensland
where I was an Honours student, second as colleague in New
Testament Studies over many years, and most valued of all, as friend.
5. See n 1 above. When I use the word 'issues', I do so for simplicity of
language but I am very aware that in relation to homosexuality or other
areas in which there is conflict within churches that there are people
and lives profoundly affected by such conflict. I wish to sensitively include each of them within this and other discussions around what we
name as 'issues' for simplicity of reference.
6. Robert Mickens, 'Vatican's civil union fight is Pope's key theme,'
http://www.thetablet.co.uk/cgi-bin/register.cgi/citw-#Rome, accessed
5 October, 2005, in relation to civil unions and Paul Michaels, 'Don't
dare to speak its name,' http://www.thetablet.co.uk/cgi-bin/regis-
ter.cgi accessed 5 October, 2005, which speculates about the contents of
the 13-page working document in preparation by the Congregation for
Education in Rome and how it might address homosexuality in the context of seminary education.
7. For a brief outline see http://www.religioustolerance.org/hom_-
uoz.htm accessed 5 October, 2005.

through history as they seek to address controversial and contemporary issues at particular points in time.

An expected starting point for such an exploration could well be a direct analysis of the authority of scripture. In this regard, however, *The Windsor Report* makes a thought-provoking claim, namely that:

> [i]t may be, historically, that the phrase 'authority of scripture' has characteristically emerged in *contexts of protest* (when one part of the Church appeals to scripture against something being done by another part).[8]

This view is shared by a number of other scholars[9] and suggests, therefore, that it is wise to step back a little from the context of protest that currently faces the churches, and to look at scripture in the light of process and pilgrimage in dialogue with some of the shifts in contemporary biblical studies which have had an impact on understandings of the authority of scripture and its interpretation in the churches. It is this route that this article will take. Such an exploration, however, is not a 'new thing'. Understandings of the authority of scripture and its interpretation have been developing and changing in the life of the church since the church's inception.[10] It is these very changes

---

8 *The Windsor Report*, 28, §54, emphasis mine. L. William Countryman, *Interpreting the Truth: Changing the Paradigm of Biblical Studies* (Harrisburgh: Trinity Press International, 2003), 31, makes a similar claim in relation to the canon and the power of communities of faith to change the canon: '… they prefer not to exercise these powers consciously unless perhaps during periods of significant cultural upheaval.'

9. Mary Ann Tolbert, 'A New Teaching with Authority: A Re-evaluation of the Authority of the Bible,' in Fernando F. Segovia and Mary Ann Tolbert (eds), *Teaching the Bible: The Discourses and Politics of Biblical Pedagogy*, (Maryknoll: Orbis, 1998), 168-189, addresses this issue extensively as she moves through the church's debates over slavery, women and now homosexuality. See also, Elizabeth Huwiler, 'Authorized Conflicts: The Bible in Church Conversations,' *BTB* 34.1 (2004), 41-45.

10. For a brief and accessible history of this see, David Jasper, *A Short Introduction to Hermeneutics* (Louisville: Westminster John Knox, 2004). Sandra M. Schneiders, *The Revelatory Text: Interpreting the New Testament as Sacred Scripture* (Collegeville: Liturgical Press, 1999), is an excellent full length study of many issues in relation to the function of scripture in the church today in dialogue with much of the contemporary theory and historical perspectives.

that have brought the church on pilgrimage to today.[11]

*Paradigms of Interpretation*

In order to demonstrate how biblical interpretation in the church can be understood as *process* and *pilgrimage*, it is important to acknowledge that one of the things which feeds the current debate around homosexuality, and has fed other current debates in the church in recent history, is a difference or differences in the paradigms of interpretation of scripture. In suggesting certain paradigms or frameworks, there are always going to be nuances that are not addressed. The positing, however, of two types of fundamentally different contemporary understandings of the Bible and its function across Christian churches may enable us to understand some of the debates involving biblical interpretation more clearly.

The first paradigm is that of the *Bible as mythical archetype*, borrowing a category used by Elisabeth Schüssler Fiorenza.[12] In this model, the Bible as myth or foundational story contains the universal or perennial truths and models for human behaviour which have traditionally been accessed, to continue with Schüssler Fiorenza's categories, by doctrinal, by 'historical-factual', or by dialogical-pluralistic historical interpretation.[13] The

11. I use the word 'church' to refer collectively to those varied communities of faith who share the name 'Christian' and among whom there are shared historical experiences and beliefs. I do not wish to obscure the differences among various churches but will only address these when it is necessary for this study.

12. Elisabeth Schüssler Fiorenza, *Bread not Stone: The Challenge of Feminist Biblical Interpretation* (rev ed, Boston: Beacon, 1984), 10. As introduction to her discussion of paradigms of biblical interpretation, Schüssler Fiorenza demonstrates the way in which biblical authority has functioned as a key issue in discussions of 'the bible as the book of Women-Church.'

13. *Ibid.*, 10-11. Countryman, *Interpreting the Truth*, 1, recognises the modern 'historical-critical' approach or paradigm as the 'dominant paradigm' in contemporary biblical studies. Others may nuance the paradigms of biblical studies differently, for example, Fernando Segovia, "And They Began to Speak in Other Tongues': Competing Modes of Discourse in Contemporary Biblical Criticism.' in Fernando F. Segovia and Mary Ann Tolbert (eds), *Reading from this Place, Volume 1: Social Location and Biblical Interpretation in the United States,* (Minneapolis: Fortress, 1995), 1-34. It is clear, however, that the latter part of the twentieth century saw a significant shift in biblical studies as methodologies

text as historical/mythical/theological archetype can be approached with contemporary questions and issues such as: is homosexuality contrary to God's law? From the text, come answers or 'truths': yes – look at Lev 18:19-23 and 20:10-16 as well as Rom 1:26-7. Within this model, one methodological approach is that of a careful historical critical and 'objective' searching for the meaning intended by the original author, a meaning which is then imported into the present as the intended meaning for all time including today. A literalist or dogmatic reading tends to approach the biblical text as if it were a twenty-first century document with the truths and doctrines being read off the text in a 'value neutral' way believed to be applicable directly to contexts in the twenty-first century, often with no account taken of their historical context.

One of the problems with this paradigm, especially among communities of faith seeking ethical direction in relation to contemporary issues, is that the Bible answers in multiple ways that can be in conflict with one another or with some of the contemporary ethical stances that a community may have discerned in response to contextual issues. By way of example, approaching the biblical text in relation to contemporary issues about waging 'war' can yield a text such as Deut 20:10-20: destroy the city and all its male inhabitants, take women and children as slaves and booty to be raped and humiliated, and devastate the earth, destroying all the trees of the city. This is but one example among many of the problems of a prooftexting approach to biblical interpretation in contemporary contexts in which communities of faith are addressing conflictual issues.

The second model suggested by Schüssler Fiorenza which I will use as a basis for further exploration is that of the *Bible as historical prototype*.[14] Within this model, scripture is also considered sacred and revelatory,[15] it is the church's foundational story that travels or journeys with the community on its pilgrimage through human history. It shapes the church as a pilgrim people: shapes their religious imagination with metaphors such as the *basileia* or reign of God as God's dream for the human

---

such as the new literary, social scientific and cultural approaches emerged and hermeneutical perspectives multiplied.

14. Schüssler Fiorenza, *Bread not Stone*, 14.

15. For a much more extensive treatment of scripture as sacred and revelatory, see Schneiders, *The Revelatory Text*.

community; shapes their liturgical life with stories and time-frames; and shapes their ethics as they continually face new situations. The church is finding itself challenged by greater social and cultural acceptance, as well as legal recognition in some countries, of same-sex unions and homosexual relationships, and by the changes that have taken place in understandings of human sexuality in the twentieth and twenty-first century. From this, questions arise which have never before been faced in the same way by the church in its history.

The Bible is also shaped by the church as communities of faith enter into dialogue with their sacred story anew in each new era as they respond to new issues, create new frameworks of thinking and being and shape changing spiritualities. Each new age develops new understandings of biblical texts and traditions that inform the horizon of present-day interpreters.[16] The church has, therefore, in its pilgrimage and its engaging with the process of ongoing biblical interpretation, to search anew in each new age for perspectives which will inform new ethical issues, search with all the tools and processes of interpretation available to it in dialogue with the wisdom of the tradition that has informed and shaped the church on its pilgrimage.[17] Such an approach is much more complex than that of simply proof-texting the bible as archetype. The church offers today's communities of faith a biblical story that has been on pilgrimage through myriads of processes of interpretation. Today's church stands at the end of one stage of the process and the beginning of another

---

16. For this aspect of biblical interpetation see Hans-Georg Gadamer, *Truth and Method*, trs William Glen-Doepel, (London: Sheed & Ward, 1979), 235-341.

17. Countryman, *Interpreting the Truth*, is also searching for an articulation of a new paradigm which will assist communities of faith in their interpretation of scripture. He says [19] in relation to the pilgrimage of the Bible in human history that 'every distinct historical era within a given culture is a particular exploration of human possibilities ... The past and its texts do not, of course, exhaust all human possibilities; nor do we need them to. We do not need them to give us a perfect paradigm of human life. We only need them to relativise the certainties of the present, break their apparent stranglehold on human possibility, offer a few alternative directions, and so set our collective imagination free to continue into the future.'

and is invited, by its very conflictual and contextual issues, into a new stage or new process of interpretation.[18]

In order to further demonstrate interpretation of the biblical text as process rather than product, I want to very briefly trace the emergence of the church's sacred scripture as an ongoing storytelling process. At some point, there was the beginning of a story or stories around which or from which other stories spiraled and developed. Before the story, however, there was *experience*, experience in the world, an experience perhaps of slavery and oppression and escape from such.[19] Experience was reflected on by individuals and communities and from this emerged story, the beginning of story. In Israel's storytelling, experience was named as not only experience in and of the world of politics and cultures but of the divine engaged in those worlds – God sees the slavery and oppression, God is engaged in it (Ex 3:7). Experience was reflected on to discern its meaning and told as a story. Thus, a story begins, a story which in its turn shapes the way the people telling the story are in the world and the way their descendants are in the world. A vision and a story of liberation shape the lives of a people, and so they relate their laws to their story of being freed from slavery (Ex 20:1-21; Deut 5:1-20).[20] That story then is both told and lived in a community to shape *vision and praxis* – the story shapes community and the community shapes the story or the understanding and interpretation of the story.

The telling and living of the story is taken with the community into new eras and new contexts and so new experiences of life and of the divine in life emerge. New meaning needs to be dis-

---

18. For those in the Anglican communion, this seems to be the approach that the *Windsor Report* recommends in its section on Scripture and Interpretation. See *Windsor Report*, 29-30.

19. My construction of this model of biblical storytelling is informed profoundly by decades of biblical studies but I do not want here to engage in the dialogues and debates over the beginning point of the story, the theories about the emergence of the exodus tradition or those of the ancient ancestors of Israel, and the dating of oral and written traditions. Rather I want to allow my knowledge around these issues to inform the construction of a storytelling process as paradigm within which many of the above issues can be discussed and debated.

20. Walter Brueggemann, *Hope within History* (Atlanta: John Knox, 1987), 20-24, calls this phase of Israel's storytelling the release of new social imagination.

cerned as they live in new situations. Israel, for instance, was faced with new questions, one of which must have been whether they could/should take and/or possess slaves as they established kingships and hierarchal structures in Israel and became 'like all the other nations' (See for example Lev 25:6, 39, 42, 44, 46). They needed to *discern anew* in dialogue with their established praxis and their foundational story because new issues, new questions had arisen. The story and the living of the story became the tradition that was *disclosive*. Critical engagement with it, however, in new eras when new issues arose, invited a new story and new praxis that was transformative of the tradition. This critical engagement is at the heart of the prophetic in the unfolding storytelling,[21] and it has been at the heart of the biblical and Christian traditions throughout their histories although at times it may have been silenced. The re-telling of the story, which is also the role of the prophet at each new point along the story's unfolding is, therefore, both disclosive and transformative. The story itself is transformed in the retelling and a new vision, a new way of being in the world emerges which begins the process over again. The community is shaping its story and the collection of its stories will become the Bible in whose ongoing interpretive processes communities of faith today stand.[22] This is the process which I suggest informs the 'Bible as prototype' model of interpretation as the Bible travels with communities of faith on their pilgrim journey.

There are a number of issues that faced the historical communities which shaped and were shaped by the developing biblical narrative/s. The history of any one of these issues could be traced to demonstrate how the communities who carried this story dealt with the issue in new and different contexts. Divorce could be one such issue. In a study of this issue across the biblical tradition, it would be noted that the Markan and Matthean communities present Jesus re-interpreting the Mosaic law which

---

21. Walter Brueggemann, *The Prophetic Imagination* (2nd ed.; Minneapolis: Fortress, 2001), names the critical aspect of the prophetic as 'prophetic criticizing' and the re-telling of the story from a new perspective as 'prophetic energizing'.

22. See William Stacy Johnson, 'Reading the Scriptures Faithfully in a Postmodern Age,' in Ellen F. Davis and Richard B. Hays (eds), *The Art of Reading Scripture*, (Grand Rapids: Eerdmans, 2003), 110, '[t]he narrative is not just a given but must be constructed and reconstructed in the life of the community of faith over time.'

allowed for a certificate of divorce to be given (Deut 24: 1-4; Mk 10:2-9; Mt 19:3-9) but these two communities then nuance Jesus' teaching differently: Matthew's community allows an exception to the divorce prohibition (Mt 19:9). Human sexuality together with attitudes to the male and female body is another topic that has import for many current questions and issues in Christian communities. Careful historico-biblical study of the many different attitudes to human sexuality and the gendering of the human body encoded in and influential of the biblical story has not yet been undertaken but it is essential to the current conflictual debate in relation to homosexuality.[23] Homosexuality itself was not a developed topic in the biblical story. It seems to have received the most cursory of responses across texts divided by centuries if, indeed, the texts generally cited in relation to this issue were addressing what we now understand as homosexuality. It is difficult, therefore, to find any developed perspective or even story line in relation to this issue in the biblical tradition that shapes and is shaped by the church. How then do the Christian churches who are so challenged by this issue address it in the context of *pilgrimage and process?*

*A Model for Theological Reflection*

In recent decades, these churches have sought to respond to a number of contemporary social issues: poverty and oppression in the two-thirds world; the place of women in society and church; the ecological challenge; and postcolonialism and the rights of indigenous peoples. The churches and the academic communities of theologians and biblical scholars who have undertaken these ethical engagements have provided us with a

---

23. William Loader is currently undertaking one small piece of such a topic in one segment of that history, namely the New Testament period and its surrounding centuries of influence. He has already published the first fruits of this research: *The Septuagint, Sexuality, and the New Testament: Case Studies on the Impact of the LXX in Philo and the New Testament* (Grand Rapids: Eerdmans, 2004), and *Sexuality and the Jesus Tradition* (Grand Rapids: Eerdmans, 2005). See also Björn Krondorfer (ed), *Body and Bible: Interpreting and Experiencing Biblical Narratives* (Philadelphia: Trinity Press International, 1992) and Margaret R. Miles, *Female Nakedness and Religious Meaning in the Christian West* (Tunbridge Wells: Burns & Oates, 1989), who takes such a study into the post-biblical era of the Christian church.

type of model/s or framework/s.[24] Different nuances on the
praxis model have emerged among many contemporary interpreters undertaking liberation, feminist, ecological and contextual theologising. Generally, however, the model will include in
some form:

    1. telling of stories from life in the here and now and high-
    lighting the issues arising from those stories;

    2. analysing of historical, social, political and other contextual
    aspects of the issue/s;

    3. engaging the sacred story or stories (biblical, traditional,
    community); and

    4. articulating a new praxis.[25]

It is a model which is already inherent in the above discussion of
biblical interpretation as process and pilgrimage and I will suggest below ways in which communities of faith might use such a
model to enter into the process of ethical decision-making in relation to current issues around homosexuality.

    In addressing the conflictual in a theological process, the cur-
rent context is a significant starting point. It is important initially,
I would suggest, to hear the stories, to listen to the experience of
those in same-sex unions, of those who desire same-sex unions,
of those who are gay, lesbian, bi-sexual or transgendered who
are members of communities of faith and/or who are ordained
into Christian communities or are seeking ordination. The life-
context, life stories, oppressions and spiritualities of those most

---

24. Countryman, *Interpreting the Truth*, 24-40, proposes a triangular
process of interpretation as an alternative model to the historical critical
with the three axes being the text, the interpreter (usually academically
trained), and the community of readers (or communities of faith).

25. See also Clodovis Boff, *Theology and Praxis: Epistemological
Foundations*, trs Robert R. Barr, (Maryknoll: Orbis, 1987); Elisabeth
Schüssler Fiorenza, *Wisdom Ways: Introducing Feminist Biblical
Interpretation* (Maryknoll: Orbis, 2001), 135-194, with a diagram of the
spiraling model or process on 194; and The Earth Bible Team, 'Guiding
Ecojustice Principles,' in Norman Habel (ed), *Readings from the
Perspective of Earth* Vol 1, (Sheffield: Sheffield Academic Press, 2000), 38-
53; and Stevan Bevans, *Models of Contextual Theology: Faith and Cultures*
(rev & expanded ed; Maryknoll: Orbis, 2004). For an example of how
the work of academic theologians has shaped a praxis model that can
be engaged by communities of faith in relation to contemporary justice
issues, see the interactive CD, *Mercy and Justice Shall Meet*, produced by
Fraynework Multimedia (Mercy International Association: 2004).

affected by the issue is of utmost import. This storytelling will involve partners, parents, family, church communities. From the stories, questions and issues can be drawn out and highlighted so that the community can enter into dialogue with the biblical tradition carrying the stories and the issues.

Before approaching the biblical tradition, however, the wisdom of the present age offers tools with which to *analyse* experience, stories, and issues or questions. Medical science, gender studies, psychology and the social sciences, literary studies and other contemporary disciplines provide not only further data beyond the personal but also tools to examine the stories, the issues, and the questions arising from context. There are varieties of ways in which small or large communities can undertake this part of the process, engaging experts in particular fields as well as members of Christian communities in their contexts. Just as the base Christian communities in central and south America trained their church members to develop basic analytical skills in their situations of political and economic oppression, so too can churches across the Christian communion develop skills of analysis and discernment of issues involved in contemporary ethical challenges among their members so that they can engage fully in the interpretive process.

Having undertaken the second stage of *analysis of experience,* therefore, the communities seeking to understand and come to an ethical stance in relation to same-sex unions, and where and how members of such unions might function in the church, are in a new and very different position to *engage the biblical story and the tradition.* They have new issues and questions nuanced by experience and analysis of experience. It is all this that they bring to the biblical text.

One important point already addressed earlier is that just as the biblical text functions in different ways and is interpreted from different contexts in the present, so too did the text or story function in different communities in the past, whether in the fourteenth or fourth century BC or first century AD. The text is 'other'. It was shaped and compiled in a different place and a different time than our own. The first stage of the theological reflection process will have demonstrated the complexity around same-sex unions and homosexual relationship and ordination as a twenty-first century issue. This alerts us to the fact that biblical communities faced complex challenges in societies and cultures

which differ from ours. Each age brings its particular questions
to this text which is 'other' and seeks to hear it as other, to hear it
in its multiple contexts or perhaps just one of those contexts,
perhaps the first century AD, the time of the Jesus movement
and the initial shaping of Christianity. The text, in its turn, asks
new questions of its inquirers, opening up a new world of
Christian praxis and vision in front of the text, a world which
today's community can inhabit ethically.[26]

In recent biblical scholarship the space between a text as first
century and as contemporary has been collapsed in some instances as attention has shifted to the reader/s of the text among
whom are contemporary readers.[27] A brief survey of some of the
shifts in biblical scholarship in recent decades can help inform
current interpretation of texts.[28] Scholars have drawn attention
to the dynamic in the biblical text, namely author/text/reader.
Historical criticism, which dominated biblical studies for over
two centuries up to the second half of the last century, placed
emphasis on the author and the world behind the text or context.
This is significant in understanding the meaning of the text and
its function in its context of origin. One question that has arisen,
however, is just how accurately can anyone know that context
and the meaning of the text. Scholars catch but glimpses of societies and cultures of old and so, despite all scholarly efforts, it is
clear now that we cannot accurately capture the 'intention of the
original author'.[29] That does not mean, however, that we abandon historical study. The social sciences and shifts in the understanding of history mean that historical biblical study can still
function in significant ways that inform the interpretation of

---

26. The question of the ethic of biblical interpretation and of interpreting the bible ethically is a significant topic in contemporary biblical
studies. See Elisabeth Schüssler Fiorenza, *Rhetoric and Ethic: the Politics
of Biblical Interpretation* (Minneapolis: Fortress, 1990); Daniel Patte,
*Ethics of Biblical Interpretation: A Reevaluation* (Louisville: Westminster/
John Knox, 1995); and Elna Mouton, *Reading a New Testament Document
Ethically* (Atlanta: Society of Biblical Literature, 2002).

27. This is one of Countryman's axes of interpretation as acknowledged
above in n. 24.

28. One among many contemporary resources which maps some of
these changes is Steven L. McKenzie and Stephen R. Haynes (eds), *To
Each Its Own Meaning: An Introduction to Biblical Criticisms and their
Application*, (Louisville: Westminster John Knox, 1999).

29. Johnson, 'Reading the Scriptures,' 118.

biblical texts for the present day. It prevents us from reading the text as if it were a twenty-first century text and it enables us to dialogue with it in its own context as we seek to respond to an issue in our context. It does not, however, provide us with the meaning of the text that can simply be transported and applied today.

In the second half of last century, the focus of biblical interpretation shifted to the text and the significance of literary tools in the interpretative process. This together with recognition of the role of the reader in the meaning making process and the perspective/s that the reader brings to a text and its interpretation has been the most challenging and paradigm changing aspect of recent scholarship. But with the shift to the reader comes the emergence of multiple meanings as readers in different contexts, with and from different perspectives, interpret the biblical story in different ways (the very experience which the churches face around conflictual issues). The world in front of the text is no longer singular but multiple, providing a wealth of new meanings. Such a situation is often named the challenge of postmodernism[30] but my own work on the gospel of Matthew leads me to believe that even in the first century AD, the emerging Jewish Christian community that shaped the gospel named Matthew was seeking ways to hold together interpretations which came from different households of interpretation.[31] One of the ways they did this was to allow some of these different interpretations to stand together in the one story and so we have two very different perspectives on leadership (Mt 16:13-20 and 18:15-18); and different perspectives on women and women's engagement as, for instance, when the patrilineage of Mt 1:1-17 is punctured with five references to women (1:3, 5, 6 and 16). When the Matthean story is combined with many other compositions from different periods into the library of books we call Bible, differences among different interpreters abound. Recognition of the different interpretations that emerge because of differences in readers has alerted us not only to the challenge and promise of contemporary interpretation but also to differ-

---

30. See Walter Brueggemann, *Texts under Negotiation: The Bible and Postmodern Imagination* (Minneapolis: Fortress, 1993).
31. Elaine M. Wainwright, *Shall We Look for Another? A Feminist Re-reading of the Matthean Jesus* (Maryknoll: Orbis, 1998) in which I explore this claim more fully.

ence in the biblical tradition itself, even within one literary composition.

In relation to its theological reflection around the current
issue of homosexuality, the church needs to engage in biblical
interpretation and, as with the initial stage in the proposed
model, to listen to different voices. Some of the interpretative
work will be carried out by expert biblical scholars who will
come with different methodologies or a combination of methodologies and with different hermeneutics.[32] This will provide a
wide range of historical, socio-cultural and literary interpretations of not only those texts which are the focus for the issue of
same-sex unions but also those texts in the context of some key
biblical principles which are more developed and which could
provide insight and direction in responding to the issue today.
Interpretations will also be undertaken by a range of members
of the church. This provides a challenge to the church, however,
which has not always carried out its responsibility of ensuring
that its members are biblically literate so that they can engage in
debates and deliberations around current issues.[33]

Returning to the process, what we have seen is that it will not
yield *an* answer or even *the* answer to the current church debate.
What it will yield are a number of different perspectives or
meanings on the issue, biblical perspectives that are multiple.
The community will need to engage with these multiple meanings courageously and in faith, not a faith that seeks to know the
single right answer or that assumes on it before the interpretative
work has begun. Rather, it will need to engage the multiple
meanings with a faith that humbly seeks to make the best decision possible at a particular point in time, shaping the best ethical praxis, taking account of as many ethical principles as possible.[34] *The Windsor Report* names some of these, communion

---

32. See for instance Bernadette J. Brooten's introduction to her book
*Love between Women: Early Christian Responses to Female Homoeroticism*
(Chicago Series on Sexuality, History, and Society; Chicago: University
of Chicago Press, 1996), 1-26, in which she seeks to lay out her own perspective and to critique, for instance, that of Boswell who does not take
account of gender differences but collapses women into his treatment
of male homoeroticism.
33. Mary Ann Tolbert, 'A New Teaching,' 183-184.
34. Johnson, 'Reading the Scriptures,' 112, where he notes that the
'foundationalist way of thinking ... represents not the strength of faith
but the result of a faith that has lost its nerve.'

being one such principle which, it could be suggested, dominates the report.[35] As a woman in a patriarchal church, I am a little more suspicious of the principle of communion put forward so strongly by a committee on which the ratio of women to men was 5:12 or 29% and it is not known whether any members of the commission were in same-sex unions or were ordained homosexuals. This raises the question of whose communion or in whose interest unity or communion and who will be sacrificed to it. My questions and hesitations do not mean that communion is not an important principle in discerning a way forward in situations of conflict informed by multiple interpretations. It needs, however, to be a nuanced principle.

*The Windsor Report* also proposes that taking care of the 'weak' who have scruples of conscience is an important ethical principle to guide the process of determining contemporary praxis.[36] This too needs to be nuanced to determine just what is meant by 'scruples of conscience' and what is the difference between people with scruples of conscience and those who oppose any change on multiple other grounds, some of which may be unethical. In this respect, too, there seemed to be a silence in the report of the cry arising from the victimised, in this instance those in same-sex unions especially those which demonstrate the key values of the gospel such as faithful love, justice and fidelity. Their voice and their pain from possibly a life time of oppression and victimisation or marginalisation would, it seems to me, be an important ethical principle that will need consideration as the community discerns its position. There is a need to take care that these people are not further oppressed by those who claim loudly other sensibilities as well as being attentive to some of those sensibilities.

Another principle which is not in *The Windsor Report* but which I believe will be essential in the process of discerning new ethics, new praxis for the future in relation to homosexuality, is that of 'power'. It might be argued that power is addressed in the report in so far as it recognises the leadership role of the bishop in the discernment process.[37] This needs, however, to be nuanced in order to emphasise the necessity of those in leadership in Christian community being well-informed in their on-

---

35. *Windsor Report*, 11-14, § 1-11.
36. *Windsor Report*, 39-40, §92.
37. *Windsor Report*, 29 §58.

going knowledge of and facility with the interpretation of scripture, as the church too needs to be as it is engaged in this
process. Around many issues, however, power is a principle
that is not addressed directly and so it gets directed covertly into
other areas.[38] Attention to how power and threats to power
might be operating among bishops and others in leadership,
among scholars, and among various others engaged in the discernment process will ensure good decision-making. In relation
to same-sex unions, there may also be an issue of 'fear' in relation
to sexuality in general or homosexuality in particular, a fear
which clouds judgment.

Communities will develop a much longer list of ethical principles and the church will need to discern which are most appropriate in relation to particular issues. This short list is but exemplary of the ethical dimensions involved in the process of moving from vision to praxis, the final stage of the theologising
process. They will lead to a decision or decisions which are the
best the church can make at a particular point of time but which,
as the process has demonstrated, will lead into new interpretations and new decision-making into the future as the church
lives into the current decision. Such a process is challenging at
all levels of the church and demonstrates that the making of a
decision, the coming to a true and faithful ethical decision at a
particular point in time is a challenge of faith, true faith that does
not deal with certainties but with the God who is on pilgrimage
with the people who belong to that God, as they seek to continue

---

38. One example of this in the Catholic tradition is contained in the 1994
document of the Pontifical Biblical Commission, 'The Interpretation of
the Bible in the Church', *Origins* 23.29 (1994), 509, where the
Commission responsible for the compilation of the document is a body
comprised of male clerics, all therefore holding significant positions of
power. They critique feminist biblical scholarship, undertaken predominantly by women scholars, as being in danger of seeking after
power that is not service. This critique is not made of any other current
hermeneutical or methodological approach nor is there any analysis of
their own positions of power in the church, especially in relation to
women engaged in feminist biblical interpretation. It should be noted,
however, that four commissioners voted against the paragraph and
four abstained with those voting against it requesting that a footnote
regarding the vote be included. This example provides fertile grounds
for an analysis of power in the context of a church undertaking biblical
interpretation that is process and pilgrimage.

the work of the gospel in bringing to birth God's vision, Jesus' *basileia* proclamation, in each new age and in response to each new ethical challenge.

*Conclusion*

Biblical interpretation in relation to current debates is truly *pilgrimage* and *process*. I have not in this article provided answers to the current debate around homosexuality. Rather, I have sought to put forward some paradigms and models which may enable members of the church or the various communions, to talk with one another, to engage in dialogue rather than debate. These paradigms and models provide a process grounded in the biblical process itself and its authorising of the community called church to continue that process. This will truly engage the church in the process of interpreting scripture towards an ethical stance. Christian communities in their various locations with all their complexities and differences are invited to undertake the process of informed ethical decision-making and to do this in dialogue with the wisdom available among scholars in a variety of disciplines as well as theologians and among the people and the leaders of Christian communities. It is not an easy journey but one which is essential to ensuring that areas of conflict within Christian communities become sites for well-informed ethical decision-making as the community continues to participate in the interpretation of biblical and other sacred stories as pilgrimage and as process.

# List of Contributors

Nigel Biggar is Professor of Theology in the University of Dublin.

Joseph Blenkinsopp is John A.O'Brien Professor of Biblical Studies (*emeritus*) in the University of Notre Dame.

John Dillon is Regius Professor of Greek (*emeritus*) in the University of Dublin.

Stephen J. Duffy is Professor of Systematic Theology in Loyala University, New Orleans.

Martin Hengel is Professor of New Testament and Ancient Judaism (*emeritus*) in the Protestant Faculty of Theology in the University of Tübingen.

Werner G. Jeanrond is Professor of Systematic Theology and Dean of the Faculty of Theology and Religious Studies in the University of Lund.

Maureen Junker-Kenny is Associate Professor of Theology in the University of Dublin.

Karl-Josef Kuschel is Professor in the Catholic Faculty of Theology in the University of Tübingen, and Vice President of the Global Ethic Foundation.

James P. Mackey is Thomas Chalmers Professor of Theology (*emeritus*) in the University of  Edinburgh, and Visiting Professsor in the University of Dublin.

John D'Arcy May is Associate Professor of Interfaith Dialogue at the Irish School of Ecumenics in the University of Dublin.

Andrew D. H. Mayes is Erasmus Smith's Professor of Hebrew in the University of Dublin.

Enda McDongah is Professor of Moral Theology (*emeritus*) in the Pontifical University of Maynooth, and Chairman of the Governing Body of University College Cork.

Dietmar Mieth is Professor of Theological Ethics/Social Ethics in the Catholic Faculty of Theology in the University of Tübingen.

Stephen D. Moore is Professor of New Testament and Chair of the Graduate Division of Religion at the Theological School in Drew University.

Elizabeth Schüssler Fiorenza is Krister Stendahl Professor of Divinity in Harvard University.

Elaine M.Wainwright is Professor of Theology and Head of the School of Theology in the University of Auckland.

Felix Wilfred is Professor and Head of the Department of Christian Studies in the University of Madras.

Ellen J. van Wolde is Professor of Old Testament Studies and Hebrew in the University of Tilburg.